# Those with Ears to Hear . . .

## all that Jesus commanded them

*A Reference Commentary on the Greek
Imperative Mood Usage of Jesus*

— RICHARD  LIGTHART —

**A Gathering
of 2 or 3**

525 6th Street
Lemont, IL 60439

Copyright © 2019 Richard Ligthart; All rights reserved.

Ligthart, Richard
    Those with Ears to Hear…all that Jesus commanded them
    A Reference Commentary on the Greek Imperative Mood Usage of Jesus
        Images: Katie Overgard; Cover Design: David Jobb, Bond Brothers Printing Co., Inc.

No part of this publication may be reproduced, stored in a retrieval system or transmitted in any form by any means, electronic, mechanical, photocopy, recording or otherwise, without the prior written permission of the author, except for brief quotation in critical reviews or articles. Unless otherwise noted, all Scripture quotations are from the Holy Bible English Standard Version, Crossway Publishing, Wheaton, IL.

For permission requests, write to: A Gathering of 2 or 3, 525 6th St., Lemont, IL 60439
        708-334-7831; www.thosewithearstohear.com

| Identifiers: | Library of Congress Control Number: 2019903702 | | | |
|---|---|---|---|---|
| | ISBN: | Soft Cover: | 978-1-7329483-0-3 | First Edition, 2019 |
| | | Hard Cover: | 978-1-7329483-2-7 | First Edition, 2019 |
| | | Electronic: | 978-1-7329483-1-0 | First Edition, 2019 |

Names:   Ligthart, Richard, 1953- author, editor.

Title:   Those with ears to hear... all that Jesus commanded them : a reference commentary on the Greek imperative mood usage of Jesus / Richard Ligthart.

Description:   Lemont, IL : A Gathering of 2 or 3, [2019] | Includes bibliographical references.

Identifiers:   ISBN: 978-1-7329483-0-3 (soft cover) | 978-1-7329483-2-7 (hard cover) | 978-1-7329483-1-0 (electronic) | LCCN: 2019903702

Subjects:   LCSH: Greek language, Biblical--Grammar. | Jesus Christ--Teachings. | Bible. New Testament. Greek. | Bible. New Testament--Language, style. | Bible. New Testament--Criticism, interpretation, etc. | Bible--Criticism, interpretation, etc. | Bible--Commentaries. | Bible-- Hermeneutics. | BISAC: BIBLES / Multiple Translations / Reference. | BIBLES / Multiple Translations / Study. | BIBLES / Multiple Translations / Text. | LITERARY CRITICISM / Subjects & Themes / Religion. | RELIGION / Biblical Commentary / New Testament / General. | RELIGION / Biblical Commentary / New Testament / Jesus, the Gospels & Acts. | RELIGION / Biblical Commentary / New Testament / Revelation. | RELIGION / Biblical Criticism & Interpretation / New Testament. | RELIGION / Biblical Reference / Language Study. | RELIGION / Biblical Reference / Quotations. | RELIGION / Biblical Studies / Exegesis & Hermeneutics. | RELIGION / Biblical Studies / History & Culture. | RELIGION / Biblical Studies / New Testament / Jesus, the Gospels & Acts. | RELIGION / Christian Theology / Christology.

Classification:   LCC: BS38 .L54 2019 | DDC: 225.4/8--dc23

*Biblical Studies. Biblical Languages. Reference. Jesus. Bible. Theology. Christianity. New Testament Koine Greek. Biblical Grammar. N.T. Language Style. Language. Culture. Criticism. Interpretation. Commentary. Quotations. Christology. Exegesis. Hermeneutics. Translation.*

    Summary: A reference commentary on the Greek imperative mood usage of Jesus. Content includes historical and Koine Greek linguistic content in First-Century Judea under Roman rule. Content also includes insight on Biblical exegesis, hermeneutics, exposition, and interpretation, and includes multiple translation references. Includes Bibliographical References --Publisher.

        Printed in the United States of America

# Contents

| | | |
|---|---|---|
| 1 | Contents . . . . . . . . . . . . . . . . . . . . . . . . . . . . . . . . . . . . . . . . . . . . | 1 |
| 2 | Preface . . . . . . . . . . . . . . . . . . . . . . . . . . . . . . . . . . . . . . . . . . . . . | 5 |

      Traditions and Traditions Challenged
      Missing Something
      You are not Alone
      Beyond Bible Stories
      Go Back to There and Then

| | | |
|---|---|---|
| 3 | Introduction . . . . . . . . . . . . . . . . . . . . . . . . . . . . . . . . . . . . . . . . | 11 |

      How to Read this Book
      The Importance of Context
      Why Read this Book
      Disclaimers

**Section One:**      **Fear Not the Greek**

| | | |
|---|---|---|
| 4. | Koine Greek for English Speaking Christians . . . . . . . . . . . . . . . . . . | 25 |

      God's Chosen Time, God's Chosen Language
      Time Between the Testaments
      NT Authors' Limited Competencies
      Idiot
      What They Heard, What They Wrote

| | | |
|---|---|---|
| 5 | Bible Translations . . . . . . . . . . . . . . . . . . . . . . . . . . . . . . . . . . . . | 41 |

      Why so many English Bible Translations?
      Word Accuracy or Thought Essence
      Presuppositions, Paul's Presuppositions
      Beyond the Bible, Theological vs Pastoral
      Where Did We Get the Greek Texts?
      From Codex and Papyri to Critical Texts and Critical Apparatus
      Contemporary English Bibles

**Section Two:**      **Meaning Then, Meaning Now**

| | | |
|---|---|---|
| 6 | Exegesis, Hermeneutics, Exposition, and Interpretation. . . . . . . . . . . | 61 |

      Why These Matter
      Defining Terms, The Process
      Jesus' Contemporary Leaders and Bad Exegesis
      High Priests and Roman Leadership
      Grammatical Historical Method
      Contextual, Historical, and Contemporary Hermeneutics
      Both a Common Sense and a Scholarly Process

7   Imperative Types .......................................... 73
       Understanding Imperative Commands in Context
       Making Sense of Greek Mood for English Readers
       Imperative Time Aspect, Defined and Undefined
       "Let" and "Must" for Third Person Greek to English
       No means no, Imperative Prohibitions
       No means no, Non-Imperative Prohibitions
       Non-Imperatives Conveying an Imperative Intent
       Participles and Imperatives

8   Interpreting Then, Interpreting Now ........................... 89
       Morphology
       Greek Grammar and Syntax
       Word Formation and Morphology
       They Wrote, We Read
       Aramaic Insight
       Imperative Types

Section Three:        **The Imperatives of Jesus**

9   Matthew's Record of the Imperatives of Jesus ................... 101
       Matthew's Background and Intellect
       Reliability of Meticulous Matthew's Text

10  Mark's Record of the Imperatives ............................. 151
       Mark's Background
       Reliability, Timing

11  Luke's Record of the Imperatives of Jesus ...................... 185
       Luke's Background
       Luke's Intellect, Luke and Paul

12  John's Record of the Imperatives of Jesus ...................... 225
       John's Background
       John's Greek

13  The Imperatives of Jesus in Acts .............................. 259
       Reliability of Luke
       Imperatives Relocated Paul in Asia

14  The Imperatives of Jesus in Revelation ......................... 267
       John's Record of Jesus' Imperatives During the Revelation
       Interpreting Insight
       Summary of Jesus' Imperative to the Seven Churches

| | | |
|---|---|---|
| 15 | The Imperatives of Jesus in the Lord's Prayer | 277 |
| | The Setting of the Lord's Prayer | |
| | Greek to English | |

## Section Four: **Beyond His Commands**

| | | |
|---|---|---|
| 16 | Imperatives to the Christ | 287 |
| | How to Salt a Steak | |
| | What They Commanded Him | |

| | | |
|---|---|---|
| 17 | Spirit's Power, Father's Will, and Trinity in Jesus' Commands | 311 |
| | Titles and Names Matter | |
| | Paraclete, Comforter, Counselor, Helper, Advocate | |
| | Jesus and the Holy Spirit | |
| | Dove Power | |
| | Blasphemy against the Holy Spirit | |
| | Beyond Jesus toward His Imperatives | |
| | The Holy Spirit and the Spoken Imperatives of Peter and Paul | |
| | The Father's Will within Jesus | |
| | The Father's Will and the Disciples | |
| | John 14: 1 | |
| | Place of the Trinity | |
| | Jesus Immanuel and His Imperatives | |

| | | |
|---|---|---|
| 18 | Keeping His Commands, Exegesis of John 14: 15 | 329 |
| | Keep or Obey | |
| | Keep is neither a Simile nor a Metaphor for Obey | |

| | | |
|---|---|---|
| 19 | Conclusion and Summary | 339 |
| | Language and Culture Matter | |
| | Timing, History, and Culture Matter | |
| | Bible Translations Matter | |
| | From Knowing, to Understanding, to Keeping | |
| | Effort to Know Matters | |
| | Belief and Obedience / Disbelief and Disobedience | |
| | Imperative Proof | |

| | | |
|---|---|---|
| | Bibliography | 345 |

"It is the Spirit who gives life; the flesh is no help at all. The words that I have spoken to you are spirit and life. But there are some of you who do not believe." (For Jesus knew from the beginning who those were who did not believe, and who it was who would betray him.) And he said, "This is why I told you that no one can come to me unless it is granted him by the Father." After this many of his disciples turned back and no longer walked with him.

Jn 6: 63-66

# Preface

Honor your father and your mother, that your days
may be long in the land that the LORD your God is giving you. Ex 20: 12

## Family and Faith Traditions

When our families and friends gathered, no one talked much about who went to what church, but we all went somewhere. Family gatherings at homes included laughter, food, and usually one of us kids getting reprimanded. Someone always knocked over a framed glass photo of a deceased relative from the old country as we tossed baseballs in the living room. After everyone heard the crash, mom stepped into the room with her hands on her hips, then picked up the photo, placed it back on the table, and said, "Baseballs are for outdoors!" Lesson learned. Sunday school, church, prayer before all three meals and bedtime were seldom missed traditions.

Families and friends were a mix of Lutherans, Evangelicals, Catholics, Orthodox, Nazarenes, Baptists, Methodists, Reformed, Episcopalians, and too many Christian denominations to count. We also had friends who never attended church, but our family went every Sunday no matter how late we stayed up Saturday night.

There was a synagogue in town, but no one ever explained to me how a synagogue was different from a church. I never heard of a mosque or temple as a kid. Evangelists, Jehovah Witnesses, and Mormons regularly knocked on our door plying their message. Dad or Mom always kindly chatted with them while we siblings sat at the supper table, watching mashed potatoes grow cold.

## Family and Faith Traditions Challenged

Beyond my teen years and into college, something new began to happen. Non-denominational and mega-churches developed. I was raised to respect Pastors. Every Pastor that I knew wore robes, collars, and sashes. These new churches, however, had young guys in suits or t-shirts speaking from the floor. Pulpits disappeared. Watching someone without a robe from one of these new non-denominational megachurches talk about God from a podium (not a pulpit) was strange. Pastors went from robes to suits with ties, to sports coats, to jeans with open-collared shirts, to shorts with t-shirts and sandals. In my home church as a kid, we used hymn books with words right underneath dots and lines to follow the melody.

My older sister whispered, "Just follow the dots on the lines." which is pretty much how everybody I knew learned to read music. They sang along with the organ that made music coming out of big pipes, located up high in the back loft of the church. Sometimes mom or dad sang a little bit differently. My sister said, "That's harmony." It sounded nice even though I'm not sure mom or dad or my sister got it right all the time. As a kid, I did not know what harmony meant but figured all those dots and lines in those thick hymn books meant something. So I followed the dots. When I started going to those mega-churches, I noticed those big white screens showed just the words. I didn't hear the same sounds I had heard as a kid when everybody sang from my home church, even the older people. The mega-church music was nice, but not quite equal to a lot of gray-haired people belting out a hymn. I missed that.

New friends who called themselves Christians like me advocated that dirty jeans and t-shirts in the pulpit meant that the Pastor was my friend. Somebody told me that with these new mega-church pastors dressed in blue jeans (just like I wore during the week) because they had my spiritual care in mind. I could trust them because they were just like me.

With clothing change, came message change. In my youth, the Pastor wore a robe, and my parents dressed me in a suit. Hard to find pastors in robes and pew-sitters in suits today in most churches. The music also changed. Screens replaced hymnals with words and lots of pictures. The sermons seemed to be shorter too. I had never seen a drama play in church before attending one of those new megachurches. The closet my parents and siblings came to any drama was at Christmas. Some of the teens dressed to look like Mary, Joseph, and the Kings all gathered around a manger scene. But there was no talking. My old church had candles, but those seemed to disappear in these new churches. I can still smell the candles.

Through these new church experiences, I kept my Bible close. Didn't read it much, but it was there. No one told me the message would change. As long as I went to church, I figured no matter what Pastors wore or what hymns or worship songs were played, the Pastors were right. Pastors would never knowingly or even mistakenly teach me something wrong. Would they?

## Missing Something

Most of the churches that I have attended over decades have been worship-focused, with powerpoint leadership and pastorally based sermons. Parents taught us to respect pastors and teachers. Although posing questions to our Sunday-school teachers was not a problem, understanding their answers was a challenge. I sometimes struggled with, "Am I too stupid to understand"? or "Are they unable to give an understandable answer because they do not know the answer?" or "Are they not able to make me understand?"

Maybe you have had similar experiences. Perhaps like me, you went to church with your parents, didn't ask much, and enjoyed those church picnics. Not until later in life did I learn that Theology, Hebrew, Greek, Culture, Context, Exegesis, Hermeneutics, and other big words had anything to do with sermons or Sunday school. I was taught to sit still in church, pay attention to the Sunday school teacher, and don't ask too many questions.

After all those church years, I began to wonder if I had missed something. After thousands of sermons, classes, catechisms, and church socials and plenty of fried chicken and chocolate cake, perhaps not until our adult years do we realize so many biblical truths. There are only two options. Either I missed something by not paying attention, or perhaps I had never been taught more profound things.

Perhaps maturity in age has increased your desire for maturity in faith. Maybe you have come to find that churchianity has not been able to answer your more profound questions. I discovered that only more highly focused intentional study could provide solid food for which I hungered. It was not until the adult years that I realized how hungry I was and how undernourished I had been. If you too are starving in the pews, know you are not alone. Perhaps you also hunger for solid food.

But solid food is for the mature. Hb 5: 14.

## You Are Not Alone

It was not until my late 40's, through my 50's, and into the 60's that I began to seek relationships with new friends of faith hungry for solid food. I found people who wanted to learn beyond either emotionally charged megachurch messaging or staid, solemn services. I could not get enough. I often visited numerous churches, sometimes three or four on any Sunday. I found people hungry, wanting, and willing to put time, effort, and finances toward loving the Lord with their minds. They too sat in their pews with little meat on their nearly empty plates even after having filled the passing collection plate with tithes and offerings. I wondered how "How can I get beyond my church"?

As hypocritical as I felt, it seemed the church (or churches, no matter which one I attended) was holding me back. I was afraid to ask if the church was intentionally keeping me away from more profound things. With college came classes, grades, freedom, and other temptations which I thought had higher priorities than faith. Rightly interpreting the Word was not crucial to me at that time. I did not know my ignorance. However, God had placed me at Christian college where chapel attendance was mandatory. I often found chapel attendance more deeply edifying than any of the churches I attended.

Only after decades of church attendance, lay volunteerism in worship teams, Sunday school, mission trips, and small groups, did I realized that I was deeply involved in church ministry, but knew very little. Evangelizing, worshiping, reciting parables, and talking about the birth, life, death, resurrection, ascension, and a return of Jesus, came easy. Church told me what to do and did it. However, I knew little about God. Not a week went by that I did not do something for or through the church. But those big words that sometimes my Pastor said, but never explained, remained remote. Church mattered. God, however, was distant. Maybe that was my fault. Maybe not.

## What Would Jesus Do (WWJD)? Challenged

In the 1990's, most of my friends who said they were Christian wore, "What would Jesus do?" bracelets. Some stuck a bumper sticker with the acronym "WWJD" on their used car. From so many Sunday school classes, catechisms, mid-week meetings, baptisms, weddings, funerals, and church attendances, I knew a lot about what Jesus had done and probably what he would want me to do. However, I did not know much about what he said to do. From pulpits, lecterns, or open stages I repeatedly heard parables, Old Testament stories, and of course the 10 Commandments. I had heard about Revelation. But most of my Sunday school teachers and Pastors conveyed that the book of Revelation was too scary or something like that. The book of Revelation was too far beyond my teachers. So I looked at Revelation the same way. In my youth, I do not recall ever hearing any pastor preach or teach on Revelation. But I listened every week about Jesus, the cross, and salvation with some stories thrown in from the Pastor's personal experiences.

I eventually took the WWJD bracelet off, wondering if what Jesus had said was equally as important as to what he had done. Years of the church, Sunday school, and catechism classes pounded the Gospel message into me. However, I never had much clarity on what he had said to his disciples in their language, let alone what he's saying to me in my language. I wanted to know why Jesus said what he said to those in his day. Having been taught that salvation and church were the main Christian priorities, I began to ignore anything beyond salvation and church. I wanted the

Kingdom, but the Kingdom was never discussed. It seemed in all the churches I'd attended that only salvation and church mattered. Jesus' words in Mt 6: 33a took on a new meaning.

>Seek first the Kingdom of God and his righteousness ζητεῖτε δὲ πρῶτον τὴν βασιλείαν καὶ τὴν δικαιοσύνην αὐτοῦ. Mt 6: 33a

How could I have a relationship with God without knowing what Jesus had commanded? I wondered what Jesus had told his disciples? What exactly had they heard? How had they interpreted his commands after they heard him? I had to get beyond Bible stories. To go ahead, I had to go back to their time.

## Beyond Bible Stories to Historical Realities

This book first identifies and then provides commentary on each command of Jesus. More clearly, Section 3 is a reference commentary on the Koine Greek mood imperatives spoken by Jesus as recorded by Matthew, Mark, Luke, and John and translated into English from through Westcott-Hort Greek New Testament.

Now do not get frightened over some new words about Greek. Don't shut the book because you think you cannot handle Greek or theology or new words not often heard from pulpits. You can. This book is written at about an early high school level, so if you can read, you can understand what is in this book.

Studying the Greek imperatives of Jesus that Matthew, Mark, Luke, and John recorded provided to me a profound understanding of Jesus and those who wrote his words. Fed in youth by the King James Version (KJV) and later by paraphrases such as the New International Version (NIV) and New Living Translation (NLT), I realized something I thought impossible.

Bibles were different!

Not wanting to doubt my Pastors or their Bibles, I started comparing various English Bibles with cautious skepticism. In my youth, I had no idea that there were so many different Bible translations. I thought there was just one Bible, the KJV. I never knew about Bibles, but I could tell you about Christmas, Easter, and salvation. I kept my KJV Bible red-letter edition always near. My parents had given it to me after confirmation. It was cool because it had my name embossed right on the front in gold letters and it had pictures inside. Years went by.

## Intentional Intellectual Faith Development

Through intentionally conscience study at Wheaton, I realized that the imperative commands of Jesus (often translated at English commands) must be considered in their original context. In other words, meaning then and meaning now can be different. Big difference.

Comparing what I read in English in the quiet of my study under a single 75-watt bulb to what John recorded in Greek of what Jesus said was an eye-opener. English is adequate. But how did culture and the Greek language effect what the Matthew, Mark, John, Peter, and others had heard and understood in their day? How much might have been lost in translation from Greek to English? Was I missing something? Were others missing something? I had no idea of not just Greek but the cultures of Jesus' day. I also had no idea of how English Bibles came to be or translation philosophies or how translators throughout history have rendered Greek to English. You'll find those answers in Section 3.

Trusting pastors, Sunday school, and catechism teachers, I eventually realized they, like me, were limited to English translations. I came to hunger for the written and oral language of the Gospel writers, their context, their time, and their culture. Not mine. I knew what I was reading in English. Someone told me to pretend that I was living in Jesus' day. I could not do that without knowing the language and culture of Jesus' day. I had a strong worshipping feelings based faith but eventually realized that an intentional intellectual faith is also worshipful. Big difference.

This book has been written with non-Greek laypersons in mind. The commentary insights are intentioned for the laity. Readers need not be a Greek enthusiast. Your goal is to comprehend what disciples, Scribes, Pharisees, Sadducees, onlookers, and sinners heard Jesus say. Deeper still, your goal is also to understand what they came to believe after having heard Jesus speak. Remember, this book is about the rendering of Greek imperatives or into English commands. Be intentional in comparing their, "there and then," to our, "here and now." Big difference.

## Gratitude

Thank you to New Testament Greek Professors, tutors, and classmates, Wheaton professors Dr. J. Julius Scott, Jr., Dr. Mark Noll, Dr. Philip Comfort, Dr. Walter E. Elwell, Dr. Scott J. Hafemann, Dr. Doug Penny, the family of the late Dr. Tim Phillips, and the family of the late Dr. Robert Webber.

Thank you to fellow language and biblical theologically focused friends. Much appreciation for productive conversations and critiques from friends of the Evangelical Theological Society over the years. I am indebted to those in the academy and pastorates who have intentionally labored in mind and time to research and writing.

Appreciation also goes to Katy Overgard, Jim Haider, Dan Keating, Susan Wilson, Matthew Pukala, William Bill Grall, Catherine Rategan, Eric Twietmeyer, John Noe, Rob Pike, David Jobb, Mike Fehan, sisters Karma Orwig and Judy Carico and all who have persevered through our many conversations.

Love and gratitude to Donna Ligthart with whom I am blessed to be her husband. Without her, research, writing, editing, and production of this book would not have been possible.

Eternal thanks and glory be to the LORD Messiah, Immanuel Jesus.

From that time Jesus began to preach, saying, "Repent, for the kingdom of heaven is at hand."

Mt 4: 17

# Introduction

Then Daniel said to the steward whom the chief of the eunuchs had assigned over Daniel, Hananiah, Mishael, and Azariah, "Test your servants for ten days; let us be given vegetables to eat and water to drink. Dn 1: 11–12

## Mom and Vegetables

When your mom said, "Eat your vegetables!" you knew what to do. You ate your vegetables. Not eating those warm or sometimes cold vegetables sitting on your plate was not an option. Your mom was the boss. If you did not do what mom said, something happened. Mom told you what to do because she knew the consequences for you beyond what you could understand. Mom knew. You did not know. Now, eat your vegetables.

Mom's intentional will preceded her clear and understandable command that you eat your vegetables. Mom had big plans for your future. Her words and her rules developed from her superior and beneficial love for you.

Mom knew what was best for both you and her. So, she told you what to do. You did it. If you loved your mom, you ate your vegetables just as she had told you. You were better for eating your vegetables, even the cold, limp broccoli. Mom and Jesus are somewhat similar with regards to commands. Mom knew what would benefit you. Jesus knew what would benefit those he commanded. Jesus however, went beyond vegetables.

## How to Read this Book

First, this book is a research tool. Section Three "The Imperatives of Jesus" identifies all of Jesus' Greek imperative words and phrases in both English and Greek. Following each passage that contains a Greek imperative of Jesus is a brief commentary that may include context, meaning, exposition, interpretation, or nuances about the imperative.

Second, this book attempts to bring readers back to the first-century culture, language, grammar, and meaning. Grasping the historical context and meaning has precedence over contemporary application and significance. This book is written in a manner for today's reader to comprehend what first-century hearers and readers may have understood.

Third, Section One "Fear Not the Greek" and Section Two "Meaning Then, Meaning Now" provide valuable insight into Greek language and culture in their historical contexts. These two sections are useful in leaving contemporary presuppositions and returning to the meaning of Jesus' day. While these two sections are primers, they are helpful in understanding Jesus imperatives in the historical context of his day.

Fourth, this book provides a general commentary on Jesus' imperatives. Comments following each imperative are not intended to be exhaustive but insightful in drawing out Jesus' imperatives. Readers are encouraged to seek more scholarly comments for contemporary application.

Following the Contents, Preface, and Introduction, this book has four sections:

- Section One: "Fear Not the Greek," provides an overview of Koine Greek for the laity. This section is purposed to help non-Greek readers approach the original language and culture without fear.

- Section Two: "Meaning Then, Meaning Now," highlights common challenges translators encounter when rendering English from Koine Greek. A lay explanation of exegesis, contextual hermeneutics, historical hermeneutics, contemporary hermeneutics, exposition, and interpretation is provided.

- Section Three: "The Imperatives of Jesus" is the meat of the book. This section identifies the English commands derived from the Greek imperative mood form recorded by Matthew, Mark, Luke, and John. You may start by immediately digging into Section Three. However, much can be learned reading Sections One, Two, and Four. Chapter 15 identifies Jesus' imperatives within the Lord's Prayer.

- Section Four: "Beyond His Commands" highlights the Greek imperative mood forms translated into English commands spoken to and heard by Jesus. Did Jesus obey commands from others? This section provides insight into the role of the Holy Spirit and the Father's will regarding Jesus' commands and analysis of Jn 14: 15.

You may delay the more profound insights offered in Section One, Section Two, and Section Four. Helpful to understanding what Jesus commanded are basic understanding of exegesis, contextual hermeneutics, historical hermeneutics, contemporary hermeneutics, and translation methodologies. A simple comprehension of these five topics will be helpful.

However, starting with Section Three, "The Imperatives of Jesus" is not problematic. If you have little interest in the preliminary information, no problem. Just proceed to Section Three: "The Imperatives of Jesus" in Chapters 9 through 15.

Since this book is about translating Jesus' Greek imperatives to English commands, precise word definitions are helpful. Where the word "imperative" is found, refers to the Greek imperative morphological mood form. The narrative will be about the historical context of Jesus' day. Where the word "command" or "demand" or "order" is found, refers to the contemporary context of our day. In English, people understand a command such as a General's command to those lower in rank or a boss's authority over an employee. Keep the idea of being told what to do where the English words command, commanded, commanding, demand, demanded, or demanding are found. The word "imperative" refers to the Greek mood and historical context. The word "command" and its cognates refer to English meanings.

This book has been written from the view that Jesus spoke Greek and that Matthew, Mark, and John with the help of editors recorded the Greek that Jesus spoke. Luke not being an eyewitness depended on corroborating witnesses. More in-depth, this book also considers beyond what first-century readers read in Greek after the books, gospels were copied and distributed. This book focuses on what hearers of Jesus heard in his Greek. To that point, this book attempts to go back beyond English translations to comprehend the Greek from the view of:

1. What Jesus said in Greek
2. What Jesus meant in their language
3. What his disciples and those within the narratives heard and
4. What those who heard Jesus speak may have thought he meant.

Reading this book with these four perspectives in mind will be helpful. The book has been written for those having no knowledge of New Testament Koine Greek. The book is a laity primer more than a scholarly critique and is intended to bring the reader back to when Jesus spoke.

For ease of use, sufficient passages surrounding Jesus' imperatives are provided for the reader to grasp the context before and after his imperatives. Extensive use of quotation marks identifying a single word or phrase is intentional. Quotation marks around keywords are intended to identify specific words in the narrative to assist the reader. Since some passages in the synoptic gospels (Matthew, Mark, and Luke) parallel each other, passages listed at the end of the comment sections are referenced to other books.

## The Importance of Historical Context

Proper exegesis, hermeneutics, and interpretation methods affirm that Jesus' words do not trump the biblical narrative in its context. Jesus said many things. This book does not focus on everything Jesus said. Instead, it focuses only on his Greek Imperatives translated into English commands. John affirmed the breadth of what Jesus did beyond what John or others wrote about what Jesus said:

> This is the disciple who is bearing witness about these things, and who has written these things, and we know that his testimony is true. Now there are also many other things that Jesus did. Were every one of them to be written, I suppose that the world itself could not contain the books that would be written. Jn 21: 24-25

Interpreting biblical texts out of context is problematic. Understanding the imperatives of Jesus can bring a more profound understanding of who he was to his disciples in their day and who he is to us in our day. That is why context is so important.

Could Jesus's disciples have denied his imperative commands? Did they follow, or did they fail? Moreover, what about you? To understand his commands to us as we read in English, we must first understand his Greek imperatives to them.

## Why Read This Book?

Renewing your mind through understanding Jesus' Greek imperatives and English commands can be transforming. You may experience a broader sense of truth, veracity, reliability, and confidence. Just as his disciples struggled to determine who Jesus was, you might experience a more profound discernment of good from evil, light from darkness and truth from deceit. This book offers three helps:

- This book helps readers build a relationship beyond salvation, knowing Jesus as King and Immanuel - God with us.

- This book helps edify, educate, and teach those within Jesus' church.

- This book helps to strengthen those proclaiming His Kingdom.

Jesus' commands in the first-century context can deepen your faith. Your goal is to move from complexity to simplicity. First, grasp the mindset of Jesus' imperatives his orders, his directives, his proclamations, and especially his commands had a purpose for those who heard him. An effort is required to first understand meaning to them before trying to understand meaning to us. Then consider the relevance and the power of his commands in our day.

## Going There

Those who heard his imperative commands gradually came to understand the power of his imperatives. His disciples matured. Their maturity was costly. Even though they walked with Jesus, time was required for them to comprehend his commands. It took them even more time after his resurrection and ascension to understand his commands. Similarly, you too may need some time. Have patience. You do not have the benefit of hearing his words — big difference. Matthew, Mark, Luke, and John progressed in their understanding of the imperatives of Jesus. His words caused them to fear. Luke affirmed:

> "He said to them, 'Where is your faith?' And they were afraid, and they marveled, saying to one another, 'Who then is this, that he commands even winds and water, and they obey him?'" εἶπεν δὲ αὐτοῖς Ποῦ ἡ πίστις ὑμῶν φοβηθέντες δὲ ἐθαύμασαν λέγοντες πρὸς ἀλλήλους Τίς ἄρα οὗτός ἐστιν ὅτι καὶ τοῖς ἀνέμοις ἐπιτάσσει καὶ τῷ ὕδατι καὶ ὑπακούουσιν αὐτῷ? Lk 8: 25

The Disciples needed time to surrender both their fear of him and the fear of his words, especially his commands they heard through his Greek imperatives. After having heard and experienced his imperative commands, they ultimately learned to live, preach, and teach without fear. Both their discipleship and confidence were increased over time. You must do the same. After reading this book, you may find that you both fear and love Jesus' commands. To quote from Proverbs, "The fear of the LORD is the beginning of knowledge; fools despise wisdom and instruction. Pr 1: 7

## To Them, For Us

When we read the Bible, we must always be cognizant that we read words, phrases, statements, paragraphs, chapters, and whole letters written to others, not us today. The saying, "The Bible was written to them for us." is foundational.

While the original writers may have considered that others like you would be reading their letters thousands of years later, I approach this book from the position that the writers wrote to their readers in their day. Their language and culture influenced their thoughts and interpretations. The Holy Spirit empowered them to write and read their words in their day.

As you read each imperative spoken by Jesus as recorded by the writers, picture yourself looking over the shoulders of original readers. You are there. You are with them. However, they are unaware of your presence. Try to read what they read or heard in the first-century context — big difference.

## Simple Past Tense Style

A deliberate effort has been made to write in the past tense, not present active tense. You will read, "Jesus said." not, "Jesus says." You will read, "Mark wrote that Jesus said." not, "Mark writes that Jesus says." This past tense style is intentional. The present active tense can inhibit the reader from going back to their time and place. Reading in past tense form can help readers grasp the importance of historical context. Present faith if first historical. We first go there. Then we come back home.

## Contextual Understanding

Four words that scholars often use are "exegesis," "hermeneutics," "context," and "exposition." Basic understanding of these words is appropriate for a study/commentary book of this type. When "exegesis" and "hermeneutics" are substituted for one another, confusion results. For this book, I have deferred to a simple and generally agreed explanation for exegesis and hermeneutics by most scholars from Gordon D. Fee and Douglas Stuart in their book, *How to Read the Bible for All Its Worth: A Guide to Understanding the Bible*. Fee and Stuart affirm:

> Exegesis is the careful, systematic study of the Scripture to discover the original intended meaning.[1] Although the word 'hermeneutics' ordinarily covers the whole field of interpretation, including exegesis, it is also used in the narrower sense of seeking the contemporary relevance of ancient texts.[2]

---

[1] Fee, Gordon D., and Douglas Stuart, *How to Read the Bible for All Its Worth*, 19.
[2] Ibid. 25.

When reading this book, these definitions will help:

- "Context" refers to historical biblical backgrounds, environments, situations, and perspectives.

- "Exegesis" refers to what they wrote.

- "Contextual Hermeneutics" refers to what the text meant there and then at or near the time of the writing.

- "Historical Hermeneutics" refers to what interpreters throughout history thought the text meant in their historical setting.

- "Contemporary Hermeneutics" refers to what today's interpreters think the biblical texts mean in our contemporary setting.

The reason for identifying three hermeneutic types is to help lay readers understand interpretation throughout history. In short, what people thought at the time when something happened may not be the same as what people thought later in history, which may not be the same as what people believe today. "Contextual Hermeneutics" meaning, what the text meant to them in their time is the priority. We cannot know what Jesus said without knowing what the Gospel writers wrote. For this book, we are first concerned with what Jesus said in their context. Chapter 6, expounds.

## Laity Demand for Emotions and Relevance

In today's pews lay demand for emotions and relevance is a high priority. There is a mandate by the sheep that the shepherd addresses the present pastoral needs of the sheep and make them feel good about it. The sheep tell the shepherd what and how to feed them. They want relevance and feelings. As a result, the immediate application drives the messenger and the message. There is a cost for only pursuing relevance for immediate application. That can be a problem.

In response to demand for relevance, sermons, homilies, small group lessons, and writings are in present tense grammar. While accommodating lay demand for relevance seems helpful, when life application contextual hermeneutics mediocre and possibly erroneous interpretations are likely. In other words, in the zeal to become relevant to an immediate clamoring laity, the use of the present tense often obscures context. As a result, much can be lost in translation.

Worse, pulpit messages from well-intentioned preachers often include mixed tenses. Preachers who mix past, present, and future tenses both in and out of context more often confuse more than clarify. Mixed tenses can produce incorrect and confusing messaging. Sadly many speaking from behind our pulpits exude grammar and tense mixtures that produce confusion. A past tense style, as much as possible within this book, was intentional.

## Past Tense or Present Tense

People in the pews often opine that their pastors are pastoral only when their messages seem relevant. After having heard sermons and teachings conveyed in present tense listeners often feel enlightened. However, cheap relevance without historical context is dim light. Relevance for the "here and now" as the only goal can be a problem. The problem is, one cannot get to the "here and now" without having first gone to the "there and then." Fee and Stewart agree:

> The reason good exegeting and good preaching must not begin with the here and now is that the only proper control for hermeneutics is found in the original intent of the biblical text.[3]

Today's demand for relevance has resulted in a disregard for the original intent of the biblical text in their time and space. The sheep opine, "I do not care what it meant back then because I am here now, and I need help. That is why I come to church, and if the pastor does not make the message relevant, especially to me, I will go down the street to another pastor." Demand for relevance has resulted in present tense form prevalence:

>  Jesus walks. (Simple Present)
>  Jesus is walking. (Present Progressive)
>  Jesus has walked. (Present Perfect)
>  Jesus has been walking. (Present Perfect Progressive)

Present tenses convey a contemporary modern current realism which to hearers sounds relevant to them. They leave church feeling, "Wow, the pastor is preaching right to me. What a relevant and meaningful message for me." However, contemporary wording and sentimentality is not the whole message.

## Tense Confusion from the Pulpit

Present tense over usage can be subjectively providing a variety of meanings from the text for whatever the orator wants the text to mean. Fee and Stewart affirm:

> Otherwise, biblical texts can be made to mean whatever they meant to any given reader. However, such hermeneutics becomes pure subjectivity, and who then is to say that one person's interpretation is right, and another's is wrong. Anything goes. In contrast to such subjectively, we insist that the original meaning of the text – as much as it is in our power to discern it – is the objective point of control.[4]

---

[3] Fee, Gordon D., and Douglas Stuart, *How to Read the Bible for All Its Worth*, 25.
[4] Ibid. 25.

Since this book was intentionally written as much as possible in the past tense, some past tense examples are:

> Jesus spoke. (Simple Past),
> Jesus was speaking. (Past Progressive),
> Jesus had spoken. (Past Perfect),
> Jesus had been speaking. (Past Perfect Progressive).

For this book, the original recording and meaning in their context of the Greek text have priority. Understanding here and now is elusive without initially knowing then and there. With the mindset that, "The Bible was written to them for us." comments following each of Jesus' imperatives in chapters 9 – 16 are intentionally written in the past tense.

The past tense style can put you, the reader in the mindset that you are looking back to their context. You may find reading in the past tense a bit awkward. However, as you progress clarity and understanding will become easier. We read words that Jesus said in the past to his hearers and words that the writers wrote to their contemporaries. Klein sums up well my approach:

> Our goal remains to hear the message of the Bible as the original audience would have heard it or as the first readers would have understood it.[5]

Respect for the text is paramount. An attempt to understand God's Word is to glorify God. Thoughtful devotion toward the biblical text does not mean that every insight or comment is sacrosanct in any text. Agreeing with a phrase from Bill Mounce regarding his book, *The Morphology of Biblical Greek*:

> At the core of this study is a profound reverence for the biblical text and a desire to understand God's word as wholly as possible.[6]

## Software and References

*Bibleworks Software V8* was the source for *English Standard Version* from Crossway and Greek New Testament Morphology from Westcott and Hort. *Nestle-Aland Greek-English New Testament*, Barbara Aland, Kurt Aland, Deutsche Bibelgesellschaft, Stuttgart, and *The New Greek-English Interlinear New Testament*, Robert W. Brown, Phillip W. Comfort edited by J.D. Douglas were also sourced.

While there are numerous New Testament Koine Greek scholars, one would be hard-pressed not to find the works of William Mounce, Henry Wallace, and Frederick William Danker's in seminaries and theological schools. William Mounce's numerous textbooks and especially his *Basics of Biblical Greek* are commonplace for beginning and advanced Koine Greek students. Daniel B. Wallace's, *Greek Grammar Beyond the Basics* are commonly found in any serious student's home or school library.

---

[5] Klein, William, Craig L. Blomberg, Robert L. Hubbard, Jr., *Introduction to Biblical Interpretation,* 12.
[6] Mounce, William D., *The Morphology of Biblical Greek: A Companion to Basics of Biblical Greek and the Analytical Lexicon to the Greek New Testament,* Xvi.

While this book is not a word study, Colin Brown's, *New International Dictionary of New Testament Theology* as well as Mounce's, *Complete Expository Dictionary of Old and New Testament Words* are noteworthy. Regarding Exegesis and Hermeneutics, Gordon Fee and Douglas Stuart's, *How to Read the Bible for All Its Worth* and William W. Klein, Craig L. Blomberg, and Robert L Hubbard Jr.'s book, *Introduction to Biblical Interpretation* are also found in seminaries and theological schools. Henry Virkler's, *Hermeneutics* is an informative and short read for those serious about getting the text right.

See the Bibliography for a detailed list of all referenced works.

## Footnotes and Margins

I have intentionally chosen footnotes over endnotes and have not followed a typical 40-word indentation format. Regardless of longevity, indentations are for reader value, ease, and note-taking. Turning to the back of a book for referencing information is both challenging and time-consuming. Margins are deliberately wide for note-taking. The font size and book size are intentional for ease of use behind pulpits or lecterns.

Where possible, the layout has been designed not to require readers to turn pages. Only the author, title, and page numbers are reference cited. Cited works are available in the bibliography. Bible verses may be written within the text or found in a footnote depending on the context, length, and reader ease. A two-letter biblical book abbreviation has been used.

## Images

Katie Overgard produced the images throughout this book in conjunction with numerous editors. Each image was prepared to elicit more profound contemplations for readers. Facial features were intentionally excluded for a broader context. Each image links to a passage or description within the book. Images were deliberately created in black and white with limited peripheral content to focus on a particular message. Below each image is a brief narrative specific to that image. Much appreciation is given to Katy and numerous editors who viewed and commented on Katy's images as this book developed.

## Disclaimer One

There are numerous books from Greek scholars that can more deeply edify the Greek text. Noted scholars like, Wallace, Carson, Porter, Mounce, and others have produced scores of New Testament Greek books for instruction. This book is a primer. Greek, exegesis, hermeneutics, exposition, and interpretation courses combined with individual study and tutoring can give confidence. I humbly concede to scholars more deeply edified than myself and trust this primer will bring a thirst for context and language. I convey my deep respect for college, university, and seminary Koine Greek teachers, translation teams, those teaching Greek with minds and hearts for God's word.

## Disclaimer Two

Within this book are some English Bible translation anomalies. Highlighting anomalies is intended for discussion and building up the body. Apologetics,[7] irenics,[8] polemics,[9] Or dialogues and debates today are seldom found in faith bodies, churches or academies. That is, Christians rarely debate, discuss, or dialogue over doctrines, dogmas, or practices. Sadly ecumenical understanding and love seem to dominate at the cost of merely searching for the truth. Too few of both secularists and people of faith are willing to say, "Oops. Hmm. I might have that wrong."

Christians go to church and listen. However, seldom are Christians afforded the openness to ask questions in a public forum with fellow congregants. As a result, over time, numerous interpretations have produced practices and beliefs widely varying across Christianity through innumerable denominations.

There can be confusion and misunderstanding about Christianity both within Christendom and outside of Christendom. Christians can get lost in both too many and too few details. Different interpretations are the result of both mistakenly misunderstanding the details and erroneously obscuring the details. In *Exploring Theological English: Reading, Vocabulary, and Grammar for ESL/EFL*, Pierson summarizes well the issues of time and interpretation:

> Through the ages, differing interpretations have developed as to how the details of Christianity are to be understood.[10]

This book is less concerned with how the details of Christianity are to be understood and more concerned with illuminating the Word, particularly the grammar and usage of Jesus' Greek imperatives. To restate, this book does not provide an apology, irenic, or polemic. This book helps English Bible readers understand the historical and linguistic mindsets of those who heard or read Jesus words in the language of their time.

## Disclaimer Three

This book is not connected to nor an advocate for the "Jesus Seminar," "Quest for the Historical Jesus," "Jesus Project," or "The Westar Institute." This book is not connected to nor an advocate for the "Red Letter Christian" movement. This book solely provides an objective exegetical study commentary on the Greek imperative mood form spoken by Jesus as recorded by Matthew, Mark, Luke, and John in the New Testament.

---

[7] Apologetics: Occasionally called eristics, apologetics is the formal defense of the Christian Faith. Grenz, Stanley, J., David Guretzki, and Cherith Fee Nordling, *Pocket Dictionary of Theological Terms*, 13.

[8] Irenics: The practice of debating and discussing Christian doctrines with other Christians who are theologically orthodox but with whom there are matters of genuine theological disagreement. It involves the friendly but rigorous task of doing theological reflection together within the community of faith. Grenz, Stanley, J., David Guretzki, and Cherith Fee Nordling, *Pocket Dictionary of Theological Terms*, Downers Grove, IL: Intervarsity Press, 1999. 68.

[9] Polemics: The art of disputation or controversy (the defense of a thesis by formal logic). A polemic can also be the aggressive refutation of another position or principle. Grenz, Stanley, J., David Guretzki, and Cherith Fee Nordling, *Pocket Dictionary of Theological Terms*, 92.

[10] Pierson, Cheri L., Dickerson, Lonna J., Scott, Florence R., *Exploring Theological English: Reading, Vocabulary, and Grammar for ESL/EFL*, xiv.

## Disclaimer Four

This book is not connected to nor an advocate for a dispensational antinomian view of Old Testament commandments. This book is not connected to nor an advocate for or against any denominational advocacy regarding dispensational eschatology, already, not yet, or inaugurated/consummated Kingdom views. This book solely provides an objective exegetical study commentary on the Greek imperative mood form spoken by Jesus as recorded by Matthew, Mark, Luke, and John in the New Testament.

## Disclaimer Five

A study of Jesus' Greek imperatives might be mistakenly interpreted to advocate law over grace simply by the context of the study. This book is not intended to advocate a doctrine or systematic theology related to law or grace. While the subject matter centers on Jesus' Greek imperative mood usage to English commands, this book is not purposed to imply that Jesus' words have precedence over biblical laws in their context. This reference commentary is not intended to be a controversial polemic advocating or discouraging biblical law or grace.

## Summary

Believers face the unceasing challenge to overcome the flesh, the world, and Satan. This book is an attempt to justifiably and accurately handle exegesis, exposition, hermeneutics, and interpretation. It is my hope that this book imparts a deeper purpose to faith and calling. Be blessed through the imperatives of Jesus Immanuel, God with us.

Richard Ligthart, MBA, MA
2019

# Section 1

# Fear Not The Greek

Blessed is the one who reads aloud the words of this prophecy, and blessed are those who hear, and who keep what is written in it, for the time is near.

Rv 1: 3

Now as he went on his way, he approached Damascus, and suddenly a light from heaven flashed around him. And falling to the ground he heard a voice saying to him, "Saul, Saul, why are you persecuting me?" And he said, "Who are you, Lord?" And he said, "I am Jesus, whom you are persecuting. But rise and enter the city, and you will be told what you are to do." The men who were traveling with him stood speechless, hearing the voice but seeing no one.

Ac 9: 3-7

# 4 Koine Greek for English Speaking Christians

> Pilate also wrote an inscription and put it on the cross. It read, "Jesus of Nazareth, the King of the Jews." Many of the Jews read this inscription, for the place where Jesus was crucified was near the city, and it was written in Aramaic, in Latin, and in Greek. So the chief priests of the Jews said to Pilate, "Do not write, 'The King of the Jews,' but rather, 'This man said, I am King of the Jews.'" Pilate answered, "What I have written I have written." Jn 19: 19-22

## Koine Greek Basics

The Koine Greek of the New Testament preceded both classic and contemporary Greek. Koine Greek today is considered a dead language, no longer in general use as a written or spoken language. However, through Christian schools, seminaries, and theological higher schools of learning Koine Greek is available and lives on.

Greek is a beautiful language for clarity. Koine Greek of Jesus's time conveyed a simplicity in their context that can be difficult to understand and convey here and now. Those unfamiliar with or having little appreciation for the contextual language and culture in the time of Jesus can miss a more in-depth understanding.

## The Perfection of God's Chosen Time

The timing of Jesus' birth, life, ministry, suffering, death, resurrection, ascension, and the promise of his ever presence was perfect. Paul in his message to the Galatians affirmed the perfection of Jesus' timing to redeem those under the law. The Koine Greek language of the New Testament was significant to the fullness of time. Paul affirmed:

> However, when the fullness of time had come, ὅτε δὲ ἦλθεν τὸ πλήρωμα τοῦ χρόνου, God sent forth his Son, born of woman, born under the law, to redeem those who were under the law, so that we might receive adoption as sons. Gl 4: 4-5

The fullness of time had arrived. That fullness of time, that historical foundation on which the Gospel started and now stands was perfect. The timing of Jesus' arrival could have been anytime. God could also have sent Jesus after the prophet Malachi ended his book and before Caesar Augustus ruled the Roman Empire.

God could have bypassed the rule of Judea under Pontius Pilate and the Temple leadership under Caiaphas and Annas. God could have sent Jesus after the fall of Rome, during the Civil War, WWI, and WWII or in the 1970s. Further, God could also have waited after Neil Armstrong walked on the moon. Alternatively, we today could still be awaiting the Messiah. The awaited Old Testament Messiah who had been prophesied had arrived.

The point is that waiting for Jesus Immanuel; the God with us Messiah is over. He arrived at the fullness of time. Significant to that time was not just Jesus' arrival. Significant also were the people, nations, religions, beliefs, and cultures. Perhaps the most significant contribution to the fullness of time was language, the chosen language of their day.

# The Perfection of God's Chosen Language

God chose the time. God chose the place. God also chose the language. Agreeing with Paul's words to the Galatians regarding the timing of Jesus, the appointed time included the language. The language recorded by those who scribed his spoken words have a bearing on meaning. What authors and scribes wrote to them, there and then, is available for us to read here and now. So as previously presented, our challenge is getting back to then. Returning to the first century when Jesus walked requires at least a minimal understanding of the language and words of their time. The language of the New Testament was Koine Greek, and that particular language, the language chosen by God for that time, had arrived during the time between the Old and New Testaments.

## The Time Between the Testaments: Books

Considering biblical history, 400 years had passed from the last Old Testament book Malachi to the New Testament Gospels. Those 400 hundred years are not without historical writings. The collection of books during that time period are referred to by Protestants as "The Apocrypha" or "Deuterocanonical" books. Both the Roman Catholic and Eastern Orthodox communities include the Apocrypha books. The Orthodox refer to the Apocrypha books as the "longer cannon" derived the Septuagint not Hebrew. The Bible of Protestants and Evangelicals does not include the Apocryphal books. Bibles used by Protestant and Evangelical communities numbers a total of 66 books, 39 Old Testament books, and 27 New Testament books and do not include the Apocrypha.[1] Metzger clarifies:

> The word "Apocrypha" is used in a variety of ways that can be confusing to the general reader. The confusion arises partly from the ambiguity or the ancient usage of the word, and partly from the modern application of the term to different groups of books.[2]

In short, the Roman Catholic magisterium throughout history has developed doctrines and practices from Apocryphal books. Since Protestants and Evangelicals have not included Apocryphal books in their 66 book canon, doctrines, beliefs, dogmas and practices have not developed from them. However, history and written documents after Malachi and before Matthew have contributed to the formation of the Christian faith.

This book does not detail doctrines or practices among churches or denominations within Christendom related to canonization of books. The "Apocryphal/Deuterocanonical" books are recommended reading for all Christians to recognize history that preceded the New Testament.

---

[1] It is fruitless to debate the exact number of books in Bibles associated with numerous denominations throughout history. The number of books within the Apocrypha varies depending on how the books are numbered or combined. For our purpose in studying the Greek imperative mood forms of Jesus, all Christian Bibles contain the 27 New Testament books which include the Gospels, Acts, and Revelation.

[2] Metzger, Bruce M., Roland E. Murphy, *The New Oxford Annotated Apocrypha, The Apocryphal/Deuterocanonical Books of the Old Testament*, iii.

## The Time Between the Testaments: Faith

During these 400 years, the Jewish faith underwent historic changes. Julius Scott in his book, *Customs and Controversies: Intertestamental Jewish Backgrounds of the New Testament* recognizes various terms for Judaism during the time between the Testaments:

> Jewish writers seem to prefer "Second Temple" or "Second Commonwealth Judaism." At times such names as "Early Judaism," "Middle Judaism," "Greco-Roman Judaism," and "Judaism of the Late Hellenistic Period" are employed. We shall call it "Intertestamental Judaism."[3]

The first Jewish Temple in Jerusalem built by Solomon was destroyed in 586 BC by the Babylonians. Following the Temple destruction, the Jews were exiled in mass to Babylon. Eventually, following the return of the Jews from captivity in Babylon to Jerusalem permitted by Persian King Cyrus under his "Edict of Cyrus" the Temple was restored. Beyond the physical Temple restoration, the Jewish faith was also restored. Zerubbabel oversaw the Temple restoration. Nehemiah focused on the Temple walls. Ezra focused on the faith restoration of the community. In spite of the Temple, Temple walls, and community restoration in place, the influence of Hellenism and the conflicts of customs and controversies had started. Scott affirms the broad influences of Hellenistic culture:

> A highly significant reason for the rise of distinctive customs and controversies was the variety of reactions to two major crises, the destruction of the Jewish state and temple by the Babylonians in the sixth century B.C. and the arrival of Hellenistic culture in the fourth century B.C.[4]

Per Scott, "Intertestamental Judaism" laid the groundwork for two major faith groups: Rabbinic Judaism and early primitive Christianity. Between 516 BC and AD 70. Judaism faced many influences under both Greeks under Alexander and eventually the Romans. In any event, Judaism faith and practices experienced invasions by Greeks and eventually the Romans who destroyed the second temple in AD 70 some brief 40 years after the crucifixion of Jesus.

## The Time Between the Testaments: Philosophy

Greek philosophical influences went far beyond only political rule. Transcending governance alone, Greek philosophy through the spread of Hellenism transcended both governance and religion. Scott elucidates the influence of past Greek culture into the present:

> The conquests of Alexander the Great changed the world; the Jewish community was no exception. The most sweeping part of that change was not political but cultural. Alexander deliberately set out to spread Greek culture. His army included city planners and architects, literary figures and philosophers, biologists, and botanists, musicians and actors, and other purveyors of culture. The infusion of

---

[3] Scott Jr., J. Julius, *Customs and Controversies: Intertestamental Jewish Backgrounds of the New Testament*, Grand Rapids, MI: Baker Books, 1995. 20. (Second printing is *Jewish Backgrounds of the New Testament*).
[4] Ibid. 23.

Hellenistic culture into the broader world was his greatest legacy. Hellenistic political dominance lasted until Roman conquests absorbed the last Hellenistic kingdoms (c. 30 B.C.). Hellenistic culture was a significant factor in Judaism for about 360 years, and its influence continues to this day.[5]

Scott provides understanding on two schools of Greek philosophy cited by Luke:

> Luke recorded two Hellenistic schools of philosophy in Acts 17:18, the Epicureans and the Stoics. Epicurus (c. 341 – 270 B.C.) assumed no supernatural being or future human existence. For Epicurus, pleasure meant friendship, mental serenity, and the absence of fear and pain; his followers defined pleasure more materially and sensually. Stoicism seems to have been the dominant philosophy of the Hellenistic world. It was founded by Zeno (c. 335 – 265 B.C.) a Phoenician, whose outlook has been summarized as "Live according to nature. The Stoics assume a cyclical character of the natural order. Happiness and virtue were found by living in harmony with this order submitting to the *logos*.[6]

Greek philosophy shaped Judaism and Christianity. Beyond Epicureans and Stoics mentioned by Luke are three Greek philosophers and a Greek conqueror: Socrates, Plato, Aristotle and Alexander the Great. Chronologically, Socrates taught Plato. Plato taught Aristotle. Aristotle taught Alexander the Great. Having been philosophically influenced by Socrates, Plato, and Aristotle, Alexander the Great conquered the Persians. He spread Hellenism to the Jews just a few centuries before Jesus was born. Alexander died in 323 B.C. After the death of Alexander, Hellenism, shaped by the philosophies of Socrates, Plato, and Aristotle advanced Greek culture, thought, and language where Jesus was born and lived. Below are the life timelines of distinguished Greeks before the birth of Jesus.

```
Socrates     469_____399
Plato              423_____347
Aristotle                        384_____322
Alexander                              356_____323
```

## The Time Between the Testaments: Hellenism

Seldom heard from pulpits are sermons or insights about Socrates, Plato, Aristotle, or Alexander the Great. However, Greek philosophy is linked to the Gospel writings. Both the Gospel message and the concept of the Kingdom of God were not familiar to Hellenism. Nevertheless, without these teachers and the conqueror Alexander, the Koine Greek language of the New Testament, the writers, and the Hellenism of Palestine would not have happened. Few give thought to God having worked through these three Greek philosophers that lead to the spread of Hellenism through Alexander's conquests. Equally as influential as Jewish Semitic culture upon Christendom is Hellenistic language, culture, and thought.

---

[5] Scott Jr., J. Julius, *Customs and Controversies: Intertestamental Jewish Backgrounds of the New Testament*, 114.
[6] Ibid. 115.

Most Christians know the Jewish roots of Christianity. The links between the Old Testament Hebrew books and New Testament Gospel and Epistles are well established. What is less known by Christians is how Greek culture notably Hellenism contributed to Christianity.

Hellenism and Hellenists were significant influencers at the time of Jesus and when New Testament authors wrote. Three times Luke recorded issues regarding Hellenists.[7] Hellenists were indigenous people who were not Greek. Being bilingual or multilingual, they spoke Aramaic and Greek and embraced the Greek way of life. F. F. Bruce summarizes:

> Many of the Hellenists would have connections with the Diaspora, whereas most of the Hebrews would be Palestinian Jews. The line of demarcation between Hebrews and Hellenists cannot have been hard and fast, for many Jews were bilingual. Paul, for example, who spoke Greek habitually (as might be expected in a native of Tarsus), nevertheless calls himself 'a Hebrew born of Hebrews' (Phil 3:5; *cf.* 2 Cor 11:22). Perhaps the determinant factor with such a person was whether the services in the synagogue which he attended were conducted in Greek (*cf.* Acts 6:9) or in Hebrew.[8]

In Acts 9: 22 – 29 both Jews and Hellenists plotted to kill Saul / Paul to end his life and message. Whether Hellenism and Hellenists positively or negatively influenced Christianity is a subjective argument. What is not subjective is that Hellenism and Hellenists played a significant role in shaping Christianity as did Judaism.

## Greek and New Testament Timing

Greek was not a native language of the indigenous people where Jesus walked. Since Aramaic was the colloquial language, how did Greek become the language at the time and place where Jesus ministered, and the Gospel writers wrote? To understand the power of the Greek language and its dissemination, a history lesson will help. As previously mentioned, key historical events and eras brought the Greek language prior to and during the life of Jesus.

The time between the conclusion of the Old Testament and the beginning of the New Testament is referred to as the "Intertestamental Period" chronologically dated approximately 400 BC to Jesus' arrival. This "Intertestamental Period" or "Time Between the Testaments" is also known as the "400 Years of Silence." Specific to Judaism this period is also known as

---

[7] Ac 6: 1 Now in these days when the disciples were increasing in number, a complaint by the Hellenists arose against the Hebrews because their widows were being neglected in the daily distribution.

Ac 9: 22 – 29 But Saul increased all the more in strength, and confounded the Jews who lived in Damascus by proving that Jesus was the Christ. When many days had passed, the Jews plotted to kill him, but their plot became known to Saul. They were watching the gates day and night in order to kill him, but his disciples took him by night and let him down through an opening in the wall, lowering him in a basket. And when he had come to Jerusalem, he attempted to join the disciples. And they were all afraid of him, for they did not believe that he was a disciple. But Barnabas took him and brought him to the apostles and declared to them how on the road he had seen the Lord, who spoke to him, and how at Damascus he had preached boldly in the name of Jesus. So he went in and out among them at Jerusalem, preaching boldly in the name of the Lord. And he spoke and disputed against the Hellenists. But they were seeking to kill him.

Ac 11: 20 But there were some of them, men of Cyprus and Cyrene, who on coming to Antioch spoke to the Hellenists also, preaching the Lord Jesus.

[8] F.F. Bruce, "Hellenists" in Douglas, J. D., ed., in *The Illustrated Bible Dictionary*, 635.

"Intertestamental Judaism" referring to the type of Judaism practiced by Jews during that time. Some scholars determined that after the last book of the Old Testament and the first book of the New Testament, no significant writings or letters or books were to be included in the 66 books of the biblical canon. Roman Catholics, however, include many books in their bible written within the "Intertestamental Period" and source those books known as the "Apocrypha" for creating doctrines and dogmas.

## Language and Word Development

All languages evolve over time. Words that have had particular meanings in history often acquire new or different meanings decades or centuries later. New words also develop as languages change. For example, no word had existed for a platform box that rolled on wheels under its self-power, and carried people. Something automatically mobile by itself needed a name. The word, "automobile" made sense in the early 1900s. There was no word for a machine that portrayed moving pictures with sounds and words that could be both heard and read. A device that provided images and at the same time provided written readable words needed a name. Those words were visible on a screen. Even better words could be heard from the box that could tell a story. The word "television" made sense. At one time, "cool" meant not cold but not warm. Today "cool" may have no connection to heat but rather mean the status of acceptance or acknowledgment of success.

The words automobile, television, and cool make sense to us now. Matthew, Mark, Luke, John, and Paul, however, would have found automobile, television, and cool incomprehensible in their contexts. You get the idea.

Since Babel Gn 11: 1-10 words and languages have developed and changed. Word meanings have changed. Because words and languages change over time, understanding first-century Koine Greek in context and syntax is central to accurate exegesis (what the text said) and contextual hermeneutic (what the text meant in their time), as well as contemporary hermeneutics (what the text means today). Metaphors, similes, allegories, and parables in their context must be identified.[9] Words, meaning, morphology, and etymology are essential.[10]

## Koine Greek

Hellenism and the Greek language infiltrated the lands that Alexander the Great had conquered. Embracing the Greek language and culture became necessities. Assimilation was difficult to avoid. When languages become necessary for both political and business ventures, change quickly follows. While indigenous people attempted to maintain their previous languages, they became bi-lingual or multi-lingual.

When languages become essential, they also become more explicit. A word takes on a particular meaning to be understood by the masses — details matter. A refinement provides clarity. Subtleties within a language can create difficulties for those learning a second language. Wallace clarifies the refinement of Koine Greek:

---

[9] Metaphor – one word to describe another; Simile – a figure of speech using "like" or "as"; Allegory – representation of something abstract, implying something other, additional meaning or meanings; Parable – an accompanying story helping to highlight or expose meaning.

[10] Morphology – word structure, word formation, roots, prefixes, suffices; Etymology – word origin, historical meaning.

The Koine was born out of the conquests of Alexander the Great. First, his troops, which came from Athens as well as other Greek cities and regions, had to speak to one another. This close contact produced a melting-pot Greek that inevitably softened the rough edges of some dialects and abandoned the subtleties of others. Second, the conquered cities and colonies learned Greek as a second language. By the first century CE, Greek was the lingua franca of the whole Mediterranean region and beyond. Since the majority of Greek-speakers learned it as a second language, this further increased its loss of subtleties and moved it toward greater explicitness.[11]

First-century, where Jesus walked, was no exception. Greek, Hebrew, and Aramaic languages were very much in use. However, Greek was the language without which few could flourish. The word Koine means "common" the regular everyday language used by ordinary people in first-century Jerusalem and surrounding areas. The English word, "common" conveys a less clear language perhaps a rough, unsophisticated, straightforward language. English speakers sometimes presume the New Testament language was mediocre at best. Disappointingly some English speakers assume that the language of Jesus' day was less than adequate or too ordinary for deep understanding. That assumption is faulty.

As languages mature through stages, they improve. They need not be literary masterpieces because speaking, writing, and reading that provide clarity and understanding are paramount. Wallace identifies five great stages of the Greek language:

- Pre-Homeric (Up to 1000 BCE)
- The age of the Dialects, or the Classical Era (1000 BCE – 330 BCE)
- Koine Greek (330 BCE – 330 CE)
- Byzantine (or Medieval) Greek (330 CE – 1453 CE)
- Modern Greek (1453 – present)[12]

Koine Greek never developed as a complex literary form. Instead, Koine Greek of that time was a functional form language. It was a useful practical language suitable and efficient for vocal and verbal clarity. Because Koine Greek in Jesus' day was a language purposed to be spoken, heard and read for clarity and understanding, Koine Greek was significant to Scripture in their time. The time and place of the language combined with the way the language was employed made way for the Gospel. Mounce affirms:

> Most of the books in the NT were never intended to be literary works – thus it is not an apt analogy to compare them to works intended to be literary. They were written, for the most part, for an audience, not just a private individual – and they were usually intended to be read aloud.[13]

Since the New Testament books were intended to be read aloud to a private and public audience, Matthew, Mark, Luke, and John employed a language that perfectly fit Jesus' mission. His kingdom, messiahship, and gospel of salvation message had a functional language effectively

---

[11] Wallace, Daniel, B., *Greek Grammar Beyond the Basics: An Exegetical Syntax of the New Testament*, 15.
[12] Ibid. 14-17.
[13] Ibid. 21.

suited to that time and place. To presume that Koine Greek is an inferior language is a mistake. The Koine Greek of the New Testament both then and now was the perfect utility language. God chose the time. God chose the place. God chose the culture. God chose the language.

## Limited Competencies of New Testament Authors

Authors from every generation have had dissimilar writing, reading, and speaking competencies. New Testament authors were no exception. Their syntax, style, and vocabulary skills differed. Their customs and backgrounds varied. Their oral, reading, writing and comprehension abilities varied. Wallace affirms:

> Since almost all of the writers of the NT books are Jews, their style of writing is shaped both by their religious heritage and by their linguistic background.[14] Since authors wrote the New Testament with various linguistic backgrounds and abilities, it is quite impossible to view their Greek as merely one kind.[15]

Following are four English translations ESV, NIV, KJV, YLT and the Westcott Hort (WHO) Greek. Notice the various English words rendered from the same Greek words found in Ac 4: 13. This verse affirms the limited linguistic competencies of Peter and John as they stood before the people, priests, captain of the Temple, and Sadducees from Ac 4: 1[16]. Note how different English translations have rendered the English to describe the competencies of Peter and John:

Now when they saw the boldness of Peter and John and perceived that they were <u>uneducated, common</u> men, they were astonished. And they recognized that they had been with Jesus. Ac 4: 13 ESV

When they saw the courage of Peter and John and realized that they were <u>unschooled, ordinary</u> men, they were astonished and they took note that these men had been with Jesus. Ac 4: 13 NIV

Now when they saw the boldness of Peter and John, and perceived that they were <u>unlearned and ignorant</u> men, they marveled; and they took knowledge of them, that they had been with Jesus. Ac 4: 13 KJV

And beholding the openness of Peter and John, and having perceived that they are men <u>unlettered and plebeian</u>, they were wondering -- they were taking knowledge also of them that with Jesus they had been – Ac 4: 13 YLT

Θεωροῦντες δὲ τὴν τοῦ Πέτρου παρρησίαν καὶ Ἰωάννου καὶ καταλαβόμενοι ὅτι ἄνθρωποι <u>ἀγράμματοί</u> εἰσιν <u>καὶ ἰδιῶται</u> ἐθαύμαζον ἐπεγίνωσκόν τε αὐτοὺς ὅτι σὺν τῷ Ἰησοῦ ἦσαν WHO

---

[14] Wallace, Daniel, B., *Greek Grammar Beyond the Basics*, 29.
[15] Ibid. 29.
[16] And as they were speaking to the people, the priests and the captain of the temple and the Sadducees came upon them, greatly annoyed because they were teaching the people and proclaiming in Jesus the resurrection from the dead. Act 4: 1-2

From the Greek in Acts 4:13: ἀγράμματοί εἰσιν καὶ ἰδιῶται these four English translations, ESV, NIV, KJV, and YLT have produced numerous and different renderings. In Acts 4: 13, the intellectual experiences of Peter and John were revealed. English translations have varied in how they have described Peter and John's education or perhaps more appropriately their lack of education. Notice the different English word choice renderings derived from the same Greek words, ἀγράμματοί and ἰδιῶται found in four different English translations:

- Uneducated and common (ESV)
- Unlearned and ignorant (KJV)
- Unschooled and ordinary (NIV)
- Unlettered and plebian (YLT).
- ἀγράμματοί and ἰδιῶται
- Transliteration: agrammatoi and idiot

We may also consider "without grammar" and "illiterate" meaning Peter and John's reading and writing skills were average at best. However, their time with Jesus had given them power knowledge from having been with Jesus. The council perceived them to be bold, courageous, and fearless. Their grammar and literateness had nothing to do with their power.

## Literacy and Illiteracy in Their Context

Many people attested to Peter and John's literary abilities. Priests, the captain of the temple, Sadducees, (Ac 4: 1) rulers, elders, scribes (Ac 4: 5), Annas the high priest, Caiaphas, John, and Alexander and all who were of the high priestly family (Ac 4: 6) were aware of the Peter and John. Luke made sure in his writing that many people knew the abilities of Peter and John. Luke further quoted that Peter acknowledged the status and credibility of those before them, "Rulers of the people and elders." Peter acknowledged the authority and abilities of the "rulers" "elders" when he addressed the crowd.

In any event, Peter and John had been identified at that time as having been deficient in commonly accepted literary skills. Luke's Greek word choice in Acts 4: 13 affirmed the inadequate literary abilities of Peter and John. Their literary limitations, however, did not mean that Peter and John were incapable of communicating in verbal or written form.

To the contrary, Peter and John are responsible for much of the New Testament messaging with Matthew, Mark, Luke, Paul, James, Jude and the author of Hebrews. Even with limited literary skills Peter and John have become the most read and studied authors in history. The language they used for their audiences was what God had prepared for them. Nevertheless, the question is begged. What were their abilities?

## Against Grammar ἀγράμματοί

The Greek word ἀγράμματοί (transliteration: agrammatoi) must first be understood in their context, their time, and their meaning. What did the words that Luke recorded in Ac 4: 13 mean to them? These words may not be as clear to us today in our English. Following are numerous definitions for ἀγράμματοί from reliable lexicon and dictionary sources:

Friberg defines the Greek word ἀγράμματος Luke recorded in Ac 4:13: strictly *unable to write*; hence *unable to read or write, illiterate; uneducated, unlearned.*[17]

Louw-Nida Lexicon defines ἀγράμματος: Pertaining to one who has not acquired a formal education (referring primarily to formal training) – uneducated, unlearned.[18]

Mounce defines the ἀγράμματος: Illiterate, unlearned.[19]

Danker defines the ἀγράμματος: Unable to write, also uneducated, illiterate; ἀγράμ = lacking in legal proficiency.[20]

Given the root prefix ἀ and root γράμ (Transliteration: gram – English, grammar) the word may more literally mean "against grammar" or "without grammar." In any event, the grammar of Peter and John was weak. Their limited grammar affirmed that they were unschooled, unlearned, uneducated or unlettered. In short, Peter and John likely had a minimum education of grammar related to reading and writing of Greek by way of home or communal schooling. However, that does not mean they were unable to communicate in Greek. They spoke understandable and meaningful Greek. They also understood meaning when they heard spoken Greek by anyone including Jesus. Their lack of grammar related to reading and writing simply meant they made wise use of scribes and editors. By their definition, they may have been illiterate by way of reading and writing at literary levels.

## Idiot ἰδιῶται

The Greek word ἰδιῶται (transliteration: idiot) must also be understood in their context, their time, and their meaning. Following are numerous definitions for ἰδιῶται:

Friberg defines ἰδιώτης: ἰδιώτης, ου, ὁ strictly, one in private life *layman* or *non-specialist*, with the specific sense taken from contrast in the context; (1) *uneducated, unlearned* (AC 4.13); (2) *nonmember* of a community, *uninstructed person, inquirer* (1C 14.16, 23, 24); (3) *unskilled, untrained* (2C 11.6).[21]

Brown defines the ἰδιώτης: In Acts 4: 13 the word is used in the sense of unlettered, uneducated: "When they...perceived that they were uneducated [ἄνθρωποι ἀγράμματοί], common men [ἰδιῶται], they wondered" (RSV).[22]

Mounce defines ἰδιώτης: ἰδιώτης idiotes 5 pr. One in private life, one devoid of special learning or gifts, a plain person, Acts 4: 13.[23]

---

[17] Friberg, Timothy, Barbara Friberg, and Neva F. Miller, *Analytical Lexicon of the Greek New Testament*, 33.
[18] Louw-Nida *Greek English Lexicon of the New Testament*: from *Bibleworks 8 Software for Biblical Exegesis and Research*, Summary Resources.
[19] Mounce, William D., *Mounce's Complete Expository Dictionary of Old & New Testament Words*, 1072.
[20] Danker, Frederick William, ed. Walter Bauer, *A Greek-English Lexicon of the New Testament and other Early Christian Literature*, 15.
[21] Friberg, Timothy, Barbara Friberg, and Neva F. Miller, *Analytical Lexicon of the Greek New Testament*, 202.
[22] Brown, Colin, ed., *New International Dictionary of New Testament Theology*, 456.
[23] Mounce, William D., *Mounce's Complete Expository Dictionary of Old & New Testament Words*, 1172.

Danker defines ἰδιώτης: ἰδιώτης 1. a person who is relatively unskilled or inexperienced in some activity or filed or knowledge, *layperson, amateur*; an untrained person Ac 4: 13; 2. one who is not knowledgeable about some particular group's experience, *one not in the know, outsider.*[24]

The English word "idiot" derived from the Greek word ἰδιῶται. In the first century context early Gospel readers understood that Peter and John simply were not schooled. There are no contemporary English translations that use the English word "idiot" to describe Peter or John in spite of the Greek word. And rightly so, given a contemporary context. Because of the contemporary meaning of the word idiot, no translator is likely to employ that word. English words that are more appropriate are "uneducated, common men" (ESV), "unschooled, ordinary men" (NIV), "unlearned and ignorant men" (KJV), and "men unlettered and plebeian" (YLV).

In short, Peter and John were two men considered by their peers to be unsatisfactorily equipped to read or write Greek. While the contemporized word "idiot" is derogatory today, in their context the Greek word ἰδιῶται was descriptive and conveyed to them that Peter and John had not received a formal education. It merely meant that the abilities of Peter and John to hear and speak Greek were stronger than their abilities to read or write Greek. Their lack of education also did not inhibit them in their successful fishing businesses on the Sea of Galilee. However, their lack of education did not limit their effectiveness in authoring their books.

## Correcting a Lack of Formal Education

We would be mistaken to think that Peter and John's writings were weak or erroneous because of their grammatical and literary limitations. Reading, writing, or grammar deficiencies were overcome by wise use of scribes and editors. Scribes played the role of editing autographs for accuracy. New Testament writers were clear on what they wanted conveyed. Even if Peter and John's reading and writing skills were not comparable to the religious leaders or the scribes of their day, Peter and John did not depend on their abilities. Their writings were highly scrutinized.

Further, the working of the Holy Spirit was with them. They did not write or edit alone. Their lack of a formal grammatical Greek language education ultimately produced their words which resulted in spreading the Gospel and Kingdom message. Not only had God chosen Peter and John, but he also chose their abilities.

## The Value of Scribes

Like a car engine, you can sit behind the wheel and ride an English translation, but Koine Greek powers the engine that moves the car. Power comes from written words. So it is with New Testament Greek. Pronunciation, definitions, grammar, construction, context, and syntax matter just as much in Greek texts as in contemporary English texts.

While determining New Testament book authorship is somewhat reliable, actual scribing of the texts is less precise. It is likely that Peter and John dictated and scribes recorded their words. They may have handwritten the autographs themselves. However, Scribes likely would have produced their finished works after copious and extensive editing and affirmations that what they

---

[24] Danker, Frederick William, ed. Walter Bauer, *A Greek-English Lexicon of the New Testament and other Early Christian Literature*, 468.

had recorded was correct. The process of utilizing scribes is called amanuensis. Demoss explains amanuensis:

> A person who takes dictation, a secretary (Lat. "by hand"). The difference in style between New Testament letters that are signed by the same person (e.g., 1 and 2 Pet) is sometimes accounted for by the use of an amanuensis who would have been given a degree of freedom in the writing process.[25]

Editing letters and rewriting texts before copying and distribution were standard procedures. Despite not having any autographs today, we can be confident that before their autographs or their dictations were recorded, copied and distributed, the finished manuscripts that eventually were distributed contained precisely what the authors permitted their scribes to record. Combine their skill levels with the inspiration and the freedom from error of the Holy Spirit, the Greek critical texts we have today give no cause for speculation.[26]

The Greek, more specifically the Greek critical texts we have today are solid. The English, less so merely due to translation challenges. In short, New Testament Greek critical texts available today that serve as the basis to produce English Bibles are trustworthy. Our challenges are not the Greek critical texts. Our challenges regard exegesis, hermeneutics, exposition, and interpretation of the Greek critical texts. Inferior exegesis, can produce inferior hermeneutics, which can produce inferior exposition, which can produce an inferior interpretation. Inferior interpretation can be a problem.

## What They Heard and What They Wrote

The New Testament authors recorded what Jesus spoke which means they recorded what people heard. Reading and writing skills were minimal for many to whom Jesus spoke. However, the words Jesus spoke and what they heard in their place, time and context were familiar and definitive. Word meanings were less ambiguous. Of course there were times when Jesus spoke in parables, metaphors, allegory, or similes. Matthew recorded Jesus' explanation about parables:

> Then the disciples came and said to him, "Why do you speak to them in parables?" And he answered them, "To you it has been given to know the secrets of the kingdom of heaven, but to them it has not been given. For to the one who has, more will be given, and he will have an abundance, but from the one who has not, even what he has will be taken away. This is why I speak to them in parables, because seeing they do not see, and hearing they do not hear, nor do they understand. Indeed, in their case the prophecy of Isaiah is fulfilled that says: "'You will indeed hear but never understand, and you will indeed see but never perceive. For this people's heart has grown dull, and with their ears they can barely hear, and their eyes they have closed, lest they should see with their eyes and hear with their ears and understand with their heart and turn, and I would heal them.' But blessed are your eyes, for they see, and your ears, for they hear." Mt 13: 10-16

Jesus affirmed that his words and parables were not intended to be understood by all. Those are blessed who hear, listen and understand. So, while language and words were necessary, simply

---

[25] Demoss, Matthew S., *Pocket Dictionary for the Study of New Testament Greek*, 17.
[26] See Chapter 5 "Bible Translations" for an explanation of the Critical Texts and Critical Apparatus.

knowing and speaking the language and the words were not sufficient to garner meaning or application. Parables, metaphors, similes, and allegory were equally as important as language and words — same today.

## Phonology toward Morphology toward Meaning

The audible sounds of Jesus spoken words carried meaning. Today we do not have the benefit of hearing the words Jesus spoke. The closest we can get to hearing Jesus' words comes only through phonology, the study of audible sounds within languages. Spoken words are formed through sound and with sound comes meaning. Word meaning is the result of a process that begins with sound. Sounds produced from speech are shaped by the tongue, lips, teeth, lungs, breath, jaw, nose and the shape of the mouth. Phonology is essential because what they heard through the formation of Greek words carried meaning to them. Demoss defines phonology:

> The discipline concerned with systems of speech sounds, how languages use the distinctive features of sounds and follow predictable patterns in forming words.[27]

Phonology precedes morphology because words are initially formed by sound. Word formation as a result of sound or morphology follows. Demoss connects and categorizes phonology and morphology:

> The study of the structure of words and the system of forms of a language. Sometimes phonology is conceived as a subcategory of morphology.[28]

Demoss makes clear that phonology, the sound of a word as a subcategory is the foundation for morphology the written formation of a word. From morphology comes meaning. The process toward meaning starts with sound. Meaning comes from morphology and morphology comes from phonology. Mounce is more affirmative clarifying that phonology controls morphology. In defining morphology, Mounce affirms:

> Morphology, (a study of the written form of the language) is directly controlled by phonology (how the language was spoken). In other words, what we read was determined by how it was spoken.[29]

Meaning comes through a process starting with sound; specifically, the sound emanating from a person's voice, the spoken word. What they audibly heard mattered to meaning. No surprise the numerous references to ears and hearing the spoken word.[30]

Speaking, hearing, writing, or reading their Greek language was more understandable then and there than our contemporary English may be to us here and now. In other words, the Greek that was spoken, heard, and read by them was likely more definitive and comprehensible to them

---

[27] Demoss, Matthew S., *Pocket Dictionary for the Study of New Testament Greek*, 98.
[28] Ibid. 86.
[29] Mounce, William D., *The Morphology of Biblical Greek: A Companion to Basics of Biblical Greek and the Analytical Lexicon to the Greek New Testament*, 1.
[30] Passages referring to "having ears to hear": Mt 11: 5; 13: 9; 13: 43; Mk 4: 9, 23; Lk 8: 8; 14: 35; Rv 2: 7, 11, 17, 29; 3: 6, 13, 22; 13: 9.

than the English we read, hear and speak today. While they too would have dealt with parables, metaphors, similes, and allegory within Jesus' words, they were closer to the Greek language.

It is no surprise that God ordained that the New Testament books were written in the Greek of their day. Greek was a powerful and useful language for the dissemination of the Gospel message in their time and place. The gospel writers knew the power of the Greek language for their immediate readers where they resided. They also considered that Greek through Hellenism would be useful and for those in lands far from where they lived. While speaking and hearing may have been a standard way to communicate face to face, the written New Testament was recorded in Koine Greek. Voicing the written word in its original language carried profound, comprehensible and understandable meaning to its original hearers. For us today, however, what they heard and comprehended in Koine Greek must be translated into English. Details matter.

## English Textual Confidence

Accurately revealing with translation challenges, however, does not mean the numerous English Bible translations we have today are suspect. Bibles in various versions are reliable, depending on how those Bibles are used. Doing a word study from a paraphrase Bible is not suggested merely because the word in a paraphrastic Bible might not be a literal equivalent. Competencies in speaking, hearing, writing, and reading the biblical languages: Hebrew, Aramaic and Koine Greek are not prerequisites to understanding Scriptures. Although, understanding the New Testament Koine Greek language, their culture, and historical context raises the bar.

God chose that time and place. He chose the words within the New Testament recorded by Matthew, Mark, Luke, and John. Although Koine Greek today may be considered a dead language, words in their day and their context were what God intended. God chose the time. God chose the language. Moreover, God chose those who heard, spoke, read and interpreted the language in their context.

Let us now consider Chapter 5: "Bible Translations," particularly translation philosophies and the challenges individual translators as well as large translation teams encounter to render English from Koine Greek.

Therefore we must pay much closer attention to what we have heard, lest we drift away from it.

Hb 2: 1

# 5 Bible Translations

Do not be deceived my brothers. Ja 1: 16

## Why So Many English Bible Translations?

So many English Bibles have developed, are developing, and will be developed that to conclude which translation was, is, or will be the best is only a debate. Since "best" is a subjective word, I have no intention of entering the best Bible translation debate. However, because languages evolve, new Bible translations will always be in process. Nevertheless, the question is begged. Why are there so many English Bibles?

## First, Changing Languages and Words

One reason so many different English translations have developed over time is because, over history, words and languages evolve. When languages no longer are in use by communities they die. Koine Greek, the written language of the New Testament is considered a "dead" language today. Languages change because words change. Over time words become metaphors, similes, symbols, representations, or figures of speech not equivalent to the word's original meaning. Because words and languages change, new Bible translations are necessary.

From Wallace (see Chapter 4) Greek has evolved from Pre-Homeric, Classic, Koine, Byzantine to today's Modern Greek. Koine Greek, the Greek of the New Testament, however, is living today in a sense because serious biblical scholars and students ardently learn, read, and study this New Testament written language. The Koine Greek, the New Testament language within the critical text[1] and what we have today comes from reputable historical scholarship. Current and future languages and words, however, will always be changing, which is why new Bibles in contemporary languages will always be needed.

## Second, Earlier Manuscripts and Queen's English

Scholars deem manuscripts nearer to the originals more reliable than later dated manuscripts. An example is the history of the formation of the English King James Version (KJV). King James wisely authorized the version to assist all (not some or selected) churches of England. Those who translated the KJV produced in 1611 made wise use of the most reliable Greek texts of that time, the *Textus Receptus*. However, the Critical Texts at that time used to translate Greek into English were more recent than what we have today. In short, the KJV was produced using the *Textus Receptus* certainly a reliable text at that time. But since then, more reliable documents closer to the originals have been found. That means that while the KJV was appropriate for its era, newer Bibles based on more reliable and earlier dated manuscripts are now available. Bibles based on more reliable documents and scholarship than what was available in 1611 does not negate the

---

[1] As a reminder, a "critical text" is a product of textual criticism. A "critical text" refers to the Greek text compiled by scholars in committees who have examined numerous manuscripts and determined the critical text closest to the original texts. The *Novum Testamentum Graece,* The Greek-English New Testament in the Tradition of Eberhard Nestle refers to the Nestle Alan 28th Edition. This critical text is a standard for academic or lay work in New Testament Greek studies.

KJV or put the KJV in a bad light. Understanding the contemporary limitations of the original KJV, the New King James Version (NKJV) started in 1975 and completed in 1982 is a more reliable text for today.

The original KJV was appropriately written in the most useful language in England at that time, the Queen's English. Since King James was looking to bring harmony among all churches in England, the Queen's English was suitable for reading. However, as languages evolve, the Queen's English in the KJV became cumbersome for English readers in the 20th and 21st centuries, especially readers not from England. The NKJV attempted to address and improve both the scholarship and language.

## Third, Improving Scholarship

In addition to the timing of critical texts is the improved scholarship of biblical languages. The Greek and Hebrew scholarship in 1611 does not compare to what we know today about biblical languages in word and context. Scholarship over the centuries has produced knowledge of Hebrew and Greek in their original contexts far more significant than what translators knew in 1611. Their understanding of Hebrew and Greek in 1611 was adequate but insufficient. As respectable as the KJV translators (and what they produced is respectable) their vocabulary and contextual understanding were limited compared to the vocabulary and contextual understanding known today. Quoting Comfort at length about the formation of the KJV is valuable:

> First, knowledge of Hebrew was inadequate in the early seventeenth century. The Hebrew text they used (i.e., the Masoretic Text) was adequate, but their understanding of the Hebrew vocabulary was insufficient. It would take many more years of linguistic studies to enrich and sharpen understanding of the Hebrew vocabulary. Second, the Greek text underlying the New Testament of the King James Version was an inferior text. The King James translators used a Greek text known as the *Textus Receptus* (or, the "Received Texts"), which came from the work of Erasmus, who compiled the first Greek text to be produced on a printing press. When Erasmus compiled this text, he used five or six very late manuscripts dating from the tenth to the thirteenth centuries. These manuscripts were far inferior to earlier manuscripts. The King James translators had done well with the resources that were available to them, but those resources were insufficient, especially concerning the New Testament text.[2]

Beyond the KJV, improved scholarship applies to all new Bible translations. First, more reliable and earlier Greek texts have been found. Second, scholarly understanding of Hebrew and Greek has improved. Third, the English language has evolved in America and the world. Knowing these three facts, the KJV is a highly used and useful English translation. There is no need to discontinue reading the KJV. However, there is wisdom in knowing the limitations of the KJV as with any Bible. The NKJV as well a new Bible from various sources benefit from more reliable texts, improved Hebrew and Greek scholarship, and effective use of contemporary languages.

---

[2] Comfort, Philip Wesley, *The Complete Guide to Bible Versions*, 53-54.

# Fourth, Translation Philosophies: Words vs. Thoughts

Another reason for new Bibles concerns translation philosophies. The debate centers on translating words or interpreting thoughts. Should translators translate words or should translators read the words, determine the idea that they believe the authors intended and then convey their ideas to readers? Translating words or interpreting thoughts are distinctly different philosophies requiring different techniques. One philosophy concerns are translating words. The other philosophy concerns are conveying thoughts — big difference.

For our use we identify two types of English Bibles, Word-for-Word and Thought-for-Thought. Both are the result of two translation philosophies and two translation techniques. Understanding translation philosophies and translation techniques can help Bible readers understand their Bible types. The literalness of Jesus' Greek imperatives is not always clearly conveyed in English Bibles no matter which philosophy, Word-for-Word or Thought-for-Thought is used. Both philosophy and technique effect the English Bibles we read. This is important.

A translation philosophy answers the question, "Why do we translate this way"? A translation technique answers the question, "How do we translate this way?" Knowing why and how a Bible has been translated bears on teaching and learning. Sometimes understanding the numerous terms related to Word-for Word and Thought-for-Thought Bibles can be confusing. Below are some common terms differentiating Word-for-Word and Thought-for-Thought Bibles:

    Word-for-Word:
        Essentially Literal
        Formally Equivalent
        Verbatim
    Thought-for-Thought
        Dynamically Equivalent
        Functionally Equivalent
        Paraphrastic

Word-for-Word Bibles seek to be as *essentially literal* as possible. The priority for Word-for-Word translation committees is understanding the original word in the biblical languages (Hebrew, Greek, or Aramaic) and then translating the original language word into a *formally equivalent* English word. *Verbatim* is another English word that conveys precision or exactness.

In simple terms, try to hear Peter say to Mark, "Write exactly and only what Jesus said. Do not change what he said. Do not interpret what he said. Just write what he said." Alternatively, try to hear Mathew ask Peter, "When you jumped out of the boat, what exactly did Jesus say to you? Is what I have written what Jesus said? Do I have this right?" Try to hear Luke interviewing Mary, "Mary, can you recall and tell me precisely what Jesus said? Do you remember his words? You and John I've been told were both at the cross when Jesus was crucified. What did he say? We want to record his words exactly as he said them." Words are important. You get the idea.

However, not every language contains the same words as other languages. So while Word-for-Word Bibles focus on being as *essentially literal* as possible, where a word in Hebrew, Greek or Aramaic does not have an equivalent English word a *formally equivalent* word is used. The *form* of the word is *equivalent*, or the *essence* of the word is as *literal* as possible.

Thought-for-Thought Bibles seek to be as *dynamically equivalent* as possible. The priority is to understand the meaning from the words and translate to a *functionally equivalent* English meaning. *Paraphrastic* is a word that conveys meaning or intent. While Thought-for-Thought Bibles focus on being as *dynamically equivalent* as possible, a Hebrew, Greek, or Aramaic word is less important than the gist or meaning. The word, *functional* conveys the idea that the word is workable, usable, or practical. Klein is worth quoting at length his insights on Word-for-Word compared to Thought-for-Thought Bible versions:

> Nevertheless, specific versions try to adhere as closely to Hebrew or Greek grammar and syntax as possible, while still being understandable in English. We call these formally equivalent translations. The NASB [New American Standard Bible] is a prime example. Other versions seek to reproduce thought-for-thought rather than word-for-word called dynamically (or functionally) equivalent translations. They seek to produce the same effect on readers today that the original produced on its readers. These versions are less concerned to translate consistently a given Greek or Hebrew word with the same English word.[3]

Should translators translate Word-for-Word? Alternatively, should translators determine the thought from original words, interpret meaning, and then create new words in the language that conveys the thought that the translators have interpreted the meaning to be? The idea behind Thought-for-Thought paraphrases is to assist readers with understanding by not translating words that the reader may not comprehend.

By definition of the word, "translation" Thought-for-Thought Bibles are interpretations more so than translations. Should translators translate words or interpret meanings and put into contemporary language? Translation philosophies and technique are the most influential factors that determine Bible types. Is the Bible you use a Word-for Word or Thought-for-Thought Bible? Big difference.

## Word Accuracy or Thought Essence

Leland Ryken provides an objective comparison of Bible translation methodologies in his book, *The Word of God in English: Criteria for Excellence in Bible Translations.* Having served on Bible translation committees during his career Ryken's insights are noteworthy. He provides sound counsel. Without a doubt, those translating Hebrew, Greek, and Aramaic to English are both academically and spiritually tasked. Getting God's word right precedes teaching, preaching, evangelizing, and discipling.

Thought-for-Thought Bibles place a higher priority on conveying the gist or essence, or substance of the idea. While words are essential in Thought-for-Thought Bibles, the higher priority is conveying the thought. Thought-for-Thought scholars first read the biblical language, then interpret what they have read, and then convey the idea for the reader. The reader does not self-determine the meaning because in Thought-for-Thought Bibles the gist has been predetermined. While arriving at the essence or gist for a Greek text to make the English text easy to read is admirable, Ryken states:

> It is only in a minority of instances that getting the gist of something is adequate. The question for Bible translation runs something like this: Is it likely to be more

---

[3] Klein, William, Craig L. Blomberg, and Robert L. Hubbard, Jr., *Introduction to Biblical Interpretation,* 126.

important or less important to preserve the original wording of the Bible than it is with everyday discourse? Stated another way, if getting the exact wording is important in many kinds of everyday discourse, is it not important to strive for this as far as possible when we translate the Bible from the original into English? [4]

Word-for-Word advocates hold that the essence, point, or general idea from the Thought-for-Thought philosophy can be problematic for laity and undoubtedly insufficient for credible scholarship. Because only in a minority of instances is the essence adequate, Bibles providing the essence are not standing on solid ground. Thought-for-Thought Bibles nevertheless serve a useful purpose. Thought-for-Thought Bibles naturally seek the idea, not the words. Bible readers should know the dissimilarities between the two.

Effectively Thought-for-Thought Bibles are in real terms, not exact translations which is why they are often referred to as "paraphrase" Bibles. The word "paraphrase" makes a distinction between Word-for-Word and Thought-for-Thought. Paraphrase Bibles focus on conveying the equivalent dynamic of the text, not the literal words of the text. Big Difference.

In politics and business, interpreting and translating are key to understanding. What the speaker said is not always what the hearer thinks the speaker meant. After any negotiating meeting, one listener at the negotiation might ponder, "What he said was not what you think he meant." Another listener might ponder, "What we think she meant was not what she said." You get the point.

Words are important. Meanings are more critical because we do not always know if the words that someone has recorded mean the same to those who later hear or read them. What Jesus said then and there may not be what contemporary readers think Jesus means for us here and now. That is why the Bible you read or the Bible your church places in the pews, or the Bible your Pastor uses is essential.

## Presuppositions

All persons have presuppositions, preconceived opinions or ideas they assume are true. However, presuppositions may not be true. Individual translators and translation teams also have presuppositions, which is why committees, subcommittees, and groups are how Bible translators work. Advisors and counselors are central to solid Bible translations. As the Proverb affirms:

Without counsel, plans fail, but with many advisors, they succeed. Pr 15: 22.

Today's translation teams are sometimes employed by Christian publication companies or financially capable ministries. Bibles are sometimes products of publishing houses, ministries, denominations or even highly recognized pastors, preachers or ministry leaders. So the question is: can past, present, and future English Bibles be trusted? The short answer is, "Yes, maybe, depending on philosophy and counsel." A more accurate answer depends less on the translator and more on the reader. There is wisdom in knowing the type of Bible you read and the type of Bible being read by those who teach are either Word-for-Word or Thought-for-Thought Bibles.

---

[4] Ryken, Leland, *The Word of God in English: Criteria for Excellence in Bible Translation*, 46.

Few laypersons know the translation philosophy of their pastors. Few in today's pews question their pastor's interpretation methodologies. The Bereans would agree that checks and balances are biblically sound:

> The brothers immediately sent Paul and Silas away by night to Berea, and when they arrived they went into the Jewish synagogue. Now these Jews were more noble than those in Thessalonica; they received the word with all eagerness, examining the Scriptures daily to see if these things were so. Ac 17: 10-11

New Testament authors when transferring Jesus's spoken words into written Greek did not work in a vacuum. Grammar, spelling, word choice, structure and editing mattered. Matthew, Mark, Luke, and John did not solely rely on their abilities. Of course, they depended on the Holy Spirit. They also depended on scribes, editors, eyewitnesses, each other, and the Holy Spirit working within them. Translators throughout history similarly benefited from scribes, editors, and teams of people. The Bible was not the first text to be scrutinized for accuracy. Numerous historical Jewish and Christian translators of valuable texts in addition to the Bible have experienced the process.[5]

Competent, trustworthy translators never work in vacuums. Writing, editing, and translating are team efforts. Of course, people advocate for their Bible of choice. Having a Bible you like is a good starting point. Dubious doctrines can develop from any Bible, regardless of the translation philosophy. Fabricated beliefs and subjective doctrines can happen with biased presuppositions. Because of the ease in taking an English translation out of context we better understand Paul's words to Timothy:

> Do your best to present yourself to God as one approved, a worker who has no need to be ashamed, rightly handling the word of truth. 2 Ti 2: 15

Rightly handling the word of truth was expected then. Rightly handling the word of truth is expected today.

## Paul's Presuppositions

Paul (Saul) after his Damascus experience likely recalled that he had misinterpreted the coming Messiah from his misunderstanding of Jewish scriptures. Grasping Paul's presuppositions, Paul's mindset before his Damascus conversion must be understood. Paul was extremely zealous for the traditions of his fathers. He had genuinely believed what he had been taught only to realize that what he had been taught was erroneous.

> For you have heard of my former life in Judaism, how I persecuted the church of God violently and tried to destroy it. And I was advancing in Judaism beyond many of my own age among my people, so extremely zealous was I for the traditions of

---

[5] Historical translators of sacred Jewish / Christian texts: Masoretes, Targum's, Septuagint, Origen, Ptolemy II, Augustine of Hippo, Jerome, Vulgate, Codes Vaticanes, Codex Sinaiticus, Codex Alexandrinus, Codex Amiatinus, Textus Receptus, Eusebius, Athanasius, Alcuin, Luther, Erasmus, Calvin, Wycliffe, Tyndale, Coverdale, King James, and numerous contemporary publishers. In short, writing, translating, publishing, and distribution have been around a long time.

> my fathers. But when he who had set me apart before I was born, and who called me by his grace, was pleased to reveal his Son to me, in order that I might preach him among the Gentiles, I did not immediately consult with anyone; nor did I go up to Jerusalem to those who were apostles before me, but I went away into Arabia, and returned again to Damascus. Then after three years I went up to Jerusalem to visit Cephas and remained with him fifteen days. But I saw none of the other apostles except James the Lord's brother. (In what I am writing to you, before God, I do not lie!) Gl 1: 13-20

Imagine the remorse Paul experienced after having realized his persecution upon the followers of The Way, the early church. His meeting with Peter and James had a three-fold meaning. First Paul realized the community of The Way was from Jesus. Second, Paul looked to affirm his conversion to Peter and James. Third, Paul likely was both appreciative of their recognition and their affirmation of him as an apostle. Paul could have gone to Jerusalem immediately after his Damascus conversion. However, he did not. Paul spent three years in Arabia before returning to Jerusalem. Paul had held deep Jewish presuppositions that required change. He held two faulty presuppositions that required change. First, Paul had not understood Jesus as Messiah. Second, Paul had not considered the church of Jesus as overriding the Temple and Temple practices. Given that Paul had so intensely persecuted Jesus and the Christian community his remorse and repentance must have been profound. No surprise he spent three years in Arabia before venturing to Jerusalem.

Nowhere in Scripture can be found Paul's marital status or his leadership position or title linked to the Temple. However, most scholars deduct from Scripture and knowledge of Jewish leadership at that time that Paul was a member of the Sanhedrin. While no biblical evidence exists, most scholars deduce that Paul likely had been married given Sanhedrin membership requirements. We are less concerned with Paul's marital status of having either never been married, or widowed, or divorced. Paul's Sanhedrin membership and rabbi status, however, means that Paul had received the in-depth teaching of Torah and Hebrew Scriptures. McCray's insight into Paul's learning is noted:

> At age fifteen, Paul would have begun in earnest to study the oral traditions that were later codified in the Talmud, which contained the Gemara in addition to the Mishnah. At about the age of eighteen, as noted above, a Jewish young man, especially one who was training to be a rabbi, was expected to marry. Whether Paul married is uncertain, but he did become a rabbi.[6]

As a rabbi and likely a member of the Sanhedrin Paul would have been trained in Hebrew Scriptures sufficiently enough to interpret the coming Messiah. Paul was highly educated for his time. Luke recorded in Acts that Paul affirmed his education and credibility:

> Brothers and fathers, hear the defense that I now make before you." And when they heard that he was addressing them in the Hebrew language, they became even more quiet. And he said: "I am a Jew, born in Tarsus in Cilicia, but brought up in this city, educated at the feet of Gamaliel according to the strict manner of the law of our fathers, being zealous for God as all of you are this day. I persecuted this Way

---

[6] McRay, John, *Paul: His Life and Teaching*, 36-37.

to the death, binding and delivering to prison both men and women, as the high priest and the whole council of elders can bear me witness. From them I received letters to the brothers, and I journeyed toward Damascus to take those also who were there and bring them in bonds to Jerusalem to be punished. Act 22: 1-5

Despite Paul's study, his exegesis, hermeneutics, exposition, and interpretation of Hebrew Scriptures and Sanhedrin membership Paul had not recognized Jesus as Messiah. He did not interpret Jesus of Nazareth, Jesus Bar-Joseph as Jesus Immanuel (God with us). By Paul's confession, his training had failed him. His education at the feet of Gamaliel had failed him. His presuppositions had failed him. So, no surprise of his warning to Timothy to rightly handle the word of truth (2 Tm 2:15). Keep in mind that Paul was not talking about any New Testament books we have today. At that time the New Testament had not been written nor compiled. Paul was likely talking about the Hebrew Scriptures that prophesied of Jesus as the anointed Messiah that Paul had missed. The angst in Paul is apparent when we consider his caution to Timothy to rightly handle the word of truth.

If Paul, the New Testament writer, theologian, pastor, teacher, and evangelist had missed Jesus as Messiah despite his ability and training as a Jewish Rabbi and likely member of the Sanhedrin, then we today should heed Paul's word to Timothy. Presuppositions matter. Rightly or wrongly handling the word of truth are consequential. No one knew the consequences for holding biased presuppositions that resulted in misinterpreting Scripture better than Paul. His Damascus conversion is proof.

## Beyond the Bible

Regarding the New Testament, particularly related to Jesus' imperatives, the Greek critical text remains. There are no presuppositions in the Greek critical text. More accurately, what the Gospel writers recorded does not change. There is no option but to interpret and develop theology from the written Scripture. The question is begged. For what are we to use the Bible? Of course, evangelism, salvation, Jesus, the Gospel, Christian living, eschatology, and numerous theologies apply. Those are some of the basics or the elementary doctrines. The writer of Hebrew, however, defines the elementary doctrines that must be left behind, if God permits:

> Therefore let us leave the elementary doctrine of Christ and go on to maturity, not laying again a foundation of repentance from dead works and of faith toward God, and of instruction about washings, the laying on of hands, the resurrection of the dead, and eternal judgment. And this we will do if God permits. Hb 6: 1-3

The elementary doctrines are the Messiahship of Jesus the Christ, repentance, the inability of works for salvation, instructions about washings (possibly baptism types), laying on of hands (possibly healing types or calling recognition), and the resurrection of the dead and eternal judgments. With these elementary doctrines that must be left behind, what is the goal of Scripture? From Genesis to Revelation God's written word has been studied and interpreted. In his book, *Beyond the Bible*, I. Howard Marshall makes this point:

We should take our guidance for our continuing interpretation of Scripture and the development of theology from what goes on in Scripture itself.[7]

Marshal establishes that theology, the study of God, is the goal of Scripture. Kevin J. Vanhoozer summarizes Marshall's point with this question: "Can we go beyond the Bible to get to theology biblically?" Vanhoozer continues:

Let us make every effort so to be nurtured on the Christ-centered canon that we become expositor-performers who not only interpret but also live out the way, the truth, and the life to the glory of God.[8]

Of course, Scriptures point to Jesus. Of course, salvation and the Gospel are central to Scripture. Of course, various orthodoxies (beliefs) and orthopraxis (practices) have developed from Scripture. Where did and does the Word point? Is our priority to use Scripture to show us God or is our priority to use Scripture to address our life problems pastorally? Is there a priority? Is there order? Big difference.

## Theological vs. Pastoral

Theology precedes and trumps pastoring and preaching. The Bible is first theological, meaning the Bible is about God. The Bible is intended to be pastorally applied only after having been first understood that God is the priority. When well-meaning Christians prioritize pulpit pastoral applications above God to whom the Scriptures point, something is amiss. Sometimes well-meaning Christians miss prioritize theology and pastoring. They forget God's sovereignty.

Marshall made the point that the Bible as anything other than first pointing to God was problematic. Marshall's book title, *Beyond the Bible*, sounds heretical. What does Marshall mean by *Beyond the Bible*? While his words sound strange to the ears of an evangelical Gospel proclaimer, with an objective view, Marshall is right.

There is a priority. There is a sequence. There is a chronology. Christian faith is historical. First, theologically read the Bible to know God. Second, pastorally read the Bible to apply and proclaim. When pastoral applications have priority, the Bible becomes a "how to" book rather than a revelatory book of creator, sustainer, and savior God. Big difference.

In our personal goal to solve our life problems or our spiritual call, we fail to understand that the Bible is primarily and principally theological. It is first about God. Indeed the Bible is for pastoral care, evangelizing, discipling, edifying and numerous other faith works. However, the Bible is first about God, the Kingdom of God and the Kingdom's King, Jesus. John beautifully and accurately described the Word in the first sentence of his gospel:

In the beginning was the Word, and the Word was with God, and the Word was God. He was in the beginning with God. Ἐν ἀρχῇ ἦν ὁ λόγος καὶ ὁ λόγος ἦν πρὸς τὸν θεόν καὶ θεὸς ἦν ὁ λόγος. Jn 1: 1-2

---

[7] Marshall, I. Howard, *Beyond the Bible: Moving from Scripture to Theology*, 77.
[8] Ibid. 95.

Matthew likewise strikingly and precisely recorded Jesus' words. Jesus pointed first to the Kingdom through an imperative command with order and priority:

But <u>seek first the Kingdom of God and his righteousness</u> ζητεῖτε δὲ πρῶτον τὴν βασιλείαν καὶ τὴν δικαιοσύνην αὐτοῦ." Mt 6: 33

When lay, clergy or scholars worship Scriptures more than the LORD, there will always be problems. Pharisees, Sadducees, and Temple leaders are historical proofs of respected learned leaders who got it wrong. They either mistakenly or intentionally misinterpreted. Mistakenly or intentionally misinterpreting exists today as then.

The first-century spiritual leaders responsible to God for those under their care missed Jesus' coming, his Messiahship. They hid his coming from those who relied upon and trusted their spiritual leadership. Their goal through Scriptures was God, knowing God as he revealed himself through the Scriptures and living in the Kingdom. Jewish leaders did not see Jesus as Messiah because they had either mistakenly or intentionally misinterpreted their own Scriptures. Beyond misinterpretations of their Scriptures, they mislead their followers. Making a mistake is one thing. Intentionally misleading is quite another — big difference.

Jesus made certain the priority that seeking the Kingdom and God's righteousness trumps being a Bible scholar, exegete, pastor, missionary, evangelist, or anyone claiming belief in Jesus. The Kingdom has been, is, and always will be God's plan for his creation and his created. The Bible, however, is not the end to God's means. Translations and interpretations as well as translators and interpreters matter to God. Both translating and interpreting are serious business not to be taken lightly by translators or interpreters. Paul would agree. So would Mathew, Mark, Luke, John, Peter, James, Jude and the author of Hebrews.

## Balanced Approach

The English translation used herein is Crossway Publishing's "*English Standard Version*" (ESV) because the ESV (similar to others such as NRSV, NASB, Holman, and Young's Literal) are Word-for-Word, (Essentially Literal, Formally Equivalent, Verbatim) translations as much as possible. However, even Word-for-Word translations do not always provide (in spite of the effort) the most accurate English equivalent words from the Greek.

However, Word-for-Word Bibles are far superior to word accuracy than paraphrase Bibles despite their few anomalies. This book can be illuminating if you can be objective about which English translation you prefer. I chose the ESV for the English because of the ESV's translation philosophy. However, even the ESV, as well as the KJV, have some anomalies with the Greek texts of which is not the intent of this book to critique. Using the right English word or phrase is not easy. The challenge that Douglas Moo exposes is real. Moo affirms:

> The problem we face on the CBT [Committee of Bible Translators], as do all translation committees, is to choose the right English word or phrase to communicate the meaning that we have decided is borne by a particular Greek or Hebrew word or phrase.[9]

---

[9] Moo, Douglas J., *We Still Don't Get It: Evangelicals and Bible Translation Fifty Years After James Barr*, 7.

Embarking on detailed word studies from Thought-for-Thought Bibles can be problematic. English words in "Thought-for-Thought" bibles may not be equivalent to the original Greek or Hebrew words. Word studies, as well as grammar, syntax, and context, are essential. Word studies within this book are from recognized scholarly lexicons and dictionaries: Brown,[10] Danker,[11] Friberg,[12] and Mounce.[13]

The Bible translation debate need not be divisive. For those familiar with translation and interpretation methodologies debate is less important. What is essential, however, is knowing the translation philosophy and translation technique of your Bible.

## Where Did We Get the Greek Texts?

Two common scholarly recognized Greek texts translators source to render Greek to English are the Nestle-Aland Greek Text known as *Novum Testamentum Graece* (NTG) and the Westcott Hort Greek text known as *Westcott and Hort* (WHO). Another Greek text by the United Bible Society (UBS) title *The UBS Greek New Testament* is also a Greek text used by translators. However, where did Nestle-Aland, Wescott and Hort, and UBS source their Greek? How did they produce the Greek texts used by today's English translators? Can we trust the Greek from Nestle-Aland, Westcott-Hort, and UBS? To dig deeper a definition of terms is helpful.

> Extant – refers to an original writing still in existence. There are no extant New Testament writings. In other words, there are no original manuscripts from the penmanship of Matthew, Mark, Luke, or John. There are numerous New Testament copies considered to be handed down from originals, but no originals have been found to date. However, there are copies possibly made from originals or copies made from copies very near to the originals.
> Codex – refers to a collection of papyri in book type format.
> Majuscule – refers to capitalized or upper case letters.
> Manuscript (MS) - refers to writing similar to a complete letter or book.
> Manuscripts (MSS) - refer to numerous writings that are entirely similar to a collection of letters or books.
> Minuscule – refers to lower case, cursive, non-capitalized letters.
> Papyrus - in a literal sense is a paper-like material used in ancient times for recording words. Papyrus is also a word used when referring to ancient writings.
> Parchment - a writing surface made from animal skins.
> Velum - a specific type of parchment writing surface made from calf skins.
> Papyri (P) - a term used to describe paper fragments having written letters that include New Testament writings. Some P are more complete than others. Some P are fragmented. An individual P is identified by letter and number such as P52, P66, and P43etc. There is always a possibility of new papyri discovery.
> Scroll – refers to a roll of writing surface that could be unrolled to convey a single continuous written document. Bound books with pages eventually replaced scrolls.

---

[10] Brown, Colin, ed., *New International Dictionary of New Testament Theology*.
[11] Danker, Frederick William, ed. Walter Bauer, *A Greek-English Lexicon of the New Testament and other Early Christian Literature*.
[12] Friberg, Timothy, Barbara Friberg, and Neva F. Miller, *Analytical Lexicon of the Greek New Testament*
[13] Mounce, William D., *Mounce's Complete Expository Dictionary of Old & New Testament Words*.

Uncial – refers to a manuscript written in all capital letters (majuscule) letters. A New Testament uncial refers to a P recorded in Greek capital letters.

Numerous Codex compiled of New Testament Papyri are securely stored throughout the world. Soulen in his book, *Handbook of Biblical Criticism* describes five significant Codexes:[14]

Codex Alexandrinus (5th C) stored within the British Museum, London
Codex Bezae (5th C) stored within Cambridge University Cambridge, England
Codes Ephraemi Rescriptus (5th C) stored in Paris.
Codex Sinaiticus (4th C) stored within the British Museum, London
Codex Vaticanus (4th C) stored within the Vatican Library, Rome

Each Codex contains numerous papyri. Some papyri within each Codex, however, have been dated from different periods and have been found in different locations. Some papyri are less fragmented than others. The closer in time that papyri are dated to the original extant writing the more favorable those papyri become. The goal is to find the text from papyri closest to the original. One of the most reputable and recognized authors and scholar with historical translation knowledge today is Dr. Philip Comfort. Agreeing with Comfort:

And most scholars still consider that the earliest reading is very often the best reading.[15]

Not all New Testament P are found or stored within recognized codexes. Some P have been found after some codexes were organized. More recent P are named and provided a safe storage location. Newly found P not included within historical codex already established are often named after the locations where they were found or person or persons who found them. Codexes come from numerous locations and are stored throughout the world. What follows are their discovery locations and housing locations.

Egypt discovery locations:

Aphroditopolis, Arsinoi, Captos, Gayum, Medinet Madi, Oxyrhynchus, and Qarara.[16]

Housing locations:

| | |
|---|---|
| P1 | Philadelphia, PA: University of Pennsylvania Museum |
| P4 | Paris, France: Bibliotheque Nationale |
| P5, P13, P18 | London, England: British Library |
| P6, P82, P85 | Strasbourg, France: Bibliotheque Nationale et Universitaire |
| P8 | Berlin, Germany: Staatliche Museen |
| P10, P17, P27 | Cambridge MA: Harvard University, Semitic Museum |
| P12 | New York, NY: Pierpont Morgan Library |
| P15, P16 | Cairo, Egypt: Egyptian Museum of Antiquities |

---

[14] Soulen, Richard N., and Kendall R Soulen, *Handbook of Biblical Criticism, Third Edition*, 34 – 36.
[15] Comfort, Philip Wesley, *Early Manuscripts & Modern Translations of the New Testament*, Grand Rapids, MI: Baker Books, 1996. 16.
[16] Comfort, Philip Wesley, *Early Manuscripts & Modern Translations of the New Testament*, 221.

| | |
|---|---|
| P20 | Princeton HJ: Princeton University Library |
| P21 | Allentown, PA: Muhlenburg College |
| P22 | Glasgow, Scotland: University Library |
| P23 | Urbana, IL University of Illinois |
| P24 | Newton Centre, MS: Andover Newton Theological School |
| P29 | Oxford, England: Bodleian Library |
| P30 | Ghent, Belgium: Rijksuniversiteit, Bibliotheek |
| P32, P52 | Manchester, England: John Ryland Library |
| P35, P48 | Florence, Italy: Biblioteca Laurensiana |
| P37, P38, P53 | Ann Arbor, MI: University of Michigan |
| P39 | Rochester, NY: Ambrose Swabey Library |
| P40 | Heidelberg, Germany: Papyrussammlung der Universitat |
| P45, P46, P47 | Dublin, Ireland: Chester Beatty Private Library |
| P49, P50 | New Haven, CT: Yale University Library |
| P51, P69, P70 | Oxford, England: Ashmolean Museum |
| P71, P77, P78 | Oxford, England: Ashmolean Museum |
| P62 | Oslo, Norway: University Library |
| P64 | Oxford, England: Magdalen College Library |
| P67, P80 | Barcelona, Spain: Fundacion San Lucas Evangelista |
| P65 | Florence, Italy: Istituto di Papirologia G. Vitelli |
| P66, P72, P75 | Geneva/Cologny, Switzerland: Bibliotheca Bodmeriana |
| P81 | Trieste: Sergio Daris (Antiquities Dealer) |
| P86, P87 | Cologne, Germany: Institut Fur Altertumskunde |
| P88 | Milan, Italy: Universita Cattolica |
| P89 | Florence, Italy: Biblioteca Medicea Laurenziana |
| P91 portion | Milan, Italy: Istituto di Papirologia |
| P91 portion | Norther Ryde, Australia: Macquarie University |
| P92 | Cairo, Egypt: Museo Egizio Del Cairo |
| 0162 | New York, NY: Metropolitan Museum of Art |
| 0171 | Florence, Italy: Bibliotheca Laurenziana |
| 0189 | Berlin, Germany: Staatliche Museen |
| 0212 | New Haven CT: Yale University |
| 0220 | London, England: Quaritch. [17] |

## Codexes and Papyri of the New Testament

From centuries of scholarly textual criticism of codexes and papyri comes reliability. Few Christians in their lifetime will view the actual Greek letters or words recorded on papyrus or parchments sourced from Codexes or Papyri. The original handwork of Matthew, Mark, Luke, John, Peter, Paul, James, Jude and the author Hebrews has never been seen and may never be seen. However, copies of those texts are reliable.

The historical rigors through the copying process combined with ongoing research have provided the Greek *critical texts* we have today. From the *Nestle-Aland* and *Westcott-Hort* Greek texts sourced from Codexes and Papyri comes the English texts. The numerous Greek texts sourced

---

[17] Comfort, Philip Wesley, *Early Manuscripts & Modern Translations of the New Testament,* 31-73. Comfort includes details for each P beyond those listed here.

from Codexes and Papyri that for the *critical texts* are not going to change. In other words, English texts change with each new translation. The Greek *critical text* seldom or arbitrarily changes unless of course new texts or new papyri are discovered and assessed. With new papyri, findings can come new *critical texts* and new *critical apparatus*. The scholarly process is continuous.

Both Word-for-Word and Thought-for-Thought Bibles can suffer from being too free with the Greek texts. Translation philosophy freedoms can produce disputations. Suffice that the *Nestle-Aland* or *Westcott-Hort* Greek critical texts are reliable as produced from Codexes and Papyri. We cannot say the same for past and future Thought-for-Thought para-phrase Bibles. In short, interpretations change. Greek words from the *critical texts* seldom change unless new papyri are discovered. As stated, the scholarly process is continuous.

## From Codex and Papyri to Critical Texts and Critical Apparatus

A *critical text* is a Greek text developed from various Codexes and Papyri by committees of scholars to determine which renderings are closest to the original. A *critical apparatus* listing alternate readings generally accompany a *critical text*. Soulen clarifies the *critical apparatus*:

> Critical Apparatus refers to the notes supplied primarily in Hebrew and Greek editions of the OT and NT that cite the MS sources and readings that either support or vary from the printed text.[18]

Both scholars and students use the Nestle-Aland *Novum Testamentum Graece* (NTG) most recent *critical text* edition for translation from Greek to English now in its 28th edition. In short, the NTG *critical texts* and *critical apparatus* sourced from Codexes and Papyri are considered to be the most reliable Greek texts. Teams of Bible scholars employ the *critical texts* and *critical apparatus* when developing Bible translations.

## Greek and Copies of Greek

There are no original autographs determined to be from the hands of the original writers. That means we have only copies of original autographs referred to as manuscripts not autographs. In other words, we are not just dependent upon copies. We are dependent on copies of copies. While not having original writings may sound problematic, dependence on copies is an affirming asset more than an uncertain liability.

Often both lay and cleric Christians are unfamiliar with the Greek *critical texts* and how English translations have come to be. Churches and pastors seldom edify their congregants on translation issues or textual criticism. Instead, they depend on the English Bibles for preaching and teaching. However, at the core lies the Greek, more specifically the Greek *critical texts* derived from copies. Philip Comfort rightly clarifies our dependence on copies of original manuscripts. Our use of copies may be more reliable perhaps than originals because consistency and accuracy are paramount. The validity of copy accuracy from the reconstruction of the original texts adds to their credibility and accuracy. Comfort affirms:

---

[18] Soulen, Richard N., and Kendall R Soulen, *Handbook of Biblical Criticism, Third Edition*, 41.

Because not one original writing (autograph) of any New Testament book still exists, we depend on copies from reconstructing the original texts.[19] At present we have more than six thousand manuscript copies of the Greek New Testament or portions thereof. No other work of Greek literature can boast of such numbers.[20]

To repeat and emphasize, many New Testament Greek teachers prominently use two Greek texts developed from historical copies. The NTG is the dominant critical publication of the Greek New Testament. Its 28th edition is currently used by translators, scholars, teachers, pastors, and students. Another reputable source is the WHO text. Familiar with advocates or opponents of NTG or WHO are critics for or against their preferred Greek text. Both Greek texts are scholarly supportable each with its strengths and weaknesses from objective and subjective ad hominem critics. Maurice A. Robinson affirms Westcott-Hort:

> The Westcott-Hort text herein [BibleWorks 8] presented was constructed from a collation published in 1889 by William Sanday. Sanday's collation presents with a high degree of accuracy the approximately 6000 significant alterations between the Westcott-Hort text of 1881 and the Stephens 1550 Textus Receptus edition. The resultant text of this collation was compared with the Westcott-Hort portion of the "Textuum Differerntia" appendix to the Nestle Aland 26th edition to verify Sanday's data. Errors on the part of both Sanday and Nestle Aland 26th edition appendix were found and corrected during this process, and the resultant Westcott-Hort text is more accurate than either source taken independently.[21]

Identifying the Greek imperative morphological structure either through the NTG or WHO meets our needs. For our purposes, the WHO within BibleWorks V8 has been chosen. Philip Comfort noted textual scholar in support of WHO states:

> The text produced by Westcott and Hort is still to this day, even with so many more manuscript discoveries, a very close reproduction of the primitive text of the New Testament.[22]

Comfort is right in reaching back to primitive texts — grammatical and historical context matters. New Testament primitive texts are where any scholar of repute must begin yet not end. In short, grammatical and historical context is just the beginning. Supportive to our study for research reliability and lay use, Greek sourced from the Westcott and Hort (WHO) within BibleWorks V8 has been a primary Koine Greek source for this work.

---

[19] Comfort, Philip Wesley, *The Origin of the Bible: A Comprehensive Guide*, 179.
[20] Ibid. 182.
[21] BibleWorks V8, Copyright Source Information Westcott-Hort text from 1881 combined with the NA26/27 Variants, Prepared and edited by Maurice A. Robinson.
[22] Comfort, Philip Wesley, *Encountering the Manuscripts: An Introduction to New Testament Paleography & Textual Criticism*, 100.

# Contemporary English Bibles

There are numerous English Bibles from which to choose. With so many Bible types, selecting a Bible suited to your needs is a wise idea. In simple terms, using a Word-for-Word Bible for academic, scholarly, or word-study work in English is the wiser choice. Sometimes however, using a Word-for-Word English Bible requires deeper study, because not all Word-for-Word Bibles accurately translate Hebrew, Aramaic, or Greek into English.

Given the two translation philosophies, English Bible readers have the luxury to choose Bibles based on Word-for-Word or Thought-for-Thought. As previously covered, for ease of use, Bibles where the Word-for-Word translation philosophy has been generally applied we'll call "formally equivalent" Bibles.

Bibles where the Thought-for-Thought translation philosophy has been generally applied we'll call "functionally equivalent" Bibles. Beyond translation philosophy alone, choosing an English Bible based on the Hebrew, Greek, and Aramaic texts from which it sourced is essential. To follow are some Bibles falling within the two translation philosophies.[23]

Common "functionally equivalent" English Bibles:

  NIV  *New International Version*, (NIrV, NIVI), Zondervan Publishing, Grand Rapids MI
  NLT  *New Living Translation*, Tyndale House Publishers, Wheaton, IL
  NET  *New English Translation*, Biblical Studies Press, Richardson, TX
  MSG  *The Message*, NavPress, Colorado Springs, CO

Common "formally equivalent" English Bibles:

  ESV   *English Standard Version*, Crossway Publishing, Wheaton, IL
  NASB  *New American Standard Bible*, Zondervan Publishers, Grand Rapids, MI
  NRSV  *New Revised Standard Version*, Harper Collins, New York, NY
  NKJV  *New King James Version*, Thomas Nelson Publishers, Nashville, TN
  CSB   *Christian Standard Version*, Baker Publishing, Grand Rapids, MI

Common English Bibles that include Deuterocanonical / Apocrypha Books:

  CEB   *Common English Bible*, Christian Resource Development Corp, Nashville, TN
  NJB   *New Jerusalem Bible*, Darton, Longman, Todd, London, UK
  NRSV  *New Revised Standard Version w/Apocrypha*, Harper Collins, New York, NY

---

[23] This book is not intended to be a reference or resource for choosing a Bible. The list is merely a guide. Readers should research each Bible's translation philosophy to determine with more detail their understanding of the translation philosophy. Translation philosophies and methods are subjective. Regarding publishing, Bible translators may choose different publishers. The publishers provided above are subject to change.

# Summary

The Christian witness is strengthened with a basic understanding of Papyri, Codex, Critical Texts and Critical Apparatus. From Papyri and Greek Codex come the Critical Texts and Critical Apparatus. From the Critical Texts and Critical Apparatus comes English Bibles. Critical Texts can improve over time with research. Currently, the Nestle Aland (NTG) Critical Text is in its 28$^{th}$ edition. Both the NTG and the Westcott Hort (WHO) are critical scholarly texts. The United Bible Society (UBS) Greek New Testament is also a recognized scholarly Greek text.

English Bibles are identified as having two basic translation types: Word-for-Word (Essentially Literal, Formally Equivalent, or Verbatim) and Thought-for-Thought (Dynamically Equivalent, Functionally Equivalent, or Paraphrased).

Word-for-Word Bibles are often termed to be literal because translation teams have attempted to find the exact English word for the Hebrew or Greek. Thought-for-Thought Bibles are not intended to produce a literal meaning because ideas or the essence of the meaning has priority.

Concerning inspiration and power of the Holy Spirit upon the texts, God inspired the original texts of which today we have no autographs. However, there are over six thousand copies or portions of copies from the originals that create the Critical Texts. Bible translation philosophies and techniques are important because knowing or not knowing the language, context, and culture of Jesus' day can affect the text and meaning.

Here is where terms like Exegesis, Hermeneutics, Exposition, and Interpretation (in the next chapter) have their place in bearing fruit from Biblical texts.

# Section 2

# Meaning Then - Meaning Now

And as they were eating, he said, "Truly, I say to you, one of you will betray me." And they were very sorrowful and began to say to him one after another, "Is it I, Lord?" He answered, "He who has dipped his hand in the dish with me will betray me. The Son of Man goes as it is written of him, but woe to that man by whom the Son of Man is betrayed! It would have been better for that man if he had not been born." Judas, who would betray him, answered, "Is it I, Rabbi?" He said to him, "You have said so." Now as they were eating, Jesus took bread, and after blessing it broke it and gave it to the disciples, and said, "Take, eat; this is my body." And he took a cup, and when he had given thanks he gave it to them, saying, "Drink of it, all of you, for this is my blood of the covenant, which is poured out for many for the forgiveness of sins. I tell you I will not drink again of this fruit of the vine until that day when I drink it new with you in my Father's kingdom."

Mt 26: 21-29

When I was a son with my father, tender, the only one in the sight of my mother, he taught me and said to me, "Let your heart hold fast my words; keep my commandments, and live. Get wisdom; get insight; do not forget, and do not turn away from the words of my mouth."

Pr 4: 3-5

# 6 Exegesis, Hermeneutics, Exposition, Interpretation

> Teach me good judgment and knowledge, for I believe in your commandments. Before I was afflicted I went astray, but now I keep your word. You are good and do good; teach me your statutes.
> Ps 119: 66-68

## Why Exegesis, Hermeneutics, Exposition, and Interpretation Matter

Exegesis, hermeneutics, exposition, and interpretation are words describing what pastors or teachers do (or should do) before they preach or teach. If you do not know how your pastors and teachers come to their conclusions, there is the risk that what they preach and teach merely may not be so. The reformer Martin Luther would agree. Luther found that the leadership within the Roman Catholic Church where he had been ordained and was ministering had been teaching and applying false beliefs for financial gain. Some false teaching were mistakes. Some false teaching were intentional. Big difference. Even in the 1500's where loyalty and obedience to clergy and church were paramount for the laity, false teaching for financial gain was rampant. Hence, exegesis, hermeneutics, exposition, and interpretation must be held in check by both laity and clergy.

Exegesis, hermeneutics, exposition, and interpretation are often taught at seminaries or post-college faith-based schools. Most denominationally ordained pastors and professors have received at least a minimal amount of formal academic training in exegesis, hermeneutics, exposition, and interpretation. While basic training may sound trustworthy, what your leaders have learned may not be sufficient. What one seminary or denomination advocates, is not the same as others by way of exegesis, hermeneutics, exposition, and interpretation. One reason for so many denominations is because exegesis, hermeneutics, exposition, and interpretation differ.

Few pastors or churches clearly describe how they have come to believe what they believe, preach or teach. Statements of faith are often scripturally referenced but seldom clearly explained. Membership meetings tend to be social events. Clarification on how the Pastor interprets or what the church believes is often intentionally vague. Denomination based churches tend to rely on historical roots to assure congregants. But not always do denominations get scripture right.

The reasons the process matters are twofold. First, your own intellectual exegesis, hermeneutics, exposition, and interpretation requires continual strengthening. Secondly, you must also discern the exegesis, hermeneutics, exposition, and interpretation validities from those preaching or teaching you. Luther would agree.

## Defining Terms

Laity trusts those in the pulpit to preach and teach the truth. Few in the pews deeply comprehend the responsibilities of their pastors and teachers. Worse some behind pulpits either do not understand or deny the depth of their responsibility. There often exists a blind trust from those in the pews that what their pastors or preachers say must be true. However, not all pastors or preachers are adequate exegetes capable of developing a hermeneutic or supportable interpretation. The pulpit is no place for a gifted speaker with only oratory and presentation skills or giftedness.

Over 2000 years of church and world history affirms that churches, pastors, preachers, leadership teams, sessions, deacons, elders, and theologians have not always gotten it right. Martin Luther, a Roman Catholic monk, realized much was amiss by way of interpretation and practice within the Roman Catholic Church which had ordained him. In the mid-1500s Luther exposed numerous historical interpretations which started the Reformation that ultimately produced the Protestant movement. As a result, the Lutheran church started as did thousands of new denominations that competed with Roman Catholicism and each other. Following Luther new churches or communities began to question Lutheran and Roman Catholic beliefs. This book is not intended to present in-depth coverage of church history. Suffice to say that exegesis, hermeneutics, exposition, and interpretation can be divisive, but need not be. A definition of terms is helpful.

## The Exegetical, Hermeneutical, Expositional, Interpretational Process

Exegesis, hermeneutics, exposition, and interpretation are the foundations of preaching and teaching. A church pulpit becomes just a building lectern without proper exegesis, hermeneutics, exposition, and interpretation. Knowing what these words mean and how they differ from one another is central to discern errors or outright subjective heresy. Getting from exegesis to interpretation is a process.

## Exegesis

F. F. Bruce and J. Julius Scott Jr. simply, clearly, and accurately distinguish exegesis, hermeneutics, exposition, and interpretation. Bruce and Scott rightly lay the foundation that the first step is exegesis which is understanding what the texts meant to the original readers and hearers in their context. Exegesis starts everything. Simply put, the original New Testament documents were not written in English. That means Greek, more specifically Koine Greek requires translation into English. However, before translation happens, Bruce and Scott would agree that Koine Greek and 1st-century culture must first be understood in context. There is a process. Regarding exegesis Bruce and Scott support:

> The biblical documents are ancient, written in Hebrew, Aramaic, and Greek at various times between 1200 B.C. (if not earlier) and A.D. 100, reflecting several different historical and cultural settings. An essential requirement for the understanding of these documents is their Grammatico-historical interpretation or exegesis – bringing out of the text the meaning the writers intended to convey and which their readers were expected to gather from it.[1]

New Testament Greek words require translation from Greek to English. Words must be rendered. Translating words from Greek to English is the first challenge. Getting the Greek context into English is the more significant challenge. Exegesis is a product of numerous disciplines including being critical of the original text. Demos clarifies exegesis and context:

---

[1] Bruce F. F., Scott Jr. J. Julius, "Interpretation of the Bible" in Elwell, Walter A., *Evangelical Dictionary of Theology*, 611.

Exegesis is a result of disciplines such as language, semantics, etymology, dialectics, morphology, linguistics, genres, grammar, syntax, lexicography, textual criticism, and most importantly, context.[2]

Exegesis and hermeneutics are two words often melded and misunderstood by both those in pews and those behind pulpits. D. A. Carson clarifies their meanings and sequential order:

> Exegesis is concerned with actually interpreting the text, whereas hermeneutics is concerned with the nature of the interpretative process. But although hermeneutics is an important discipline in its own right, ideally it [hermeneutics] is never an end in itself: it [hermeneutics] serves exegesis.[3]

## Hermeneutics

Hermeneutics precedes exposition and interpretation and always follows exegesis. Regarding hermeneutics Bruce and Scott affirm:

> The study of the principles of interpretation – both the Grammatico-historical interpretation of the practical application of the interpretation in the pulpit – is called hermeneutics.[4]

Since hermeneutics deals with interpretation, hermeneutics can have three historical perspectives dealing with when an event happened. Because hermeneutics is always related to an event in time, hermeneutics always has three possibilities: contextual, historical, and contemporary. First, how past events have been interpreted at or near the time those events happened, we call *Contextual Hermeneutics*. Second, how past events have been interpreted over time, we call *Historical Hermeneutics*. Third, how events are presently interpreted we call Contemporary Hermeneutics. For clarity within this book we define three hermeneutic types:

> What the text initially meant there and then is termed, *Contextual Hermeneutics*.
> What the text has meant in historical periods is termed, *Historical Hermeneutics*.
> What the text means here and now is termed, *Contemporary Hermeneutics*.

In short, a sour exegesis produces a sour hermeneutic. A sour hermeneutic produces a sour exposition. And a sour exposition produces a sour interpretation. When Greek to English translations are weak, the hermeneutics may be weak as well. If you do not know what the text meant then, determining what the text means now can be less precise. No surprise that James warned of severe judgments upon teachers:

---

[2] Semantics – study of meaning; Etymology – derivation of words; Dialectics – a regional variety of a language; Morphology – word structure; Linguistics – study of a language; Genres – literary composition form; Grammar – language components; Syntax – sentence formation; Lexicology – words of a language; Contextual Method – social and historical milieu. See Demoss, Matthew S., *Pocket Dictionary for the Study of New Testament Greek*.
[3] Carson, D. A., *Exegetical Fallacies*, 2d ed. 25.
[4] Bruce F. F., Scott Jr. J. Julius, "Interpretation of the Bible" in Elwell, Walter A., *Evangelical Dictionary of Theology*, 611.

Not many of you should become teachers, my brothers, for you know that we who teach will be judged with greater strictness, Μὴ πολλοὶ διδάσκαλοι γίνεσθε ἀδελφοί μου εἰδότες ὅτι μεῖζον κρίμα λημψόμεθα. Ja 3:1.

## Exposition

Jesus intended Scripture exposition to proceed from his church. Those with spiritual oversight over a community have a responsibility to correctly exposit Scripture. With excellent exposition comes clarification, explication, and most importantly exactness of what Jesus said. For our purposes within this book exposition must clarify Jesus' Greek imperatives, his commands. Mark Devers contrasts the pastor's mind to God's mind:

> To charge someone with the spiritual oversight of a church who does not in practice show a commitment to hear and to teach God's Word is to hamper the growth of the church, in essence allowing it to grow only to the level of the pastor. The church will slowly be conformed to the pastor's mind rather than to God's mind. And what we want, what as Christians we crave, are God's words. We want to hear and know in our souls what He has said.[5]

First, knowing what Jesus said must precede exposition and explanation. Greek definitions and Greek grammar matter. Bryan Chapel affirms the limitations and importance of grammar related to exegesis:

> Exegesis is the process by which preachers discover the precise definitions and grammatical distinctions of the words in a text. Preachers with Greek and Hebrew expertise translate passages recognizing that even the best English translation of the Bible cannot adequately communicate the nuances of the words in the original languages.[6]

Bruce and Scott clarify the place and position of exposition. Sustaining that exposition is contemporary Bruce and Scott affirm the contemporary application intent of exposition:

> This Grammatico-historical exegesis is commonly practiced in the classroom and distinguished from the exposition, which is more appropriate to the pulpit. Exposition aims to apply the text and its meaning to men and women today, enabling them to answer the question: What message has this for us, or me, in the present situation?[7]

Bruce and Scott also affirm that pulpit exposition must first be preceded by and based upon exegesis:

---

[5] Dever, Mark, *Nine Marks of a Healthy Church*, 28.
[6] Chapell, Bryan, *Christ-Centered Preaching: Redeeming the Expository Sermon,* 105.
[7] Bruce F. F., Scott Jr. J. Julius, "Interpretation of the Bible" in Elwell, Walter A., *Evangelical Dictionary of Theology,* 611.

To be valid, exposition must be firmly based on exegesis: the meaning of the text for hearers today must be related to its meaning for the hearers to who it was first addressed.[8]

Useful exposition is only possible following proper exegesis. The process, the progression, the sequence to is absolute. The word "exposition" has to do with applying the text to today. To exposit a text means to convey application of a text. Proper exposition is not possible if exposition is not preceded by exegesis and hermeneutics.

When pew sitters ask their pastors to preach relevant messages, and what the text means to them, they are looking for exposition. Some pastors, however, give more effort to making sermons relevant often at the cost of ignoring context. Bryan Chappel explains expository preaching:

> A sermon that explores any biblical concept is in the broadest sense "expository," but the technical definition of an expository sermon requires that it expound Scripture by deriving from a specific text main points and sub points that disclose the thought of the author, cover the scope of the passage, and are applied to the lives of the listeners.[9]

The point is that before exposition competent pastors or teachers must first exegete the text, and then engage *contextual hermeneutics*. More specifically they must know what the text said in the original language and what the text's original hearers of the spoken words or listeners who heard the written words read to them thought that text meant to them. Secondly is to know what a text has meant over history or *historical hermeneutics*. Only then should preachers approach expository preaching to be relevant and interpretive through *contemporary hermeneutics*.

## Interpretation

Knowing and applying proper exegesis, hermeneutics, exposition, and interpretation identified by Bruce and Scott are absolute for anyone preaching behind church pulpits or teaching behind classroom lecterns. Bruce and Scott affirm that interpretation is:

> An explanation of what is not immediately plain in the Bible.[10]

Contrary to the opinion of some lay and clergy not all Scripture is immediately plain. God produced words in a book that require renderings and interpretation. Not everything in Scripture is immediately understandable to readers or hearers. That is why competent interpretation is not to be haphazard or selfish and can be more reliable if done through a community. However, Martin Luther would tell you that even long-established faith communities and churches can get the text wrong. Depending on our own understanding is problematic. The author of Proverbs affirms:

---

[8] Bruce F. F., Scott Jr. J. Julius, "Interpretation of the Bible" in Elwell, Walter A., *Evangelical Dictionary of Theology*, 611.
[9] Chappel, Bryan, *Christ Centered Preaching: Redeeming the Expository Sermon*, 128 – 129.
[10] Bruce F. F., Scott Jr. J. Julius, "Interpretation of the Bible" in Elwell, Walter A., *Evangelical Dictionary of Theology*, 611.

Trust in the LORD with all your heart, and do not lean on your own understanding. In all your ways acknowledge him, and he will make straight your paths. Be not wise in your own eyes; fear the LORD, and turn away from evil. Pr 3:5-7

## Jesus' Contemporary Leaders and Their Bad Exegesis

Subjective or bias interpretations is nothing new. Jesus condemned Temple leaders, Scribes, Sadducees, and Pharisees who had intentionally misled the people with false teachings that ultimately destroyed the Jerusalem Temple in AD 70. Their poor exegesis of Scriptures combined with biased, subjective hermeneutics blinded these leaders. Despite their knowledge and training, they did not recognize Jesus as Messiah nor the Kingdom he had commanded them to seek. Temple leaders, Sadducees, Pharisees or anyone having held a spiritual leadership position at that time were esteemed and revered by the masses. Many well-meaning Jewish peasants followed their spiritual leaders. Like sheep, they were misled. Their spiritual leader did not comprehend Jesus Immanuel the Messiah. No small event.

Greek exegesis is the first step. English hermeneutics follows. The more viable the Greek translation to English, the more dependable the hermeneutics may be. As previously noted, prudent interpretation always places exegesis before hermeneutics. Knowing the text must precede any advocacy for what the text meant then, meant over history, or means today. Had religious leaders in the time of Jesus employed sound exegesis, contextual / historical / contemporary hermeneutics of their time, and exposition, Jewish leaders may have perceived that Jesus was and is the Messiah. Consequences in their day for sloppy or bias exegesis, hermeneutics, expositions, and interpretations eventually came to bear. Same today.

## High Priests and Roman Leadership

Caiaphas and Pilate would have much to say if we could ask them today. After Caiaphas had sent Jesus to Pilate Jesus affirmed to Pilate that Caiaphas had the greater sin. Perhaps Caiaphas recognized that Jesus was the Jewish Messiah. The words of Jesus to Pilate affirmed that Caiaphas, the Temple High Priest had either been mistaken in his interpretation or was intentionally misinterpreting to suit his needs. Caiaphas given his understanding of Jewish scriptures was more learned than Pilate to recognize Jesus as the Messiah:

"Jesus answered him [Pilate], "You [Pilate] would have no authority over me [Jesus] at all unless it had been given you [Pilate] from above. Therefore he [Caiaphas] who delivered me [Jesus] over to you [Pilate] has the greater sin." ἀπεκρίθη αὐτῷ Ἰησοῦς Οὐκ εἶχες ἐξουσίαν κατ ἐμοῦ οὐδεμίαν εἰ μὴ ἦν δεδομένον σοι ἄνωθεν· διὰ τοῦτο ὁ παραδούς μέ σοι μείζονα ἁμαρτίαν ἔχει. Jn 19:11 (Names in brackets mine.)

The word, "therefore" implies a conclusion that there are greater and lesser sins related to interpretive responsibility. Pilate had his responsibilities given his knowledge as did Caiaphas. Caiaphas had the greater sin as the appointed High Priest by Rome who sent Jesus to Pilate.[11]

---

[11] For clarification, before Jesus' crucifixion, Caiaphas (son-in-law to Annas) was High Priest appointed by Rome, but Annas was considered the High Priest according to Jewish law. John recorded that Jesus first appeared before Annas

Greek language, grammar, and historical context in time and place are crucial to understanding the imperatives of Jesus. Whereas exegesis means reading out (ex) of the text, eisegesis means reading something into (eis) the text. Subjective exegesis or subjective eisegesis can produce erroneous hermeneutics which is why employing the Grammatical-Historical Method is central to getting text and meaning right.

## Grammatical Historical Method

In simple terms, the Grammatical-Historical Method first seeks to understand the grammar and history in its original setting. Avoiding unfitting literalism or improper allegory means that grammar and historical context are primary. Grammar and historical facts are essential. As Fee and Stuart affirm:

A text should be interpreted according to grammar and the facts of history.[12]

To audibly hear today Jesus' spoken words recorded by Matthew, Mark, Luke, or John is not possible. Due to the life expectancy in the first century, those who heard Jesus speak never read what the New Testament authors eventually wrote. The New Testament and was not canonized until the mid-3rd Century. By the time the Gospels were written and distributed most of those living when Jesus spoke likely were deceased. Of course, there may have been exceptions with a few, but those who heard Jesus speak likely never read what others wrote about him.

The oldest of all current New Testament manuscripts is P52 from the Gospel of John stored at the John Ryland Library in Manchester, England. While scholars debate the actual date, most agree that the fragment is late first to early second century.[13] While the dated writing of each New Testament book is debated, most scholars agree the earliest is near AD 50 which means that the likelihood of anyone who heard Jesus speak did not read or hear his spoken words from any written texts. What Jesus audibly said and what they heard may have been interpreted differently in their day than what we read in our day. Here is where the Grammatical-Historical Method shines.

Jesus' imperatives likely were more meaningful in the Greek of their day to his audience than what is possible for us today when reading in contemporary English. When Greek grammar and historical context are weak, Jesus' Greek imperatives can be diminished. Subtleties, nuances, and historical context can get lost in translation. Greek, however, is a language that accentuates intelligibility. Mounce emphasizes the clarity of classic Greek in use before Koine Greek of the New Testament:

The form of Greek used by writers from Homer (8th century B.C.) through Plato (4th Century B.C.) is called 'Classic Greek.' It was a marvelous form of the language, capable of exact expression and subtle nuances.[14]

---

and then before Caiaphas (First they led him to Annas, for he was the father-in-law of Caiaphas, who was the high priest that year. Jn 18:13). While Annas was complicit, Caiaphas ultimately sent Jesus to Pilate. Some interpreters identify Judas as the one who sent Jesus to Pilate. However, in the context of the Temple and Roman rule, Caiaphas was the one who sent Pilate to Jesus. While Judas betrayed Jesus which delivered Jesus to Caiaphas, Caiaphas delivered Jesus to Pilate. Caiaphas had the greater sin over Pilate.

[12] Fee, Gordon D., and Douglas Stuart, *How to Read the Bible for All Its Worth,* 62.
[13] P52 is uncial (capital letters) Greek on both sides of one sheet from a codex, not a scroll.
[14] Mounce, William D., *Greek for the Rest of Us, Mastering Bible Study without Mastering Biblical Languages*, 2.

To reemphasize, our first concern *exegesis* or explicating the Greek text and grammar—more specifically, identifying the Greek imperative mood form the authors recorded to convey the words of Jesus. Our second concern is *contextual hermeneutics* to determine what the text meant to them there. Our third concern is *historical hermeneutics* to learn what those before us interpreted. Our fourth concern is *contemporary hermeneutics* or what the text means to us here and now. Imperatives of Jesus are first and foremost contextual. What Jesus commanded then and there within what the authors wrote in their context is the focus of this book.

## Hermeneutics Need Not to Be Confusing

Throughout history, hermeneutics has embraced a variety of methods. In simple terms, hermeneutics means getting a historical message. Hermeneutics is messaging about someone or something. Determining if that message is good or bad depends on interpretation. The phrase, "Don't shoot the messenger." is appropriate. Messengers bring messages. Messages from messengers have priority. Virkler provides origin information about the word hermeneutics:

> The word hermeneutics is said to have had its origin in the name Hermes, the Greek god who served as messenger for the gods, transmitting and interpreting their communications to their fortunate—or often unfortunate—recipients.[15]

Hermeneutics has to do with delivering messages. No doubt that Jesus dealt with exegesis, hermeneutics, exposition, interpretation and messaging from those around him, particularly those in the Temple and those teaching in the Synagogues. He too exegetically read and interpreted in his day. He identified subjective exegesis, hermeneutics, exposition, and interpretation. Jesus called out errors that were mistakes or errors that intentionally mislead. Moreover, he denounced religious leaders who made them. Virkler explains:

> Even Jesus denounced the way religious leaders in his day had developed casuistic methods that set aside the very Word of God they claimed to be interpreting and replaced it with their traditions. (Mk 7: 6–13; Mt 15: 1-9).[16]

In Jesus' day, throughout history, today and in the future spiritual leaders can either erroneously get the text wrong or intentionally make the text subjectively wrong. Some make mistakes, and some have a subjective or personal bias to mislead. Big difference. The problem of mistakes or intention exists today as in Jesus' day. Jewish leaders in Jesus day, those who should have known their Scriptures about the Messiah either missed or intentionally denied him as Messiah.

Just as hermeneutics is not exegesis, translating should not be interpretation. Hermeneutics is both an art and a science. Hermeneutics means to find meaning from the texts. Interpretation is not to be confused with translation. Fee accurately summarizes:

> Although the word 'hermeneutics' ordinarily covers the whole field of interpretation, including exegesis, it is also used in the narrower sense of seeking

---

[15] Virkler, Henry A., *Hermeneutics: Principles and Processes of Biblical Interpretation*, 15.
[16] Ibid. 54.

the contemporary relevance of ancient texts. Proper 'hermeneutics' begins with solid 'exegesis.' The reason one must not begin with the here and now is that the only proper control for hermeneutics is to be found in the original intent of the biblical text.[17]

## Contextual Hermeneutics (Meaning Then and There)

Bible translators can mistakenly or intentionally become interpreters. This book is not intended to give a full meta-narrative of Scripture and doesn't explicate every word of Scripture or every word of Jesus. Our focus is Jesus' words, particularly the Greek imperative mood form in grammatical-historical context.

Hermeneutics is the process of finding meaning and conveying meaning from the text. Those who heard Jesus speak or read what he spoke in the first-century is contextual hermeneutics. For our purposes within this book, the goal is to determine what Jesus' Greek imperatives most often rendered as English commands meant to them in their context. Meaning in their context we call *Contextual Hermeneutics*.

## Historical Hermeneutics (Meaning Over Time)

Throughout history, Christian leaders have produced interpretations associated with their historical periods. There have been many approaches throughout both biblical and world history to the study of God's word. Errors are inevitable. Mistakes can be helpful. Virkler agrees:

> By observing the mistakes of those who preceded us, we can be more aware of possible dangers when we're similarly tempted.[18]

Interpretation philosophies past and present contain presuppositions. Historically interpreters have connected Scripture to address issues of their time. This practice is likely not to change. Virkler lists interpretation philosophies for seven historical eras:

1. Ancient Jewish Exegesis
2. New Testament Use of the Old Testament
3. Patristic Exegesis
4. Medieval Exegesis
5. Reformation Exegesis
6. Post-reformed Exegesis
7. Modern Hermeneutics.[19]

---

[17] Fee, Gordon D., and Douglas Stuart, *How to Read the Bible for All Its Worth*, 25.
[18] Virkler, Henry A., *Hermeneutics: Principles and Processes of Biblical Interpretation*, 48.
[19] Ibid. 47. (Pages 47 – 74 detail each era.)

Klein also lists numerous interpretation philosophies for various historical eras:

    Jewish, Hellenistic Judaism        Qumran Community
    Rabbinic Judaism                  Apostolic
    Patristic                               Apostolic Fathers
    Alexandrian                       Middle Ages
    Reformation                       Post-Reformation
    Modern                             Nineteenth Century
    Twentieth Century               Post WW I
    Post-WW II
    Recent Literary and Social-Scientific Approaches to Interpretation.[20]

These lists from both Virkler and Klein support that interpretation philosophies from historical epochs were often intended to deal with issues of their time. That same problem using scripture solely to deal with contemporary problems in our time exists today. Contemporary interpreters similar to historical interpreters attempt to scripturally and pastorally address contemporary spiritual, personal, familial, financial, cultural, national, or global issues. As a result of historical epochs and interpreters dealing with issues significant to their time than accurate interpretations are possible. The Grammatical-Historical Method is intended to produce as much as possible unbiased interpretations. The point is that historical interpretations were influenced by issues interpreters faced in their day. Again, grammar and historical facts matter. We call meaning that has developed in history, *Historical Hermeneutics*.

## Contemporary Hermeneutics (Meaning Today)

What does the text mean now? The problem is that well-meaning Christians wanting to preach, teach and apply Scriptures in the here and now often have little understanding of what texts originally meant then and there. If a pastor or teacher cannot tell you what a text meant then and there (*Contextual Hermeneutics*), or in past history (*Historical Hermeneutics*) there is little chance that what you are told in the here and now (*Contemporary Hermeneutics*) is trustworthy. Fee affirms:

> Proper 'hermeneutics' begins with solid 'exegesis.' The reason one must not begin with the here and now is that the only proper control for hermeneutics is to be found in the original intent of the biblical text.[21]

Reliable *Contemporary Hermeneutics* is not likely without reliable *Contextual Hermeneutics*. If we do not know what the text meant then, claiming to know what the text means now is not reliable. Quoting Fee:

> A text cannot mean what it never meant.[22]

Fee's quote hits the heart of interpretation that results from exegesis, hermeneutics, and exposition.

---
[20] Klein, William, Craig L. Blomberg, Robert L. Hubbard, Jr., *Introduction to Biblical Interpretation,* Chapters 2 - 3.
[21] Fee, Gordon D., and Douglas Stuart, *How to Read the Bible for All Its Worth,* 25.
[22] Ibid. 26.

# Both a Common Sense and a Scholarly Process

Some pastors and teachers are so eager to produce relevant life application messages that in their preparation they intentionally avoid *exegesis* and *contextual hermeneutics*. Love for teaching, preaching, and life application sermons can sometimes override the importance of contextual study and research. Pulpit orators who prioritize relevance over context are trying to teach college without having graduated eighth grade. While commentaries are helpful, commentaries cannot always produce what's possible through in-depth contextual study.

Without proper exegesis and hermeneutics failure is inevitable. It may take years but eventually, those who preach and teach solely about the here and now, without knowing the then and there, ultimately develop and teach doctrines and applications that sometimes just aren't so.

Lost sheep, lemmings, conformists or followers without discernment in the pews are seldom able to identify weak theology. Those who prioritized what the text says and means today before considering what the text said and meant then is a problem. They follow a recipe that inhibits maturity by feeding those in the pews sour milk rather than solid food. The author of Hebrews clarified the necessity of maturity to distinguish good from evil:

> For everyone who lives on milk is unskilled in the word of righteousness, since he is a child. But solid food is for the mature, for those who have their powers of discernment trained by constant practice to distinguish good from evil. Hb 5: 13-14

Living on milk is the first problem. Milk or worse, sour milk inhibits the ability to discern good from evil. Pretty simple.

Life application sermons, Bible classes, small groups, teaching without historical context may not be apostate or heretical, but without exegesis and context, those lessons may be at the tipping point. Context is primary. Klein affirmed the importance of context for each biblical statement. For Klein context is the single most important principle:

> Each statement must be understood according to its natural meaning in the literary context in which it occurs. This is probably the single most important principle of hermeneutics since literary context is at the heart of all language communication.[23]

## Summary

Proceeding to Chapters 9 – 15 keep in mind that comments are intentionally as much as possible both exegetically and contextually based. When reading the word "contextual" think "then." When reading the word "historical" think a past time in history but not when the event happened. When reading the word, "contemporary" think now or in today's time.

Undertaking exegesis, hermeneutics, exposition, and interpretation and the processes carry responsibility. First attempt to understand Jesus' Greek imperatives in their historical context before considering meaning as English commands in our contemporary context.

---

[23] Klein, William, Craig L. Blomberg, Robert L. Hubbard, Jr., *Introduction to Biblical Interpretation*, 217–218.

And as the men were parting from him, Peter said to Jesus, "Master, it is good that we are here. Let us make three tents, one for you and one for Moses and one for Elijah"--not knowing what he said. As he was saying these things, a cloud came and overshadowed them, and they were afraid as they entered the cloud. And a voice came out of the cloud, saying, "This is my Son, my Chosen One; listen to him!"

Lk 9: 33-35

# 7 Imperative Types

Listen! A sower went out to sow. Mk 4: 3

## Understanding Imperative Commands in Context

Returning to mom and vegetables let's move to dad and taking out the garbage. When your dad said, "Take out the garbage!" you knew what to do. You removed the garbage from the house where you lived. Leaving the garbage sit was not an option. Dad was the boss. If you did not do what dad said, something happened. Dad said what to do. He knew the short, intermediate, and long-term consequences for you. He also knew the consequences for those in your home, the kingdom where you and your family lived. He knew beyond what you understood at that time. Dad knew. You did not know. You took out the garbage. Pretty simple.

Dad's plan existed before he told you to take out the garbage. His words came from his superior knowledge and beneficial relationship with you. Dad knew what was best for both you and the household, the kingdom where you lived. So, he told you what to do. You did it.

If you loved your dad and your kingdom home, you took out the garbage just as he had commanded. If not your home stunk. You were better for taking out the garbage and so was your home, the same kingdom where you lived with your family. So it was with the Jesus' Greek imperatives, his commands to those he addressed. He spoke imperatives as King of the Kingdom which is his. His followers, however, needed time to understand what they had heard.

## Making Sense of the Greek Mood for English Readers

The Greek imperative is a mood of volition, meaning that when someone spoke an imperative, the listener knew what he had been told to do or say. In general, the will of the person who spoke the Greek imperative (English command) was placed upon the group or individual who heard the Greek imperative to fulfill the imperative command. The Greek imperative mood form was not confusing to those to whom Jesus spoke or to those who heard Jesus speak. The Greek imperative mood then or the English command today is not overly complicated.

First century Koine Greek imperatives when Jesus walked and talked were not suggestions. His listeners did not hear invitations. Readers of his words recorded by Matthew, Mark, Luke, and John were not confused by reading or hearing the words read to them. They heard the Greek imperative mood which is most often translated into English commands. There are four Greek mood types: indicative, subjunctive, optative, and imperative. In this chapter, the imperative, indicative and subjunctive mood types are presented. Wallace clarifies the meaning of the Greek mood:

> Just as with tense and voice, the mood is a morphological feature of a verb. Voice indicates how the subject relates to the action or state of the verb; tense is used primarily to portray the kind of action. In general, the mood is the feature of the verb that presents the verbal action or state with reference to its actuality or potentiality.[1]

---

[1] Wallace, Daniel, B., *Greek Grammar Beyond the Basics: An Exegetical Syntax of the New Testament*, 443.

In simple terms, the imperative mood conveys more than just the will of Jesus. Reading or hearing the mood is not difficult. Since the Greek mood, as Wallace stated, is a morphological feature of a verb, the imperative mood is recognizable by the letter formation of a word. When the writers recorded that Jesus spoke an imperative, they wrote so that their readers of the text could identify the word form. Because Matthew, Mark, Luke, and John recorded his words in Greek, the mood form conveyed meaning. Wallace explains the Greek mood:

> Mood is the morphological feature of a verb that a speaker uses to portray his or her affirmation as to the certainty of the verbal action or state (whether an actuality or potentiality).[2]

What the Gospel writers recorded was intended first and foremost to convey what Jesus had said. When Jesus spoke an imperative mood and writers recorded it, he was intentional, and the writers were intentional. Both the audible sound and the written word form were identifiable. As in previous chapters, the Koine Greek language was understandable both audibly and visually. Outside of metaphors, similes, figures of speech, and parables Matthew, Mark, Luke, and John used an operational and comprehensible language in their context.

Other Greek moods are indicative, subjunctive, and optative. Indicative and subjunctive moods and participles are briefly discussed below. This book, however, is primarily concerned with Jesus's imperative mood verbs, his commands to those to whom he spoke then and there during his life. His imperative verbs were intended for the receiver and listeners who heard him speak.

Dad told you to take out the garbage, and mom told you to eat your vegetables because they had intentions for you. Their intentions existed before they told you what to do. Same with Jesus. His intentions preceded his imperatives. Similar to Dad telling you to take out the garbage so the house would not stink and Mom telling you to eat your vegetables to keep you healthy, Jesus' imperatives were purposed to fulfill his future objectives.

For those in the first century who wrote, spoke, or heard Koine Greek imperatives, there was little ambiguity. Jesus knew the consequence for those to whom he spoke imperatives. Jesus' Greek imperatives were evident to those who first heard and read in their language. However, sometimes his imperatives are not so easily translatable into English because the power of the Greek imperative can be challenging to convey in English. Verlyn Verbrugge provides insight into the force of the Greek imperative:

> There is no more forceful way in the Greek language to tell someone to do something than a simple imperative – particularly the second person imperative. Especially when such a command is given regarding a specific situation, the one giving the command sees himself as an authority figure. He expects those addressed to do exactly as he has ordered.[3]

Matthew, Mark, Luke, and John did not record every command Jesus spoke. They also did not record everything Jesus did.[4] Today we are only able to read what they recorded. Greek

---

[2] Wallace, Daniel, B., *Greek Grammar Beyond the Basics,* 445.
[3] Mounce, William D., *Basics of Biblical Greek*, 302.
[4] Now there are also many other things that Jesus did. Were every one of them to be written, I suppose that the world itself could not contain the books that would be written. Jn 21:25.

imperative verbs are identifiable through their written form. Reading what the disciples heard can be a challenge. Further, imperatives spoken by Jesus were not exclusively intended for the hearer who was addressed. Jesus was intentional that others heard the imperatives he gave to a single person or group. When he told someone to do something, in addition to the person who heard the imperative, others heard his command to that person as well.

If Jesus told Peter to do something, Peter knew what Jesus meant. Those near Peter who also heard Jesus knew what Jesus meant. In the narrative of Peter walking on water recorded by Matthew, when Jesus commanded Peter, "Come," (Mt 14: 29) and the disciples in the boat heard Jesus' imperative command, they knew what Peter had been ordered to do. Peter had been commanded to walk on water. Jesus had commanded Peter with the Greek imperative. Matthew was intentional to record Jesus' imperative. Both Jesus' spoken imperative command and Matthew's recording of that Greek imperative command were deliberate. Moreover, Peter walked on water. How could Peter not have walked on water? Jesus had commanded Peter with an unambiguous imperative, "Come!" Peter and everyone in the boat heard Jesus' imperative.

## Imperative Time Aspect, Defined and Undefined

The length of time that the imperative extends can be confusing. Aspect is the word used to describe time and time extension. How long does a person who has been told what to do, keep doing what that person has been told to do? Communally, how long does a community that has been told what to do keep doing what they were told to do? Context is essential to the Greek imperative time aspect. Mounce explains the challenge of the imperative time aspect:

> It [the imperative] has no time significance. Because of the differences between Greek and English it [the imperative] will often be impossible to carry this over into English. At first you may want to use "continue" or "keep on" in your translation of the present imperative.[5]

Concerning time that is defined and continuous (keep doing), there is also an aorist imperative which is undefined and not continuous. Mounce clarifies:

> There are primarily two imperatives in Greek, present, and aorist.[6] The imperative built on the present tense stem is called the present imperative and indicates a continuous action. The imperative built on the aorist tense stem (without augment) is called the aorist imperative and indicates an undefined action. There is no time significance with the imperative. Once again we urge the adoption of the terminology "continuous imperative" [for present imperative, emphasis mine] and "undefined imperative" [for aorist imperative, emphasis mine].[7]

In simple terms, time is a matter of both context and aspect. In general where a present imperative is found it its morphological form a continuous action applies. Where an aorist imperative is found in its morphological form, an undefined action applies.

---

[5] Mounce, William D., *Basics of Biblical Greek*, 307.
[6] Ibid. 304.
[7] Ibid. 303.

## "Let" and "Must" for Third Person Greek to English

Because all English imperatives are second person (you) and in Greek there are second and third person imperatives (you, he, she, it, they) two English words, "let" and "must" are often employed by translators to render Greek to English. Mounce explains:

> Because there is no English equivalent to a third person imperative, your translation must be a little idiomatic. βλέπε (second person singular) means "(You) look!" βλεπέτω (third-person singular) means "Let him look!" or "He must look!" The key words "let" or "must," and a pronoun supplied from the person the verb ("him"), can be added to make sense of the construction.[8]

English passages where "let" or "must" are found likely means English translators encountered third person Greek imperatives. "Let" and "must" are suitable and the translation appropriate. However, the imperatival intent in the Greek can be greatly reduced in the English mindset. "Let" and "must" read with English eyes and processed with English minds convey possibilities or permissions perhaps more so than the command intended when understood in Greek context of their time. Comparing the NIV and ESV translations from Mt 27: 22 is helpful.[9] Lamerson elucidates Greek and English imperative differences:

> In Greek, one is not only able to command a person to whom you are speaking (i.e., like the English imperative), but also a person about whom you are speaking. This is what leads to the difference in translation in the above passage of scripture. The NIV translates this passage as if it were a second person imperative (a perfectly allowable translation choice): "Crucify him!" In reality, however, the word is a third person imperative and thus can be translated, "Let him be crucified." The difference is in the subject of the verb. The second person has as its subject Pilate, and the third person has its subject, Jesus.[10]

---

[8] Mounce, William D., *Basics of Biblical Greek*, 303.

[9] How Mt 27: 22 has been translated can determine where the translators placed responsibility. Comparing the ESV (Essentially Literal) and NIV (Dynamic Equivalent) is helpful. The NIV reads: "What shall I do then with Jesus who is called Christ?" Pilate asked. They all answered, "Crucify him λέγουσιν πάντες Σταυρωθήτω!" Mt 27:22 NIV. The ESV reads: Pilate said to them, "Then what shall I do with Jesus who is called Christ?" They all said, "Let him be crucified λέγουσιν πάντες Σταυρωθήτω!" Mt 27:22 ESV. Note that the NIV English conveyed the Greek imperative with an English command, "Crucify him." The ESV reduced the imperative command intent with, "Let him be crucified." Because of the Greek construction, "Let him be crucified." or "He must be crucified." are both acceptable because the Greek form is verb, imperative, aorist, passive third person singular, not a second person singular. However, "Crucify him." prioritizes the Greek verb, aorist, imperative before the passive third person singular. It seems Matthew did not intend for the crowd to be without culpability. His use of the imperative affirmed their guilt. It may sound trivial, but in English, there is a difference between "Let it happen." and "Make it happen" or "Let him be crucified." and "Crucify him." The English phrase "Let him be crucified." absolves the Jews of responsibility and places the crucifixion on Pilate. The English phrase "Crucify him." as an imperative, however, places the crucifixion on the Jews or both Pilate and the Jews.

[10] Lamerson, Samuel, *English Grammar to Ace New Testament Greek*, 98.

English readers unaware of this insight can miss the deeper Greek context not so easily or clearly translated into English. While the ESV translation is correct, it is somewhat vague. Discerning between the first person (I) and the second person (you) can be challenging to English readers. Lamerson distinguishes the difference between direct and distant commands:

> This difference between first and second person is often difficult for students to grasp hold of. Simply remember that the command to a person with whom you are speaking is a direct command and a command about another person to whom you are not to speak is a more distant command, who is usually translated "let him/her be...."[11]

Given that there is no English equivalent for a third person imperative the translation challenge can be significant. English translators and translation teams throughout history have given their sincerest best to get words or thoughts right regardless of differences between "essentially literal" or "dynamic equivalent" philosophies. (See Chapter 5.) Beyond translation philosophies, are genres or types of literature and words within a genre. While genres are important, words can trump genre. Words change thought. Ryken states:

> While most people readily acknowledge this principle of the primacy of form with such genres as stories and poems, it is easy to overlook something even more important: The most basic of all literary forms through which meaning is conveyed is words. There is no such thing as disembodied thought. Thought depends on words, and when we change the words, we change the thought.[12]

## No Means No, Imperative Prohibitions

"No" in biblical English occasionally bears a weak no, compared to "no" in New Testament Greek and historical context. Of course, translators do their best. However, there are challenges getting from one language to another. Greek nuances can be difficult to express in English. Mounce simplifies:

> In Greek there are several different ways to say, "No!" The beauty of the constructions is that each one has its own slightly different nuance, information available to those who understand Greek. Unfortunately these nuances are seldom carried over into the translations.[13]

The two Greek words for no, οὐ and μὴ and also their combination, οὐ μὴ are prohibitions. That is, they mean, "no" if singular or in combination. However, their aspect or time extension is not always clear because the aspect is difficult to convey in English.

Regarding present and aorist imperatives, Jesus "No" in present imperatives are continuous such as "stop and keep on stopping." His aorist imperatives are undefined such as "stop and don't start."

---

[11] Lamerson, Samuel, *English Grammar to Ace New Testament Greek*, 98.
[12] Ryken, Leland, *The Word of God in English: Criteria for Excellence in Bible Translation*, 31.
[13] Mounce, William D., *Basics of Biblical Greek*, 309.

Mounce clarifies:

> μὴ plus the present imperative. Because it is a present imperative, you know that the action being prohibited is a continuous action.
>
> *μὴ plus the aorist imperative.* Because it is an aorist imperative, you know that the action being prohibited is an undefined action.[14]

The present tense prohibition is used to prohibit an action already in process.[15]

In other words, prohibiting as a continuous action, "stop and keep on stopping" and prohibiting as an undefined action, "stop and don't start" can be understood in both word structure and context. Translating these nuances however from Greek to English is not always easy. Again, words and context matter.

## No Means No, Non-Imperative Prohibitions

Saying no was not always said through Greek imperatives. In addition to using imperatives, the Gospel writers recorded other forms to say "no." To again quote Mounce:

In Greek, there are several different ways to say, "No!"

οὐ with the indicative, or μὴ with a non-indicative form. This is the simple negation. Included here is the use of οὐ with the future indicative. "Thou shalt not covet."

μὴ plus the aorist subjunctive. This construction says, "No!" οὐ μὴ plus the aorist subjunctive. When Greek uses a double negative, one does not negate the other as in English. The οὐ and μὴ combine in a very firm, "This will certainly not occur!"[16]

General English negations are, "Do not!" or "Don't!" or "No!" English figures of speech negations examples such as, "No way!" or "That is not going to happen!" or "That is impossible!" or "No matter how hard you try, it just won't happen." convey an emphatic fruitlessness beyond a simple no.

## Non-Imperatives Conveying an Imperative Intent

Commands are also derived from Greek forms that convey an English command idea but are not actual Greek imperatives. This book is concerned with only the imperatives of Jesus recorded in the Greek imperative mood form. Nevertheless, Greek moods, indicatives, subjunctives, and participles can also convey imperative intent. Following is a list of forms that can be translated as commands but are not imperative morphological word forms:

---

[14] Mounce, William D., *Basics of Biblical Greek*, 307.
[15] Ibid. 309.
[16] Ibid. 307-308.

- Verbs, Indicative, Present Tense, (V), Second Person, Singular
- Verbs, Indicative, Present Tense, (V), Second Person, Plural
- Verbs, Indicative, Future Tense, (V), Second Person Singular
- Verbs, Indicative, Future Tense, (V), Second Person, Plural
- Verbs, Subjunctive, Aorist Tense, with a negative
- Participles parallel to imperatives

## Indicative Verbs Indicate a State of Being or a Condition

The Greek indicative mood expresses affirmation. Similar to the imperative mood, the indicative mood is identified by its morphological word form. The critical difference between the imperative and indicative is that the imperative mood *commands* and the indicative mood *describes*. Mounce explains the indicative mood as a descriptor:

> Mood refers to the relationship between the verb and reality. A verb is in the indicative if it is describing something that is, as opposed to something that may or might be.[17]

Greek indicative verbs can imply an imperative result. Greek indicatives function as the word implies, indicative verbs indicate. Indicative verbs can also clarify. Indicative verbs can also affirm present or future conditions. Indicative verbs of Jesus often followed his imperatives which confirmed his expectations.

Indicatives point to a state of being. They indicate something about the verb. After Jesus spoke an imperative, the Gospel writers often included Greek indicatives, which clarified what he had commanded. His Greek indicative verbs indicated what Jesus wanted. Indicatives indicate the result. Indicatives are often proof of imperatives. An example of an indicative following an imperative is Jesus' words and Matthew's response:

> As Jesus went on from there, He saw a man called Matthew, sitting in the tax collector's booth; and He said to him, "<u>Follow me ἀκολούθει μοι!</u>" <u>And he got up and followed Him</u> καὶ ἀναστὰς ἠκολούθησεν αὐτῷ [within the italics is the verb, indicative, aorist, active, 3$^{rd}$ person, the singular form "followed"]. Mt 9: 9.

However, before concluding that indicatives are irrefutable or absolute certainties and realities, Wallace provides an important distinction:

> The indicative mood is, in general, the mood of assertion, or presentation of certainty. It is not correct to say there it is the mood of certainty or reality. Thus it is more accurate to state that the indicative mood is the mood of assertion, presentation of certainty.[18]

---

[17] Mounce, William D., *Basics of Biblical Greek*, 121.
[18] Wallace, Daniel, B., *Greek Grammar Beyond the Basics,* 448.

Notice that Jesus had first spoken an imperative to Matthew. Following that imperative, Matthew next recorded about himself that he immediately left what he was doing and followed. Matthew obeyed the imperative of Jesus. He followed.

## Aorist Subjunctives Preceded with a
## Single Negative No (μὴ) or Double Negative no, no (οὐ μὴ)

Translators often rightly render the Koine Greek aorist tense to English words with "ed" endings. The Greek aorist tense means that something happened in the past, nothing more. The aorist tense is undefined and indefinite, meaning simply, "It happened." English words such as ran, saw, said and looked, worked, and talked are simple past tense words that affirm something happened.

Subjunctive aorist verbs, however, don't convey what is but what "may" or "might" be. The Greek subjunctive mood is a mood of probability. The English words "might" or "may" are often used to translate the idea of the Greek subjunctive into English. Mounce clarifies the difference between the indicative and subjunctive moods:

> The indicative is a mood of reality. It states what is. The book is red. Greek is fun. Hebrew is too hard. Why am I procrastinating? The subjunctive does not describe what is, but what may (or might) be. It is the mood not of reality but of possibility (or probability).[19]

An aorist subjunctive is something that happened in the past that may or might have possible consequences in the future. Koine Greek negatives (single (μὴ) or double (οὐ μὴ)) preceding aorist subjunctives often appear and are interpreted as English commands. Jesus' aorist subjunctives are difficult to translate as forcefully in English. English readers may find difficulty gleaning the depth of Jesus's words, especially single or double negatives preceding aorist subjunctives. The Greek οὐ μὴ [no, no], with the subjunctive, denies possibility or potentiality. There is a difference between "certainty" and "possibility" or "potentiality." Wallace explains:

> While μὴ + the indicative denies a certainty, οὐ μὴ + the subjunctive denies a potentiality.[20]

Double negative use by Jesus with aorist subjunctives emphasized to them what wasn't possible. While aorist subjunctives are neither imperative commands nor indicatives, Jesus' aorist subjunctives with the negative defined what was and was not for them. When single negatives "no" (μὴ) or double negatives "no, no" (οὐ μὴ) precede aorist subjunctives, certainties or potentialities come to bear.

Greek single negatives (μὴ) that precede aorist subjunctives often appear as English commands. Double negatives preceding aorist subjunctives are often translated into English as "will" or "shall," inferring a future when a more accurate translation affirms a present

---

[19] Mounce, William D., *Basics of Biblical Greek,* 282.
[20] Wallace, Daniel, B., *Greek Grammar Beyond the Basics,* 468.

impossibility, not a future. Aorist subjunctives such as, "it happened" or "what happened" can not be changed. What happened has happened.

While aorist subjunctive forms are neither imperative nor indicatives, Jesus' use of double negatives preceding aorist subjunctives illuminated what was and was not possible. Jesus said more than a simple "No." He affirmed impossibility. John recorded Jesus words:

> My sheep hear my voice, and I know them, and they follow me. I give them eternal life, <u>and they will never perish</u> καὶ οὐ μὴ ἀπόλωνται, and no one will snatch them out of my hand. Jn 10: 27-28

The passage translated "and they will never perish" reads and sounds like an English future by use of the word "will." An amplified translation "it is not possible that they can perish" provides clarity and absoluteness. The ESV English translation is acceptable. As always, context is king. Nevertheless, insight on impossibility or potentiality is compelling in context. Regarding salvation, Jesus' words in John, Jesus affirmed in his prayer those who were his and those who were not his:

> I am praying for them. I am not praying for the world but for those whom you have given me, for they are yours. All mine are yours, and yours are mine, and I am glorified in them. And I am no longer in the world, but they are in the world, and I am coming to you. Holy Father, keep them in your name, which you have given me, that they may be one, even as we are one. While I was with them, I kept them in your name, which you have given me. I have guarded them, and not one of them has been lost except the son of destruction, that the Scripture might be fulfilled. Jn 17: 9-12

John made certain in his writing that Jesus spoke of impossibilities, not ambiguities. When Jesus spoke about the eternality of those who were indeed his, he spoke in absolutes.

The four Gospels portray the learning process of the disciples. With time they grasped their eternal security likely through understanding the many imperative commands from Jesus. Beyond their security, they eventually started to understand the power of Jesus's imperatives, and after his ascension and through the indwelling Holy Spirit the power through them of their imperatives, they would speak in the power of the Holy Spirit. Over time, they learned to trust his imperatives, spread his Gospel, and proclaim the Kingdom message that Jesus had taught them.

## Participles and Imperatives

Participles are adjectives that describe verbs. Similar to indicative verbs, participles can indicate verbal actions. English active participles generally have an ending suffix with the letters "ing." English passive participles commonly end in "ed." Participles often emphasize imperative commands. Participles may indicate the condition or state of the imperative. Participles spoken by Jesus are noteworthy. His spoken participles often accompanied his spoken imperative commands.

In other words, his spoken participles described how his commands were to be fulfilled. Similarly, in many biblical texts, imperatives are followed by participles or "ing" ending English words that describe the action to occur that satisfies the imperative. Mt 28: 18–20 is an example:

And Jesus came and said to them, "All authority in heaven and on earth has been given to me. Go therefore and <u>make disciples of all nations</u> μαθητεύσατε πάντα τὰ ἔθνη, baptizing them in the name of the Father and of the Son and of the Holy Spirit, teaching them to <u>observe</u> (τηρεῖν - keep, watch over, guard) all that I have commanded you. And behold, I am with you always, to the end of the age."
Mt 28: 18-20

The English words "make disciples" is more accurately rendered, "disciple nations." In any event, there is only one imperative mood form in Mt 28: 18 – 20. While the English word, "go" sounds like an English command, "make disciples" (ESV) "teach all nations" (KJV) "make disciples of all nations" (NIV) "disciple all the nations (YLT) is the only Greek imperative form. Both "baptizing" and "teaching" are active plural participles and follow the imperative "make disciples." Baptizing and teaching were linked to disciple-making. Jesus' imperatives combined with participles in Greek supplied a deeper meaning in what his disciples heard, compared to what often is conveyed through English translations. Baptizing and teaching as participles are marks of discipleship. False baptisms and false teachings do not indicate a disciple. The single imperative is "disciple nations." also translated in many English Bibles as "make disciples."

## Imperative Uses

Today we have the luxury of categorizing imperatives according to their use. Today's academic understanding of Koine Greek is advanced. While it is helpful to categorize imperatives according to their use, the reliable scholarship today was not available to the masses in Jesus's day, nor to the Gospel writers. Scribes mattered. Scribes were necessary to accurately convey words and context. Scribes were of value because of their knowledge compared to the masses. We have already discussed the limitations of Peter and John affirmed by Luke in Acts. However, with Scribes, Peter and John were not limited. Today's scholarship identifies numerous imperative categories.

Wallace categorizes eight uses of the Greek imperative:

1. Command
2. Prohibition
3. Entreaty
4. Toleration
5. Conditional
6. Potential
7. Pronouncement
8. Greeting[21]

## Command Imperatives

Most imperatives spoken by Jesus were commands of volition. Volition means that Jesus expected his commands to be completed. Referring to mom telling us to eat our vegetables as

---

[21] Wallace, Daniel, B., *Greek Grammar Beyond the Basics*, 485 – 493.

children we may have hesitated, but we knew mom was in charge. Imperatives carry the contextual idea that one person has authority over another. Wallace explains:

> Ontologically, as one of the potential or oblique moods, the imperative moves in the realm of *volition* (involving the imposition of one's will upon another) and *possibility*. There are many exceptions to this twofold "flavor" of the imperative in actual usage, although in almost every instance the rhetorical power of the imperative is still felt. Technically, then, it is not best to call this the mood of *command* because it may be used for *other than* a command. But that volitional force is nevertheless still lurking beneath the surface, even when the speaker is not barking orders. As a command, the imperative is usually from a superior to an inferior in rank.[22]

Command imperatives are like words from military officers to enlisted soldiers. When a higher ranked general gives orders, obedience is expected from a lower ranked private. The disciples knew their positions under their teacher.

## Prohibition Imperatives

Prohibition imperatives are intended to prohibit an action. Most New Testament imperatives are present tense. Prohibition imperatives include a negative such as "no" plus an imperative. Finding the English words "no" or "don't" or "do not" often means that the English derived from a Greek imperative. An example from Matthew:

> But when you give to the needy <u>do not let your left hand know what your right hand is doing</u> μὴ γνώτω ἡ ἀριστερά σου τί ποιεῖ ἡ δεξιά σου. Mt 6:3

Wallace identifies only eight prohibition aorist imperatives, each with Jesus as the speaker. Wallace affirms that Jesus was firm in his language speaking an imperative to discontinue an act:

> "The imperative is commonly used to forbid an action."[23]

Wallace affirms the authenticity of Jesus' prohibition imperatives:

> There are, by my count, only 8 instances of the aorist imperative in prohibitions, all with Jesus as the speaker (Matt 6: 3; 24: 17, 18; Mark 13: 15 [*bis*], 16; Luke 17: 31 [*bis*]). Such multiple attestations, coupled with the criterion of dissimilarity (in that no one else uses this morpho-syntactical convention) suggests that such sayings are authentic.[24]

To summarize Wallace, the morphology and syntax are so unique that Jesus was intentional about how he formed and spoke his words. Matthew, Mark, and Luke intentionally and accurately

---

[22] Ibid. 485.
[23] Ibid. 487.
[24] Ibid. 487.

recorded Jesus' words. To those holding that Jesus only spoke Aramaic, Matthew, Mark, Luke, and John would have made sure their Greek from Aramaic was precise, which is why the Greek from the critical texts is trustworthy.

## Entreaty Imperatives

Jewish Temple or Synagogue leaders would have had a problem telling God what to do. They certainly would have been critical of anyone who would have spoken an imperative to God. Hence, identifying entreaty imperatives reduces the risk of perceived heresy or at the very least the arrogance of a sinful human telling God what to do using the Greek imperative mood form. From a pastoral perspective, isn't it arrogant to issue a command imperative to God? In the imperatives of Jesus in the Lord's Prayer Mt 6: 11; Lk 11: 3, he stated an unquestionable imperative aorist active second person singular verb translated as "Give us this day, our daily bread." While "Give" is a Greek imperative mood form, most scholars classify it as an entreaty imperative "used to encourage or ask someone to do something. Mounce distinguishes the uniqueness of a command and a request:

> The imperative mood is used when a verb expresses a command. It is also used to encourage or ask someone to do something. This is called the "Imperative of Entreaty." You do not command God to do something; you 'entreat' him, both in English and in Greek, e.g., "Give us this day our daily bread." (Give" is an imperative.)[25]

Conveying entreaties (requests) from imperatives are appropriate. However, the Greek imperatives of Jesus recorded by Matthew and Luke in the Lord's Prayer morphologically and syntactically first conveyed an imperative idea.

## Toleration Imperatives

Jesus frequently spoke toleration imperatives. Mt 8: 31-32 is an example where demons demanded through their imperative "send us away into the pigs" and Jesus followed up with a toleration imperative as described by Wallace. Jesus tolerated or let them enter the swine:

> And the demons begged him, saying, "If you cast us out, send us away into the herd of pigs, ἀπόστειλον ἡμᾶς εἰς τὴν ἀγέλην τῶν χοίρων." And he said to them, "Go, Ὑπάγετε." So they came out and went into the pigs, and behold, the whole herd rushed down the steep bank into the sea and drowned in the waters. Mt 8: 31-32

The demons spoke and imperative to Jesus. So Jesus immediately responded. He spoke the imperative "go" to them. So they immediately went into the pigs. Interpreting Jesus' response as tolerating, the imperative from the demons is appropriate. However, as we have seen with other imperatives, the command idea is ever present. Another example is Jesus' denouncement to the Scribes and Pharisees:

---

[25] Mounce, William D., *Basics of Biblical Greek*, 307.

Fill up then the measure of your fathers, καὶ ὑμεῖς πληρώσατε τὸ μέτρον τῶν πατέρων ὑμῶν. Mt 23: 32

Mocking and tolerating them his aorist active imperative affirmed what they had done and would continue doing. The Scribes and Pharisees through their hypocrisy would continue murdering the prophets. Mt 23: 23

## Conditional Imperatives

Conditional imperatives include if/then conditions. The idea is, if you do X (and you should do X), then Y will happen. Conditional imperative are somewhat easy to identify because the morphology, the word formation are constructed with, a) An imperative, b) The conjunction word, "and" καὶ plus, c) A future indicative "will." A conditional imperative example is:

So the Jews said to him, "What sign do you show us for doing these things?" Jesus answered them, "Destroy this temple λύσατε τὸν ναὸν τοῦτον, and in three days I will raise it up." Jn 2: 18–19 (See Chapter on Imperatives in John)

What follows is a paraphrase and amplification of the conditional imperative to convey meaning and context:

So the Jews said to him, "What sign do you show us for doing these things?" Jesus answered them, "Destroy this temple [A. You should destroy this temple which is my body, and you will destroy this Temple which is my body] and in three days I will raise it up." [B. You will see the result after you have destroyed my body, my temple. The result of you destroying my body is that I will raise my body up.] Jn 2: 18-19

Wallace affirmed that the force of the imperative is still applicable:

All of the conditional imperatives in the New Testament (both undisputed and potential) retained their imperatival force.[26]

As strange as Jn 2: 18–19 reads to English readers and sounds to English hearers, Jesus' imperative to the Jewish leaders that they destroy his body was fulfilled. The imperative was in force. Through Jesus' imperative to them, he affirmed that they would, in fact, kill his body.

## Potential Imperatives

Potential imperatives are disputed among Greek scholars. Some scholars argue that the second imperative is equivalent to a future indicative. Wallace identifies potential imperatives as a debatable category[27] Similar to conditional imperatives such as "if, then" situations. A secular

---

[26] Wallace, Daniel, B., *Greek Grammar Beyond the Basics,* 491.
[27] Ibid. 492.

example is "Go and be happy." The idea is, if you go (and you should go) you will be happy. Both go and be happy are imperatival more so than "go" with the potential to "be happy" in the future.

## Pronouncement Imperatives

Pronouncement imperatives often appear as imperative forms that are impossible to meet yet expected to be met. The pronouncement imperative sounds rhetorical or pretentious. On the surface, pronouncement imperatives sound impossible to meet. Nevertheless, the imperative remains. Wallace clarifies the pronouncement imperative:

> On the surface it looks like a command but its nature is such that it cannot be obeyed by the recipient and yet it comes true at the moment it is uttered. The pronouncement is couched in imperatival terms for rhetorical effect.[28]

A pronouncement imperative example is:

> And Jesus answered them, "Truly, I say to you, if you have faith and do not doubt, you will not only do what has been done to the fig tree, but even if you say to this mountain, 'Be taken up and be thrown into the sea,' ἄρθητι καὶ βλήθητι εἰς τὴν θάλασσαν, it will happen. Mt 21: 21

Jesus conveyed the power of both his and their pronouncement imperatives. Other examples are:

> And a leper came to him, imploring him, and kneeling said to him, "If you will, you can `make me clean." Moved with pity, he stretched out his hand and touched him and said to him, "I will; be clean καθαρίσθητι." And immediately the leprosy left him, and he was made clean. Mk 1: 40-42
>
> And looking up to heaven, he sighed and said to him, "Ephphatha," that is, "Be opened διανοίχθητι." And his ears were opened, his tongue was released, and he spoke plainly. And Jesus charged them to tell no one. But the more he charged them, the more zealously they proclaimed it. And they were astonished beyond measure, saying, "He has done all things well. He even makes the deaf hear and the mute speak." Mk 7: 34

"Be cleaned" (rather than "be clean") Mk 1:41 and "be opened" Mk 7: 34 are pronouncement aorist imperative examples. Some translations for Mk 1: 41 do not convey the aorist past tense. Some English Bibles translate "be clean" rather than the Greek aorist past tense, "be cleaned."

## Greeting Imperatives

Greeting imperatives are typically found in opening statements. They announce the importance at what will follow. English words, listen, behold, hail, greetings, and take heart are examples. While greeting imperatives read as if they are reduced to English exclamations, the

---

[28] Ibid. 492.

Greek form is still imperative in nature and volition. Matthew recorded a greeting imperative from the Roman soldiers who mocked Jesus:

> And the soldiers led him away inside the palace (that is, the governor's headquarters), and they called together the whole battalion. And they clothed him in a purple cloak, and twisting together a crown of thorns, they put it on him. And they began to salute him, "<u>Hail, King of the Jews</u> Χαῖρε βασιλεῦ τῶν Ἰουδαίων· Mk 15: 16–18. (Parallel passages in Mt 27: 28–29)

"Hail" is a word in the Greek imperative mood form. Although it sounds mocking, in reality, Jesus was King of the Jews in their time and context. Their imperative was volitionally and theologically correct even though the soldiers chose not to understand the truth of their spoken imperative. Matthew's accurate recording of their words revealed their mockery.

## Summary

Jesus' Greek imperatives, indicatives, aorist subjunctives, and participles contain rich insights about his will. While word studies are essential for deeper understandings, passages in their full grammatical-historical context reveal much more than a single word. A sentence in context is more reliable than a single English word translated from Greek. An English command developed from a Greek imperative is a good start.

Translation accuracy and exegesis before contextual hermeneutic and contemporary hermeneutics is the appropriate method for rightly handling the word of truth 2 Tm 2: 15.[29] God "spoke" an imperative and the world came into existence Ge 1: 3.[30] The spoken and written imperative, "let there be light" was followed with an indicative, "and there was light."

Throughout history, many have suffered persecution for holding the written English word in high esteem. Translators William Tyndale and Jon Wycliffe were hated to the point of martyrdom for their translation efforts. Wycliffe was so despised by the church of his day that even after he died of a stroke in 1384, his remains were exhumed and burned in 1428. William Tyndale was so loathed that he was strangled to death before his body was burned at the stake in 1536. Words matter because words can lead to death.

So it is with the words of Jesus, through his imperatives, indicatives, aorist subjunctives, or participles that the Gospel writers meticulously recorded. Studying the imperatives of Jesus herein can bring you the reader to comprehend Jesus as LORD. This LORD Jesus, this Jesus Immanuel, this God with us commanded with purposefully chosen imperatives.

---

[29] Do your best to present yourself to God as one approved, a worker who has no need to be ashamed, rightly handling the word of truth. 2 Ti 2: 15.
[30] And God said, "Let there be light," and there was light. Gn 1: 3.

Come to me, all who labor and are heavy laden, and I will give you rest.

Mt 11: 28

# 8 Interpreting Then, Interpreting Now

For you have exalted above all things your name and your word. Ps 138: 2b

## Morphology

Sedans, SUV's, pickup trucks, dragsters, 4X4's, semi-trucks, and dump trucks each provide a different function. Sedans are not dump trucks. A dragster built for speed on a quarter mile strip cannot haul tons of bricks across the country like a semi-truck and trailer. How a vehicle is made determines what job that vehicle can do. You get the idea.

The word "morphology" refers to how words are made and how letters work to form words which convey meaning. Like a vehicle, how a word is made determines how that word works, what that word can and cannot do, and what that word means. Like vehicles, how words are made determines how they work. Further, from word formation (morphology), comes sound (phonology), and word arrangement (syntax) which produce meaning. Demoss defines morphology, phonology, and syntax:

> Morphology: the study of the structure of words and the system of forms of a language. Derivational morphology pertains to the formation of words; inflectional morphology involves the study of inflections. Sometimes "phonology" is conceived of as a subcategory of morphology.[1]

> Phonology: the discipline concerned with systems of speech sounds, how languages use the distinctive features of sounds and follow predictable patterns in forming words.[2]

> Syntax: the study of the arrangement of words in phrases, clauses, and sentences, and the rules involved in sentenced formation.[3]

Greek imperatives are recognized through their distinct morpheme, the way the letters of the word are formed. Without getting too technical for non-Greek students, certain Greek letters that form the word distinguishes the imperative mood from other moods. When translators identify a Greek imperative mood form morpheme, they commonly translate that word form into an English meaning that conveys a command.

English readers recognize that a command is an order to do something. In other words, if the Greek word form was identified as a Greek imperative form, translators did their best to convey a command in English. Pretty basic.

## Greek Grammar and Syntax

In English, syntax provides meaning to sentences from words within a sentence. In English, how words are arranged or word order is critical to understanding what a sentence means. Syntax

---
[1] Demoss, Matthew S., *Pocket Dictionary for the Study of New Testament Greek*, 86.
[2] Ibid. 98.
[3] Ibid. 120.

is key to providing meaning in English. Greek, however, is less dependent upon syntax. In Greek, word structure or morphology is key to providing meaning. A basic grasp of Greek grammar can illuminate the meaning of Jesus' words, particularly his Greek imperatives translated into English commands. Sometimes, however, English translators have difficulty conveying the richness of the Greek imperative form. Translators rooted in English can have a predisposition toward syntax simply because of their rootedness in English. While syntax also contributes to Greek, word morphology is more critical.

English translators attempting to convey Greek imperatives through English commands are challenged merely because Greek imperatives are not always easily translated into English commands. Further, sometimes English translators have produced English commands from Greek participles (See Mt 28: 19) and Greek indicatives (See Jn 14: 1). Translation anomalies tend to be "interpretative" rather than "translation" formed.

The English command intent may be understandable, but the power and range of the Greek imperative can be reduced. Original Greek imperatives that eventually became English commands may have a grander array of significance than what was translated. Mounce affirms:

> The imperative is the mood of command. However, as is the case with participles and infinities, the imperative has a greater range of meaning in Greek.[4]

While translations from Greek imperatives to English commands are fitting, to the Greek reader or listener the Greek imperative was likely more vibrant or more defined in their context. The spoken, heard, and read Greek in Jesus' time had context. Written and audible English tends to soften the richness that the Greek provides.

## Word Formation and Morphology

There is a sequence to messaging: physically writing, visually reading, vocally speaking and audibly hearing. Three human body parts must be engaged: eyes, voice, and ears. The eyes must read. The voice must speak. The ears must hear.

- Audible messages are first vocally spoken and secondly audibly heard.
  - Example: Jesus vocally spoke to his disciples without a text. His disciples audibly heard. No visual reading was involved. They only heard what Jesus had said.
- Texts of what someone has said must be first audibly heard, second physically written, third vocally read, and finally audibly heard again.
  - Example: You read the Bible alone. You did not hear Jesus' words. No audible hearing was involved. You can only read what has been written of what Jesus said.
- Audible messages from written texts are first physically written, then visually read, then vocally spoken, and finally audibly heard.
  - Example: Someone was teaching from the Bible while another was audibly hearing. Someone vocally read aloud a previously written Bible text, and someone heard what had been written.

---

[4] Mounce, William D., *Basics of Biblical Greek*, 303.

While these clarifications may seem simplistic, how people receive and process a message can sway what they come to believe. Today we read the words of what others recorded. The Gospel writers wrote what Jesus said. In Jesus' day, his listeners heard him.

When the Gospels started to spread during the first century, the written Greek imperatives within them were both visually read and audibly heard. When Jesus spoke a Greek imperative, his audience heard a Greek imperative. Matthew, Mark, Luke, and John lead by the Holy Spirit intentionally recorded Jesus' imperatives as if he actually said them and his audience heard them. Whether Jesus spoke in Aramaic or Greek is irrelevant. In Greek then, sound carried meaning.

The morphological written form of the Greek imperative, the way the Greek word has been constructed, sticks out like a sore thumb. The Greek imperative morphological form is identified by a connecting vowel plus the imperative morpheme. Without getting too technical, this means that, following the present stem or root word, there is a vowel followed by the imperative morpheme ending. We will not delve into the actual Greek. Sufficient for you to know is that a read or spoken Greek imperative is both literally and audibly distinguishable.

## The Spoken Word: They Heard Nouns and Verbs

In the Greek language "cases" (noun types) and "moods" (verb relationships) are critical to comprehension.[5] In Greek, word formation (morpheme) is more critical to understanding than word order common to English sentences. If Jesus spoke and listeners heard in Greek (or after Jesus spoke in Aramaic and the Gospel writers recorded in Greek) their verbal, auditory, written, or read contextual implications were not mysteries. They knew what he said because his language and their language was not convoluted. It was clear.

Those who heard Jesus speak, his spoken and heard Greek imperatives were distinct. That is the acoustic sounds of spoken and heard Greek words are different from one another. Jesus' spoken words conveyed meaning. Hearers who understood Greek identified his imperatives by sound. For the most part, it is hard to miss the distinct auditory sound of a Greek imperative.

## Auditory Sounds of Spoken Greek Imperative

Let us leave this present century. Imagine yourself in the first century, living after Jesus' ascension. You can read Greek. Let's say you have a copy of any four of the Gospels Matthew, Mark, Luke, or John. Go further. Imagine you are in the first century but unable to read Greek and must depend on your ears to hear a spoken word from the writings of Matthew, Mark, Luke, or John. Go further. Imagine you are in the first century at the time of Jesus and are in the crowd of his followers listening to Jesus speak. Big difference between hearing Jesus speak, hearing the Gospels read to you or reading the Gospels in the language at the time they were written.

Had you lived and walked with Jesus, you would have heard his words. Had you lived during the first century when the Gospels were distributed to communities and were able to read Greek, you would have read his words in the language that he may have spoken. However, since you are here today, you are dependent on reading English words from Greek texts. The closest you can get to hear his words is if someone reads aloud to you the Greek texts.

---

[5] We will not deeply expound on the Greek suffice to pragmatically say Greek "cases" refer to nouns and their relationships, and Greek "moods" refer to verbs and their relationship. For more in-depth study see Wallace, *Greek Grammar Beyond the Basics* and Mounce, *Basics of Biblical Greek*.

If you knew Greek and heard the texts in spoken Greek, you likely would have discerned his imperatives from what you heard. However, few Christians today are able to read and hear the Greek texts. We do however have English translations.

Without getting too deep into the Greek, the word formation (morphemes) that produce the imperative word contains two basic audible sounds. The imperative morpheme contains the audible sounds of an English "t" and "sth' within the word. To get to the point, when Jesus vocally spoke a Greek imperative, his listeners audibly heard the sound of the distinct Greek imperative.

## They Wrote, We Read

To those in the first century who read what Jesus had said, the written Greek imperatives were distinct in their eyes. To repeat, they were able to identify a Greek imperative by its word formation. The spoken word was written and then read in Greek. Jesus' voice conveyed a meaning which was translated into written Greek and eventually read by those who could read Greek. In short, Greek readers would have identified an imperative after having read it. It is hard to miss the written word formation (morpheme) of a Greek imperative.

The illiterate, those unable to read the Gospels relied on hearing the Gospels read or preached to them. In this situation, early hearers who had the Gospels read to them are similar to many who hear the word but do not read the word. Hearers of the word depend on readers of the word. English readers depend on the English written word. In the first century, they depended on the Greek written word.

## Person – I (1st person), You (2nd person), He, She, It, We, They (3rd person)

In English, commands are directed to a person (singular / you) or persons (plural / you). Examples are: "John, fix the broken bike." or "Win the game teammates!" Greek however in addition to second person imperatives employs a third person (he, she, and they). English, however, has no equivalent to a third person (he, she, and they) imperative. Because of the differences between Greek and English, idiomatic leeway is acceptable. Mounce clarifies and provides translating insight:

> In English all imperatives are in second person; in Greek, there are second and third person imperatives. Because there is no English equivalent to a third person imperative, your translation must be a little idiomatic. The key words "let" or "must," and a pronoun supplied from the person of the verb ("him"), can be added to make sense of the construction.[6]

Agreeing with Mounce, "let" and "must" are two English words often used by translators to make sense of the Greek construction. When the words "let" or "must" are found in English Bibles, translators likely encountered a third person Greek imperative morpheme structure. While the use of "let" and "must" to accommodate the Greek and English differences is logical and correct, English phrases such as "let him go." or "he must go." somewhat softens the Greek imperative. In short, the English is unable to completely convey the Greek imperatives because English has no third person imperative.

---

[6] Mounce, William D., *Basics of Biblical Greek*, 303.

The English word "let" conveys to both hearers and readers of the English language the idea of permission, consent, or authorization. The English word "must" similarly limits the responsibility of the person or group making the imperative. That is not to say English translations are incapable of accurate literal translation. English translations today that are essentially literal as much as possible are reliable because translators are much more knowledgeable of Greek to English nuances. Today's translations that are essentially literal provide more clarity than what was possible in prior English Bibles.

## Indicative and Imperative Mood Endings

Since Greek is a language where word formation is more critical than sentence formation, prefixes, roots, connecting letters, and endings are crucial to comprehension. However, some Greek words have similar forms which mean the moods can be confusing. First-year Greek students learn that when word endings are the same, context and syntax must be considered. This translation challenge occurs when determining if a word was intended to be a statement or a command. Mounce is correct:

> Do not be fooled by the imperative second person plural (active and middle) endings. They are the same as the indicative. In the present, context will usually decide whether a particular form is a statement or a command.[7]

An example of a singular person imperative in English is: "You Matthew, go." An example of a plural person imperative in English is: "You disciples, go." Greek imperatives differ from English commands, however, because Greek provides both second and third person imperatives. Examples of first-person narratives are: "I go" or "We go." Examples of third-person Greek imperatives translated into English are: "He goes." "She goes." or "They go." which weakens the Greek imperative. Translators and expositors have ways to resolve this situation. Note the responsibility Wallace places on expositors:

> The third person imperative is normally translated 'Let him do,' etc. This is easily confused in English with a permissive idea. Its force is more akin to 'he must,' however, or periphrastically, 'I command him to...' Regardless of how it is translated, the expositor is responsible to observe and explain the underlying Greek form. The Greek is stronger than a mere option, engaging the volition and placing a requirement on the individual.[8]

## Number: Singular or Plural

The Gospel writers recorded that sometimes Jesus spoke an imperative to one person such as an individual command to Matthew, Peter, or Satan. Sometimes he spoke imperatives to groups of people such as his disciples, Jewish leaders, Pharisees, or those physically near him. Greek morphology the way the word is formed identifies the number. The number can be determined when Greek is written and read or spoken and heard.

---

[7] Mounce, William D., *Basics of Biblical Greek*, 305.
[8] Wallace, Daniel, B., *Greek Grammar Beyond the Basics: An Exegetical Syntax of the New Testament*, 486.

For example, just before Peter stepped out of the boat and walked on water, those in the boat likely audibly heard Jesus' single imperative command to Peter "Come." Mt 14: 29 Matthew was intentional in how he recorded that event. Disciples in the boat knew that Jesus had not commanded them. Jesus had commanded Peter in the singular form.

## Time - Start, Stop, or Keep Going

Greek imperatives have no time significance. An undefined imperative is often referred to as a "continuous imperative" meaning that after a command had been given, the command did not stop until the result had been reached. There was no time significance. "Aspect" is the word Greek teachers use to identify time. Time, however, can be a challenge to convey in English. Mounce affirms a translation difficulty:

> As has been the case in all non-indicative moods, the only significance of the imperative is its aspect. It has no time significance. Because of the difference between Greek and English, it will often be impossible to carry this over into English.[9]

The general idea is that when Jesus stated a present active imperative, he and those who heard him were not confused. His disciples knew the contextual continuity of his commands. They heard his spoken word and knew the meaning from Jesus' words and context.

## Prescriptive and Descriptive Imperatives

Because Jesus gave an imperative to a disciple then, does not mean that that same imperative applies to you now. Prescriptive imperatives were intended for either hearers or readers. Whoever stated the imperative expected that the recipient was capable and would fulfill the imperative. The imperative was prescribed.

However, some of Jesus' imperatives were descriptive, meaning his imperatives were intended to describe a situation. Many of his descriptive imperatives he stated within parables. Wondering if one of the imperatives of Jesus is prescriptive for to you today, you must first determine its grammatical and historical context.

## Aramaic Insight

From the New Testament can be reasoned that at least four languages, Hebrew, Aramaic, Greek, and Latin were in use during Jesus' ministry. Aramaic likely was the conversant colloquial language. Hebrew likely was spoken by indigenous Jews, rabbis, and those associated with the Temple such as Scribes, Pharisees, Sadducees, and members of the Sanhedrin. Latin likely was the language of Roman soldiers, Pilate and those administering the Roman law.

The dominant commercial language that bound Romans, Jews, and Gentiles, likely was Greek with Aramaic also a common language for general communications. Multi-lingual skills were essential for commercial success, Roman political leadership, and Jewish Temple leadership. Most likely Jesus was multi-lingual. Douglas and Tenney describe Jesus' language abilities:

---

[9] Mounce, William D., *Basics of Biblical Greek*, 307.

It has been generally assumed as proven that Aramaic was the colloquial language of Palestine from the time of the return of the exiles from Babylon. But some believe that Hebrew was spoken in Galilee in NT times. It is probably safe to assert that our Lord habitually spoke Aramaic and occasionally Greek and could read and speak Hebrew.[10]

Perhaps Jesus spoke Aramaic or a dialect of Aramaic to the masses. Those in the Temple and Synagogues may have heard Jesus speak Hebrew. Luke recorded that Jesus read from the scroll of the prophet Isaiah at the synagogue in Nazareth Lk 4: 17. Given the influence of Hellenism and use of the Septuagint, the scroll of Isaiah that Jesus read may have been in Hebrew but more likely was in Greek from the Septuagint. Demoss clarifies Hellenism and the Septuagint:

> The Greek translation of the Old Testament produced around 200 B.C. to accommodate Hellenization. The Septuagint rapidly became *the* Bible of synagogue worship and Jewish instruction, and in the New Testament is cited more frequently than the original Hebrew.[11]

Jesus may have been tri-lingual Hebrew, Aramaic, and Greek. He may have spoken the language most appropriate to the ears of his audience. Jesus may have taught his disciples in Aramaic or Greek and also spoken Hebrew to those linked to the Temple or Synagogues. While some lay and scholars enjoy heated debate, the debate over Aramaic or Greek is fruitless.

All languages provide for four communication messaging: hearing, speaking, reading, and writing. The majority of first-century people where Jesus ministered were likely multi-lingual at with hearing and speaking abilities, but not advanced to the point of reading or writing. Similarly today, many people can comprehensively speak and hear a language. However, both writing and reading require intentional study. John affirmed that no fewer than three languages were in use. He recorded that Pilate placed on the cross of Jesus words in Aramaic, Latin, and Greek (Jn 19: 20). Some English Bibles have substituted Aramaic for Hebrew and vice versa. Following are various English Bible renderings of Jn 19: 20. Some identify Hebrew and others Aramaic:[12]

> This title therefore many of the Jews read, for the place of the city where Jesus was crucified was near; and it was written in Hebrew, Greek, and Latin. Jn 19: 20 DBY

> Many of the Jews read this inscription, for the place where Jesus was crucified was near the city, and it was written in Aramaic, in Latin, and in Greek. Jn 19: 20 ESV

> This title then read many of the Jews: for the place where Jesus was crucified was nigh to the city: and it was written in Hebrew, *and* Greek, *and* Latin. Jn 19: 20 KJV

---

[10] Douglas, J. D. and Merrill C. Tenney, eds. "Aramaic" from *The New International Dictionary of the Bible*, 76.
[11] Demoss, Matthew S., "Septuagint" in *Pocket Dictionary for the Study of New Testament Greek*. 112.
[12] DBY – The English Darby Bible (1884 – 1890 a literal translation by John Nelson Darby. ESV – The English Standard Version by Crossway Bibles a division of Good News Publishers. KJV – The King James Version 1769 version of the 1611 King James Version of the English Bible. NIV – The New International Version 1984. NRS – The New Revised Standard Version 1989. YLT – The English Young's literal translation of the Holy Bible by J. N. Young. WHO – Westcott and Hort Greek New Testament. (From Bible Works Version 7)

Many of the Jews read this sign, for the place where Jesus was crucified was near the city, and the sign was written in <u>Aramaic</u>, <u>Latin</u> and <u>Greek</u>. Jn 19: 20 NIV

Many of the Jews read this inscription, because the place where Jesus was crucified was near the city; and it was written in <u>Hebrew</u>, in <u>Latin</u>, and in <u>Greek</u>. Jn 19: 20 NRS

This title, therefore, read many of the Jews, because the place was nigh to the city where Jesus was crucified, and it was having been written in <u>Hebrew</u>, in <u>Greek</u>, in <u>Roman</u>. Jn 19: 20 YLT

τοῦτον οὖν τὸν τίτλον πολλοὶ ἀνέγνωσαν τῶν Ἰουδαίων ὅτι ἐγγὺς ἦν ὁ τόπος τῆς πόλεως ὅπου ἐσταυρώθη ὁ Ἰησοῦς· καὶ ἦν γεγραμμένον <u>Ἑβραϊστί</u> <u>Ῥωμαϊστί</u> <u>Ἑλληνιστί</u> Jn 19: 20 WHO

From the Greek words Ἑβραϊστί Ῥωμαϊστί Ἑλληνιστί the auditory transliteral sounds are more comparable to *Hebraisti (Hebrew)*, *Romaisti (Roman)*, and *Hellenisti (Hellenism / Greek)*. Bibles with various words to convey Pilates's words are not problematic. The point is that no less than three languages were in use. Greek language influences in both written and oral form were substantial. The Hebrews, the Jews, and Temple leadership had available to them their Hebrew Scriptures (Old Testament) in Greek. The Septuagint[13] and had been in use for over 150 years or so at the time of Jesus. However, Aramaic was the language in common with the indigenous. Regarding Aramaic, Brownrigg agrees:

> Some scholars propose that Aramaic may have been the language that Jesus spoke and the common verbal colloquial language at that time and place.[14]

The question is begged if Aramaic was the conversant language of Jesus and his contemporaries, why are there no copies of written Aramaic Gospels similar in number to the thousands of Greek copies? Lack of Aramaic texts paralleling the Greek texts indicates that the New Testament writers likely did not use Aramaic to disseminate their texts. Matthew, Mark, Luke, John, Peter, Jude, James, Paul, and the writer of Hebrews intended to reach beyond Palestine. They employed Greek because Greek was the most useful language beyond where Jesus walked.

Affirming that Aramaic was the lingua franca of Jesus' time let us assume Matthew, Mark, John, and the Scribes originally recorded Jesus' words in Aramaic and that the original Aramaic texts (as well as any original Greek texts) no longer exist. Given the Greek copies from texts closest to originals there is no doubt that if Aramaic was the original script perhaps even in notes taken during Jesus orations, the Aramaic was translated into Greek. F.F. Bruce squelches any notion that the gospel of John was originally written in Aramaic:

> Naturally, if Jesus and his disciples habitually spoke in Aramaic, we might expect to find Aramaisms in the Greek form of the sayings; and this indeed we find in all four Gospels. But unless a piece of objective evidence is forthcoming (such as part

---

[13] Septuagint is a translation from the Hebrew Old Testament into Greek. Scholars estimate the translation from Hebrew to Greek was completed over time and became available after 200 B.C.
[14] Brownrigg, Ronald, *Who's Who the New Testament*. 159.

of an Aramaic text of the Gospel which bears no sign of being a translation from the Greek), there is no reason to doubt that the Gospel of John as such was a Greek composition from the beginning.[15]

Matthew, Mark, Luke, and John were strategic. They knew the geographical limitation of Aramaic and the geographical breadth of the Greek language. More effectively, they knew the power and clarity of the Greek language. Presuming for a moment that Jesus spoke and they recorded in Aramaic. Their original scripts, notes, words, whole sentences, notes, and grander texts required translation into Greek, if translated in their day at all. Regardless of languages spoken by Jesus or his contemporaries, most likely New Testament originals and most certainly earliest copies were scribed in Koine Greek.[16] The possibility that texts initially were recorded in Aramaic and rendered to Greek cannot be ruled out, but is not likely. Regardless of Aramaic, Hebrew, Roman, Greek, or Hellenism as languages during Jesus' lifetime, Matthew, Mark, Luke, and John recorded Jesus' words Greek.

## Summary

Trustworthy interpreters hold that rendering any text without context is a con. Interpreting the imperatives of Jesus outside of context is problematic. Readers must understand in light of the context, not Jesus' imperatives alone which is why the Grammatical Historical Method in context is absolute. Most likely, when those who heard Jesus interpreted an imperative and recognized that Jesus intentionally spoke an imperative. Each of Jesus's imperatives must be studied for what he said, what they heard, and what the writers wrote. A word of caution, however. Dogma developed solely from Jesus imperatives is not the intent of this book. Agreeing with Mounce:

> Of the many things I learned writing this text, [*The Morphology of Biblical Greek*, Mounce] two stand out. Students cannot approach Greek as if it were a "dead" language. True, Koine Greek is no longer spoken, but what we have in the New Testament is a snapshot of a language that was alive and changing. Secondly, Language study must be descriptive, not prescriptive. The best we can do is describe what we see and allow for the variations that accompany any living language.[17]

In Chapters 9 – 15 each of Jesus' commands rendered from the imperative mood form found within the Greek text are listed. The English passages from the ESV are underlined for brevity and clarity. Greek from Wescott and Hort (WHO) follows the underlined English.

---

[15] Bruce, F. F., *The Gospel of John*. 2.
[16] Oldest of all current New Testament Papyri, P52 estimated 117 - 168 CE is in uncial form – uppercase Greek letters.
[17] Mounce, William D., *The Morphology of Biblical Greek: A Companion to Basics of Biblical Greek and the Analytical Lexicon to the Greek New Testament*. xvi.

# Section 3

# The Imperatives of Jesus

Heaven and earth will pass away, but my words will not pass away.

Mk 13: 31

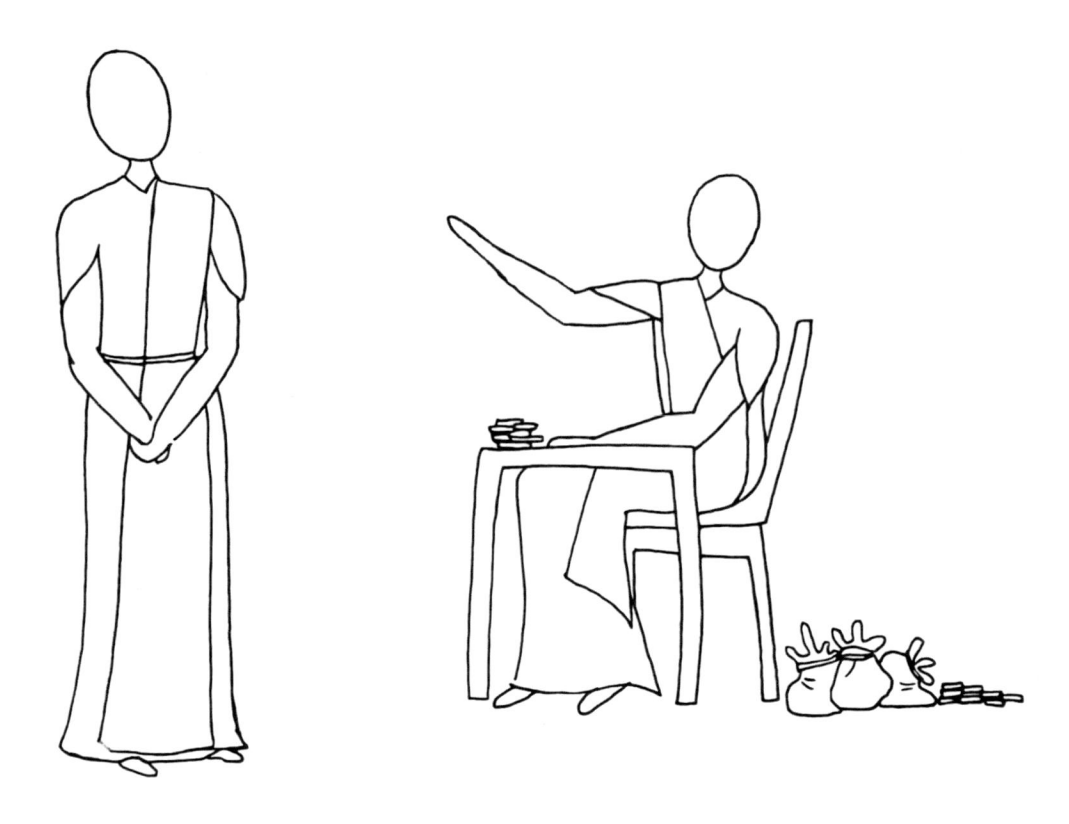

As Jesus passed on from there, he saw a man called Matthew sitting at the tax booth, and he said to him, "Follow me." And he rose and followed him.

Mt 9: 9

# 9 Matthew's Record of the Imperatives of Jesus

> And proclaim as you go, saying, 'The kingdom of heaven is at hand.' Heal the sick, raise the dead, cleanse lepers, cast out demons. Mt 10: 7-8a

## Matthew

In Mt 9: 9 Matthew recorded that Jesus spoke to him a simple imperative command, "Follow me" and Mathew followed. Matthew was a Jewish tax collector seated behind his tax booth in Capernaum when Jesus spoke a simple, concise and clear imperative command to Matthew. But, what about the person of Matthew beyond the tax collector who followed Jesus? What about Matthew's familial links? Why did Jesus choose Matthew? What do we learn about Matthew from Mark, Luke, and John the other Gospel writers? Mark identified Matthew as Levi, son of Alphaeus:

> He went out again beside the sea, and all the crowd was coming to him, and he was teaching them. And as he passed by, he saw Levi the son of Alphaeus sitting at the tax booth, and he said to him, "Follow me." And he rose and followed him. Mk 2: 13-14

Both Mark and Luke also identified James as a son of Alphaeus:

> He appointed the twelve: Simon (to whom he gave the name Peter); James the son of Zebedee and John the brother of James (to whom he gave the name Boanerges, that is, Sons of Thunder); Andrew, and Philip, and Bartholomew, and Matthew, and Thomas, and James the son of Alphaeus, and Thaddaeus, and Simon the Cananaean, and Judas Iscariot, who betrayed him. Mk 3: 16-19

> And when day came, he called his disciples and chose from them twelve, whom he named apostles: Simon, whom he named Peter, and Andrew his brother, and James and John, and Philip, and Bartholomew, and Matthew, and Thomas, and James the son of Alphaeus, and Simon who was called the Zealot, and Judas the son of James, and Judas Iscariot, who became a traitor. Lk 6: 13-16

Brownrigg makes an observation about the sons of Alphaeus from Mark and Luke:

> In the three Synoptic Gospels and in the Acts, the name of this Alphaeus is linked with that of James the Younger but is not otherwise mentioned. If James the Younger was the same person as Alphaeus, father of Levi the tax-collector, Matthew and James the Younger would have been brothers.[1]

---

[1] Brownnrigg, Ronald, "Alphaeus" in *Who's Who the New Testament*, 4.

Matthew recorded the highest word count and much more material than Mark, Luke, or John. Matthew also detailed Jesus' imperatives more than the other Gospel writers. Matthew enhanced Mark's shorter book with details. Brownrigg affirms:

> He became one of the twelve apostles and was by tradition the author of the first Gospel, written for the Jews by a Jew to present Jesus as the Messiah.[2] Ninety-five percent of Mark's Gospel is included in that of Matthew.[3]

While the book of Matthew came to be positioned as the first book of the New Testament, Mark chronologically wrote his Gospel before Matthew. Given Matthew's use of Mark, scholars agree that Matthew wrote both from his own experiences and from other sources. Mark most likely was a source for Matthew, but not the only source. Bruce affirms:

> This evangelist used at least two written sources, one being the Gospel of Mark or something very like it, and the other being the sayings collection which underlies the "Q" material.[4]

## Intellect

A tax collector, Matthew would have been known by Roman leaders, Temple leaders Pharisees, and common people to have an eye for written, oral and numerical details. Tax collectors were profitable intermediaries between those who paid and those who received taxes. Effective in record keeping, oral discourse, reading, and writing, Matthew's written Gospel reflects similar details about his intellect. He was equally as meticulous in writing his gospel as he was in his tax collections.

Luke having described the party for Jesus at Matthew's home where numerous tax collectors had gathered (Lk 5: 27-29) revealed that Matthew was well connected, affluent, smart and hospitable. Today, Mathew might be an accountant working for a Fortune 500 company, an auditor, or a state or federal government IRS employee. Today he would fit in well with any bureaucratic government position overseeing collections and accomplished at resolving written or verbal disputes.

Having quoted from the Old Testament Hebrew Scriptures more than any other gospel writer, Matthew's intended readers were Jews, particularly Pharisees, Sadducees, Scribes, and Synagogue and Temple leaders. Authority groups and those subject to following directives were knowledgeable laws, particularly laws commanded through the Greek imperative mood form. Within the Ten Commandments (Decalogue) are many Hebrew imperatives and imperative clauses. Jewish leaders in Jesus' day had been steeped in the 600+ Mitzvot commandments as well as adherence to them. The imperatives of Jesus recorded by Matthew weighed heavily with Jewish leaders at all levels. The imperatives spoken by Jesus resonated with people no matter if they heard them spoken by Jesus or read them in Matthew's Gospel some twenty or thirty years past Jesus' earthly walk.

---

[2] Brownrigg, Ronald, "Matthew" in *Who's Who the New Testament*, 175 – 176. Matthew is listed first in the New Testament, but chronologically Mark wrote his Gospel before Matthew.
[3] Brownrigg, Ronald, "Matthew" in *Who's Who the New Testament*, 177.
[4] Bruce, F. F., *The Canon of Scripture*, 290. Q being a convenient shorthand symbol for the non-Marcan material common to Matthew and Luke.

Some of Jesus' disciples may have paid taxes through Matthew. He may have known that Jesus had followers such as Peter, Andrew, James, John or others. He may have known them as simple fisherman and businessmen on the Galilean Sea. The importance of the Greek imperative is established in that Matthew recorded the imperative that he had received from Jesus, "Follow me" in Mt 9: 9. Before being called by Jesus, Matthew may have been familiar with Jesus. The imperative Matthew received from Jesus and his immediate response that he followed provide two insights.

First, his instant reaction that he recorded about himself affirmed that he knew what he would leave behind. Peter, Andrew, James, and John given what we know about their professions could have always returned to fishing. A return to tax collecting, however, likely would not have been an option for Matthew. Perhaps this is why Matthew recorded Jesus imperative to him, "Follow me." which left Matthew no option. When Matthew left his tax collection booth to follow Jesus, he likely knew there was no going back.

## Meticulous Matthew's Reliable Text

That Matthew was multi-lingual (Hebrew, Aramaic, and Greek) is likely, but not necessary. Matthew's editing process probably was similar to Mark, Luke, and John. Jesus is often portrayed as having chosen only simple fishermen, ordinary men from poor households for his disciples. Matthew does not fit the mindset, status or education of a simple fisherman. Given Matthew's education, position, income, wealth, and experience, Jesus selecting Matthew was intentional and strategic. Wessell states:

> Matthew's occupation as a tax collector qualified him to be the official recorder of the words and works of Jesus. His job accustomed him to note-taking and the keeping of records.[5]

Some scholars advocate Matthew's first use of Aramaic or Syro-Chaldaic language for his Jewish audience before producing a Greek manuscript. Regarding Matthew's use of Aramaic or Greek, Wessell clarifies that Matthew's Greek text preceded any Aramaic texts if any Aramaic texts are to be found:

> In either case, the authorship of Matthew of our present Greek Gospel is not excluded. If an Aramaic Gospel preceded our Matthew, the publication of the Greek edition completely superseded the Aramaic, since no fragment of an Aramaic Matthew remains.[6]

While no original notes in Aramaic or Greek exist from Matthew, it is likely he chronicled during his time with Jesus with editing and distribution decades after Jesus' ascension. The length and content of his Gospel would have required copious notes and numerous edits for accuracy. Matthew was well suited for writing his Gospel. Jesus knew the long-term consequences of commanding Matthew to follow him. Matthew may have been unaware of how he would serve. Jesus, on the other hand, was strategic in having commanded Matthew with the Greek imperative

---

[5] Wessell, Walter W. "Gospel of Matthew" in Douglas, J. D. and Merrill C. Tenney, eds., *The New International Dictionary of the Bible*, 631.
[6] Ibid. 631.

"Follow me." In Matthew, Jesus had not chosen a fisherman. He chose a tax collector who read, wrote, was skilled at record keeping and numbers, and could negotiate. It is highly likely that Matthew began scribing copious notes, words, and phrases, from the day he left his tax booth.

## Sermon on the Mount Imperatives

Matthew is the only Gospel writer who recorded Jesus' Sermon on the Mount found in Mt 5 – 7. The imperatives within that message weighed powerfully on anyone familiar with Jewish laws or Temple practices, both leaders and peasants. The imperatives recorded by Matthew were weighty on the hearts of Matthew's intended readers in his time. They continue to be weighty on our hearts today. Significant in the Sermon on the Mount are the imperatives found within the Lord's Prayer.[7]

Reading Matthew's record of the imperatives of Jesus put yourself in the first-century context. For Jewish minds, Matthew's Gospel had a purpose. His record of Jesus' imperatives was intentional. Jesus having chosen Matthew as his disciple conveys much about Jesus' strategy. Jesus' had commanded Matthew to be his disciple. Within all four Gospels, there are no lengthy narratives on Matthew. Jesus chose Matthew for his giftedness to write his Gospel. Going deeper, Matthew's record of Jesus' imperatives was deliberate. When Matthew heard Jesus' imperative command to him, "Follow me." there was no doubt in Matthew's mind that he would be strategic to Jesus. Matthew may not have immediately known how Jesus would put his gifts to use when he heard Jesus' command. But Matthew knew he would not be returning to tax collection. The clarity of Matthew's Greek within his Gospel listed as the first book of the New Testament is no mistake.

## Matthew's Record

Mt 3: 13-15 Then Jesus came from Galilee to the Jordan to John, to be baptized by him. John would have prevented him, saying, "I need to be baptized by you, and do you come to me?" But Jesus answered him, "<u>Let it be so now for thus it is fitting for us to fulfill all righteousness</u>." ἄφες ἄρτι,
οὕτως γὰρ πρέπον ἐστὶν ἡμῖν πληρῶσαι πᾶσαν δικαιοσύνην Then he consented.

Many well-meaning sermons have conveyed that Jesus had commanded John to baptize him. However, Jesus did not command John to baptize him. Instead, Jesus commanded John to surrender his belief that John should not baptize Jesus. Jesus ordered John to stop making excuses.

An expanded wording emphasizing the imperative is, "John, let go of your idea that you should not baptize me." An expanded translation conveying only imperative intent not using the phrases, "Let it be so." or "Let go of your idea John…" or "John, stop thinking that you should not baptize me." Matthew did not record that Jesus had commanded John to baptize Jesus. Jesus did not speak an imperative to John saying, "John, baptize me!" or "John, you must baptize me."

John was not the only one who heard Jesus' words. Others standing near Jesus and John also heard Jesus command John to change his thinking. Those within earshot

---

[7] See Chapter 15, "Imperatives within The Lord's Prayer."

heard Jesus' imperative to John. The English phrase that follows Jesus command, "then he consented" affirms that John changed his mind as Jesus had commanded him through the imperative mood form. John changed his mind and baptized Jesus. If Matthew had recorded that Jesus had commanded John to baptize him, Christian baptism would have become a legalistic requirement similar to laws developed out of the Temple system.

As Jesus clarified at his cleansing of the Temple, Temple leaders had abused God's laws and exploited the people. John was the baptizer. Jesus was the baptized. John performing the act as baptizer and Jesus as being baptized were acts in response to commands. The baptism of Jesus fulfilled all righteousness. Big difference.

Interesting that Jesus' last imperative in Matthew 28: 19 is, "disciple nations" followed by the participle, "baptizing" and "teaching." Jesus affirmed to John and those who had heard Jesus' imperative command to John that baptism was indicative of those who pursued righteousness. The concept of pursuing righteousness as a baptized Christian is seldom a focus in contemporary baptisms. Jesus' baptism was a public expression. Jesus' second person singular imperative command to John initiated his Kingdom work.

The same is true today. Adult baptism today is a premeditated public declaration that models Jesus' baptism by John. Jesus as an adult went to John. Jesus' baptism preceded his Kingdom work. Baptism throughout Christian history has often portrayed one of two meanings. Infant baptisms practiced in numerous churches publically conveys a visible church or community relationship. Some self-confessing Christian faith communities link infant baptism to salvation. Some don't. With adult baptism, adults who request to be baptized likely had the opportunity to understand the meaning of baptism. However, some are moved by emotion with little understanding.[8]

Mt 4: 10-11 Then Jesus said to him, "Go ὕπαγε (depart), Satan! For it is written, 'YOU SHALL WORSHIP THE LORD YOUR GOD, AND SERVE HIM ONLY.'" Then the devil left him, and behold, angels came and were ministering to him.

    Jesus' next second person singular imperative was to Satan. Jesus gave a singular imperative, "go!" was his response to Satan's temptations. Jesus' imperative to Satan combined with Jesus' quoted scriptures was combative and victorious. Satan did not have the power to disobey Jesus' imperative to depart. Satan departed. He did not disobey Jesus' imperative. This is the first indication found early in Matthew centered on the power of Jesus' imperative commands. Jesus gave an imperative to Satan, and Satan obeyed. Jesus said, "Go" and Satan "left him." Matthew's record of Jesus first two imperatives was second person singular first to John and second to Satan.

---

[8] This brief narrative is not intended to enter the infant vs. adult baptism debate nor present various denominational views on baptism.

Mt 4: 17 From that time Jesus began to proclaim and say, 'Repent for the kingdom of heaven is at hand μετανοεῖτε ἤγγικεν γὰρ ἡ βασιλεία τῶν οὐρανῶν."

>Jesus first two imperatives were second person singular to John and Satan. Jesus' first publicly spoken plural imperative command that Matthew recorded was, "repent." Jesus' second person plural imperative meant that his imperative was intended first to all who heard it as well as to all who would come to read it or would head his imperative command read to them. Jesus here affirmed repentance as a prerequisite for those who followed him. Repenting and calling to repentance was foremost in Jesus' mind. Unrepentant sinners were unable to experience the kingdom of heaven. Jesus taught them that experiencing the kingdom of heaven was not available to them without repentance. We do not know if all who heard Jesus' imperative to repent repented. Scripture does, however, affirm that following his plural and public imperative to repent his mission started and repentant followers followed. Mk 1: 15

Mt 4: 18-19 While walking by the Sea of Galilee, he saw two brothers, Simon (who is called Peter) and Andrew his brother, casting a net into the sea, for they were fishermen. And He said to them, "Come, follow me δεῦτε ὀπίσω μου, and I will make you fishers of men."

>The exhorted adverb (imperative verb) Simon and Andrew heard was "come." Jesus did not invite. He did not ask. He did not offer. He did not casually bid them come. He exhorted them.

>Having responded to his command yielded them an absolute result. They were guaranteed to be fishers of men because Jesus made them fishers of men. When Jesus said he would make something, it was not possible that Jesus would fail. Jesus' imperative assured Simon and Andrew of their future fishing success.

>They became fishers of men because Jesus made them fishers of men. Early in Jesus' ministry, Simon and Andrew were likely unaware of the power of Jesus' Greek imperative (our English command). As Jesus' disciples spent years with him and after having heard Jesus' numerous imperatives they eventually grasped who Jesus was. His imperatives verified his power.

Mt 5: 12 Rejoice and be glad χαίρετε καὶ ἀγαλλιᾶσθε for your reward is great in the heavens, for so they persecuted the prophets who were before you.

>Immediately after having explained the beatitudes to his disciples Jesus linked two imperatives. He first commanded to, "rejoice" and then commanded that they, "be glad" because their rewards were great in the heavens. Failure to rejoice and be glad were common lapses then as today. Because suffering was and is inherent in kingdom work, Jesus' imperatives reminded his disciples of their reward in the heavens.[9]

---

[9] Note plural heavens. See 2 Co 12: 2, (3rd heaven); Charlesworth, James H. *The Old Testament Pseudepigrapha, Volumes 1 and 2,* 2 Enoch 3, 7, 8, 11, 18, 19, 20, 21, 22; (1st – 10th heavens).

The Kingdom work for which he called them was burdensome which is why he commanded them to rejoice and be glad. His disciples were commanded to remember that their rewards would come in the heavens. Matthew recorded rejoice as present active and be glad as a present middle. Both imperatives were plural. What this meant to them was that their rejoicing and gladness were to be done in community with one another. Jesus addressed them in the plural, such as, "you all" which proclaimed multiple reward recipients.

Mt 5: 16 "<u>Thus, shine the light before men</u> οὕτως λαμψάτω τὸ φῶς ὑμῶν ἔμπροσθεν τῶν ἀνθρώπων in such a way that they may see your good works, and glorify your Father who is in heaven.

    Jesus' imperative was, "shine." Many translations correctly rendered the aorist imperative third-person singular as, "let your light shine." The English word, "let" however, weakens the imperative focus. "Let the light shine" depreciates Jesus' command to "make the light shine" or "make your light shine."

The English word, "Let" is correct, but somewhat a weak option with little imperatival force supporting the word. His command to "shine" was not egotistical but demonstrative. Jesus here had commanded his disciples to show the light. Good works glorified the father in heaven and others were to see them.[10]

Mt 5: 24 <u>Leave your gift there before the altar and go</u> ἄφες ἐκεῖ τὸ δῶρόν σου ἔμπροσθεν τοῦ θυσιαστηρίου καὶ ὕπαγε. First <u>be reconciled to your</u> brother πρῶτον διαλλάγηθι τῷ ἀδελφῷ σου and then come and<u> offer your gift</u> πρόσφερε τὸ δῶρόν σου.

    Jesus words contained three imperatives, each having purpose. Here, Jesus' commands were progressive to them, one followed another. Reconciliation preceded the altar gift. If the gift was first brought, Jesus commanded to leave it and depart or go to the person with whom reconciliation was commanded. While leaving the gift before the altar Matthew recorded as an imperative, reconciliation was Jesus' greater command in the progression. While leaving gifts at the altar was important, Jesus' primary priority was reconciliation, not gifts.

The English word, "come" preceding the phrase, "offer your gift" conveys a command, but, "come" is not an imperative but a participle. A better translation to convey the Greek active, aorist, participle is, "and then having come" (YLT) or "and after having returned."

---

[10] Note here the ESV rendered heaven singular, but the Greek is a dative, masculine, plural, noun - heavens.

Mt 5: 25 <u>Make it happen</u> ἴσθι εὐνοῶν that you come to terms quickly with your accuser while you are going with him to court, lest your accuser hand you over to the judge, and the judge to the guard, and you be put in prison.

>Some translations render, "come to terms quickly" or "make in happen." But, the Greek word ἴσθι, a present, active, second person, singular, imperative Greek *emi* verb or in English a, "me" verb. An expanded translation conveying who was to do what and when is, "You make it happen that you quickly come to terms."

>Jesus a present active command meant to them that when there was disagreement with an accuser, believers were commanded to quickly take the initiative to come to an agreement with the accuser. Hesitation was not an attribute of those who claimed to follow Jesus. Believers were not to wait. They were to be active, intentional, and initiate the process of coming to a resolution.

Mt 5: 29 If your right eye causes you to sin, <u>take it out and throw it away</u> ἔξελε αὐτὸν καὶ βάλε ἀπὸ σοῦ. For it is better that you lose one of your members than that your whole body be thrown into hell.

>Here are two progressive imperatives. The first imperative here was "take" or "tear" or "pluck out." The second imperative was "throw," "cast," or "toss away." These imperatives were action-oriented in their context. Speaking in metaphor, Jesus was not teaching that believers should be blind or have only one eye. Jesus taught that the first action was to remove what had caused the sin and then create a significant separation by throwing away at a significant distance what caused sin.

>First identifying and then removing what caused sin was then and is still today not natural. His command to throw away indicated to them a significant separation or distance from what had caused the sin. The English is weak on clarifying the distance there must be between what causes the sin and the sinner. Jesus taught that both actions, removing and throwing were are indicative of his followers. The cause of sin was to be first thrown away and also kept away.

Mt 5: 30 If your right hand makes you stumble, <u>cut it off and throw it from you</u> ἔκκοψον αὐτὴν καὶ βάλε ἀπὸ σοῦ. For it is better that you lose one of your members than that your whole body go into hell.

>Similar to v29, the action was commanded. Jesus affirmed positive consequences for following his imperatives. Hyperbole may or may not have been applied here as the message was clear, sin if not cut out and separated destroys the whole. Jesus commanded cutting and throwing because he his focus was the whole body. The emphasis here was not merely cutting and throwing away. Rather, what was most important was protecting the fullness or the completeness of the body

Mt 5: 31-32 "It was said, 'Whoever sends his wife away, <u>let him give her a certificate of divorce</u> δότω αὐτῇ ἀποστάσιον; But I say to you that everyone who divorces his wife, except on the ground of sexual immorality, makes her commit adultery, and whoever marries a divorced woman commits adultery.

>Context is extremely important here. His aorist active third person imperative affirmed the Mosaic Law. English translations often use, "let him give" or "he must give" to accommodate the Greek to English structure.

>Regarding divorce and the certified document attesting it, Jesus affirmed and restated Dt 24: 1 - 5.[11] Jesus upheld the Greek indicatives found in the Septuagint from Dt 24: 1 - 5 regarding the certificate of divorce and then clarified the imperative. Jesus acknowledged the procedures for the "bill of divorce." Writing, producing, and giving a certificate or bill of divorce, however, was not the central issue. Jesus acknowledged the process from Moses' teachings.

>There was no divorce without a recognized certificate of divorce having been written and given by the spouse divorcing and sending away the spouse being divorced. Here Jesus identified a husband who had sent his wife away or divorced his wife which meant the divorcing husband created the certificate of divorce to give to his wife. In our contemporary context the intent still applies. Today, within secular government law, one spouse initiates preparation of the certificate of divorce usually through lawyers and ultimately provides the divorce decree to the spouse being sent away regardless of husband or wife.[12]

Mt 5: 37 "<u>Let what you say be simply 'Yes' or 'No'</u>; ἔστω δὲ ὁ λόγος ὑμῶν ναὶ ναί οὒ οὔ; anything more than this comes from evil.

>Many English translations read, "let your statement be" or "simply let your statement be" or "simply let your word be." The English word, "let" conveys a lack of responsibility. Richer translations are, "make your statement be" or "but make your word be." Jesus' imperative here left no doubt that his followers were responsible for their words. He did not demand unadorned responses. Because simple verbal retorts were not easy in the heat of debate or being questioned by religious leaders, Jesus commanded direct answers. While Jesus often spoke in parables, answering questions required clarity and simplicity.

---

[11] "When a man takes a wife and marries her, if then she finds no favor in his eyes because he has found some indecency in her, and <u>he writes her a certificate of divorce</u> and puts it in her hand and sends her out of his house, and she departs out of his house, ² and if she goes and becomes another man's wife, ³ and the latter man hates her and writes her a certificate of divorce and puts it in her hand and sends her out of his house, or if the latter man dies, who took her to be his wife, ⁴ then her former husband, who sent her away, may not take her again to be his wife, after she has been defiled, for that is an abomination before the LORD. And you shall not bring sin upon the land that the LORD your God is giving you for an inheritance. ⁵ "When a man is newly married, he shall not go out with the army or be liable for any other public duty. He shall be free at home one year to be happy with his wife whom he has taken. Dt 24: 1-5.

[12] This summary is not intended to fully detail divorce, certificate of divorce, or marital issues. Suffice to say that Jesus' imperative was a summary of the Mosaic Law from Dt 24: 1–5.

Mt 5: 39 but I say to you, do not resist the one who is evil, but if anyone slaps you on the right cheek <u>turn to him the other also</u> στρέψον αὐτῷ καὶ τὴν ἄλλην;

>Jesus knew that when the weak encountered evil the weak would likely run. Running and hiding are human responses. However, his disciples were to respond differently to evil. Turning from evil must be taught. Turning rather than running was discipleship teaching on a higher level. This teaching was not to be overlooked because all believers who followed Jesus then continuously faced temptation and evil. Same today. The Kingdom of evil is not compatible with the Kingdom of God. Turning the other cheek to evil and standing in the face of evil had to be taught. Believers were commanded not to resist but turn.

Mt 5: 40 "And if anyone would sue you and take your tunic, <u>let him have your cloak as well</u> ἄφες αὐτῷ καὶ τὸ ἱμάτιον

>Some English translations use the words, "give him" in place of "let him have." The "let him have" translation implies that if he asks for your cloak, then let him have it. The English word, "let" while appropriate and correct in translation, weakens the imperative.

>The context implies that after someone has taken your shirt, giving your coat will affirm either his or her greed or perceived need and your generosity. After someone has sued you and taken your tunic, your giving more by making sure he or she also has your cloak is not a natural response. The point is to make sure that people who sue you know that you know that they have sued you either out of their greed or their perceived need. Either way, their greed or need shows their lack of trust. Your generosity beyond their greed shows your trust. Big difference.

>Jesus imperative taught his disciples that there would be those who would sue them out of greed or their perception of need. For those who sought a suit by way of the courts, their greed would be hidden under their use of the courts. No surprise that Jesus commanded his followers to quickly settling matters before going to court in Mt 5: 25.

>Jesus imperative here was, give your coat even after your shirt has been taken. Giving your cloak after they've sued you for your tunic conveys to the one who sued you of your knowledge of their fear because of their greed. Giving your cloak further affirms to them your trust that God will provide you a new tunic and new cloak.

>You do not need to sue because your God is not the courts used to bring suit. Your God is a God who provides. Big difference.

Mt 5: 41 And if anyone forces you to go one mile, <u>go with him two miles</u> ὕπαγε μετ αὐτοῦ δύο
> Furthering the imperatives in Mt 5: 39 - 40 Jesus spoke another direct command, "go." This active command required effort. Going extra miles was not natural necessitating premeditative and preplanned training. The human response was to stop. Jesus commanded to be in relationship longer than what was expected or required. Jesus did not say go for the entire journey. Jesus limited distance enough so that the one who forced the other person to go one mile was aware that the believer went beyond what was required.

Mt 5: 42 "<u>Give to the one who begs from you</u>, τῷ αἰτοῦντί σε δός and <u>do not refuse the one who would borrow from you</u> τὸν θέλοντα ἀπὸ σοῦ δανίσασθαι μὴ ἀποστραφῇς.
> Here Jesus gave two commands. The first, "you give" is in the imperative mood form. The second, "do not refuse the one who would borrow from you" is not an imperative, but an aorist subjunctive preceded by a single negative and can be conveyed as a command. It is acceptable to render as an imperative. Providing for those who asked because they were in need of borrowing affirmed the blessings that believers were in positions to lend rather than borrow. Dt 15: 6; 28: 12[13]

> Believers were not to be debtors out of necessity. No matter how little or much believers had, preparation to give when asked was Jesus' command to them. Believers were always in a position to lend when asked. Giving needed to be taught early in the believer's life because benevolence was not an inherent characteristic even among those who followed Jesus.

Mt 5: 44 "But I say to you, <u>love your enemies</u> ἀγαπᾶτε τοὺς ἐχθροὺς ὑμῶν and <u>pray</u> προσεύχεσθε <u>for those who persecute you</u> προσεύχεσθε ὑπὲρ τῶν διωκόντων ὑμᾶς
> Jesus' two imperatives, "love" and "pray" for enemies and persecutors were not natural human inclinations to those who heard them. Jesus commanded both an understanding and applying a higher calling to love and pray for enemies. He spoke these two imperatives in plural form. The Beatitudes and the imperatives that followed the Beatitudes as recorded by Matthew were given to the disciples as the crowd looked on. The message to his disciples was to love their enemies (past, present, and future enemies) bringing them to repentance and inclusion in the kingdom of God.

> His disciples were learning to understand the reason for loving and praying. They had no alternative. Jesus' imperatives were not debatable, only doable. The disciples had to learn how to love their enemies and pray for those who persecuted them. Their lives of ministry that followed Jesus' death, resurrection, and ascension exemplified their love and prayers for enemies and persecutors. Jesus did not give them an option to love.

---

[13] For the LORD your God will bless you, as he promised you, and you shall lend to many nations, but you shall not borrow, and you shall rule over many nations, but they shall not rule over you. Dt 15: 6
The LORD will open to you his good treasury, the heavens, to give the rain to your land in its season and to bless all the work of your hands. And you shall lend to many nations, but you shall not borrow. Dt 28: 12

Mt 6: 1 "<u>Beware</u> Προσέχετε of practicing your righteousness before men to be noticed by them;
Here Jesus commanded a stern warning to his disciples to shun self-righteousness. The temptation to use righteousness for vanity was ever present. Many of the Pharisees showed their righteousness and vanity.

The English word, "beware" sounds cautionary more so than the imperative they heard or read in their context. The second commandment found in Ex 20: 7 and Dt 5: 11 forbade using Yahweh for self-aggrandizement and vanity for the guilt that falls on the self-righteous.[14] The "beware" imperative commanded Jesus' followers to be vigilant of self-righteousness.

Mt 6: 3 But when you give to a needy, <u>do not let</u> μὴ γνώτω your left hand know what your right hand is doing,

Jesus prohibited publicized giving to the needy. Jesus presses the point. You must know what to do concerning almsgiving, and not publically make known what you do. Give silently is the command. This was not a recommendation but a command toward private gifting.

The personal reference of right and left hand emphasized that God glorifying benevolence was not to be prideful. Jesus could have focused only on the external pride of others. His example of left and right hand emphasized the absolute elimination of both internal and external pride with regards to giving.

Mt 6: 6 But when you pray, <u>go into your room</u> εἴσελθε and shut the door and <u>pray</u> πρόσευξαι to your Father who is in secret. And your Father who sees in secret will reward you.

The imperative they heard was "go into a place" or "go into a room." He commanded they enter a private place with the intention to pray. "Shut the door" in English sounds like an imperative, but a more definitive translation is, "and after you have shut the door" or "and having shut the door." The imperatives he spoke were "enter" and "pray." This command did not negate public or communal prayer but commanded private intentioned prayer in a closed room for intentional secret prayer. The closed door in their context affirmed the intention of privacy.

Mt 6: 7–13 contains Jesus' instruction to his disciples within *The Lord's Prayer*. Imperatives within this prayer are listed in Chapter 15: *Imperatives of Jesus in the Lord's Prayer*

Mt 6: 16 "And when you fast, <u>do not be look gloomy like the hypocrites</u> μὴ γίνεσθε μὴ γίνεσθε ὡς οἱ ὑποκριταὶ σκυθρωποί

Jesus commanded that fasting for his disciples was to be distinctly different from hypocrites who made known their fast. Jesus' disciples were not to show or proclaim their fasting. Their fasting as disciples was to be done without edict.

---

[14] You shall not take the name of the LORD your God in vain, for the LORD will not hold him guiltless who takes his name in vain. Ex 20: 7
You shall not take the name of the LORD your God in vain, for the LORD will not hold him guiltless who takes his name in vain. Dt 5: 11

Mt 6: 17 But when you fast, <u>anoint your head</u> ἄλειψαί ἄλειψαί σου τὴν κεφαλὴν and <u>wash your face</u> τὸ πρόσωπόν σου νίψαι.

>Jesus commanded his followers while they fasted two additional imperatives. First, anoint the head and second, wash the face. The English conveys anointing and washing to be in preparation for the fast. But with the Greek imperative anointing and washing are not only part of the fast. His imperatives affirmed that anointing and washing are as significant as the fast.

Mt 6: 19 "<u>Do not store treasures on earth for yourselves</u> Μὴ θησαυρίζετε ὑμῖν θησαυροὺς ἐπὶ τῆς γῆς where moth and rust destroy and where thieves break in and steal,

>Jesus commanded his disciples to abstain from storing earthly treasures. The idea was that what God had given, God also intended to be actively working and productive. The gifts that God's had given them were to be used, not stored. His gifts were to be employed. This command confirmed to them God's sovereignty to provide. Jesus commanded to make use of God's provisions, not idly store them. Remove from your storage and provide to those who can make use of what you have stored. Disciples were to employ all that God had given them, not parts that they had in storage. The command is to employ God's provisions.

>Productivity, not hoarding was Jesus intent. Unused gifts from God were to be put to use or given to others who would make use of them. If God has given you a gift, a provision, to use and you are not making us of that gift, then give it to someone who will employ that gift and do not store that gift. Metaphorically, cleaning house, of stored unused goods or possessions, was commanded. A sinful nature tends to store God's blessings rather than employ God's blessings. His imperatives affirmed to his disciples that they were to have absolute trust in God's sovereignty and provisions.

>In short, the disciples were to give to others what they were not employing. This imperative is less about a command to put what is in storage to use and more his followers trusting in God's provisions to the point that they have no need for storage.

Mt 6: 20 but <u>lay up for yourselves treasures in heaven</u> θησαυρίζετε δὲ ὑμῖν θησαυροὺς ἐν οὐρανῷ where neither moth nor rust destroys and where thieve do not break in and steal.

>Jesus commanded storing treasures in heaven because of the simplicity at having focused on an earthly realm rather than the heavenly Kingdom realm. Here Jesus commanded his disciples to employ their earthly gifts for heavenly treasures. There was a place for storage but storage on earth was not what Jesus meant.

>Storage of heavenly treasures is a God concept. Earth is God's place to put God's gifts to work. Earth is a place where functioning happens, particularly working of God's provisions. Heavenly storage was not for God. In other words, God has no use for what you store in heaven. What is stored in heaven is not for God. During their earthly lives, his disciples were commanded to make use of God's provisions

because heaven, not earth, was and is where treasures unable to be destroyed or stolen are stored.

Earth is a place God's people to make use of God's provisions to them. Jesus spoke this imperative in plural, not singular. He had commanded those who had sat under his teachings which means earth is a place where God's people function together using God's provisions, not storing them, but employing them.

In short, treasures are stored up in heaven when God's provisions to his people have functioned on earth. Big difference.

Mt 6: 25 "Therefore I tell you, <u>do not be anxious</u> μὴ μεριμνᾶτε about your life, what you will eat or what you will drink, nor about your body, what you will put on. Is not life more than food and the body more than clothing?
>   Jesus commanded that worries about eating, drinking, clothing or adornments were forbidden. Food, drink, clothing, and adornments were part of life, but worry over them was consequential. Anxiousness over their possession inhibited their Kingdom experience. Jesus affirmed that God would provide for his disciples through his sovereignty to the point that they were not to worry about worldly essentials.

Mt 6: 26 "<u>Look at the birds of the air</u> ἐμβλέψατε εἰς τὰ πετεινὰ τοῦ οὐρανοῦ. They neither sow nor reap nor gather into barns and yet your heavenly Father feeds them; Are you not of more value than they?
>   Jesus commanded his disciples to look at birds for affirmation that God had provided, provides, and will provide for his creation. Jesus could have said, "Consider" or "Think about" but he commanded them to visually look understanding that God provides. Many English Bibles translate, "birds of the air" but the literal Koine Greek is "birds (plural) of heaven (singular)." Jesus affirmed the sovereignty of God to provide for his disciples and all of God's creation.

Mt 6: 28 And why are you <u>anxious</u> μεριμνᾶτε about clothing? <u>Consider the lilies of the field</u> καταμάθετε τὰ κρίνα τοῦ ἀγροῦ, how they grow: they neither toil nor spin,
>   His imperative commanded his disciples (plural), to they think about or observe the flowers. "Lilies (plural) of the field" implies variety and wealth of flowers. Some English translations render, "Observe the lilies..." Both "consider and "observe" are acceptable but weak in explaining the weight of the imperative. Here Jesus commanded to observe God's provisions as God had provided for flowers. The Greek word καταμάθετε has a more descriptive meaning such as learn, observe well, know, and notice. The idea is one of understanding beyond merely looking at the lilies of the field.

Mt 6: 33 But <u>seek first the kingdom of God and his righteousness</u> ζητεῖτε δὲ πρῶτον τὴν βασιλείαν καὶ τὴν δικαιοσύνην αὐτοῦ, and all these things will be added to you.

> Jesus made clear that his followers must first, seek. His imperative to them was, "first seek." "Seek" is the imperative verb and "first" is the adverb. The Greek word ζητεῖτε also carries the meaning of desire or have desire for or demand.
>
> Matthew recorded the phrases "kingdom of God" and "God's righteousness" in the accusative case, the direct objects that Jesus had commanded them to seek. Jesus taught them that at the point of salvation came seeking of God's kingdom and God's righteousness. Seeking kingdom and righteousness are indicatives of salvation and precede ministry and service.
>
> Jesus commanded first, not second or third, to seek God's kingdom and righteousness. Ministry, service, and mission follow first having sought kingdom and righteousness. Seeking, not serving was their priority. In his initial teaching, Jesus did not teach his disciples about conversion, evangelism, prayer, feeding the poor, or missions. Those works came later. He first taught them what preceded all things of his faithful followers.
>
> The results for having sought the kingdom and righteousness were the addition of "all these things," the very things of which he had been speaking. Following the seeking of the kingdom and righteousness, needs would be met.
>
> Prioritizing faith efforts is common. Prayer, worship, giving, evangelism, missions and numerous Christian works are often thought to have higher priorities. Yet, Jesus did not use "prayer" here. He spoke a word that described effort, searching, trying, attempting, and striving for one's interest or advantage, wanting, asking, investigating and demanding. Jesus taught that those who served without first seeking were not fully developed followers because their services were likely self-righteousness, like the Pharisees. God's kingdom and righteousness had priority for Jesus' disciples.

Mt 7: 1-2 "<u>Do not judge that you be not judged</u> Μὴ κρίνετε ἵνα μὴ κριθῆτε· For with the judgment you pronounce you will be judged, and with the measure you use it will be measured to you.

> This passage has been interpreted in several ways throughout history (historical hermeneutics). The most common misinterpretation results from interpreting only the first part of this passage, "Do not judge." and disregarding the English phrase, "that you be not judged." The English phrase "Do not judge." produces an erroneous English command (contemporary hermeneutic) that Christians should never judge anyone or anything or any sin. Jesus did not teach his followers not to judge.
>
> The English word, "judge" is rendered from the Greek word κρίνετε a second person plural present active imperative verb. In English the contemporary word "judge" carries a negative connotation and often a disparaging accusation more so than what the Greek word carries or for our purposes, what the Greek word

conveyed to hearers when Jesus spoke or Matthew's words were read. Numerous Greek lexicons offer insight on word meaning.

Brown: κρίμα
    (a) *krino* has the following meanings: to distinguish, give preference, approve; In addition it means to consider, regard as; to speak or think ill of, to decide, to judge; *krino* also means to decide, resolve.
    (b) *krino* and *krima* are very frequently used in the NT in a strictly judicial sense.[15]

Danker: κρίνω
1. To make a selection, select, prefer
2. To pass judgment upon (and thereby seek to influence) the lives and actions of other people
3. To make a judgement based on taking various factors into account
4. To come to a conclusion after a cognitive process
5. To engage in judicial process
6. To ensure justice for someone[16]

Friberg: κρίνω
1. As making a personal evaluation *think of as better, prefer*
2. As forming a personal opinion *evaluate, think, judge*
3. As reaching a personal or group decision *resolve, determine, decide*
4. As passing a personal judgment on someone's actions *judge, criticize* often in a negative *condemn, find fault with*
5. As a legal technical term
6. Hebraistically, in a broader sense *rule, govern*[17]

Rendering the Greek to mean "do not judge" in English is problematic and a deceptive teaching because it is out of context with the full passage. While the plain meaning of the words appear to indicate, "do not judge" the fuller context inclusive of the Greek ἵνα clause is required to understand today what the disciples understood then (contextual hermeneutics). The ἵνα is a conjunction used to introduce a clause that expresses the purpose or the goal.

The imperative "do not judge" is plural, meaning that Jesus had commanded it to his disciples as a group. Having heard this imperative, the disciples knew that they and their judgments would be judged by others both individually and as a community. Here Jesus taught his followers that the consequences for their judging

---

[15] Brown, Colin, ed., *New International Dictionary of New Testament Theology*, Vol 2, 364-365.
[16] Danker, Frederick William, ed. Walter Bauer, *A Greek-English Lexicon of the New Testament and other Early Christian Literature, 3d ed.*, 567 – 568.
[17] Friberg, Timothy, Barbara Friberg, and Neva F. Miller, *Analytical Lexicon of the Greek New Testament*, 238.

would be that they would be judged. Jesus demanded that his disciples be judged by others as having judged gracefully, mercifully, and righteously. Big difference.

Here Jesus used an imperative command plus an *aorist subjunctive with a negative with the iva clause.* Jesus explained the consequences for not judging. An expanded rendering incorporating Greek cases, clause, and the verb is, "Do not be judging so that you may not be judged." Those who did not judge were identified as being unwilling or unable to discern right from wrong.

Today, poor exegesis (reading something out of the text that is not within the text) or eisegesis (reading something into the text that is not within the text) often teaches that judging is not part of the Christian witness.[18] However, in both historical and contemporary context disciples have been, are, and will be judged by both believers and non-believers. Jesus taught his disciples that how they judged would be how they would be judged. Judging and being judged were both inevitable for his disciples. Jesus commanded his disciples not to judge so that they would not be judged. Somewhat conversely when disciples judged those who saw the disciples' judgments would judge by similar judgments. To quote a long-standing insight, "What is good for the goose is good for the gander." Do not withhold your judgments in hopes that they will not judge your judgments. Instead, make judgments knowing that others will judge you. Contemporarily, how you judge today and how others have seen you judge is how others will judge you.

Eisegesis interpretation has historically focused only on the first part of the passage, "do not judge" without the second part of the passage. Jesus commandment affirmed that others would judge his disciples' judgments. Jesus followed with the clarification that the log is removed from their eye before they removed the speck from their brother's eye. Jesus imperative command was not to be a scapegoat for not judging. The context must be considered in its entirety. In a contemporary context, Jesus' imperatives apply today. Don't judge so you will not be judged, instead, take the log out of your eye and judge knowing that you will be judged by others on how you have judged. Judging and being judged was then and is today inevitable. Jesus taught that not judging was not an option for his disciples and teachers. His disciples were to be able to discern good from evil because they would be judged for either judging rightly or wrongly.[19] Not judging was not an option for Jesus' disciples because they were witnesses for Jesus.

---

[18] Sometimes exegesis and eisegesis are confusing. In short, lousy exegesis is a result of incorrectly interpreting something out of the text that is not within the text and lousy eisegesis is incorrectly putting something into the text that is not within the text.

[19] 12 For though by this time you ought to be teachers, you need someone to teach you again the basic principles of the oracles of God. You need milk, not solid food, 13 for everyone who lives on milk is unskilled in the word of righteousness, since he is a child. 14 But solid food is for the mature, for those who have their powers of discernment trained by constant practice to distinguish good from evil. 6:1 Therefore let us leave the elementary doctrine of Christ and go on to maturity, not laying again a foundation of repentance from dead works and of faith toward God, 2 and of instruction about washings, the laying on of hands, the resurrection of the dead, and eternal judgment. 3 And this we will do if God permits. Hb 5: 12-6: 3

Mt 7: 4 Or how can you say to your brother, 'Let me take the speck out of your eye Αφες ἐκβάλω τὸ κάρφος ἐκ τοῦ ὀφθαλμοῦ σου when there is the log in your own eye?

>Jesus orated an imperative command within an example. His imperative must be considered in context. Jesus did not command to leave the speck. He commanded to remove the speck after having first removed the log. Removing both log and speck was imperative. Each brother had logs and specks.

>If logs and specks remained, everyone would be blind. Regardless of size or location, effort must be made to remove what obscures or blinds. Jesus commanded his disciples to help one another. An even deeper mark of a disciple is a disciple seeking other disciples to remove logs or specks. His use of, "brother" indicated that their community of disciples was purposed to help each other remove logs and specs.

Mt 7: 5 You hypocrite, first take out the log of your own eye ἔκβαλε πρῶτον ἐκ τοῦ ὀφθαλμοῦ σοῦ τὴν δοκόν, and then you will see clearly to take the speck out of your brother's eye.

>Jesus commanded that the log from their eye must first be removed. Jesus' first demanded self-inspection and removal of their own hindrances. Jesus demanded that they ask one another for clarity. Removing a large log was one matter, removing a speck required assistance from fellow disciples. The log was commanded to be self-removed before helping others. We underestimate the possibility of vision. Inspect yourself. When there is a log in your eye, remove it. When help is needed, ask for help. However, once the log has been removed, then help remove the speck from a brother's eye.

Mt 7: 7 "Ask, and it will be given to you, Αἰτεῖτε καὶ δοθήσεται ὑμῖν seek and you will find, ζητεῖτε καὶ εὑρήσετε knock and it will be opened to you, κρούετε καὶ ἀνοιγήσεται ὑμῖν·

>Jesus combined three imperatives in one sentence, ask, seek, and knock. Each present active plural imperative meant that there was to be among the disciples an ongoing continuity of asking, seeking, and knocking. Jesus went beyond the imperatives alone. He assured them of a future positive result. A positive result followed each imperative. Ask, and they would be given to. Seek, and they would find what they were seeking. Their knocks would be answered with opened doors.

>Jesus commanded his disciples to ask, seek, and knock to build faith in his ability to provide for them rather than faith in the provisions. Fulfilled wants and needs, finding a treasure or receiving an open door was less important than their faith in God who provided. Perhaps more evident, Jesus was less concerned with what they would receive after having asked, sought, and knocked. He was more concerned that they had faith that he would provide for them.

Mt 7: 12 "So whatever you wish that others would do to you, <u>do also to them</u> ποιεῖτε καὶ ὑμεῖς ποιεῖτε αὐτοῖς, for this is the Law and the Prophets.

> Jesus commanded to "do" or "be active" toward others. His disciples were to have an active faith beyond prayer. What his disciples were to do was what they desired to have done to themselves. Jesus commanded this because their human sinfulness would not respond this way. Jesus gave this imperative because they would not have done what they should have had done by themselves. They needed this imperative. This was a mark of discipleship. Note that before they did something for someone else, they were first to consider what they would have had done for themselves. These are second person plural, not first person singular imperative commands. They as a group were to be seen as doing for others what they would have wanted themselves. Contemporary exegesis often conveys a singular work which is applicable, yet the imperative Matthew recorded that Jesus spoke was plural.

Mt 7: 13 "<u>Enter by the narrow gate</u> Εἰσέλθατε διὰ τῆς στενῆς πύλης. For the gate is wide and the way is easy that leads to destruction, and those who enter by it are many.

> The Disciples did not doubt about which gate to enter. This imperative from Jesus clarified that the choosing the narrow gate was to be their choice. There was a certainty. There was no ambiguity. The narrow gate was the one to choose, but few choose it. They had to be taught to choose to enter the narrow path and not take the wider path which the majority chose. His command did not permit them to consider the wider easier path. The wider gate was a stress-free easy journey toward destruction chosen by many. Jesus did not give his disciples an option.

Mt 7: 15 <u>Beware of false prophets</u> Προσέχετε ἀπὸ τῶν ψευδοπροφητῶν, who come to you in sheep's clothing but inwardly are ravenous wolves

> Misleading and false prophets were as real in Jesus day as today. Jesus stated a present active plural imperative to the disciples to beware of deceivers. Consequences for not identifying a sheep's clothing resulted in confrontation by ravenous wolves. Jesus' metaphors were disturbingly descriptive to his hearers. Sheep's clothing and ravenous wolves imparted unforgettable descriptions. Jesus' imperative to beware combined with visual imaging were memorable to those who heard. Those unable to identify false prophets were not Jesus' disciples. Identifying false prophets was both a command to the disciples and an indication of a disciple.

Mt 7: 23 And then will I declare to them, 'I never knew you; <u>depart from me you workers of lawlessness</u> ἀποχωρεῖτε ἀπ ἐμοῦ οἱ ἐργαζόμενοι τὴν ἀνομίαν.'

> Jesus described the future. He will command a departing, a casting out. His disciples were taught an absolute impending separation. Before Jesus' imperative to depart, he described the reason for his command. There were those who expected to be in his presence because of their outward righteousness. His command was not only for those he would cast out but for those who would witness the separation that Jesus commanded. Those he would cast out presumed they knew Jesus because they did certain works.

What mattered was whom Jesus knew, not those who thought they knew Jesus. Knowing Jesus was irrelevant to Jesus knowing them. Workers of lawlessness thought they knew Jesus but were commanded to depart. In context, seeking to keep the moral law or "the will of my father" indicates those whom Jesus knows.[20]

Mt 8: 3-4 And Jesus stretched out his hand and touched him, saying, "I will; be clean; καθαρίσθητι and immediately his leprosy was cleansed. And Jesus said to him, "See that you say nothing to anyone ὅρα μηδενὶ εἴπῃς but go, ἀλλὰ ὕπαγε show δεῖξον yourself to the priest and offer προσένεγκον the gift that Moses commanded, for a proof to them."
    Jesus healed with imperatives. Demon cleansing and healing were done with authority to cleanse. Jesus did not speak a Greek indicative or say, "You are clean." He gave the imperative, "be clean." Immediately following the leper's healing Jesus used four successive imperative commands, "see," "go," "show," and "offer" each which required action. Jesus imperatives here affirmed the scriptural command of Moses to offer thanks as proof of this healing. Mk 1:40-45; Lk 5:12-16

Mt 8: 5-13 When he entered Capernaum, a centurion came forward to him, appealing to him, "Lord, my servant is lying paralyzed at home, suffering terribly." And he said to him, "I will come and heal him." But the centurion replied, "Lord, I am not worthy to have you come under my roof, but only say the word, and my servant will be healed. For I too am a man under authority, with soldiers under me. And I say to one, 'Go,' and he goes, and to another, 'Come,' and he comes, and to my servant, 'Do this,' and he does it." When Jesus heard this, he marveled and said to those who followed him, "Truly, I tell you, with no one in Israel have I found such faith. I tell you, many will come from east and west and recline at table with Abraham, Isaac, and Jacob in the kingdom of heaven, while the sons of the kingdom will be thrown into the outer darkness. In that place there will be weeping and gnashing of teeth." And to the centurion Jesus said, "Go; let it be done for you as you have believed Ὕπαγε ὡς ἐπίστευσας γενηθήτω σοι." And the servant was healed at that very moment.
    Jesus spoke two imperatives to the centurion whose servant needed healing. After Jesus healed the centurion's servant, he commanded the centurion to both go and then receive what the centurion had asked for. Jesus had an agenda beyond healing the centurion's servant. Matthew recorded "Go" as an active present. He recorded Jesus' next imperative, "let it be done" as aorist passive deponent indicated by "let" or some translations, "permit it to be done" or "it will be done" or "it shall be done." All are acceptable renderings but both "let" and "permit" and "will" and "shall" reduce the power of the deponent imperative that Jesus spoke. The deponent imperative appears passive form but is active in meaning. A richer translation would convey the absoluteness of the imperative that the healing had occurred. This is a significant passage by Matthew which Luke also recorded because the centurion knew the value and power of giving and receiving imperatives.[21]

---

[20] Not everyone who says to me, 'Lord, Lord,' will enter the kingdom of heaven, but the one who does the will of my Father who is in heaven. Mt 7: 21

[21] Lk 7: 2-10 included the centurion narrative. Luke, however, did not record Jesus' imperatives to the Centurion as Matthew had recorded. Both Matthew and Luke recorded the centurion's imperatives which affirmed the centurion's authority to speak commands to those below him in rank.

Mt 8: 22 And Jesus said to him, "Follow me Ακολούθει μοι, and leave the dead to bury their own dead ἄφες τοὺς νεκροὺς θάψαι τοὺς ἑαυτῶν νεκρούς
> Jesus gave two back to back imperative commands, "follow me" and "leave the dead." Jesus' metaphoric phrase, "leave the dead bury their own dead" was perplexing to them. It was physically impossible for the dead to bury the dead. Jesus two imperative commands affirmed that following Jesus meant leaving dead things behind. His visual metaphor of the dead burying the dead conveyed the difference between the living and the dead, between those who would follow Jesus and those who would die and bury themselves as a result of disregarding Jesus.

Mt 8: 28-32 And when he came to the other side, to the country of the Gadarenes, two demon-possessed men met him, coming out of the tombs, so fierce that no one could pass that way. And behold, they cried out, "What have you to do with us, O Son of God? Have you come here to torment us before the time?" Now a herd of many pigs was feeding at some distance from them. And the demons begged him, saying, "If you cast us out, send us away into the herd of pigs." And he said to them, "Go Ὑπάγετε." So they came out and went into the pigs, and behold, the whole herd rushed down the steep bank into the sea and drowned in the waters. The herdsmen fled, and going into the city they told everything, especially what had happened to the demon-possessed men. And behold, all the city came out to meet Jesus, and when they saw him, they begged him to leave their region.
> Jesus casting out the demon from the Demoniacs is found in Mt 8: 28 – 24; Mk 5: 1 – 20 and Lk 8: 26 – 39. However, only Mt recorded Jesus' imperative, "go" to them. The power of Jesus imperative to the demons is clear. Immediately after Jesus' imperative, "go" Matthew recorded, "So they came out and went into the pigs." There was no delay following Jesus command. He said, "go" and the demons went into the pigs.
>
> Mark and Luke did not record an imperative from Jesus in their narratives. Mk 5: 13 and Lk 8: 32 are identical regarding Jesus' response to them, "so he [Jesus] gave them permission." The demons had given Jesus the imperative phrase, "send us away into the heard of pigs." For insights on this imperative to Jesus, see Chapter 15: *Imperatives to the Christ* Jesus. Mk 5: 1–20; Lk 8: 26–39

Mt 9: 2 and behold, they were bringing to him a paralytic, laid upon a couch, and Jesus having seen their faith, said to the paralytic, 'Be of good courage θάρσει child, your sins have been forgiven.'
> Jesus gave a command directly to the person with paralysis to be of good courage. He taught courage based on faith at the same time he acknowledged the paralytic's sins had been forgiven. He linked forgiveness and healing. Courage based on happenstance was limited. Teaching courage based on faith through forgiven sins resulted in healing for the person with paralysis.

Mt 9: 5 For which is easier, to say, 'Your sins are forgiven,' or to say, 'Rise ἔγειρε and walk περιπάτε'?

>  Jesus linked forgiveness with imperatives to rise and walk. Both of these imperatives are linked by context, and both are miraculous acts. Forgiveness is provocative and an act of God's accomplishment. Mk 2: 9; Lk 5: 23

Mt 9: 6-7 But that you may know that the Son of Man has authority on earth to forgive sins"- he then said to the paralytic- "Rise ἆρόν pick up your bed and go ὕπαγε home." And he rose and went home.

> Jesus confronted by Scribes and asked a question through imperatives. These imperatives included two actions, rise and walk v5 and rise and go (home) v6. The paralytic after having been healed followed Jesus' imperative commands. There was no further dialogue. He did exactly as Jesus had commanded. The person with paralysis directly and in front of others got up and went home. Mk 2: 11; Lk 5: 24

Mt 9: 9 As Jesus went on from there, He saw a man called Matthew, sitting in the tax collector's booth; and He said to him, "Follow me ἀκολούθει μοι!" And he got up and followed Him.

> Here Mathew recorded Jesus' imperatives to him in his self-authored Gospel account. Jesus provided no doubt for Matthew. His command, "Follow me" was simple and direct. The Greek is a present active imperative and can be translated, "be following me" to convey the ongoing command by Jesus to Matthew. The command to follow must be taught because to follow is not inherent in humanity.

> Matthew did not record any pre or post-narrative on Jesus' imperative to Matthew. Matthew, sitting in the collection booth, immediately got up and followed Jesus' imperative. Matthew, the writer of this gospel, recorded no dialogue or reasoning with Jesus. Matthew recorded his gospel after Jesus' life, death, resurrection, and ascension, likely had an unmovable conviction to obeying Jesus' imperatives. Matthew did not record why he followed without question. When Jesus gave an imperative Matthew's record indicated he was unable not to follow.

> Matthew did not record his ability to stay or go following Jesus' command. He did not write, "After I heard his command it was not possible for me to stay as a tax collector. It was not possible for me to deny Jesus' command." Rather, meticulous Matthew beautifully wrote, "and He [Jesus] said to him [Matthew] "Follow me. And he [Matthew] followed him [Jesus]. Jesus commanded, and Matthew followed. Mk 2: 14; Lk 5: 27

Mt 9: 13 Go and <u>learn</u> μάθετε what this means, 'I desire mercy, and not sacrifice.' For I came not to call the righteous, but sinners."

> Jesus' imperative to the Pharisees to learn the meaning of Hs 6:6 conveyed that understanding did not come without instruction.[22] Ordinary Jews presumed the Pharisees knew the Scriptures, but here Jesus clarified that the Pharisees did not understand the meanings of the texts. Quoting scripture and verse was common than with the Pharisees as it is today.
>
> Teaching to memorize the Scriptures often trumps understanding or comprehending. Jesus was not concern with memorizing or quoting at which the Pharisees excelled. Jesus demanded right interpretation and teaching. He required that knowing both what scripture says (exegesis) and what it means (hermeneutics) was imperative especially for leaders. Pharisaical quoting without knowing was not sufficient. Jesus gave the Pharisees the imperative, "learn" because they did not know in spite of their Pharisaical positions or perhaps memory quoting.
>
> The word, "go" at the beginning of the sentence appears like an imperative, but "go" is an aorist passive participle more definitely translated by Young's literal, "but having gone."

Mt 9: 22 Jesus turned, and seeing her he said, "<u>Take heart, daughter</u>; Θάρσει θύγατερ your faith has made you well." And instantly the woman was made well.

> Jesus commanded the woman having a blood discharge for the past 12 years. He publically, personally and lovingly identified her as daughter following his command. Her healing had been done public. Numerous people heard Jesus' words "be of good courage daughter." The change did not happen without instruction. Jesus' imperative "take heart" attested that her faith was crucial for her healing.
> Mk 5: 34; Lk 8: 48

Mt 9: 24–26 He said, "<u>Leave</u> ἀναχωρεῖτε for the girl has not died, but is asleep." And they began laughing at Him. But when the crowd had been put outside, he went in and took her by the hand, and the girl arose. And the report of this went through all that district.

> Jesus recognized that their sorrow and disbelief surpassed their faith. To those mourning their misperception that the girl had died, he commanded them to leave. After the laughing crowd had been separated from Jesus, the ailing girl was healed in front of some of the believing faithful who had remained in the room. Matthew did not record that everyone was put outside, only the crowd and likely those who were mocking. Matthew recorded that someone reported that Jesus took her by the hand, so there was a witness to what Jesus did. Jesus here refused to publically heal in the presence of the unfaithful. The fact that the girl had been healed could not be contained. The report of her healing likely would have included that Jesus had not heal her while in the presence of those without faith or those who had been laughing and scornful.

---

[22] For I desire steadfast love and not sacrifice, the knowledge of God rather than burnt offerings. Hs 6: 6
[7] And if you had known what this means, 'I desire mercy, and not sacrifice,' you would not have condemned the guiltless. Mt 12: 7

Mt 9: 29-31 Then he touched their eyes, saying, "According to your faith <u>be it done to you</u> γενηθήτω ὑμῖν." And their eyes were opened. And Jesus sternly warned them, "<u>See that no one knows about it</u> <u>Ὁρᾶτε</u> μηδεὶς <u>γινωσκέτω</u>." But they went away and spread his fame through all that district.

> Here Jesus spoke three imperatives not well rendered in the ESV English. A translation that captures both Greek imperatives in Jesus' warning is, "See here and let no one know about it." The first imperative, "be it done to you" affirmed their faith in healing. Here Jesus commanded them to know the link between faith and healing. Immediately after this imperative linking their faith and healing, their eyes were opened.

> The narrative gives the impression that Jesus' next two imperatives were be disregarded by the blind men. Jesus commanded both blind men to 'make sure' or 'see to it' that no one knew about their healing. Matthew was diligent to record that the two men did not speak about their healing, but about Jesus' fame. Following healing, Jesus often affirmed the faith held by those he healed.

> It appears these two healed men, due to their exuberance following their healing, did not follow Jesus' imperative to keep the miraculous restoration of the eyesight to themselves. The text does not indicate that they spoke of their healing or sight restoration, but only that they spread his fame throughout the district. Jesus was not looking to increase his fame within the district. He was intentioned that they understood the connection between faith and healing. Jesus did not seek notoriety. He emphasized faith in those healed.

Mt 9: 38 Then he said to his disciples, "The harvest is plentiful, but the laborers are few; <u>therefore pray earnestly to the Lord of the harvest</u> δεήθητε οὖν τοῦ κυρίου τοῦ θερισμοῦ to send out laborers into his harvest."

> A more accurate translation is "beseech," "beg," or "implore" rather than "pray." The English word, "pray" deemphasized the imperative. Further, the Greek word for pray is προσεύχεσθε but the Greek Matthew recorded was δεήθητε which more accurately meant in their context ask, beseech, inquire, or implore. Today, pray is and English words that commonly implies petition or supplication.

> However, here Matthew did not record pray. He recorded that Jesus demanded his disciples to beseech in earnest. This insight may sound insignificant, but Matthew indicated the difference in prayer and beseeching.

> Jesus commanded his disciples as a group to beg or plead in earnestness. In context, this imperative was stronger than pray or ask. Jesus commanded his disciples to go beyond asking to begging or pleading God to send out workers. Real workers, learned workers, edified workers who knew Jesus' commands and sought to follow them were few. The harvest was not theirs nor that of the laborers. The Lord of the harvest gleaned then and gleans now with few laborers.

Mt 10: 7-8 And <u>proclaim as you go saying, 'The kingdom of heaven is at hand</u> πορευόμενοι δὲ κηρύσσετε λέγοντες ὅτι Ἤγγικεν ἡ βασιλεία τῶν οὐρανῶν. <u>Heal the sick</u> ἀσθενοῦντας εραπεύετε, <u>raise the dead</u> νεκροὺς ἐγείρετε, <u>cleanse the lepers</u> λεπροὺς καθαρίζετε, <u>cast out demons</u> αιμόνια ἐκβάλλετε. Freely you received, freely <u>give</u> δωρεὰν δότε.

> Jesus spoke six imperatives in these two verses. He specifically commanded his disciples what to do, proclaim that the Kingdom of heavens[23] was at hand and then how to do it. Following his imperative to proclaim the kingdom, he provided five successive imperatives: "heal," "raise," "clean," "cast out," and "give." These five imperatives proved the inadequacy of their flesh to pursue these commands. Jesus commanded them specific imperatives. They did not have doubt about what to do and how to do it.

Mt 10: 11 "And whatever city or village you enter, <u>inquire who is worthy in it</u> ἐξετάσατε τίς ἐν αὐτῇ ἄξιός ἐστιν, and <u>stay at his house until you leave that city</u> κἀκεῖ μείνατε ἕως ἂν ἐξέλθητε.

> Jesus had commanded them first to know who was worthy. After learning who was worthy, they were then commanded to remain at the worthy person's house until time to leave. Jesus commanded his disciples in this way, so they were in a friendly company during their arduous tasks. That Jesus commanded his disciples to "inquire" affirmed that Jesus knew that not everyone would be a willing recipient to house the disciples. Rest can be found in the company of believers when healing, raising the dead, cleansing lepers, and casting out demons. Jesus commanded them to inquire who was worthy. There was a method for rest and safety as they proclaimed the Kingdom of heaven(s) at hand. Kingdom work was feeble without the support of worthy people in companionship. Finding worthy people must be taught. Finding a safe home was a prerequisite to healing the sick, raising the dead, cleansing lepers, casting out demons, and giving without immediate reward. If they had gone into an unbelieving home not supportive of their mission, their mission would be arduous.

Mt 10: 12-14 As you enter the house, <u>greet</u> ἀσπάσασθε αὐτήν it. And if the house is worthy, <u>let (make) your peace</u> ἐλθάτω ἡ εἰρήνη ὑμῶν ἐπ᾽ αὐτήν come upon it, but if it is not worthy, <u>let (make) your peace</u> ἡ εἰρήνη ὑμῶν πρὸς ὑμᾶς ἐπιστραφήτω return to you. And if anyone will not receive you or listen to your words, <u>shake off the dust from your feet</u> ἐκείνης ἐκτινάξατε τὸν κονιορτὸν τῶν ποδῶν ὑμῶν when you leave that house or town.

> Here Jesus told the twelve disciples (Mt 10:5) what, where, when, how and to whom to greet and share their peace. Later this instruction to the 12 were given to the 72 (Lk 10:1). Jesus commanded in the plural that all disciples upon entering the house were to make greetings, not just one. They worked as a team. Jesus gave them the authority to discern if a house was worthy.

> He commanded his disciples to either make peace come upon a house or recall peace from a house. The indwelled disciples held sway upon the peace brought into any home or the peace that exited any home they visited. If a house was unworthy, Jesus commanded the disciples to shake off the dust so as not to carry its filth to another home or town.

---

[23] ESV translated as singular heaven, but Greek is plural: heavens

His disciples were commanded to leave sin and filth behind. They did not take the immorality of no peace with them. Because Jesus commanded them to shake the dust, they understood that what carried with them would have clung to them. So they shook from their feet the dust that had clung to them from unworthy houses.

Mt 10: 16-17 "Behold, I send you out as sheep in the midst of wolves; so <u>be shrewd as serpents and innocent as doves</u> γίνεσθε οὖν φρόνιμοι ὡς οἱ ὄφεις, καὶ ἀκέραιοι ὡς αἱ περιστεραί. <u>Beware of men</u> Προσέχετε δὲ ἀπὸ τῶν ἀνθρώπων, for they will deliver you over to courts and flog you in their synagogues.

> Jesus had commanded them to be both shrewd and innocent. Those not edified, not adequately instructed would have thought that shrewdness and innocence were non-compatible for disciples as witnesses. However, Jesus commanded his metaphorical sheep in the midst of metaphorical wolves to be both shrewd and innocent. He immediately gave a second imperative command that they are wary of worldly men who looked to leaders of magisterial courts as a means to flog them.

He did not want his sheep in the secular courts, so he affirmed to them his knowledge of worldly courts and instructed them with imperatives. Shrewdness and innocence were necessities for them. Jesus commanded them to recognize evil men for what they would do. He taught his disciples that not everyone was in or of or seeking the kingdom of God. No matter how righteous or faithful or spiritual they appeared, evil men would flog them in the synagogues, the synagogues where true teachings should have been found. Courts and synagogues, where one would expect to find justice and truth, were two recognized organizational bodies Jesus warned them to avoid.

Mt 10: 23 "But whenever they persecute you in one city, <u>flee to the next</u> φεύγετε εἰς τὴν ἑτέραν; for truly I say to you, you will not finish going through the cities of Israel until the Son of Man comes.

> Jesus had commanded his disciples to flee persecution. He ordered escape to the next city. God's sovereignty was at work and believers were wise to concede to it. The command was that they flee to another city to avoid persecution. Fleeing persecution had to be taught to them. Faithful servants rightly discerned the length and breadth of persecution before fleeing. Fleeing may be too quick or too late.

At the point of persecution, escape was commanded. Jesus decreed life, not persecution, suffering, or death. At the sight of persecution, Jesus mandated escape not martyrdom for his disciples. In today's contemporary context this text may offer valuable insight under persecution. The coming of the Son of Man in a biblical theological context implied then and also implies today a judgement. There is no command to intentionally pursue martyrdom as the coming Son of Man's judgement was then and is today absolute.

Mt 10: 27 What I tell you in the dark, <u>say in the light</u> εἴπατε ἐν τῷ φωτί, and what you hear whispered, <u>proclaim on the housetops</u> κηρύξατε ἐπὶ τῶν δωμάτων.

> Jesus commanded to speak whatever was revealed in darkness or by a whisper. Jesus had told them many things in private, with a whisper, behind closed doors, messages just for them. Jesus taught his disciples to appropriately speak and proclaim at the right time and in the right place. They were taught to be ready at the time and place of God's choosing, not theirs. They were to wait for the right time to proclaim what they had been taught. They were not to keep the teachings that he had given them in darkness or through a whisper solely for themselves.

Mt 10: 28 "<u>Do not fear</u> μὴ φοβεῖσθε those who kill the body but are unable to kill the soul; but rather <u>fear</u> φοβεῖσθε Him who is able to destroy both soul and body in hell.

> Jesus gave two serial commands to his listeners. First, he told them who not to fear. Second, he described to them who should be feared. The disciples were required to know both false fear and genuine fear that protected them. His commands to them as a group also applied to their bodies and souls. The words, "body" and "soul" are both preceded by singular articles, "the" verifying that Jesus warned them as a group to be concerned about their bodies and souls. Jesus focused both on the group and their bodies and souls of those within the group.

Mt 10: 31 "<u>So do not fear</u> μὴ οὖν φοβεῖσθε; you are more valuable than many sparrows.

> Jesus had commanded his disciples not to fear and supported his command with reason that they were more valuable than sparrows. Jesus demanded that his disciples knew their value to God. Lk 12: 1-7

Mt 11: 4 And Jesus answered them, "Go and <u>tell John what you hear and see</u> ἀπαγγείλατε Ἰωάννῃ ἃ ἀκούετε καὶ βλέπετε.

> The word English word, "go" appears to be the imperative command. But "go" here was not the imperative. "Go" is an aorist passive deponent verb. The only Greek imperative in this passage is, "tell." Richer translations are "After you return to John, tell him…" or "After you are gone from here, tell John…" Jesus' single aorist imperative, "tell" spoken to John's disciples assured that John would know and be comforted.

> Jesus did not command John's disciples to explain everything. He simply told them to convey to John what they were hearing and seeing. Jesus did not edict "what you have seen and heard as individuals" in the past tense. Jesus commanded John's disciples to state what they were hearing and seeing in present active plural. In other words, "Don't tell John what you have seen and heard. Tell John what you are seeing and hearing." Big difference.

> As a group they would bring John good news. John would have been comforted in knowing that he had baptized the anointed Messiah. Continuation of what they had seen and heard was absolute. Through Jesus' present active imperative commands to John's disciples, John would knew without doubt that Jesus was the Messiah. John the Baptist knew he had fulfilled his calling.

Mt 11: 15 He who has ears to hear, <u>let him hear</u> ἀκουέτω.
>Jesus' command emphasized understanding. He mandated judicial hearing on a deeper level not only a surface oration, but listening and comprehending. The words "let him" found in many translations while correct, deemphasize the imperative command to understand on a deeper intensity. This imperative was third person singular not plural meaning that an individual is responsible. The English "let" deemphasizes the imperative. A more definitive translation is "he must hear" where the imperative is conveyed. Individual understanding trumps corporate participation. Jesus affirmed that kingdom work without understanding was fruitless. Hearing with an understanding was primary. Mt 13: 9; 13: 43

Mt 11: 29 <u>Take my yoke upon you</u> ἄρατε τὸν ζυγόν μου ἐφ᾽ ὑμᾶς, <u>and learn from me</u> καὶ μάθετε ἀπ᾽ ἐμοῦ, for I am gentle and lowly in heart, and you will find rest for your souls.
>Jesus' two imperatives, "take" and "learn" exposed the disciples' weak wills to take on the burdens of learning. These commands left no doubt as to what must be done. Taking his yoke and learning from him were not options. Having taken his yoke and they learned and found their souls at rest.

>A sophomoric immature understanding would have difficulty understanding that a heavy yoke could be gentle, lowly in heart, and restful. The imagery conveyed a contradiction. Jesus' imperative disregarded the contradictory image and commanded them to take his yoke. His command would be proven when their restful souls were realized. He commanded because they lacked faith. They ultimately would find the restfulness of his yoke.

Mt 12: 13 Then he said to the man, "<u>Stretch out your hand</u> ἔκτεινόν σου τὴν χεῖρα." And the man stretched it out, and it was restored, healthy like the other.
>The man with the withered hand followed Jesus' imperative. He responded to Jesus command. Would his hand have been healed had he not followed Jesus command and not stretched out his hand? The text does not indicate what did not happen only that when the man stretched out his hand, he was healed. In deeper context, the challenge laid out by the Pharisees to get Jesus to violate the Sabbath failed.

>Even greater and beyond the miraculous healing however were Jesus' knowledge, exegesis, hermeneutic, and interpretation of the Hebrew Scriptures. It was untenable that a crippled man who was offered hope of healing by a healer would disobey a command that most certainly promised healing. Following Jesus' imperative was not a problem for the man though his healing likely did not make him any friends among the Pharisees. Mk 3: 5; Lk 6: 10

Mt 12: 33 'Either <u>make the tree good</u> ποιήσατε τὸ δένδρον καλὸν, and its fruit good, or <u>make the tree bad</u> ποιήσατε τὸ δένδρον σαπρὸν, and its fruit bad, for the tree is known from its fruit.
>Jesus spoke two identical imperatives to the Pharisees regarding the tree. Make it good or bad. Regardless of what was made, do something. The Pharisees were masters at division. Jesus exposed them so their fruit good or bad could be seen.

Fence sitting disciples unable to take a position (similar to Pharisees) would not be ministry effective for the kingdom. Ambiguity was not a mark of a true disciple. The human spirit desires to be indistinct and vague. Thus, taking and making decisions was taught by command. Disciples similar to the Pharisees were not called to elusiveness but to give light and produce fruit that identified the tree.

Mt 13: 9 He who has ears, <u>let him hear</u> ἀκουέτω.
    Mt 11: 15; 13: 9, 43; and Chapter 14: "The Imperatives of Jesus in Revelation"

Mt 13: 18 <u>Therefore hear</u> ὑμεῖς οὖν ἀκούσατε then the parable of the sower.
    Jesus clarified the soils parable. Jesus had just given the parable of the sower to the masses in Mt 13: 1 – 9 and was asked by his disciples why he spoke in parables to them Mt 13: 10 – 18. Jesus had used the metaphor of a tree and its fruit, good or bad. His disciples were aware that those in the crowd may not have understood his parable so they questioned Jesus' teaching method of using parables. After Jesus heard the disciples' comments he commanded them to pay attention, understand, or give a judicial discerning at hearing what he had said in his parable of the sower.

In context hearers of these parables who grasped Jesus' intent would have linked the fruit of the Pharisees, the Temple, the religious practices and demands. Jesus was aware of the condition of the disciples, their lack of understanding and confusion so he delivered an imperative command to them as disciples to understand. In prior context to this command, Jesus affirmed that there were and are those who will not understand. But for his disciples understanding was a command.

Mt 13: 30 <u>Let both grow together</u> ἄφετε συναυξάνεσθαι ἀμφότερα until the harvest, and at harvest time I will tell the reapers, <u>Gather the weeds first</u> συλλέξατε πρῶτον τὰ ζιζάνια and <u>bind them in bundles</u> δήσατε αὐτὰ εἰς δέσμας to be burned, but <u>gather the wheat</u> τὸν δὲ σῖτον συναγάγετε into my barn.'"
    In the parable of the weeds Jesus stated 4 imperatives. The first is often translated "allow" or "permit" or "let" them to grow together. Matthew recorded, "grow together" in the passive voice, affirming that their growth was not their own, but the will of God. Such a translation however, while acceptable and accurate diminishes the imperative that he commanded them to grow together. He did not permit separation during the growing season. Jesus' imperative acknowledged the anguish that resulted when holiness grew next to evil.

The righteous, the wheat grew next to the weeds eking out to survive and grow from the same water and soil as the weeds took. Both the weeds and wheat required water and were commanded to persevere and grow together through the growing season. Not until the harvest was ready would he command reapers to first gather and bind the tares in preparation for burning. The master was patient permitting each plant to bear out its fruit before the harvest.

Notice the order. He first commanded gathering, bounding, and burning of the weeds. He then commanded the gathering of wheat into the barn. The saved grew next to the lost as the righteous grew next to the unrighteous. Holy ones grew next to evil ones. Suffering was a reality as wheat grew next to weeds. Harvest was to occur, neither sooner nor later, but at the right time. Suffering would stop and the harvest would be stored. Suffering, gathering weeds, binding bundles, and gathering wheat, were commanded. Until the harvest however, suffering next to the tares was ever present.

Mt 13: 43 He who has ears, <u>let him hear</u> ἀκουέτω.
See Mt 11: 15; 13: 9, 43; Chapter 14: "The Imperatives of Jesus in Revelation"

Mt 14: 15 – 16 Now when it was evening, the disciples came to him and said, "This is a desolate place, and the day is now over; send the crowds away to go into the villages and buy food for themselves." But Jesus said to them, "They do not need to go away; <u>you give them something to eat</u> δότε αὐτοῖς ὑμεῖς φαγεῖν!"

After the disciples asked Jesus to send the crowds away Jesus immediately commanded his disciples to give the crowd something to eat. He told them to give yet they presumed they had not enough to give. At this point in Jesus' ministry the disciples were likely realizing that after Jesus gave an imperative command they did not have options but to obey. The disciples here gave Jesus an imperative to send the crowds away, yet Jesus completely disregarded their imperative to him His command reply to their command was that that they feed the crowd. Mk 6: 37; Lk 9: 13; Chapter 16: "Imperatives to the Christ."

Mt 14: 17-18 They said to him, "We have only five loaves here and two fish." And He said, "<u>Bring them here to me</u> φέρετέ μοι ὧδε αὐτούς."

Jesus commanded that the disciples bring him the five loaves and two fish. They brought what they had to the Lord for his use. They were not to be concerned with how little they had or what they brought. Throughout Jesus' ministry the disciples learning over time and through experience to trust the Jesus far beyond obeying his imperative commands alone. Obedience is inferior to trust. Jesus told the disciples what to do because they were yet to trust what Jesus could do. Big difference.

Mt 14: 25-27 And in the fourth watch of the night he came to them, walking on the sea. But when the disciples saw him walking on the sea, they were terrified, and said, "It is a ghost!" and they cried out in fear. But immediately Jesus spoke to them, saying, "<u>Take heart</u> θαρσεῖτε; it is I. <u>Do not be afraid</u> μὴ φοβεῖσθε."

Jesus used two imperatives. The first imperative was positive. The second imperative was prohibitive. First be courageous and second, do not be afraid. Jesus immediately spoke to their fears. He did not permit them to be distressed nor remain in distress. As he stood on the water he quickly called out two imperative commands. The disciples had experienced the power of Jesus spoken commands particularly prior to the miraculous feeding of the large crowd with two fish and five loaves of bread. His imperative commands brought them comfort, not confusion or fear. Mk 6: 50; Jn 6: 20

Mt 14: 28-33 And Peter answered him, "Lord, if it is you, <u>command me to come to you on the water</u> κέλευσόν με ἐλθεῖν πρός σε ἐπὶ τὰ ὕδατα." He said, "<u>Come</u> ἐλθέ." So Peter got out of the boat and walked on the water and came to Jesus. But when he saw the wind, he was afraid, and beginning to sink he cried out, "<u>Lord, save me</u> Κύριε σῶσόν με." Jesus immediately reached out his hand and took hold of him, saying to him, "O you of little faith, why did you doubt?" And when they got into the boat, the wind ceased. And those in the boat worshiped him, saying, "Truly you are the Son of God."

> Peter having heard Jesus' words and having seen Jesus walk on water responded with an imperative command to Jesus in v28. Here is a very insightful exchange of imperative commands between Peter and Jesus. Peter had commanded Jesus to command Peter. Peter with his growing faith had commanded Jesus what to do with his words, "command me to come to you on the water" and Jesus did exactly what Peter had commanded. Without hesitation as soon as Jesus heard Peter's imperative Jesus responded with another imperative to Peter, "come."
>
> The power in both Peter's and Jesus' commands were verified as the disciples in the boat witnessed both Jesus and Peter walking on water. Peter specifically and with intention had commanded Jesus to give Peter an imperative command to walk on water. Peter and the disciples who saw and heard their oral exchange were beginning to trust the power of Jesus' spoken imperatives. They would learn the power of their own imperatives through Jesus. As Peter sank, Peter spoke another imperative to Jesus, "Lord, save me" at which immediately Jesus saved Peter from sinking.[24] See Chapter 16: "Imperatives to the Christ."

Mt 15: 4 For God commanded, '<u>Honor your father and your mother</u> τίμα τὸν πατέρα καὶ τὴν μητέρα,' and, 'Whoever reviles father or mother must surely <u>die</u> θανάτῳ τελευτάτω.'

> The English phrase, "must surely die" is weak in rendering from two Greek words, θανάτῳ τελευτάτω which more literally means "let him die the death" as found in the ERV, KJV, and YLT. Mk 7: 10

Mt 15: 10 And he called the people to him and said to them, "<u>Hear and understand</u> ἀκούετε καὶ συνίετε.
> Mk 7: 14

Mt 15: 14 <u>Let them alone</u> ἄφετε αὐτούς; they are blind guides. And if the blind lead the blind, both will fall into a pit."

> Some translations render "tolerate" in place of "let them alone." Jesus commanded his disciples to tolerate the Pharisee's blindness. The Pharisee's self-destruction was inevitable. Jesus' imperative here seems to contradict contemporary evangelical ideals to save the lost from destruction. Here Jesus had commanded the crowd to let the blind lead the blind and fall into a pit. This teaching inclusive of Jesus' imperative in light of evangelism today is a hard saying and a lesson that Jesus taught his disciples and the crowd. Jesus commanded his disciple to let the lost, these blind guides, continue in the blindness. These blind Pharisees had misguided

---

[24] Both Mark (Mk 6: 47-52) and John (Jn 6: 16-21) recorded Jesus walking on water. Only Matthew recorded Peter walking on water and the dialogue between Peter and Jesus. Matthew likely witnessed and heard their words.

their followers. Identifying blind guides is equivalent to discerning good from evil as the writer of Hebrews affirms. Given that Matthew's Gospel focused on the Jews, the writer of Hebrews affirms Matthew's insight.[25]

Mt 15: 28 Then Jesus answered her, "O woman, great is your faith! <u>Be it done for you as you desire</u> γενηθήτω σοι ὡς θέλεις." And her daughter was healed instantly.
    Some translations, to create Jesus' imperative, use "let it be", or "it will be done" or "be it done." The verb here is an aorist, passive, third person, singular, deponent, imperative. Deponent means passive in form but active in meaning. In other words, Jesus made the healing happen. In this passage, Jesus affirmed to the woman through an imperative that her longing to have her daughter healed had could stop. Jesus commanded and her request was granted.

Mt 16: 6 Jesus said to them, "<u>Watch and beware of the leaven of the Pharisees and Sadducees</u> ὁρᾶτε καὶ προσέχετε ἀπὸ τῆς ζύμης τῶν Φαρισαίων καὶ Σαδδουκαίων.
    Here Jesus could have just said, "Beware" but he spoke two imperative "watch" and "beware" emphasizing that his disciples must be both observant and cautious. Being attentive or watchful was not sufficient. They were commanded to give attention to, heed, or be concerned about what they had seen.
    Mk 8: 15

Mt 16: 11 How is it that you fail to understand that I did not speak about bread? <u>Beware</u> προσέχετε of the leaven of the Pharisees and Sadducees."
    Jesus provided another imperative to beware. The English rendering "beware" is somewhat less powerful than the Greek word which provides a higher sense of urgency and importance than simply "beware." Kingdom workers were commanded to be knowledgeable and cautious of motives from those seeking to ruin the worker's mission. Jesus' imperative conveyed an idea to be a step ahead, proactive, preemptive, anticipatory, not reactionary or surprised by actions of the Pharisees.

Mt 16: 23 But he turned and said to Peter, "<u>Get behind me, Satan</u> ὕπαγε ὀπίσω μου, σατανᾶ! You are a hindrance to me. For you are not setting your mind on the things of God, but on the things of man."
    Mk 8: 33

Mt 16: 24 Then Jesus told his disciples, "If anyone would come after me, let him <u>deny</u> himself ἀπαρνησάσθω ἑαυτὸν and <u>take up his cross</u> ἀράτω τὸν σταυρὸν αὐτοῦ and <u>follow me</u> ἀκολουθείτω μοι.
    Mk 8: 34; Lk 9: 23

---

[25] But solid food is for the mature, for those who have their powers of discernment trained by constant practice to distinguish good from evil. Hb 5: 14

Mt 17: 5 He was still speaking when behold, a bright cloud overshadowed them, and a voice from the cloud said, "This is my beloved Son, with whom I am well pleased; <u>listen to him</u> ἀκούετε αὐτοῦ."
    Mk 9: 7; Lk 9: 35

Mt 17: 3-7 And behold, there appeared to them Moses and Elijah, talking with him. And Peter said to Jesus, "Lord, it is good that we are here. If you wish, I will make three tents here, one for you and one for Moses and one for Elijah." He was still speaking when, behold, a bright cloud overshadowed them, and a voice from the cloud said, "This is my beloved Son, with whom I am well pleased; <u>listen to him</u> ἀκούετε αὐτοῦ." When the disciples heard this, they fell on their faces and were terrified. But Jesus came and touched them, saying, "<u>Rise, and have no fear</u> ἐγέρθητε καὶ μὴ φοβεῖσθε." And when they lifted up their eyes, they saw no one but Jesus only.
    Jesus two imperatives to Peter and James followed the Father's specific command to them, "listen to him." Their fear having heard the Father's words from the cloud was clarified by Jesus' two imperatives: "rise" and "have no fear." Peter and James received instructions to follow both the Father's imperatives and Jesus' future imperatives. Yet, Peter at Jesus' trial denied Jesus three times. Peter was growing toward understanding that Jesus' imperatives are God's imperatives.

    In 1 Peter, 2 Peter and Acts, Peter exemplified his embracing and trusting Jesus' imperatives to have no fear. Peter's denial and fear in the courtyard at Jesus' trial affirmed that Peter at that time had not yet fully grasped Jesus' imperatives, but Peter's hesitation to trust Jesus' imperatives would change as Peter grew to trust Jesus' commands. Peter's ministry after Jesus' ascension affirms Peter's eventual grasp of Jesus' imperatives as well as his imperatives through the power of the Holy Spirit within Peter evidenced within miracles at Peter's imperatives.

Mt 17: 17 And Jesus answered, "O faithless and twisted generation, how long am I to be with you? How long am I to bear with you? <u>Bring him here to me</u> φέρετέ μοι αὐτὸν ὧδε."
    Jesus commanded the faithless and twisted ones whom Jesus had been teaching, to bring the sick boy to him. Jesus publically criticized what seems to be his disciples or others to whom the man had brought his child. He identified them with, "Oh faithless and twisted generation" for their and inability to heal because of their lack of faith. He commanded that the boy be bought to him. He explained to them the reasons for their inability to heal. His imperative "bring" is key to this teaching. Beyond Jesus' frustration and castigation, he stressed that faithless and twisted people were unable to heal the sick. Jesus desired that they heal, but as a faithless and twisted generation healing was beyond them. Mk 9: 19; Lk 9: 41

Mt 17: 20 He said to them, "Because of your little faith. For truly, I say to you, if you have faith like a grain of mustard seed, you will say to this mountain, '<u>Move from here to there</u> μετάβα ἔνθεν ἐκεῖ,' and it will move, and nothing will be impossible for you."
    Before Jesus explained to his disciples why they were unsuccessful at healing the lunatic son, he commanded them to command an imperative. This teaching is central to Jesus use and his command for his followers to employ imperatives. As an example Jesus commanded them that they command a mountain to move. Jesus

then assured them that the mountain would move. His disciples had to learn Jesus' power within them that could move mountains. Jesus had commanded his disciples to heal by their speaking imperative commands. Mt: 21: 18 - 21

Mt 17: 27 However, not to give offense to them, go to the sea and <u>cast a hook</u> βάλε ἄγκιστρον and <u>take the first fish</u> πρῶτον ἰχθὺν ἆρον that comes up, and when you open its mouth you will find a shekel. Take that and <u>give it to them</u> λαβὼν δὸς αὐτοῖς for me and for yourself."

    Jesus ordered three imperative commands, cast, take, and give. The story of casting a hook, catching a fish and finding a shekel that is sufficiently valued to pay the tax is memorable. His three imperatives provided insight as to what the disciples were commanded. Jesus commanded them to cast out, not keep what has been given. They used the hook that God provided. After catching the fish, the coin must be removed and used to pay the tax. Even the disciples as fishers of men paid taxes out of a miraculous catch.

Mt 18: 8-9 And if your hand or your foot causes you to sin, <u>cut it off and throw it away</u> ἔκκοψον υτὸν καὶ βάλε ἀπὸ σοῦ. It is better for you to enter life crippled or lame than with two hands or two feet to be thrown into the eternal fire. And if your eye causes you to sin, <u>tear it out and throw it away</u> ἔξελε αὐτὸν καὶ βάλε ἀπὸ σοῦ. It is better for you to enter life with one eye than with two eyes to be thrown into the hell of fire.
    Mk 9: 43–47

Mt 18: 10 "<u>See that you do not despise one of these little ones</u> Ὁρᾶτε μὴ καταφρονήσητε ἑνὸς τῶν μικρῶν τούτων. For I tell you that in heaven their angels always see the face of my Father who is in heaven.

    Jesus commanded his disciples to beware of looking down on "little ones." "Little ones" may mean young in age or immature in faith. His word was not cautionary, but a command. Jesus commanded his disciples to have no contempt nor create stumbling blocks for those growing in faith or those whose faith is immature by age or lack of understanding. He referenced intercessory angels on their behalf which emphasized consequences for disobeying his imperative command not to despise the little ones. More edified believers are not to despise those who are less edified.

Mt 18: 15 If your brother sins against you, <u>go and tell him</u> ὕπαγε ἔλεγξον αὐτὸν his fault, between you and him alone; If he listens to you, you have gained your brother.

    Jesus commanded his disciples to take action when a brother sinned against brother. Disciples were commanded to initiate the first effort to go and privately explain the faults to the brother. The English word "tell" is weak in reflecting the Greek imperative which conveys more than merely telling. The Greek word carries a convicting, rebuking, or exposing to the brother his faults. If he went beyond hearing to listening and understanding what was brought to light, the relationship would be strengthened. If the brother would not listen a relational separation would be created until repentance occurred and reconciliation became possible. Regardless of the brother's culpability or response to the confrontation, Jesus commanded that his disciples make the first initiative to convict and bring resolution. Concession to the fault was a prerequisite for restoration.

Mt 18: 16 But if he does not listen, <u>take one or two others along with you</u> παράλαβε μετὰ σοῦ ἔτι ἕνα ἢ δύο that every charge may be established by the evidence of two or three witnesses.
>Jesus charged his disciples that if the brother did not listen, the next step was to partner with at least one or two others and again confront the brother. Jesus gave no alternative to this command. Because Jesus knew the consequences of sin among brothers, he demanded exposure, not as the end goal. Exposure was to lead to repentance and ultimately to reconciliation.

Mt 18: 17 If he refuses to listen to them, <u>tell it to the church</u> εἰπὲ τῇ ἐκκλησίᾳ; and if he refuses to listen even to the church, <u>let him be to you as a Gentile and a tax collector</u> ἔστω σοι ὥσπερ ὁ ἐθνικὸς καὶ ὁ τελώνης.
>Jesus commanded that if the brother refused to listen that the community must be informed. Responsibility was on the offender to ask the church for help. If refusal to ask the church for help continued Jesus commanded that the community must confront the unrepentant brother and treated as one outside a brotherly relationship. Continued effort to be in a relationship with someone who would not listen, not confess or repent was harmfully consequential to the community. Jesus demanded separation from those who refused to listen, something not common in today's faith communities.

Mt 18: 26-29 So the servant fell on his knees, imploring him, '<u>Have patience with me</u> μακροθύμησον ἐπ᾽ ἐμοί, and I will pay you everything.' And out of pity for him, the master of that servant released him and forgave him the debt. But when that same servant went out, he found one of his fellow servants who owed him a hundred denarii, and seizing him, he began to choke him, saying, '<u>Pay what you owe</u> ἀπόδος εἴ τι ὀφείλεις.' So his fellow servant fell down and pleaded with him, '<u>Have patience with me</u> μακροθύμησον ἐπ᾽ ἐμοί, and I will pay you.'
>Jesus, here simply requoted imperatives from within the narrative.

Mt 19: 6 So they are no longer two but one flesh. What therefore God has joined together, <u>let not man separate</u> ἄνθρωπος μὴ χωριζέτω."
>Mk 10: 9

Mt 19: 12 For there are eunuchs who have been so from birth, and there are eunuchs who have been made eunuchs by men, and there are eunuchs who have made themselves eunuchs for the sake of the kingdom of heaven. <u>Let the one who is able to receive this receive it</u> ὁ δυνάμενος χωρεῖν χωρείτω."
>Receive is a third person singular imperative. The English word "let" is appropriate. Jesus taught his disciples about divorce and singleness. He commanded those who chose singleness for the sake of the kingdom of heaven to understand without confusion. In context, married disciples presumed that single disciples faced unconquerable challenges. The text affirms that there were both married and single disciples confused about understanding singleness for the sake of the Kingdom.

Jesus' imperative verified that singleness for the sake of the kingdom of heaven was not within everyone's ability to understand. Those who understood their singleness for a Kingdom purpose were to be confident in their singleness. They were not to be concerned about what others thought because some were unable to comprehend singleness and discipleship.

Mt 19: 14 but Jesus said, "Let the little children come to me ἄφετε τὰ παιδία and do not hinder them, for to such belongs the kingdom of heaven."
Mk 10: 14; Lk 18: 16

Mt 19: 17 And he said to him, "Why do you ask me about what is good? There is only one who is good. If you would enter life, keep the commandments τήρησον τὰς ἐντολάς."

Jesus gave an imperative to the man to keep the commandments. Without knowing or keeping the law, there was no entrance into life. Knowing the commands preceded keeping them. The word Matthew recorded that Jesus said was "keep" in a singular form which personally addressed the man. Jesus did not assert here that salvation happens through commandment keeping. He also did not command or infer to disobey. Instead, he conveyed the goodness of God over the commandments without denying the commandments or obedience to them.

Some translations use "obey" (ὑπακούουσιν Mt 8: 27) rather than "keep" (τήρησον), but here the Greek word Matthew recorded that Jesus said was "keep" not "obey." He conveyed that without commandments, without rules, without laws without understanding the history of the consequences of obedience and disobedience the life which the man wanted was not possible. Of course, obedience is God's will, but obedience was not the issue. Without knowing or in the sense of not throwing out laws, entering the life the man sought was not possible. Chapter 18 "Keeping His Commands: John 14:15" details "obey" and "keep."

Mt 19: 19 Honor your father and mother τίμα τὸν πατέρα καὶ τὴν μητέρα and, you shall love your neighbor as yourself."

The strong imperative, "honor" stated by Jesus in this passage came from Ex 20: 12 and Dt 5: 16.[26] "You shall love" reads like an English command, but the literal Greek is future indicative. Acts of honoring and loving in their context were indications of authentic Kingdom workers. Honoring parents without loving neighbors or loving neighbors without honoring parents were polarizations. Honoring father and mother and loving neighbors are simultaneous commands.

The future, active, indicative, "you shall love" carries an imperatival force. If Jesus had spoken an imperative such as, "love your neighbor" rather than "you shall love your neighbor," Matthew would have recorded the imperative. Honoring father and mother was no less important than loving one's neighbor. Similarly, loving one's neighbor was no less important than honoring father and mother.

---

[26] Honor your father and your mother, that your days may be long in the land that the LORD your God is giving you. Ex 20: 12 Honor your father and your mother, as the LORD your God commanded you, that your days may be long, and that it may go well with you in the land that the LORD your God is giving you. Dt 5: 16

Mt 19: 21 Jesus said to him, "If you would be perfect, go, sell what you possess and give to the poor ὕπαγε πώλησόν σου τὰ ὑπάρχοντα καὶ δὸς [τοῖς] πτωχοῖς and you will have treasure in heaven; and come, follow me ἀκολούθει μοι."
    "Go," "sell," "give," and "follow" were four sequential Greek imperatives that Jesus said and the man heard. Those near Jesus also heard the imperative Jesus gave the man. Lk 18:22

Mt 20: 4 and to them he said, 'You go into the vineyard ὑπάγετε καὶ ὑμεῖς εἰς τὸν ἀμπελῶνα too, and whatever is right I will give you.'
    Jesus directed laborers in this parable to go into the vineyard. Here the imperative confirmed God's sovereignty that God would give what was right. Without trusting God, the laborer's work would not be fruitful.

Mt 20: 7 They said to him, 'Because no one has hired us.' He said to them, 'You go into the vineyard too ὑπάγετε καὶ ὑμεῖς εἰς τὸν ἀμπελῶνα.'
    Jesus again directed laborers to go into the vineyard.

Mt 20: 8 And when evening came, the owner of the vineyard said to his foreman, 'Call the laborers and pay them their wages κάλεσον τοὺς ἐργάτας καὶ ἀπόδος αὐτοῖς τὸν μισθὸν, beginning with the last, up to the first.'
    Here Jesus used two imperatives, "call "and "pay." There was no wasted time. Those who responded to the call were paid and those who were paid responded to the call. The foreman had no choice or argument. Jesus' use of this parable and the imperatives guaranteed that all the laborers were paid.

Mt 20: 14 Take what belongs to you and go ἆρον τὸ σὸν καὶ ὕπαγε. I choose to give to this last worker as I give to you.
    Jesus commanded laborers both to "take" and "go." Kingdom workers did not remain in the field and he did not ask them to return. There was a time to receive the wage, leave the field, not complain about the work or the wage, and enjoy the fruits of spent labor.

Mt 21: 2 saying to them, "Go into the village in front of you πορεύεσθε εἰς τὴν κώμην τὴν κατέναντι ὑμῶ, and immediately you will find a donkey tied, and a colt with her. Untie them and bring them to me ἀγάγετέ μοι.
    Mk 11: 2-3; Lk 19: 30

Mt 21: 18–21 In the morning, as he was returning to the city, he became hungry. And seeing a fig tree by the wayside, he went to it and found nothing on it but only leaves. And he said to it, "May no fruit ever come from you again!" And the fig tree withered at once. When the disciples saw it, they marveled, saying, "How did the fig tree wither at once?" And Jesus answered them, "Truly, I say to you, if you have faith and do not doubt, you will not only do what has been done to the fig tree but even if you say to this mountain, 'Be taken up and be thrown into the sea,' ἄρθητι καὶ βλήθητι εἰς τὴν θάλασσαν, it will happen.
    Jesus' two imperatives here referred to Mt 17:20. Jesus affirmed that speaking commands moved mountains. He did not say, "Get a shovel and begin shoveling

the mountain into the sea." He conveyed that the spoken imperative held power. Jesus was in the process of building up his disciples. He was asserting the power available to them. He commanded them to understand the power of faith and spoken imperatives.

In v19 "May no fruit come to you again" Jesus spoke as an aorist subjunctive with a negative. Jesus use of aorist subjunctives with the negative defined what was and was not with an imperatival force. Jesus' imperative affirmed the impossibility for the tree to bear fruit. The disciples having recalled that Jesus had spoken to the tree, were again reminded of the power of his spoken imperative commands.

Mt 21: 28 "What do you think? A man had two sons. And he went to the first and said, 'Son, go and work in the vineyard today ὕπαγε σήμερον ἐργάζου ἐν τῷ ἀμπελῶνι.'
> Jesus often linked two imperatives within a parable. "Go and work" were successive imperatives. "Go" assured that something was left behind. "Work" assured that leisure was left behind. The English word, "work" derived from the ἐργάζου which is an imperative form that is deponent meaning while the word form in passive, the word is active in meaning. In other words, the work was to be active, meaning to be doing something by way of work.

Mt 21: 33 Hear another parable, Αλλην παραβολὴν ἀκούσατε.
> Jesus in this passage commanded his disciples to hear another parable. At the point when the disciples were thinking Jesus was finished speaking, he commanded them with an imperative to "Hear another parable." as he continued to teach. They were wise to listen because Jesus had commanded them to persevere in learning.

Mt 22: 4 Again he sent other servants, saying, 'Tell those who are invited εἴπατε τοῖς κεκλημένοις, See, I have prepared my dinner, my oxen and my fat calves have been slaughtered, and everything is ready. Come to the wedding feast δεῦτε εἰς τοὺς γάμους.'
> Jesus quoted two imperatives within this parable. The servants were to tell about the preparations and exhort attendance to the wedding.

Mt 22: 9 Go therefore to the main roads πορεύεσθε οὖν ἐπὶ τὰς διεξόδους τῶν ὁδῶν and invite to the wedding feast as many as you find ὅσους ἐὰν εὕρητε καλέσατε εἰς τοὺς γάμους.'
> Jesus had commanded servants to go to a specific location, the main roads, and invite to a particular place for a specific reason. His imperatives lefts no doubt as to where they would go, what they would say, and what they would do. His imperative did not guarantee success in their eyes. They were commanded to make the invitation, not guarantee attendance.

Mt 22: 13 Then the king said to the attendants, 'Bind him hand and foot and <u>cast him into the outer darkness</u> ἐκβάλετε αὐτὸν εἰς τὸ σκότος τὸ ἐξώτερον. In that place there will be weeping and gnashing of teeth.'
>Jesus quoted the King's commands. The King's words indicated a separation between those inside and those outside the Kingdom. Description of the outer darkness was secondary to the imperative command to cast him out.

Mt 22: 19 - 21 <u>Show me the coin for the tax</u> ἐπιδείξατέ μοι τὸ νόμισμα τοῦ κήνσου." And they brought him a denarius. And Jesus said to them, "Whose likeness and inscription is this?" They said, "Caesar's." Then he said to them, "<u>Therefore render to Caesar the things that are Caesar's, and to God the things that are God's</u> ἀπόδοτε οὖν τὰ Καίσαρος Καίσαρι καὶ τὰ τοῦ θεοῦ τῷ θεω."
    Mk 12: 15; Lk 20: 24

Mt 22: 44 "'The Lord said to my Lord, <u>Sit at my right hand</u> κάθου ἐκ δεξιῶν μου, until I put your enemies under your feet'?
    Jesus quoted David's imperative from Psalm 110:1[27]

Mt 23: 3 so <u>practice and observe whatever they tell you</u> πάντα οὖν ὅσα ἐὰν εἴπωσιν ὑμῖν οιήσατε καὶ τηρεῖτε, <u>but not what they do</u> κατὰ δὲ τὰ ἔργα αὐτῶν μὴ ποιεῖτε. For they preach, but do not practice.
>Jesus commanded to practice and observe what the Scribes and Pharisees said. He then commanded his disciples not to do what the Scribes and Pharisees did. He demanded through imperatives that there were things to do, things to be watched, and things not to do particularly from the Scribes and Pharisees.

Mt 23: 26 You blind Pharisee! <u>First clean the inside of the cup</u> and the plate καθάρισον πρῶτον τὸ ἐντὸς τοῦ ποτηρίου, that the outside also may be clean.
>Jesus used an imperative through symbolism and commanded the blind Pharisees. His command was an affront to the Pharisees' self-ignorance as spiritual leaders. The Pharisees were less offended by being called 'blind' compared to being commanded to clean the inside of the cup. An accusation was one thing, a command by Jesus to them was more offensive and derogatory.

Mt 23: 39–32 "Woe to you, scribes and Pharisees, hypocrites! For you build the tombs of the prophets and decorate the monuments of the righteous, saying, 'If we had lived in the days of our fathers, we would not have taken part with them in shedding the blood of the prophets.' Thus you witness against yourselves that you are sons of those who murdered the prophets. <u>Fill up, then, the measure of your fathers</u> πληρώσατε τὸ μέτρον τῶν πατέρων ὑμῶν.
>Jesus mockingly commanded the Pharisees to fill the measure of their fathers. He exposed their genealogical worship. They had done just as their fathers before them. These Scribes and Pharisees believed what they had always believed from prior generations of murdering the prophets. Jesus commanded them to continue proving their heresy. His imperative revealed their past, present, and future mindset from which they were loath to turn.

---

[27] *A Psalm of David.* The LORD says to my Lord: "Sit at my right hand, until I make your enemies your footstool." Ps 110: 1

Mt 24: 3-4 As he sat on the Mount of Olives, the disciples came to him privately, saying, "Tell us, when will these things be, and what will be the sign of your coming and of the close of the age?" And Jesus answered them, "<u>See that no one leads you astray</u> βλέπετε μή τις ὑμᾶς πλανήσῃ.

>Here Jesus had commanded his disciples to be on guard so that they would not be misled. The English command rendered from the Greek imperative in the ESV is "see that." The KJV is "take heed." The NRS is "beware." In the context of Jesus day the imperative warning conveyed to them that Jesus placed a higher priority on deception than persecution.

>None of the Gospel writers recorded that Jesus warned against persecution. Rather, he conveyed that his disciples should expect persecution. However, falling into deception from false teachers was worse for them than any persecution they might experience.

>As his disciples questioned Jesus about the end of the age Jesus commanded them as a group (second person plural) to beware that no one leads them astray. Being led astray would do more harm to them than suffering persecution. In other words, being led astray was more consequential, injurious, and destructive to the disciples than oppression by those who would disagree with them or martyr them.

>In short, accurate doctrine has priority over persecution. Big difference.

Mt 24: 6 And you will hear of wars and rumors of wars. <u>See to it that you are not alarmed</u> ὁρᾶτε μὴ θροεῖσθε, for this must take place, but the end is not yet.

>Here Jesus commanded his disciples to recognize not to be alarmed. First knowing, "see to it" and then recognizing what would take place, there was no cause for alarm. Because the disciples would know and recognize what would take place, they would not have cause for alarm.

Mt 24: 15 "So when you see the abomination of desolation spoken of by the prophet Daniel, standing in the holy place (<u>let the reader understand</u>, ὁ ἀναγινώσκων νοείτω),

>Here Jesus referred to words spoken by Daniel.[28] Jesus commanded the reader to let him observe and understand. Through a reading of the Word, Kingdom workers were to observe what was to come. This is a third person singular imperative. Use of the English word let" is appropriate but weakens the Greek imperative intent.

---

[28] And he shall make a strong covenant with many for one week, and for half of the week he shall put an end to sacrifice and offering. And on the wing of abominations shall come one who makes desolate, until the decreed end is poured out on the desolator. Dn 9: 27

Forces from him shall appear and profane the temple and fortress, and shall take away the regular burnt offering. And they shall set up the abomination that makes desolate. Dn 11: 31

And from the time that the regular burnt offering is taken away and the abomination that makes desolate is set up, there shall be 1,290 days. Dn 12: 11

Mt 24: 15-18 "So when you see the abomination of desolation spoken of by the prophet Daniel, standing in the holy place (<u>let the reader understand</u> ὁ ἀναγινώσκων νοείτω), then let those who are in Judea <u>flee to the mountains</u> φευγέτωσαν εἰς τὰ ὄρη. Let the one who is on the housetop <u>not go down to take what is in his house</u> μὴ καταβάτω ἆραι τὰ ἐκ τῆς οἰκίας αὐτου, and let the one who is in the field <u>not turn back to take his cloak</u> μὴ ἐπιστρεψάτω ὀπίσω ἆραι τὰ ἱμάτια αὐτου.

    Jesus four imperatives emphasized fleeing without hesitation and without turning back. While these for successive imperatives may appear overstated and excessive, they would be followed. He knew that even after they would see the abomination of desolation spoken by Daniel, they would not understand the urgency. So, he commanded them. Flee and do not turn back for anything.

Mt 24: 20 <u>Pray that your flight may not be in winter or on a Sabbath</u> προσεύχεσθε δὲ ἵνα μὴ γένηται ἡ φυγὴ ὑμῶν χειμῶνος μηδὲ σαββάτῳ.

    Jesus commanded them to pray that their fleeing would not be in winter or on the Sabbath. He did not command them to pray to stop the impending desolation (v15). He emphasized that the dreadfulness would be sufficiently painful in itself. His command to pray asserted that they were unable to stop the end and that they would not know when it would arrive.

Mt 24: 32-33 "From the fig tree <u>learn its lesson</u> μάθετε τὴν παραβολήν: as soon as its branch becomes tender and puts out its leaves, you know that summer is near. So also, when you see all these things, <u>you know that he is near, at the very gates</u> γινώσκετε ὅτι ἐγγύς ἐστιν ἐπὶ θύραις.

    Jesus commanded they learn a lesson from the fig tree. His imperative prevented the disciples from taking this lesson lightly. Jesus commanded to know that the Son of Man would be near when they saw those things. He demanded they have no doubt when they saw what was to come.

Mt 24: 42-44 Therefore, <u>stay awake</u> γρηγορεῖτε οὖν, for you do not know on what day your Lord is coming. But <u>know this</u> ἐκεῖνο δὲ γινώσκετε, that if the master of the house had known in what part of the night the thief was coming, he would have stayed awake and would not have let his house be broken into. <u>Therefore you also must be ready</u> διὰ τοῦτο καὶ ὑμεῖς γίνεσθε ἕτοιμοι, for the Son of Man is coming at an hour you do not expect.

    Jesus three imperatives "stay awake," "know," and "be ready" demanded their expectation without anticipation. That is, they were to be ready without forecasting or predicting or prophesying. Jesus demanded that they know the story about the master in waiting without knowing the details of his arrival.

Mt 25: 6-13 But at midnight there was a cry, 'Here is the bridegroom! <u>Come out to meet him</u> ἐξέρχεσθε εἰς ἀπάντησιν [αὐτοῦ].' Then all those virgins rose and trimmed their lamps. And the foolish said to the wise, '<u>Give us some of your oil</u> ἡμῖν ἐκ τοῦ ἐλαίου ὑμῶν, for our lamps are going out.' But the wise answered, saying, 'Since there will not be enough for us and for you, <u>go rather to the dealers</u> πορεύεσθε μᾶλλον πρὸς τοὺς πωλοῦντας and <u>buy for yourselves</u> ἀγοράσατε ἑαυταῖς.' And while they were going to buy, the bridegroom came, and those who were ready went in with him to the marriage feast, and the door was shut. Afterward the other virgins came also, saying, 'Lord, lord, <u>open to us</u>.' But he answered, 'Truly, I say to you, I do not know you.' <u>Watch therefore</u> γρηγορεῖτε οὖν, for you know neither the day nor the hour.

Jesus told his disciples what to expect. The foolish would command the wise to give oil to the foolish. But Jesus made clear that the wise were not to follow the command from the foolish. Rather, Jesus commanded the wise to command the foolish to go buy oil themselves.

Jesus' imperatives were strategic. He acknowledged that the Lord would be commanded by those who were unprepared to open the door to those who were foolish. Jesus positively responded to imperatives given to him by the faithful. Yet, imperative commands from the foolish were disregarded. Precisely because the hour and day were not known, Jesus commanded his disciples to watch.

Mt 25: 1-13, See Chapter 16 "Imperatives to the Christ"

Mt 25: 21-30 His master said to him, 'Well done, good and faithful servant. You have been faithful over a little; I will set you over much. Enter into the joy of your master εἴσελθε εἰς τὴν χαρὰν τοῦ κυρίου σου.' And he also who had the two talents came forward, saying, 'Master, you delivered to me two talents; here I have made two talents more.' His master said to him, 'Well done, good and faithful servant. You have been faithful over a little; I will set you over much. Enter into the joy of your master εἴσελθε εἰς τὴν χαρὰν τοῦ κυρίου σου.' He also who had received the one talent came forward, saying, 'Master, I knew you to be a hard man, reaping where you did not sow, and gathering where you scattered no seed, so I was afraid, and I went and hid your talent in the ground. Here you have what is yours.' But his master answered him, 'You wicked and slothful servant! You knew that I reap where I have not sown and gather where I scattered no seed? Then you ought to have invested my money with the bankers, and at my coming I should have received what was my own with interest. So take the talent from him ἄρατε οὖν ἀπ αὐτοῦ τὸ τάλαντον and give it to him who has the ten talents καὶ δότε τῷ ἔχοντι τὰ δέκα τάλαντα. For to everyone who has will more be given, and he will have an abundance. But from the one who has not, even what he has will be taken away. And cast the worthless servant into the outer darkness καὶ τὸν ἀχρεῖον δοῦλον ἐκβάλετε εἰς τὸ σκότος. In that place there will be weeping and gnashing of teeth.'

> Jesus used the same Greek imperative "enter into the joy of your master" for both faithful investors. Their recompense was the joy and protection of the master. On the other hand, Jesus' next two imperatives "take" from and "give" to, left no room for negotiation. Jesus visually described an emotional and painful place where he commanded the unfruitful servant be thrown.

Mt 25: 34 Then the King will say to those on his right, 'Come, you who are blessed by my Father, inherit the kingdom prepared for you κληρονομήσατε τὴν ἡτοιμασμένην ὑμῖν βασιλείαν from the foundation of the world.

> Jesus spoke a plural imperative to those who were blessed that they would receive what had been prepared for them. The narrative conveyed an image of saved souls aghast, standing before a door, waiting to enter, too amazed at what was before them to enter. So the King joyfully commanded them, "inherit" the kingdom prepared for you.

Mt 25: 40-41 And the King will answer them, 'Truly, I say to you, as you did it to one of the least of these my brothers, you did it to me.' "Then he will say to those on his left, '<u>Depart from me, you cursed into the eternal fire</u> πορεύεσθε ἀπ᾽ ἐμοῦ [οἱ] κατηραμένοι εἰς τὸ πῦρ τὸ αἰώνιον, prepared for the devil and his angels.

    Jesus commanded the destiny of the cursed into the fire which is eternal.

Mt 26: 18 He said, "<u>Go into the city</u> ὑπάγετε εἰς τὴν πόλιν to a certain man and <u>say to him</u> καὶ εἴπατε αὐτῷ, 'The Teacher says, My time is at hand. I will keep the Passover at your house with my disciples.'"

    Jesus imperatives "go" and "say" left no doubt over what Jesus wanted to be done. After having followed Jesus for three years, Matthew did not record that the disciples argued or debated when Jesus told them what to do without them knowing why. Matthew did not record that the disciples asked for clarification. Jesus provided them with a ready response. They learned the power of Jesus' commands.

Mt 26: 26-27 Now as they were eating, Jesus took bread, and after blessing it broke it and gave it to the disciples, and said, "<u>Take</u> λάβετε, <u>eat</u> φάγετε, this is my body." And he took a cup, and when he had given thanks he gave it to them, saying, "<u>Drink of it, all of you</u> πίετε ἐξ αὐτοῦ πάντες,

    Jesus did not include with his two imperative, how to "take" or "eat." His commands were simple and understandable. "Drink of it, all of you" indicated the cup was shared by all present. He did not invite. He commanded them to eat and drink. Some weak English translations are vague conveying that they were to drink all of what was in the cup rather than that they were all to drink of the cup. The imperative is second person plural meaning that they were all to drink of the cup.

Mt 26: 36-46 Then Jesus went with them to a place called Gethsemane, and he said to his disciples, "<u>Sit here, while I go over there and pray</u> καθίσατε αὐτοῦ ἕως [οὗ] ἀπελθὼν ἐκεῖ προσεύξωμαι." And taking with him Peter and the two sons of Zebedee, he began to be sorrowful and troubled. Then he said to them, "My soul is very sorrowful, even to death; <u>remain here, and watch with me</u> μείνατε ὧδε καὶ γρηγορεῖτε μετ᾽ ἐμοῦ." And going a little farther he fell on his face and prayed, saying, "My Father, if it be possible, <u>let this cup pass from me</u> παρελθάτω ἀπ᾽ ἐμοῦ τὸ ποτήριον τοῦτο; nevertheless, not as I will, but as you will." And he came to the disciples and found them sleeping. And he said to Peter, "So, could you not watch with me one hour? <u>Watch and pray that you may not enter into temptation</u> γρηγορεῖτε καὶ προσεύχεσθε, ἵνα μὴ εἰσέλθητε εἰς πειρασμόν. The spirit indeed is willing, but the flesh is weak." Again, for the second time, he went away and prayed, "My Father, if this cannot pass unless I drink it, <u>your will be done</u> γενηθήτω τὸ θέλημά σου." And again he came and found them sleeping, for their eyes were heavy. So, leaving them again, he went away and prayed for the third time, saying the same words again. Then he came to the disciples and said to them, "Sleep and take your rest later on. See, the hour is at hand, and the Son of Man is betrayed into the hands of sinners. <u>Rise, let us be going</u> ἐγείρεσθε ἄγωμεν; see, my betrayer is at hand."

    Matthew's Gethsemane account somewhat differs from Mark's. Matthew did not cite Jesus' imperative to the father "remove the cup" whereas Mark recorded Jesus' imperative to the father. Note: in English "Sleep and take your rest later on." reads and sounds to the English ear like commands. However, "sleep" and "take" are Greek indicatives, not imperatives. Mk 14: 32-42

Mt 26: 52 Then Jesus said to him, "Put back your sword into its place ἀπόστρεψον τὴν μάχαιράν σου εἰς τὸν τόπον αὐτῆς. For all who take the sword will perish by the sword.

    Peter, the Temple guards, and Jesus' disciples all heard Jesus' imperative to Peter to sheath his sword. Although the text did not indicate if Peter shielded his sword, by now Peter's time with Jesus gave him no argument. Matthew did not record any further action by Peter. Given Peter's experience having heard many imperatives from Jesus, Matthew had no reason to record that Peter sheathed his sword.

Mt 28: 10-11 Then Jesus said to them, "Do not fear; go and tell my brothers to go to Galilee ὑπάγετε ἀπαγγείλατε τοῖς ἀδελφοῖς μου ἵνα ἀπέλθωσιν εἰς τὴν Γαλιλαίαν, and there they will see me." While they were going, behold, some of the guard went into the city and told the chief priests all that had taken place.

    Jesus gave three successive imperatives to Mary Magdalene and the other Mary. They were commanded by Jesus, do not fear, go, and tell his disciples to go to Galilee. Only after his commands did he affirm that his disciples would see him. They did what Jesus had commanded. They were not afraid. They went and told the Disciples to go to Galilee.

    Matthew's words in v11 in the ESV, "While they were going" are rendered from the single Greek word, Πορευομένων a present, middle or passive, deponent, genitive feminine plural participle. The translation, "And while they are going on" correctly conveys the participle and other Greek attributes.

Mt 28: 18-20 And Jesus came and said to them, "All authority in heaven and on earth has been given to me. Go therefore and make disciples of all nations μαθητεύσατε πάντα τὰ ἔθνη, baptizing them in the name of the Father and of the Son and of the Holy Spirit, teaching them to observe (τηρεῖν - keep, watch over, guard) all that I have commanded you. And behold, I am with you always, to the end of the age."

    These passages are often studied by students of Greek for translation anomalies. Nearly every seminary or academic Koine Greek 101 student learns that the English "go" found in Mt 28: 19 has been rendered from πορευθέντες an aorist, passive, deponent, nominative, masculine, plural, participle.

In a contemporary context, the English word "go" has historically been accepted as an appropriate translation. The meaning of the word "go" conveys a command.

Some from the pulpit know that "go" while an accepted translation can be problematic regarding doctrine. Some pastors to convey the participle in place of "go" use "going" or "while going" or "while you are going" in sermons which is an effort to convey the actual Greek participle to an English participle. In other words, the use of English "ing" to convey the Greek participle is acceptable.

While conveying the participle attribute is correct, the aorist, passive deponent attributes within the word πορευθέντες must also be rendered for accuracy. Few English translations include Greek grammar attributes beyond the participle except for Young's Literal Translation (YLT).

The YLT of this verse, "having gone then" is most appropriate because "having gone then" reflects the Greek aorist passive deponent participle which is what Jesus spoke and Matthew recorded. Matthew had also recorded that Jesus had spoken many imperatives meaning "go" before Mt 28: 19.

Jesus' use of the English command "go" from a Greek imperative is also found in John 8: 1 - 11 specifically v11. Here Jesus spoke two imperatives, "go" and "sin no more." Specifically, the Greek is "go from" derived from the Greek words, πορεύου ἀπὸ. Many English translations use only the English word "go." Some use "go your way" (NAS), "go now" (NIV) or "be going on" (YLT). The point is that here in the book of John was recorded that Jesus spoke a clear imperative πορεύου which is not a participle turned into an English command in many translations.

In Matthew, there are 18 Greek imperatives and 3 Greek participles that have been translated to "go" in English. However, Mt 28: 19 is not one of them. Below are both Jesus' imperatives and participles in the ESV translated as "go" in Matthew:

| Verse | ESV | Imperative | Number with Imperative |
|---|---|---|---|
| Mt 4: 10 | be gone | ὕπαγε | (S) Satan |
| Mt 5: 41 | go | ὕπαγε | (S) with him two (miles) |
| Mt 6: 6 | go | εἴσελθε | (S) into your room |
| Mt 8: 4 | go | ὕπαγε | (S) show yourself to the priest |
| Mt 8: 13 | go | ὕπαγε | (S) let it be done for you |
| Mt 9: 6 | go | ὕπαγε | (S) into your house |
| Mt 11: 4 | go | ἀπαγγείλατε | (P) and tell John what you hear and see |
| Mt 18: 15 | go | ὕπαγε | (S) and tell him his fault |
| Mt 19: 21 | go | ὕπαγε | (S) sell what you possess |
| Mt 20: 4 | go | ὑπάγετε | (P) into the vineyard too |
| Mt 20: 7 | go | ὑπάγετε | (P) into the vineyard too |
| Mt 20: 14 | go | ὕπαγε | (S) take what belongs to you and go |
| Mt 21: 2 | go | πορεύεσθε | (P) into the village |
| Mt 21: 28 | go | ὕπαγε | (S) and work in the vineyard today |
| Mt 22: 9 | go | πορεύεσθε | (P) therefore to the main road |
| Mt 25: 9 | go | πορεύεσθε | (P) rather to the dealers and buy |
| Mt 26: 18 | go | ὑπάγετε | (P) into the city to a certain man |
| Mt 28: 10 | go | ὑπάγετε | (P) and tell my brothers to go to Galilee |
|  |  | Participle (aorist passive) |  |
| Mt 9: 13 | go | πορευθέντες | (P) and learn what this means |
| Mt 17: 27 | go | πορευθεὶς | (P) to the sea and cast a hook |
| Mt 28: 19 | go | πορευθέντες | (P) therefore and make disciples |

Clearly, Jesus knew how to speak and Matthew knew how to write both the Greek imperative "go" and the Greek aorist passive participle "having gone." To loosely translate Jesus' words in Mt 28: 19 can be problematic.

When Jesus' imperative is rendered as an English command "go" rather than the actual Greek aorist deponent participle "having gone," those hearing the message as a command to go, often understand that disciples commissioned as missionaries who have left their homeland have the responsibility to "make disciples." That is not what Jesus said, meant, or intended by those who heard his words then or those who read his words now. Wherever Christians find themselves is where they are to disciple nations

In v18 "all authority in heaven and on earth" has been given to Jesus. Jesus has authority and sovereignty over his disciples and sends them. His use of the aorist deponent participle rightly translated as Matthew recorded, "having gone then" aligns with his authority.

In addition to the participle element, the Greek passive, aorist, and deponent attributes also contribute to meaning. However, many pastors or translators only focus on the participle adding letters "ing" somewhere in the translation of Matthew's written word πορευθέντες. Adding the "ing" to produce an English participle produce words or phrases like "going" or "while going" which are close and acceptable, but not entirely on target with Matthew's Greek or Jesus' words.

Since Jesus has been given all authority, he does the sending. First-century hearers or readers of Matthew's text would have understood that Jesus' authority would direct everything that followed. In contemporary meaning, today's believer, whether missionary, evangelist, preacher, pastor, teacher, or prophet should understand that those Jesus leads will be placed where Jesus wants his disciples. Since Jesus has been given all authority, does he need to command his disciples to go someplace raises an interesting study.

Further, since Jesus has all authority, he will accomplish sending his disciples. Jesus does not need to "command" sending or going because he has all authority. He has placed his people where he wants them. The most important imperative within the commission is not "going" or "go" but the imperative "disciple nations." What Jesus imperatively commanded was that they "disciple nations" wherever Jesus had placed them through his authority. This idea would have been easily understood in their context but is not so easy to grasp through English in today's context. Contextual hermeneutics and contemporary hermeneutics require study.

The most persuasive argument for speculation in the English word "go" comes from considering what the disciples heard.

In context, the English word "go" is applicable and not too problematic. However, the aorist passive participle verb "having gone then" from the YLT indicates that God has already done the sending given from v18 that "all authority in heaven and on earth" has been given to him. A first-century reader of Matthew's text would have understood that wherever disciples (plural) find themselves was where they were to disciple nations. They would not have interpreted an imperative command to go anywhere. They would have understood that wherever Jesus would lead them was where they were to "disciple nations" compared to "make disciples."

Jesus chose the time and place for his disciples for his purpose. The consequence of loosely translating to an English "go" that sounds like an English command weakens the focus on the only imperative in v19, "disciple all the nations." The Greek imperative "disciple all the nations" is not equivalent the English rendering "make disciples." Baptizing, teaching, and going are participles, not imperatives.

The only imperative Matthew recorded in this verse was μαθητεύσατε often rendered to English as "make disciples" conveying the idea to English hearers that the goal or the command is to "make disciples." While that logic is plausible, Jesus did not say "make disciples." He said and they heard, "disciple all the nations."

This difference in word selection may appear insignificant to English readers. Those who heard Jesus' Greek spoken to them, those who read Matthews Greek text or those who heard Matthew's text read to them, however, did not hear "make disciples." They heard "disciple all the nations."

The English word "make" correctly rendered from the Greek root word ποιέω. This verb, generically translated as "to do," has a wide range of meanings such as "to make, cause to happen, accomplish."[29] Matthew, however, did not use this Greek word in v19 as an imperative "make." Matthew recorded that Jesus said, μαθητεύσατε πάντα τὰ ἔθνη which the KJV rendered "teach all the nations" and the YLT rendered "disciple all the nations" more accurately reflects each of the Greek aorist, active, plural imperative attributes. The YLT "disciples all the nations" is preferred over the KJV because the Greek root word for teach is "διδάσκω" and is found in v19. "Baptizing" and "teaching" are participles in v20.

The English word "Go" sounds to the English ear a command. YLT "Having gone, then" is preferred.

"Make disciples" has historically been translated to sound to the English ear and convey to the English mind an English command. To grasp what the disciples heard however, the YLT "disciple all the nations" is preferred.

Additional insight has been provided on Mt 28: 18–20 because the Greek imperative they heard or read is distinct in the Greek but sometimes indistinct in English translations. Remembering we are focused on the Greek, the imperatives are our focus.

Beyond merely the imperative which is the focus of this book, the sovereignty of Jesus having been given all authority in heaven and on earth are often overshadowed by the English word that sounds like a command, "go" in English

---

[29] Mounce, William D., *Mounce's Complete Expository Dictionary of Old & New Testament Words*, 432.

Bibles. While "go" is an acceptable translation, there is wisdom in going deeper to understand Jesus' words to them, what they heard, and what Matthew wrote. Further, the disciples were to teach the nations to guard or keep all that Jesus had commanded. See Chapter 18 "Keeping His Commands" for insight on keep or guard and obey from John 14: 15.

The issue involves first the contemporary view to evangelize making people Christians and secondly making them disciples before addressing the needs of the nation. Before grabbing on to that contemporary view, we must consider what they heard and read in their context. This process of evangelization then discipleship is a typical contemporary view and methodology. However, in a more in-depth view, our contemporary process may be lacking. Considering a more literal translation from Greek to English, the YLT includes the Greek attributes of each word:

> Having gone then, disciple all the nations (baptizing them -- to the name of the Father, and of the Son, and of the Holy Spirit and teaching them to observe all, whatever I did command you,) and lo, I am with you all the days -- till the full end of the age. YLT

> Go therefore and make disciples of all nations, baptizing them in the name of the Father and of the Son and of the Holy Spirit, teaching them to observe all that I have commanded you. And behold, I am with you always, to the end of the age. ESV

Moral oversight related to every previous command from Jesus would have been in the minds of Jesus' disciples who had heard him speak as well as those who had read or heard Matthew's words read to them beyond Jesus' ascension. The disciples were aware of the wickedness of Rome, the immorality of surrounding nations, and the corruption of Temple Judaism given the crucifixion of Jesus. Jesus' Greek imperative, "disciple all the nations" in the minds of his disciples was not solely about making disciples by way of evangelism and discipleship. His imperative, "disciple all the nations" carried his authority and Kingdom ethic to the ethnos or nations.

The fullness of Greek attributes and word meaning are within the YLT. To restate, there is nothing wrong with English translations which intend to assist today's contemporary readers. However, as held throughout this book, our goal is to understand what they heard and read in their context, not ours. Within this chapter can be found all of Jesus' Greek imperative mood forms which Matthew recorded. We must first understand in their terms, not ours.

This book focuses on Jesus' spoken Greek imperatives recorded by the Gospel writers. What Jesus said, what they heard, and what Matthew wrote in Greek of their day has precedence.

And as he came out of the temple, one of his disciples said to him, "Look, Teacher, what wonderful stones and what wonderful buildings!" And Jesus said to him, "Do you see these great buildings? There will not be left here one stone upon another that will not be thrown down." And as he sat on the Mount of Olives opposite the temple, Peter and James and John and Andrew asked him privately, "Tell us, when will these things be, and what will be the sign when all these things are about to be accomplished?" And Jesus began to say to them, "See that no one leads you astray.

Mk 13: 1-5

# 10 Mark's Record of the Imperatives of Jesus

And as he came out of the temple, one of his disciples said to him, "Look, Teacher, what wonderful stones and what wonderful buildings!" And Jesus said to him, "Do you see these great buildings? There will not be left here one stone upon another that will not be thrown down." And as he sat on the Mount of Olives opposite the temple, Peter and James and John and Andrew asked him privately, "Tell us, when will these things be, and what will be the sign when all these things are about to be accomplished?" And Jesus began to say to them, "See that no one leads you astray. Mk 13: 1-5

## Mark

Mark, is sometimes mistakenly presumed to have been one of the original twelve disciples. Perhaps surprising to some, neither Mark nor Luke were disciples of Jesus. Conceivably because Mark was not one of the twelve he included conversations between Jesus and his disciples which included Greek imperatives or equivalent English commands from Jesus. Because Mark's gospel is about both Jesus and his disciples the words within Mark's record provide insight into Jesus' relationship with his Disciples then and followers now. George Ladd affirmed the breadth of Mark's Gospel,

> Mark's gospel is not the story of Jesus alone, but of Jesus and his disciples.[1]

Agreeing with Ladd, the imperatives that Jesus spoke and Mark recorded hold significant insight to those identifying themselves as Christians today. Mark developed much of his gospel through his relationship with Peter. Regarding Mark's accuracy and credibility, Eusebius quoted Papias who affirmed Mark's relationship with Peter and confidence in Mark's writing:

> And John the Presbyter also said this, Mark being the interpreter of Peter whatever he recorded he wrote with great accuracy." Regarding Mark's reliability, Eusebius further quoted Papias, "wherefore Mark has not erred in anything by writing something as he has recorded them; for he was carefully attentive to one thing, not to pass by anything that he heard, or to state anything falsely, in these accounts. Such was the account of Papias respecting Mark.[2]

It is unlikely Peter would have permitted Mark to inaccurately record Peter's words or the words Jesus had spoken to Peter. The relationship between Mark and Peter means that Mark likely consulted Peter especially regarding the details of any event where Mark was not present. Peter may not have been Mark's only resource. The other disciples may have provided Mark details as well that verified Peter's words or vice versa. In any event. Mark and Peter shared a relationship that brought Mark's Gospel into being.

---

[1] Ladd, George Eldon, *A Theology of the New Testament*, 233.
[2] Eusebius, *Ecclesiastical History*, Translated by C. F. Cruse, 105 – 106.

# Reliability

Having recorded Jesus' imperatives to his disciples, Mark's attention to detail is revealing. Had Mark been haphazard with words and meaning Peter would have corrected Mark's errors. Mark's notes and likely his journaling while with Jesus and the disciples is key. Mark was not simply a note taker or journalist. Mark's journaling and notes he likely recorded while with Jesus served him well in writing his gospel. Each of the gospels portrays a chronology of Jesus' life. Matthew, Mark, and John walked with Jesus. While none of the gospel writers recorded that notes or journaling occurred within their gospels, Matthew and John as disciples likely recorded Jesus' words as a rabbi, either during or after he taught. Mark as a follower likely recorded and journaled. Similarities of the synoptic gospels, (Matthew, Mark, and Luke) indicate that note-taking and journaling occurred. It is highly unlikely that Matthew, Mark, or John began writing from scratch about their experiences long after Jesus' ascension. Eusebius' words on *The Writings of Papias* affirmed Mark as an interpreter for Peter:

> And John the Presbyter also said this, Mark being the interpreter of Peter whatsoever he recorded he wrote with great accuracy but not however, in the order in which it was spoken or done by our Lord, for he neither heard nor followed our Lord, but as before said, he was in company with Peter, who gave him such instruction as was necessary, but not to give a history of our Lord's discourses: wherefore Mark has not erred in anything, by writing some things as he has recorded them; for he was carefully attentive to one thing, not to pass by anything that he heard, or to state anything falsely in these accounts. Such was the account of Papias, respecting Mark.[3]

Litfin commenting on Papias via Eusebius writes:

> The prose here [in Eusebius] is complex, in English as well as in the original Greek. Let us analyze what is being said. First, we see that Mark is called Peter's "interpreter." The Greek word *hermeneutics* typically meant a person who served as a mediator between foreign languages. In other words, Mark was a translator.[4]

Given the limitations of Peter's Greek (See Chapter 4, 'Idiot" in "Koine Greek for English Speaking Christians" and Ac 4: 13) and that Aramaic was likely Peter's most comfortable language, Litfin's insights are of value:

> The apostle Peter was originally a fisherman of modest education whose native tongue was Aramaic. Scholars debate whether he spoke any Greek. Probably he would have picked up a little of the language in his homeland of Galilee, but even if he did not, his missionary work would have given him basic proficiency. This is not the same as being able to write a polished document intended for wider circulation. Literacy was not easily obtained by small-town workingmen in the ancient world. Mark, however, was from a wealthy family (recall that he had a large house with servants). In the cosmopolitan city of Jerusalem, it is likely he would

---

[3] Eusebius, *Ecclesiastical History*, Translated by C. F. Cruse, 105 – 106.
[4] Litfin, Bryan, *After Acts: Exploring the Lives and Legends of the Apostles*, 46.

have been taught better Greek than someone could pick up from day-to-day usage. Therefore, it appears he was assigned to help Peter with literary tasks that were beyond the reach of a fisherman's basic language capabilities, such as writing letters or recording oral history. Mark served as Peter's translator from Aramaic into Greek as needed.[5]

Whether Mark himself heard and walked with Jesus or relied on Peter amidst the Aramaic challenge, Mark's Greek is solid. His recorded imperatives from Jesus' words are intentional. Reputable journalists who are translators or reputable translators who are journalists focus on truth. Because of Mark's journaling or translating accuracy, his recording of Jesus' imperatives is no small issue. Peter would not have permitted mediocrity in what Jesus had told Peter or others in their conversations that Mark recorded. Accuracy mattered. More specifically accuracy of the Greek mattered. Even more specifically, the accuracy of Mark's writings mattered to the indwelling Holy Spirit within Mark.

In Mark's view, an imperative from Jesus to a disciple was a privilege. Throughout Mark's gospel first-century readers perceived that Mark held the disciples in high regard. Mark knew them to be a privileged group of not only followers but disciples. Mark knew the difference between followers and privileged disciples. Ladd expounds:

> But over and against the dullness and failure of the disciples we find in Mark also an important emphasis on the privilege of discipleship; and on the fundamental distinction between Jesus' disciples and "those outside." Mk 4: 11.[6]

For Mark, a follower of Jesus and a disciple of Jesus were not the equivalents. Underneath Mark's Gospel, he conveyed that few including those closest to Jesus were prepared to receive an imperative from him. The initial hearings of Jesus' teachings were sometimes difficult for his disciples to understand fully.

Nowhere did Mark record that he had received an imperative from Jesus. Mark's record of imperatives from Jesus to others, particularly the disciples presented challenges to whom Jesus commanded. Blomberg affirms:

> More so in Mark than in any other Gospel, Jesus frequently commands people not to tell anyone about his identity. In 8: 30 he abruptly silences Peter without any of the praise or promises so well-known from Matthew's version (Matt 16: 17 – 19). Insight into parables is not to be given to "outsiders" (Mark: 4: 10 – 12); demonic confessions are rebuked (1: 25, 34; 3: 12); and spectacular miracles are to be reported to no one (1: 44; 5: 18 - 19, 43; etc.).[7]

Receiving an imperative from Jesus was a daunting experience given that those who received an imperative command from Jesus knew they were expected to fulfill his imperative. In Mk 4: 35 – 41 Jesus' command to the wind and waves was brief, powerful, and gave a reason for the disciple's fear of Jesus. These early imperatives, which were first spoken by Jesus, then heard by his disciples and recorded by Mark provided a foundation. Their fear of Jesus' words more so

---

[5] Litfin, Bryan, *After Acts: Exploring the Lives and Legends of the Apostles*, 46.
[6] Ladd, George Eldon, *A Theology of the New Testament,* 235.
[7] Blomberg, Craig L., *Jesus, and the Gospels,* 119.

than their fear of the storm affirmed that when Jesus spoke, they had reason to listen. After the disciples had heard Jesus' imperatives to the wind to be still and immediately the wind obeyed and became still, the disciples realized this Jesus was no ordinary man. They had a reason for fear, or they had a reason for joy. Not to fear Jesus' imperatives was a lesson they had to learn.

## Timing

Mark likely started his gospel during Peter's life and finished after Peter's death or after Peter left for Rome. "Irenaeus, on the other hand, can be interpreted as believing that Peter had already died when Mark wrote, as he maintains that after Peter's and Paul's "departure" (Greek exodus), "Mark the disciple and interpreter of Peter also transmitted to us what he had written about what Peter had preached" (Against Heresies 3.1.38-41).[8]

Mark wasted no time. His first two sentences in Mk 1: 1-2 identified messiah Jesus as good news affirmed by the prophet Isaiah.[9] Mark highlighted the difficulties the disciples had seeing Jesus as Messiah. Mark's record of Jesus' imperatives directly to the disciples are not kind in that Mark conveys the struggles the disciples had understanding Jesus' parables and imperatives. However, Mark does not end his book leaving the disciples in a quandary about Jesus parables and imperatives. Mark's last two verses read:

> So then the Lord Jesus, after he had spoken to them, was taken up into heaven and sat down at the right hand of God. And they went out and preached everywhere, while the Lord worked with them and confirmed the message by accompanying signs. Mk 16: 19 - 20[10]

Notice how Mark affirmed that the disciples "went out and preached everywhere, while the Lord worked with them and confirmed the message by accompanying signs." As you read Mark's record of Jesus' imperatives, keep in mind that the sick, demons, Jewish rulers, synagogue leaders, followers, and especially disciples were not confused about his words. They may have had some uncertainties about meaning, but as they preached, they were certain about Jesus' imperatives.

## Mark's Record

Mk 1: 15 and saying, "The time is fulfilled, and the kingdom of God is at hand; <u>repent</u> μετανοεῖτε and <u>believe in the gospel</u> πιστεύετε ἐν τῷ εὐαγγελίῳ."

Following Jesus' baptism and temptation in the desert, "repent" and "believe" were Jesus' two spoken imperatives Mark recorded. Before these two imperatives, however, Jesus first proclaimed the fulfilled time and presence of the Kingdom of God. His imperatives declared the futileness for anyone to attempt experiencing the Kingdom of God without repentance of sin and belief in the good news.

---

[8] Blomberg, Craig L., *Jesus, and the Gospels*, 122.
[9] A voice cries: "In the wilderness prepare the way of the LORD; make straight in the desert a highway for our God. Is 40: 3
[10] Some manuscripts end the book [Mark] with 16:8; others include verses 9 – 20 immediately after v8. See ESV footnote, 853.

In today's context, the word "repent" conveys a weak meaning, more like, "Yes, I should probably give some thought that I might be wrong." In their context, however, they heard Jesus command them to change their minds, stop thinking and living as they had thought and lived in the past because of the Kingdom of God. Things had changed. Without repentance and belief in the good news, the Kingdom of God was unavailable to them.

Perhaps at least one reason today's believers are weak in comprehending, seeing, entering, or experiencing the Kingdom of God is that to convey the power of Jesus' imperatives to repent and believe is difficult to do in English compared to what they read and heard in Greek. The Kingdom of God or Kingdom of Heaven was easier to understand through Jesus' words in their context. Mt 4: 17

Mk 1: 22–27 And they were astonished at his teaching, for he taught them as one who had authority, and not as the scribes. And immediately there was in their synagogue a man with an unclean spirit. And he cried out, "What have you to do with us, Jesus of Nazareth? Have you come to destroy us? I know who you are--the Holy One of God." But Jesus rebuked him, saying, "<u>Be silent</u> φιμώθητι, and <u>come out of him</u> ἔξελθε ἐξ αὐτοῦ!" And the unclean spirit, convulsing him and crying out with a loud voice, came out of him. And they were all amazed, so that they questioned among themselves, saying, "What is this? A new teaching with authority! He commands even the unclean spirits, and they obey him."

> Jesus did not dialogue with demons, he commanded them. He ordered the unclean spirit in the man to be silent and come out. Jesus did not negotiate. He knew their intent and wasted no time at their expulsion. He knew their location and commanded their silence. Note that one demon speaks for a plurality of demons, "What have you to do with us, Jesus of Nazareth? Have you come to destroy us? I know who you are—the Holy One of God."

> Jesus did not engage in conversation with this one demon speaking on behalf of others. Jesus did not permit a demon presence in those he delivered. Demons were under the power of Jesus' imperatives. Jesus' imperative "come out" establishes that the demons were within. Demons knew they were not able to disobey his imperatives and remain within.

> This exchange between Jesus and the demons, however, was not only about the demons and the person in the synagogue. Those who heard Jesus' imperatives to the demons and then saw what happened were convinced that Jesus' imperatives were unchallengeable. Those in the synagogue watched the unclean spirits obey Jesus' command. Lk 4: 35

Mk 1: 40-44 And a leper came to him, imploring him, and kneeling said to him, "If you will, you can make me clean." Moved with pity, he stretched out his hand and touched him and said to him, "I will; <u>be clean</u> καθαρίσθητι." And immediately his leprosy left him and he was made clean. And Jesus sternly charged him and sent him away at once, and said to him, "<u>See that you say nothing to anyone</u> ὅρα μηδενὶ μηδὲν εἴπῃς, but <u>go</u> ὕπαγε, <u>show yourself to the priest</u> δεῖξον σεαυτὸν δεῖξον τῷ ἱερεῖ and <u>offer for your cleansing what Moses commanded</u> προσένεγκε περὶ τοῦ καθαρισμοῦ σου ἃ προσέταξεν Μωϋσῆς, for a proof to them." But he went out and began to talk freely about it, and to spread the news, so that Jesus could no longer openly enter a town, but was out in desolate places, and people were coming to him from every quarter.

Jesus preceded his imperative with "be clean with "I will." The follow-up imperative "be clean" was not only physical healing. Cleanliness would return the leper to society. Jesus could have chosen other imperatives such as be healed, be restored, or be whole. Jesus spoke a passive imperative "be clean" which held a future purpose. The leper had no doubt of his healing. The imperative, however, was not solely for the leper. The leper was both physically cleansed and socially restored to the community. Those who watched and heard Jesus' imperative were aware that there was no need to banish the former leper. His leprosy was gone. He was no longer a threat to society.

Following Jesus' first imperative, "be clean" he spoke three additional imperatives within one sentence, "see," "go," and "show." Jesus had purposed that the leper follows his commands. Jesus demanded the leper's secrecy and quick journey to the priest. The former leper had been commanded by Jesus to show the priest his cleanliness. Jesus' commands had intentions beyond what the leper could understand. Jesus had a post-healing purpose. For the leper, his healing was of utmost importance, yet for Jesus, the leper's healing had a grander plan. The healing was central to the leper, but the leper's responsibilities after being healed were of greater importance to Jesus.

These imperatives are unique in that it appears that the Leper had disobeyed Jesus' command first to keep silent then go to the priest. The passage affirms that the leper, "went out and began to talk freely about it." To English readers, it appears that Jesus' imperative to the leper meaning, "See to and stay to it that you do not tell anyone what happened or how you were healed before going to the priest." was disobeyed.

Context is needed here. The only way lepers were permitted return to the community was that their healings had to be verified by a priest. Without priestly verification, even a healed leper would have continued to be excluded. That is, the leper would not have been permitted entrance into the community which did not have lepers until and unless a priest affirmed he was clean. Jesus knew that the leper eventually would tell a priest how he had been cleansed to return the community. Mark did not provide a time context. Mt 8: 3-4; Lk 5: 12-16

Mk 2: 3-9 And they came, bringing to him a paralytic carried by four men. And when they could not get near him because of the crowd, they removed the roof above him, and when they had made an opening, they let down the bed on which the paralytic lay. And when Jesus saw their faith, he said to the paralytic, "Son, your sins are forgiven." Now some of the scribes were sitting there, questioning in their hearts, "Why does this man speak like that? He is blaspheming! Who can forgive sins but God alone?" And immediately Jesus, perceiving in his spirit that they thus questioned within themselves, said to them, "Why do you question these things in your hearts? Which is easier, to say to the paralytic, 'Your sins are forgiven,' or to say, 'Rise ἔγειρε, take up ἆρον your bed and walk' περιπάτει?

Jesus used imperatives within his question. He emphasizes that sin was not the root cause of the paralysis. Healing the paralytic man was secondary to the forgiveness of his sins. Jesus proved his power to forgive by his power to heal with his imperatives. Similar to healing the leper, Jesus' higher motive proved his authority to forgive sins. He taught to the Scribes that beyond healing, his higher purpose was forgiving sins. Mt 9: 5; Lk 5: 23

Mk 2: 10–11 But that you may know that the Son of Man has authority on earth to forgive sins"--he said to the paralytic--"I say to you, <u>rise</u> ἔγειρε, <u>pick up</u> ἆρον your bed, and <u>go</u> ὕπαγε home."
    Jesus had spoken three imperatives to the paralytic, "rise," "pick up," and "go." The paralytic had no comprehension that Jesus' intent through healing him was directed at the Scribes. The message was that Jesus forgave and would continue to forgive sins. Jesus gave the imperatives and the healed man complied. The paralytic rose, picked up his bed and went home. What is central through these imperatives to the paralytic was what the Scribes saw and heard. Mt 9: 6 - 7; Lk 5: 24

Mk 2:12-4 And he rose and immediately picked up his bed and went out before them all so that they were all amazed and glorified God, saying, "We never saw anything like this!" He went out again beside the sea, and all the crowd was coming to him, and he was teaching them. And as he passed by, he saw Levi the son of Alphaeus sitting at the tax booth, and he said to him, "<u>Follow me</u> ἀκολούθει μοι." And he rose and followed him.
    These passages from Mark parallel recordings by both Mathew and Luke regarding Matthew's calling through Jesus' imperative. Mt 9: 9; Lk 5: 27

Mk 3: 1–3 Again he entered the synagogue, and a man was there with a withered hand. And they watched Jesus, to see whether he would heal him on the Sabbath, so that they might accuse him. And he said to the man with the withered hand, "<u>Come here</u> Εγειρε εἰς τὸ μέσον."
    Jesus' imperatives were stated inside the synagogue. Jesus commanded the man with the withered hand and observers heard Jesus' words. An expanded rendering is, "Come stand in the middle of those here who are watching everything that is happening within this synagogue." Those who heard Jesus command and witnessed the healing were fully exposed to the power of Jesus' imperatives. Jesus' imperative was not solely intended for the healed man, but an affirmation to those who witnessed and heard. Mt 3: 13; Lk 6: 8

Mk 3:5-6 And he looked around at them with anger, grieved at their hardness of heart, and said to the man, "<u>Stretch out your hand</u> Εκτεινον τὴν χεῖρα σου." He stretched it out, and his hand was restored. The Pharisees went out and immediately held counsel with the Herodians against him, how to destroy him.
    As those in the synagogue looked and listened, Jesus stated an imperative to the man to stretch out his hand, and the hand was healed. Certainly, the man was amazed at the healing as would have been onlookers. Jesus, similar to prior healings, was less concerned about healing and more concerned about the hardness of hearts of those who looked on in disbelief. Immediately in v6 the Pharisees met with the Herodians to plot against Jesus.

Jesus' imperatives at the beginning of his ministry likely meant little to the Pharisees, Scribes, and Herodians who witnessed what happened in the synagogue. They marginalized Jesus' imperatives that healed. Despite his miraculous healing imperatives, they chose to destroy him. Mt 12: 13; Lk 6: 10

Mk 4: 1-3 Again he began to teach beside the sea. And a very large crowd gathered about him so that he got into a boat and sat in it on the sea, and the whole crowd was beside the sea on the land. And he was teaching them many things in parables, and in his teaching, he said to them: "<u>Listen</u> Ἀκούετε! A sower went out to sow."

> Jesus' imperative "listen" emphasized that his parable of the four soils held profound meaning for them. His greeting imperative intended a weighty meaning followed this particular parable. This "listen" imperative in Mark is not found in parallel parable passages by Matthew or Luke.

Mk 4: 4–9 And as he sowed, some seed fell along the path, and the birds came and devoured it. Other seed fell on rocky ground, where it did not have much soil, and immediately it sprang up since it had no depth of soil. And when the sun rose, it was scorched, and since it had no root, it withered away. Other seed fell among thorns, and the thorns grew up and choked it, and it yielded no grain. And other seeds fell into good soil and produced grain, growing up and increasing and yielding thirtyfold and sixtyfold and a hundredfold." And he said, "He who has ears to hear, <u>let him hear</u> ἀκουέτω."

> At the parable's completion, Jesus was aware that some listeners would not understand. He gave a closing imperative commonly and correctly translated "let him hear." The Koine Greek imperative, however, trumps the English milder translation from "let" to "hear!" Jesus made a point that everyone with ears must hear.

> Since those who heard the parable of the four soils had ears, they were also required to understand. Jesus was not presenting an option as some readers interpreted his words. He commanded everyone who had ears and could hear to understand his parable. In English, the word, "hear" often takes on multiple meanings such as an audible sound and a meaning of understanding. In English, the word "listening" is that of understanding and the word "hear" means to perceive the audible sound. In context, Jesus did not command to hear an audible sound but to receive with the understanding that the audible sound teaches. Mt 13: 9; Lk 8: 8

Mk 4: 10-23 And when he was alone, those around him with the twelve asked him about the parables. And he said to them, "To you has been given the secret of the kingdom of God, but for those outside everything is in parables, so that "they may indeed see but not perceive, and may indeed hear but not understand, lest they should turn and be forgiven." And he said to them, "Do you not understand this parable? How then will you understand all the parables? The sower sows the word. And these are the ones along the path, where the word is sown: when they hear, Satan immediately comes and takes away the word that is sown in them. And these are the ones sown on rocky ground: the ones who, when they hear the word, immediately receive it with joy. And they have no root in themselves, but endure for a while; then, when tribulation or persecution arises on account of the word, immediately they fall away. And others are the ones sown among thorns.

They are those who hear the word, but the cares of the world and the deceitfulness of riches and the desires for other things enter in and choke the word, and it proves unfruitful. But those that were sown on the good soil are the ones who hear the word and accept it and bear fruit, thirtyfold and sixtyfold and a hundredfold." And he said to them, "Is a lamp brought in to be put under a basket, or under a bed, and not on a stand? For nothing is hidden except to be made manifest; nor is anything secret except to come to light. If anyone has ears to hear, let him hear ἀκουέτω."

    This imperative came after Jesus had explained in detail the parable of the four soils. His explanation was not a suggestion but a command. English readers often differentiate between hearing and listening. Jesus used the same root word, "hear" in two different moods. The first "hear" in "If anyone has ears to hear," is in the Greek infinitive mood form meaning "to hear." The second "hear" is in the imperative mood.

    To have heard in English often means to have audibly received the sound or to have heard the words. To have listened in English often means to have understood what was heard. Big difference. Listening often means acceptance of the imperative command. Jesus had commanded them to go beyond simply hearing his parables to listening and understanding them.

Mk 4: 24-25 And he said to them, "Pay attention to what you hear βλέπετε τί ἀκούετε with the measure you use, it will be measured to you, and still more will be added to you. For to the one who has, more will be given, and from the one who has not, even what he has will be taken away."

    Jesus commanded to go beyond hearing to understanding. Following v23 Jesus' had commanded understanding on a deeper level. He did not suggest but required that his followers understand the reward for an honest, truthful measure and righteous judgments. Lk 8: 18

Mk 4: 35-41 On that day, when evening had come, he said to them, "Let us go across to the other side." And leaving the crowd, they took him with them in the boat, just as he was. And other boats were with him. And a great windstorm arose, and the waves were breaking into the boat so that the boat was already filling. But he was in the stern, asleep on the cushion. And they woke him and said to him, "Teacher, do you not care that we are perishing?" And he awoke and rebuked the wind and said to the sea, "Peace σιώπα! Be still πεφίμωσο!" And the wind ceased, and there was a great calm. He said to them, "Why are you so afraid? Have you still no faith?" And they were filled with great fear and said to one another, "Who then is this, that even the wind and the sea obey him?"

    The disciples in the boat with Jesus heard his two rebuking imperatives, "peace" and "be still" to the wind and sea. The leading imperative "peace" is in the present active and the following imperative, "be still" is perfect passive. Both are second person singular (you). More clarifying translation inclusive of the present active is, 'be at peace and keep being at peace" and for the perfect passive is, "be still as you have been made to be still." Mark recorded that the wind ceased and there was a great calm. The great calm affirmed the perfect passive. In v40 and v41 the disciples recognized that even the wind and sea obeyed his imperatives. Because the wind and sea had obeyed his two spoken imperatives, the disciples recognized the power of Jesus' imperatives. How Jesus had commanded the wind and waves through his spoken imperative mood usage weighed heavy upon them.

Nature's obedience to Jesus' commands caused the disciples to understand that Jesus' imperatives were consequential. The disciples progressed in their understanding of Jesus' power, but after hearing Jesus' commands to nature, they were beginning to understand his power as the power of God. His words held power over nature. While Jesus' parables and conversations were moving, his disciples found his irresistible imperatives to the sea and wind both fearful and comforting. They likely believed the impossibility that Jesus' imperatives could be disobeyed.

As the disciples would come to learn, the winds, waves, seas, demons, and diseases could not disobey his spoken imperatives. The question is simple. If nature obeyed Jesus' imperatives, could a man's will override Jesus?

Mk 5: 8-13 For he was saying to him, "<u>Come out of the man you unclean spirit</u> Εξελθε τὸ πνεῦμα τὸ ἀκάθαρτον ἐκ τοῦ ἀνθρώπου!" And Jesus asked him, "What is your name?" He replied, "My name is Legion, for we are many." And he begged him earnestly not to send them out of the country. Now a great herd of pigs was feeding there on the hillside, and they begged him, saying, "Send us to the pigs; let us enter them." So he gave them permission. And the unclean spirits came out and entered the pigs, and the herd, numbering about two thousand, rushed down the steep bank into the sea and were drowned in the sea.

After his imperative to the demon to "come out" Jesus publically defined the spirit as unclean. The unclean spirit implored for the many additional spirits he led. It was not within Jesus' will nor the will of the Father for uncleanliness or sickness to remain in anyone cleansed or healed. Mt 8: 28-32; Lk 8: 26-39

There is significant depth to this passage beyond the imperative. R. Alan Street's insight is of value:

> When the man from the tombs meets Jesus on the seashore, the demon inside him cries out, "What have to do with You, Jesus, Son of the Most High God? I implore You by God that You do not torment me (Mark 5: 7). These words are a response to Jesus's command. "For He said to him, 'Come out of the man, unclean spirit?' Then He asked him, 'What is your name?'" (verse 8-9).
>
> The first clue this passage should be read at two levels is found in the demon's response. "And he answered, saying, 'My name is Legion;' for we are many': (verse 9). On a literal context, (contextual hermeneutic) the demoniac's response meant to them that a myriad of demons had possessed him. The readers of the Gospels, however, the word, "Legion" had political connotations a well. It was commonly used to refer to a contingent of 6,000 Roman foot soldiers. Jews rubbed shoulders every day with Roman occupation troops.
>
> The second clue that this passage has a future political connotation, as well as a literal one, is found in the mention of pigs. After begging

Jesus not to send them out of the country, the demons request that he send them into the swine. Jesus grants permission (verse 11 – 13). According to Josephus, a pig's or boar's head was the symbol of the Roman Tenth Legion (*Fretensis*), which besieged Jerusalem (Jewish War 5.71-97) and occupied the Mount of Olives in the Jewish War (AD 67–70).

The conclusion of the exorcism provides the final clues. "Then the unclean spirits went out and entered the swine (there were about two thousand), and the herd ran violently down the steep place into the sea, and drowned in the sea? (verse 13 – 14). Does this account jog your memory about another army drowning in a sea? The wording is nearly identical to that of the Exodus scene at the Red Sea (Exodus 15: 1, 10). God delivers Israel from Egyptian domination, but Pharaoh's army perishes in the sea.[11]

The "unclean spirit" that left the man went into the pigs and perished in the sea. Beyond the Greek imperative, many metaphors in their historical context are not available in English.

Mk 5: 19 And he did not permit him but said to him, "<u>Go home to your friends</u> Ὑπαγε εἰς τὸν οἶκόν σου πρὸς τοὺς σούς and <u>tell them how much the Lord has done for you</u> ἀπάγγειλον ἀπάγγειλον αὐτοῖς ὅσα ὁ κύριός σοι πεποίηκεν, and how he has had mercy on you."

    Jesus' two imperatives "go" and "tell" had intentions beyond the healing. Here Jesus had commanded that the person who had been healed should tell friends what the Lord had done and the mercy the Lord had given. While this healing seems to conflict with others where Jesus had told others to remain silent after their healing, the point is that the healings are not solely to the benefit of the healed person. Jesus always had deeper intentions beyond his healing imperatives. His healing imperatives affirmed the Kingdom of God and the presence of the King. Lk 8: 39

Mk 5: 25-34 And there was a woman who had had a discharge of blood for twelve years, and who had suffered much under many physicians, and had spent all that she had, and was no better but rather grew worse. She had heard the reports about Jesus and came up behind him in the crowd and touched his garment. For she said, "If I touch even his garments, I will be made well." And immediately the flow of blood dried up, and she felt in her body that she was healed of her disease. And Jesus, perceiving in himself that power had gone out from him, immediately turned about in the crowd and said, "Who touched my garments?" And his disciples said to him, "You see the crowd pressing around you, and yet you say, 'Who touched me?'" And he looked around to see who had done it. But the woman, knowing what had happened to her, came in fear and trembling and fell down before him and told him the whole truth. And he said to her, "Daughter, your faith has made you well; <u>go in peace</u> ὕπαγε εἰς εἰρήνην, and <u>be healed of your disease</u> ἴσθι ὑγιὴς ἀπὸ τῆς μάστιγός σου."

---

[11] Streett, R. Alan., *Heaven on Earth: Experiencing The Kingdom Of God In The Here And Now*, 87 – 88.

Jesus' first affirmed the daughter's faith to her healing then spoke two imperatives, "go in peace" and "be healed of your disease." She can be at peace because her faith made her well. Jesus' imperative commanded her to continue to be overjoyed at her healing. Jesus affirmed her faith to both her healing and continued health. To grasp the present active imperative an expanded translation is, "be going in peace." Faith had healed, and continuous faith would keep her disease at bay. Mark does not expound on her future health nor do any other Gospel writers acknowledge or deny that her disease returned. We only know what Jesus commanded her. Mt 9: 22; Lk 8: 48

Mk 5: 35–37 While he was still speaking, there came from the ruler's house some who said, "Your daughter is dead. Why trouble the Teacher any further?" But overhearing what they said, Jesus said to the ruler of the synagogue, <u>Do not fear</u> μὴ φοβοῦ, only <u>believe</u> πίστευε." And he allowed no one to follow him except Peter and James and John the brother of James.

    Jesus was always aware of those listening to his words and watching what he did. In v36 Jesus overheard the ruler who had been told that his daughter was dead and that there was no need to trouble Jesus, the teacher. The synagogue ruler had given up hope yet Jesus quickly commanded him not to fear and only believe. These double imperatives were progressive in that his first imperative "do not fear" was purposed to remove fear followed by his second imperative "believe." Belief and fear are not compatible. These imperatives affirmed the more belief, the less fear. Lk 8: 50

Mk 5: 38-43 They came to the house of the ruler of the synagogue, and Jesus saw a commotion, people weeping and wailing loudly. And when he had entered, he said to them, "Why are you making a commotion and weeping? The child is not dead but sleeping." And they laughed at him. But he put them all outside and took the child's father and mother and those who were with him and went in where the child was. Taking her by the hand he said to her, "Talitha cumi," which means, "Little girl, I say to you, <u>arise</u> ἔγειρε." And immediately the girl got up and began walking (for she was twelve years of age), and they were immediately overcome with amazement. And he strictly charged them that no one should know this, and told them to give her something to eat.

    Before Jesus' spoken imperative to the little girl others in the house had laughed at Jesus wherein he promptly put them outside the house. Only the father, mother, the little girl and those with Jesus were permitted in the house with Jesus.

    After Jesus' imperative, "Arise" he immediately directed those who had witnessed her restoration to withhold telling anyone what happened. There was no need to tell what happened. It is likely that both Mark and Peter were part of the group with Jesus. There would be no reason to tell of her healing because those who presumed the child to have died would soon see her alive and walking.

Mk 6: 7-10 And he called the twelve and began to send them out two by two, and gave them authority over the unclean spirits. He charged them to take nothing for their journey except a staff--no bread, no bag, no money in their belts--but to wear sandals and not put on two tunics. And he said to them, "Whenever you enter a house, <u>stay there until you depart from there</u> ἐκεῖ μένετε ἕως ἂν ἐξέλθητε ἐκεῖθεν.

This verse read in English sounds strange. "Stay there until you depart from there." seems logical, so why did Jesus speak an imperative command to stay? He was making sure that his disciples would be very sensitive to the inevitable time to leave. He commanded that they stay up to the moment that they perceived that their presence was burdensome and no longer. Jesus did not want them merely going from house to house as on some tour or timeline schedule. They were commanded to wait until they perceived it was time to leave and not sooner. Time was not important. What was important was their perception of blessings or burdens.

Mk 6: 11 And if any place will not receive you and they will not listen to you, when you leave, <u>shake off the dust that is on your feet as a testimony against them</u> ἐκτινάξατε τὸν χοῦν τὸν ὑποκάτω τῶν ποδῶν ὑμῶν εἰς μαρτύριον αὐτοῖς."

    Jesus had commanded that they shake off the dust. The dust that remained behind was intended to remain with those who refused to listen. His disciples likely were curious why it was necessary to Jesus that they shake off the dust. Jesus referred to Ex 9: 9 the fine dust of Egypt that caused boils and sores and the consequences that befell those who refused to listen.[12]

    He made clear to his disciples the power his word. They were not to carry any plague of unbelief with them from house to house, but shake off the dust and leave as testimony and confirmation of those who had not listened.

Mk 6: 27-31 And immediately the king sent an executioner with orders to bring John's head. He went and beheaded him in the prison and brought his head on a platter and gave it to the girl, and the girl gave it to her mother. When his disciples heard of it, they came and took his body and laid it in a tomb. The apostles returned to Jesus and told him all that they had done and taught. And he said to them, "<u>Come away by yourselves to a desolate place</u> Δεῦτε ὑμεῖς αὐτοὶ κατ ἰδίαν εἰς ἔρημον τόπον and <u>rest a while</u> ἀναπαύσασθε ὀλίγον." For many were coming and going, and they had no leisure even to eat.

    These two imperatives "come away" and "rest" immediately came after the disciples had told Jesus about all they had taught and that they had buried John the Baptist. Fittingly Jesus then commanded them to get away to a quiet place and intentionally rest.

    He was more aware of their weariness and emotional fatigue after the beheading death of John the Baptist and their work to bury him. Jesus knew the ministry strain given all that had happened during their two by two time together. Although they were incentivized to continue, given the power they had experienced and the emotions following John the Baptist's beheading and burial, he commanded both the to leave where they were and go to a place where rest would be possible.

Mk 6: 37 And they went away in the boat to a desolate place by themselves. Now many saw them going and recognized them, and they ran there on foot from all the towns and got there ahead of them. When he went ashore he saw a great crowd, and he had compassion on them because they

---

[12] It shall become fine dust over all the land of Egypt, and become boils breaking out in sores on man and beast throughout all the land of Egypt." Ex 9: 9

were like sheep without a shepherd. And he began to teach them many things. And when it grew late, his disciples came to him and said, "This is a desolate place, and the hour is now late. Send them away to go into the surrounding countryside and villages and buy themselves something to eat." But he answered them, "You give them something to eat δότε αὐτοῖς ὑμεῖς φαγεῖν." And they said to him, "Shall we go and buy two hundred denarii worth of bread and give it to them to eat?"

> Jesus commanded his disciples a seemingly impossible task to feed a minimum of 5,000 people. Beyond his imperative, "you give them something to eat," the seemingly impossible command to them became understandable to them following the actual feeding. Jesus' present imperatives were often incomprehensible in their context and often only fathomable in their future as they reflected back upon what had happened. Here Jesus taught his disciples that feeding the 5,000 was possible for them.
>
> The English word "give" while appropriate conveys the idea that the disciples were to give from their personal holdings to feed the 5,000. However, the Greek word δότε in their context also meant, "grant," "yield," "permit," "cause" which the disciples perceived something like, "you figure out how to feed" or "you might think it is not possible to feed them, but it is possible." Mt 14: 16; Lk 9: 13

Mk 6: 38-46 And he said to them, "How many loaves do you have? Go ὑπάγετε and see ἔχετε." And when they had found out, they said, "Five, and two fish." Then he commanded them all to sit down in groups on the green grass. So they sat down in groups, by hundreds and by fifties. And taking the five loaves and the two fish he looked up to heaven and said a blessing and broke the loaves and gave them to the disciples to set before the people. And he divided the two fish among them all. And they all ate and were satisfied. And they took up twelve baskets full of broken pieces and of the fish. And those who ate the loaves were five thousand men. Immediately he made his disciples get into the boat and go before him to the other side, to Bethsaida, while he dismissed the crowd. And after he had taken leave of them, he went up on the mountain to pray.

> Jesus imperatives to them proved their self-perceived inability. His two imperatives, "go" and "see" affirmed the reality of their helpless incompetence. They went and saw that clearly five loaves and two fish were insufficient to feed 5,000 people. The English phrase "when they had found out" (ESV) is appropriate but lacks the Greek participle and aorist attributes which "having known" (YLT) is better. The English "found out" conveys more or a surprise rather than knowledge. Because they knew not by the amazement that they "found out" but that they knew for certain that their total of five loaves and two fish was not sufficient.
>
> Some English translations insert the English conjunction "and" between "go" and "see." Mark recorded that Jesus said, "Go see" ὑπάγετε ἴδετε without the Greek conjunction.

Mk 6: 47-50 And when evening came, the boat was out on the sea, and he was alone on the land. And he saw that they were making headway painfully, for the wind was against them. And about the fourth watch of the night he came to them, walking on the sea. He meant to pass by them, but when they saw him walking on the sea they thought it was a ghost, and cried out, for they all saw him and were terrified. But immediately he spoke to them and said, "Take heart θαρσεῖτε, it is I.

Do not be afraid μὴ φοβεῖσθε." And he got into the boat with them, and the wind ceased. And they were utterly astounded, for they did not understand about the loaves, but their hearts were hardened.

Jesus' imperative here followed after disciples had witnessed Jesus walk on Galilean Sea while they were in the boat at night. Given the miraculous feeding of the 5,000 and after having experienced Jesus' imperatives, hearing Jesus' imperative "take heart" and "do not be afraid" likely made them realize that there was no need to fear. The disciples were growing to understand and trust the power of Jesus' imperatives. Here Mark did not convey fearful disciples as they had been when Jesus had earlier calmed the wind and waves. Here instead Mark affirmed their growth. Mt 14: 27; Jn 6: 20

Mk 7: 10 For Moses said, 'Honor your father and your mother τίμα τὸν πατέρα σου καὶ τὴν μητέρα σου; and, 'Whoever reviles father or mother must surely die θανάτῳ τελευτάτω.'

Here Jesus quoted two of Moses' imperatives. Emphasizing Moses' words to honor mother and father, Jesus affirmed the consequences of death (separation) upon those who revile either father or mother. The imperative "die" in this passage is present active third-person singular meaning that those shaming father or mother are immediately and actively separated by death, not in a physical sense, but an instantaneous detachment from illumination of revelation.

Separation (death) resulted from dishonoring a parent. The English translation "must surely die," while a suitable rendition, implies a future. Jesus' use of the Greek present active however asserted an immediate disconnection or death at the moment of reviling father or mother. Jesus affirmed the fifth commandment from Ex 20: 12 and Dt 5: 16 (Septuagint) through Moses' "Honor" τίμα imperative.

Because there is no English equivalent to a third person imperative, many English translations insert the phrase two English words, "let" and "must" are prominent. A phrase such as "let him be put to death," "let him die the death," or "let him surely die," are found as a consequence for those who have not honored their parents. These are correct translations. However, the English word "let" sounds like and carries the idea of permission or option. The English word "must" is also commonly used in English translations for a Greek third person imperative. Hence, "must surely die" or "must be put to death" are common English translations.

Similarly the English words "let" and "must" convey a necessary human effort to bring the death. However, the Greek language was very clear to them. There is no human involved in the death of anyone dishonoring a mother or father. Instead, at the moment of dishonoring a mother or father, there is death or separation unable to avoid.

The only two imperatives here are "honor" and "die." These imperatives were clear to them. Here Jesus gave no command to save or intercede. Jesus simply affirmed that death was an unavoidable result when a father or mother was dishonored. It affirmed withdrawal from evil after a dishonoring had happened. The salvation of the lost was a priority, yet here Jesus affirmed Moses' command to honor a parent and let those who chose to disregard the law be left to their death. This was a hard command from Moses and an imperative that Jesus affirmed.

Jesus was not teaching adherence to the law as much as affirming absolute and unavoidable consequences. He was not simply exposing Pharisaical errors. Here Jesus spoke to the Pharisees, Scribes and likely his disciples and other onlookers teaching them to withdraw and let death occur because, after the sin of dishonoring a father or mother, death is inevitable. Death by separation would take its course upon the unrepentant who dishonored a father or mother. Note, neither Moses nor Jesus referred to parents in the plural, only to father and mother as individuals.
Mt 15: 3

Mk 7: 14 And he called the people to him again and said to them, "Hear me, all of you Ἀκούσατέ μου πάντες, and understand σύνετε: There is nothing outside a person that by going into him can defile him, but the things that come out of a person are what defile him."
> Jesus gave two imperatives preceding his explanation of what goes into and comes out of the body. Jesus' brought them to attention that this was not a simple message. While his burden may not be heavy, he taught that his message was not simple. These imperatives are not participles such as to be hearing and to be understanding. These are imperatives Mt 15: 10

Mk 7: 26-28 Now the woman was a Gentile, a Syrophoenician by birth. And she begged him to cast the demon out of her daughter. And he said to her, "Let the children be fed first Αφες πρῶτον χορτασθῆναι τὰ τέκνα, for it is not right to take the children's bread and throw it to the dogs." But she answered him, "Yes, Lord; yet even the dogs under the table eat the children's crumbs."
> Jesus' imperative here was to the Gentile Syrophoenician woman who had asked Jesus to cast out an unclean spirit, a demon from her daughter. His imperative was not directly related to her daughter or her, but a reference to children being fed first. Jesus cast the demon out of her daughter and referenced the woman's statement, "Yes, Lord; yet even the dogs under the table eat the children's crumbs." Jesus affirmed in v29 that her faith was central in that Jesus' would cast out the demon.

Mk 7: 29 And he said to her, "For this statement you may go your way ὕπαγε ἐξελήλυθεν the demon has left your daughter."
> The imperative in v29 is often also correctly translated as "you may go" rather than the imperative "go" or "go your way." English translations using the word "may" though accurate conveys a sense of permission rather than the Greek imperative to English command "go." Jesus was very clear that the mother was to return to her daughter with both haste and knowledge that her daughter was free of the demon. There was no doubt in the woman's assurance that her daughter had been healed.

Mk 7: 34–37 And looking up to heaven, he sighed and said to him, "Ephphatha," that is, "Be opened διανοίχθητι." And his ears were opened, his tongue was released, and he spoke plainly. And Jesus charged them to tell no one. But the more he charged them, the more zealously they proclaimed it. And they were astonished beyond measure, saying, "He has done all things well. He even makes the deaf hear and the mute speak."

Here Mark recorded that Jesus spoke an indeclinable Aramaic word "Ephphatha" which Mark translated "Be opened" with the use of the Greek imperative. Following Jesus' imperative to the deaf and speechless man "be opened" Jesus charged the people in v36 to tell no one. Mark did not record Jesus' use of an imperative in the charge, only that Jesus told them to tell no one. Jesus' healing imperatives were absolute, but healing was not his sole purpose as much as means to Jesus' ends. His healing imperative affirmed the Father's will and his divine power.

Mk 8: 15 And he cautioned them, saying, "Watch out ὁρᾶτε; beware βλέπετε of the leaven of the Pharisees and the leaven of Herod."

The Pharisees and the Sadducees tested Jesus. After testing, Jesus commanded his disciples to "watch" and "beware" using leavening as an illustration. He spoke two declarative imperatives not merely cautioning, but commanding his disciples to be aware of the root motives of the Pharisees and Herod. He did not condemn the Pharisees nor Herod. They were commanded to beware of the leaven a metaphor for the motives of the Pharisees and Herod.

He did not say watch out or beware of the Pharisees or Herod. He said to watch and beware of the leaven of the Pharisees and Herod as false teachers. Big difference.
Mt 16: 6

Mk 8: 31–22 And he began to teach them that the Son of Man must suffer many things and be rejected by the elders and the chief priests and the scribes and be killed, and after three days rise again. And he said this plainly. And Peter took him aside and began to rebuke him. But turning and seeing his disciples, he rebuked Peter and said, "Get behind me Satan ὕπαγε ὀπίσω μου, σατανᾶ! For you are not setting your mind on the things of God, but on the things of man."

Immediately after Jesus had explained his impending death, Peter denied Jesus' words. Jesus responded with a command imperative that identified and addressed Satan, not Peter. Mark recorded no dialogue, only a single command imperative "go behind me Satan" or more often in English "get behind me Satan." Disciples were not to dialogue with evil where Satan had control or influence. Where false statements, lies, and untruths were brought to light, Jesus confronted and placed Satan and the demons behind him, not in front of him.

The English command "get behind me Satan" translation suffers to convey the strong imperative to depart. Having commanded Satan to depart, Jesus acknowledged Satan's power over Peter. Satan had put the will of man before the will of God. Jesus called out Satan's work in Peter. This imperative affirmed Jesus' sovereign control over Satan within Peter. Peter himself, Peter's friends, and the disciples were unaware of Satan's power over Peter. Jesus' imperative and explanation to Satan prioritized God's purpose. Anyone who heard Peter's rebuke to Jesus and then Jesus' rebuke of Satan would have considered their condition of Satan's power over them. Mt 16: 23

Mk 8: 34 And calling the crowd to him with his disciples, he said to them, "If anyone would come after me, let him <u>deny himself</u> ἀπαρνησάσθω ἑαυτὸν and <u>take up his cross</u> ἀράτω τὸν σταυρὸν his cross and <u>follow</u> ἀκολουθεί me.

> Jesus provided three imperatives which defined characteristics of those who follow Jesus. "Deny" self, "take up" your cross, and "follow" are not suggestions. Each of them is an individual imperative command. Because of the lack of a 3$^{rd}$ person imperative in English, the rendering "let him" somewhat conveys an option or a suggestion such as "he is permitted to…"

> These imperatives to them were not options nor suggestions, but commands. Some English translations use, "he must" (NIV, NAU) which conveys clarity that those who follow Jesus have denied, taken up their cross and have followed. Kingdom servants cannot be in complete service without first having denied self, taken up his cross, and followed Jesus to the Father's will. Mt 16: 24; Lk 9: 23

Mk 9: 2–7 And after six days Jesus took with him Peter and James and John, and led them up a high mountain by themselves. And he was transfigured before them, and his clothes became radiant, intensely white, as no one on earth could bleach them. And there appeared to them Elijah with Moses, and they were talking with Jesus. And Peter said to Jesus, "Rabbi, it is good that we are here. Let us make three tents, one for you and one for Moses and one for Elijah." For he did not know what to say, for they were terrified. And a cloud overshadowed them, and a voice came out of the cloud, "This is my beloved Son; <u>listen to him</u> ἀκούετε αὐτοῦ."

> The word, "listen" here was not an imperative command from Jesus, but from "a voice" that "came out of the cloud." This imperative occurred during Jesus' transfiguration with Moses and Elijah as Peter, James and John looked on. The imperative "listen to him" came from the cloud after Jesus was declared to be the "beloved son."

> Mark recorded this imperative "listen to him" to Peter, James, and John which would later be read by readers of Mark's gospel. Mark record clarified that Jesus is God's son and that Jesus' words held power. Immediately after the imperative "listen to him" recorded in second person plural (you listen to him), Moses and Elijah were gone. The imperative word "listen" was intentional. The words of Jesus, the very words they heard and would continue to hear from Jesus especially Jesus' imperatives held power.

> Following this experience, Peter, James, and John would have had no doubt that Jesus' words held divine power especially his imperatives. The voice that pronounced the imperative, "listen to him" established the absolute that Jesus is the beloved son.

> Narratives of Matthew and Luke of this parallel text differ somewhat. Matthew included, "in whom I am well pleased." Luke included "whom I have chosen." Mark did not include either phrase from Matthew and Luke. In any event, Matthew, Mark, and Luke had to have heard the event told them by Peter, James or John. John in

his gospel did not record his experience at the transfiguration of Jesus nor words from the cloud.

The Father then gave a single imperative command "listen" to Peter, James, and John. The word listen did not mean to them to hear, but to head, understand, or give a judicial understanding. The Father could have given any statement or command. The single imperative "listen to him" was absolute and unmistakable. There was no ambiguity. Peter, James, and John heard what the father said and more importantly knew what the Father meant. Jesus always pointed to the Father, and the Father's imperative here was clear to them. Mt 17: 5; Lk 9: 35

Mk 9: 17-19 And someone from the crowd answered him, "Teacher, I brought my son to you, for he has a spirit that makes him mute. And whenever it seizes him, it throws him down, and he foams and grinds his teeth and becomes rigid. So I asked your disciples to cast it out, and they were not able." And he answered them, "O faithless generation, how long am I to be with you? How long am I to bear with you? <u>Bring him to me</u> φέρετε αὐτὸν πρός με."

    Jesus publically lamented a faithless generation just before he commanded that the child be brought to him. The question is begged, who is the "faithless generation?" The "faithless generation" may have been the disciples at their faithlessness to heal the child themselves. It may have been the Scribes who were questioning Jesus. Alternatively, it may have been the crowd who continued exhibiting faithlessness at Jesus' healings.

This generation is both a time and type of generation, a generation of faithless people of that time. No matter the faithless generation of whom Jesus spoke and Mark recorded, Jesus had tired of their faithlessness. Jesus commanded that the boy be brought to him. Jesus was preparing the "faithless generation" to witness the miracle healing about happen.

Note: Mark and Matthew recorded "bring" φέρετέ in second person plural ("you as a group bring him to me") whereas Luke recorded "bring," προσάγαγε in the second person singular, "bring your son here") because Luke recorded that Jesus had commanded the father to bring his son to Jesus. The number issue of how many were required to bring the man to Jesus may be moot because Luke obtained his Gospel from sources other than Peter's words to Mark. Mt 17: 17; Lk 9: 41

Mk 9: 20–25 And they brought the boy to him. And when the spirit saw him, immediately it convulsed the boy, and he fell on the ground and rolled about, foaming at the mouth. And Jesus asked his father, "How long has this been happening to him?" And he said, "From childhood. And it has often cast him into fire and into water, to destroy him. But if you can do anything, have compassion on us and help us." And Jesus said to him, "'If you can'! All things are possible for one who believes." Immediately the father of the child cried out and said, "I believe; help my unbelief!" And when Jesus saw that a crowd came running together, he rebuked the unclean spirit, saying to it, "You mute and deaf spirit, I command you, <u>come out of him</u> ἔξελθε ἐξ αὐτοῦ and never enter him again."

Jesus' followed up his imperative "come out of him" with an aorist subjunctive preceded by a negative "and never enter him again." Onlookers were assured that the unclean spirit would not return. Here, once clean always clean applied in that the unclean spirit would not be returning. Jesus did not make this word formation type in all situations after casting out demons because each demon or demons and each person was unique. Here through Jesus' affirmation by use of the subjunctive with a negative, Jesus assured continuity of healing in that this particular demon would never return. Jesus' power within his imperative to cast out demons held the same power to keep them out.

Mk 9: 38-40 John said to him, "Teacher, we saw someone casting out demons in your name, and we tried to stop him, because he was not following us." But Jesus said, "Do not stop him Μὴ κωλύετε αὐτόν for no one who does a mighty work in my name will be able soon afterward to speak evil of me. For the one who is not against us is for us.

John warned Jesus that someone was casting out demons in Jesus' name and that those with John tried to stop him for the reason that this particular person was not one within their group.

Jesus imperative to John made clear that John was not to interfere. Jesus clarified that the one healing in Jesus' name would not speak evil of Jesus. Jesus affirmed to John and to those who heard Jesus correct John that the longer mission of Jesus glorified the Father. Casting out demons, while important, was secondary to Jesus' wider mission. Casting out demons served a higher purpose far beyond healing alone. Casting out demons was not limited to Jesus' alone. Casting out demons pointed to Jesus who glorified the Father. Lk 9: 50

Mk 9: 41–48 For truly, I say to you, whoever gives you a cup of water to drink because you belong to Christ will by no means lose his reward. "Whoever causes one of these little ones who believe in me to sin, it would be better for him if a great millstone were hung around his neck and he were thrown into the sea. And if your hand causes you to sin, cut it off ἀπόκοψον αὐτήν. It is better for you to enter life crippled than with two hands to go to hell, to the unquenchable fire. And if your foot causes you to sin, cut it off ἀπόκοψον αὐτόν. It is better for you to enter life lame than with two feet to be thrown into hell. And if your eye causes you to sin, tear it out ἔκβαλε αὐτόν. It is better for you to enter the kingdom of God with one eye than with two eyes to be thrown into hell, 'where their worm does not die and the fire is not quenched.' Is 66: 24

Jesus' imperatives to cut off a sinning hand or foot or tear out an eye targeted a future consequence. Jesus' taught separation of evil from holiness. Jesus' concern was the holiness of heaven for whole body. Jesus taught that evil parts could destroy the whole. If evil parts were not separated from holiness, the whole body was destined for destruction and separation from holiness.

Parallel passages in Mt 19: 9 included an imperative "throw." Jesus combined visually disturbing words here with "cut," "tear," and "throw." This graphic and rather crude symbolism established that effort to separate sin from holiness is necessary. These imperatives did not merely imply. The disciples heard the demand for action to separate sinful parts from intended holiness. Mt 18: 8–9

Mk 9: 49-50 For everyone will be salted with fire. Salt is good, but if the salt has lost its saltiness, how will you make it salty again? <u>Have salt in yourselves</u> ἀρτύσετε ἔχετε ἐν ἑαυτοῖς, and <u>be at peace with one another</u> εἰρηνεύετε ἐν ἀλλήλοις."

> Jesus' two imperatives "Have salt" and "be at peace" refer to Lv 2: 13 that salt accompanied all offerings. To listening Jews who would have understood his reference to Lv 2:13, he commanded them to have salt and be at peace with one another. Salted offerings were sufficient. They were ready so they were commanded to be at peace with one another.

Mk 10: 2–9 And Pharisees came up and in order to test him asked, "Is it lawful for a man to divorce his wife?" He answered them, "What did Moses command you?" he said, "Moses allowed a man to write a certificate of divorce and to send her away." And Jesus said to them, "Because of your hardness of heart he wrote you this commandment. But from the beginning of creation, 'God made them male and female.' 'Therefore a man shall leave his father and mother and hold fast to his wife, and the two shall become one flesh.' So they are no longer two but one flesh. What therefore God has joined together, <u>let not man separate</u> ἄνθρωπος μὴ χωριζέτω."

> The translation is correct, yet the English rendering "let not man separate" reads and sounds weak because there is no English equivalent to a third person imperative. As explained in earlier chapters, the English words "let" and "must" are rightly used to make sense of the Greek construction. While the English word "let" somewhat conveys the imperative intent, in this passage, English readers can miss the absoluteness of the marriage covenant because the English word "let" carries a permissive meaning.

> Jesus affirmed the covenant marriage bond. The reason no one was to attempt separating what God had joined was that attempting to separate what God has joined together was not possible. In John 4: 1-30 Jesus affirmed the Samaritan woman's five husbands. Jesus used the aorist active, "you have had" five husbands. Note Jesus did not say "had five husbands" or "had had five husbands." John recorded that Jesus said "have had" five husbands. Mark's record affirmed that what God had joined was not separable by man even for the woman at the well as John had recorded. The aorist active while undefined and indefinite, is a fact. She has had five husbands. God's marital covenant was not dismissible. Her five previous husbands continued being her five former husbands.

> Agreeing with Mark's imperative in v9 Jesus was not advocating multiple marriages. Rather he affirmed that what God has joined was not separable. The present active imperative rightly translates, "let not" affirming that no man should attempt to separate what God has joined together because separating what God has joined is impossible. Mt 19:6

Mk 10:13-15 And they were bringing children to him that he might touch them, and the disciples rebuked them. But when Jesus saw it, he was indignant and said to them, "<u>Let the children come to me;</u> Ἀφετε τὰ παιδία ἔρχεσθαι πρός με; <u>do not hinder</u> μὴ κωλύετε αὐτά τῶν them, for to such belongs the kingdom of God. Truly, I say to you, whoever does not receive the kingdom of God like a child shall not enter it."

Jesus' two imperatives "let" and "do not hinder" made clear that there were to be no obstructions of any kind that hindered children. Jesus' seemed to imply a double meaning in children by age and by faith maturity (v15). Some have childlike faith not fully matured. Jesus commanded that his disciples understand that patience was required for those exhibiting an undeveloped faith. Jesus commanded to permit or let children seek him. God's calling was irrelevant of age. No hindrances to maturity by age or progress were to be placed regardless of years or maturity.

The Greek word here for "let" is Αφετε (root: ἀφίημι) which is the Greek word often translated into English as "forgive," "let go," "permit," "divorce," "leave," "abandon," and "let someone have something." Some translations use the phrase, "Suffer the little children to come to me."

What is clear from Jesus' imperative is that all hindering obstructions where to be removed. The children trying to come to Jesus had been held back. The command Jesus gave loosed the grip that held children of age or immaturity. Mt 19: 14; Lk 18: 16

Mk 10: 19 You know the commandments: 'Do not murder, Do not commit adultery, Do not steal, Do not bear false witness, Do not defraud, <u>Honor your father and mother</u> Τίμα τὸν πατέρα σου καὶ τὴν μητέρα.'"
    The first five commands in v19 are aorist subjunctives with negatives and not any less meaningful than the imperative, "honor." Mt 19: 19; 7: 10; Lk 18: 20

Mk 10: 21 And Jesus, looking at him, loved him, and said to him, "You lack one thing: <u>go</u> ὕπαγε, <u>sell all that you have</u> ὅσα ἔχεις πώλησον, <u>give to the poor</u> δὸς δὸς [τοῖς] πτωχοῖς, and you will have treasure in heaven; and come, <u>follow me</u> ἀκολούθει μοι." Disheartened by the saying, he went away sorrowful, for he had great possessions.
    Mark recorded four consecutive imperatives: "go," "sell," "give," and "follow." The consequential reward for the first three resulted in treasure in heaven. The man had done everything to receive eternal life except for one thing. Jesus did not correct him or deny his statement that he had kept the law from his youth. Jesus remained silent there. Jesus did not affirm or deny that the man had murdered, adultered, stolen, provided a false witness, committed fraud, or dishonored father or mother. Jesus was silent concerning the rich man's sins. Jesus did not say that the man had coveted his possessions.

Some in the crowd likely knew the man to be upstanding. Jesus commanded the man first go, second then sell his possessions, third then give to the poor and fourth then follow Jesus. Jesus' imperatives were powerfully meaningful and difficult commands for both the man and those in the crowd who heard Jesus' words to follow. Jesus' imperatives here were not only for this particular rich man but also for those who heard Jesus' imperatives to him.

In v22 Mark recorded that the man had departed with sorrow because he had great possessions. But the text does not indicate what happened in the future. While there is no indication that the man kept his wealth and did not follow Jesus, there is no indication that he did not sell his possessions and follow Jesus. Only through speculation can a prediction be made on what the rich man did. The power of Jesus' imperatives is compelling.

Mark does not tell his readers if the rich man sold his possession, gave to the poor and followed Jesus. We only know that what Jesus commanded him. What believer has not had a sorrowful temporary experience for what they must give up and yet joyful at what they receive in the future after having followed. Mt 19: 21; Lk 18: 22

Mk 10: 46-52 And they came to Jericho. And as he was leaving Jericho with his disciples and a great crowd, Bartimaeus, a blind beggar, the son of Timaeus, was sitting by the roadside. And when he heard that it was Jesus of Nazareth, he began to cry out and say, "Jesus, Son of David, have mercy on me!" And many rebuked him, telling him to be silent. But he cried out all the more, "Son of David, have mercy on me!" And Jesus stopped and said, "Call him." Φωνήσατε αὐτόν And they called the blind man, saying to him, "Take heart. Get up; he is calling you." And throwing off his cloak, he sprang up and came to Jesus. And Jesus said to him, "What do you want me to do for you?" And the blind man said to him, "Rabbi, let me recover my sight." And Jesus said to him, "Go your way ὕπαγε, ἡ πίστις σου; your faith has made you well." And immediately he recovered his sight and followed him on the way.

>Jesus' first imperative "Call him!" was to his disciples and the great crowd. His next imperative was to Bartimaeus where he verbally and publically commanded Bartimaeus whose sight had been restored to "go." Jesus' imperative here affirmed to both Bartimaeus and the crowd (and Jesus' disciples) the power of faith in healing beyond an imperative alone.

Rather than take sole credit for healing, Jesus credited the faith of Bartimaeus. Following his restored sight, he straightaway followed Jesus. Jesus openly asserted the power of faith and particularly the power of Bartimaeus' faith. Following Jesus, the formerly blind Bartimaeus exhibited to the crowd faith's healing power. Bartimaeus used his sight to follow Jesus. Jesus had commanded Bartimaeus man to 'go your way' but he followed Jesus. Jesus had given the man freedom with his sight to go wherever he wanted. Bartimaeus with his restored sight could have gone a different way. Mark recorded that he followed Jesus on the way or on the journey.

Mk 11: 1-3 Now when they drew near to Jerusalem, to Bethphage and Bethany, at the Mount of Olives, Jesus sent two of his disciples and said to them, "Go into the village in front of you, Ὑπάγετε εἰς τὴν κώμην τὴν κατέναντι ὑμῶν and immediately as you enter it you will find a colt tied, on which no one has ever sat. Untie it λύσατε αὐτὸν and bring it φέρετε. If anyone says to you, 'Why are you doing this?' say, εἴπατε 'The Lord has need of it and will send it back here immediately.'"

>As Jesus prepared his entrance into Jerusalem, he commanded two disciples with three imperatives, "go into the village," "untie it (the colt), and "bring it" (the colt) to him. After his imperatives, however, Jesus quickly acknowledged to those who were about to go into the village that what he had commanded them to do would be

challenged. He then commanded them the exact words to say after they had been challenged. Jesus knew what would happen. He protected those he had commanded. He specifically commanded them and gave them the exact words to say. Mt 21: 2; Lk 19: 30

Mk 11: 19-23 And when evening came they went out of the city. As they passed by in the morning, they saw the fig tree withered away to its roots. And Peter remembered and said to him, "Rabbi, look! The fig tree that you cursed has withered." And Jesus answered them, "<u>Have faith in God</u> Εχετε πίστιν θεοῦ. Truly, I say to you, whoever says to this mountain, '<u>Be taken up and thrown into the sea</u> Αρθητι καὶ βλήθητι εἰς τὴν θάλασσαν,' and does not doubt in his heart, but believes that what he says will come to pass, it will be done for him.

>These are Jesus' imperative after Peter affirmed that the tree Jesus had previously cursed (v14) had in fact withered. Peter made a public statement heard by others. Jesus' command, "have faith" was not to Peter in the singular but plural to all who were listening.

>Jesus stated two aorist passive imperatives, "be taken up" and "thrown." Jesus appeared to be speaking with hyperbole given the immensity of raising a mountain and throwing it into the sea. Yet his illustration is not exaggerated. Jesus' conclusion, "it will be done for him" affirmed that people of faith may speak imperatives with power and effectiveness. Mt 21: 20 – 22

Mk 11: 24 Therefore I tell you, whatever you ask in prayer, <u>believe that you have received it</u> πιστεύετε ὅτι ἐλάβετε, and it will be yours.

>Jesus concluded his illuminating lesson on casting a mountain into the sea by faith with the imperative "believe that you have received it." Those who believe they have the power will receive what they ask through that power. His intent is that they are sufficiently solid enough in their faith to ask to move mountains. The power of their faith is exhibited by the size of their requests.

Mk 11: 25 And whenever you stand praying, <u>forgive</u>, ἀφίετε if you have anything against anyone, so that your Father also who is in heaven may forgive you your trespasses."

>Jesus commanded that both forgiving and being forgiven must precede prayer. He did not suggest forgiveness. He commanded forgiveness.

Mk 11: 29 And they came again to Jerusalem. And as he was walking in the temple, the chief priests and the scribes and the elders came to him, and they said to him, "By what authority are you doing these things, or who gave you this authority to do them?" Jesus said to them, "I will ask you one question; <u>answer me</u> ἀποκρίθητέ μοι, and I will tell you by what authority I do these things.

>Jesus' imperative "answer me" to the chief priests, scribes and elders exposed their conundrum. Relevant here is not merely what the chief priests, scribes, and elders heard, but what those around them heard. Lk 20: 3

Mk 11: 30 Was the baptism of John from heaven or from man? <u>Answer me</u> ἀποκρίθητέ μοι."

Jesus' more than pressed the chief priests, scribes, and elders to respond to his question. He commanded them a second time following v29 to answer. Repetition added to the power of his question. He knew they were stuck between heaven and the people. They were not silent and responded to his command with "We do not know." Their answer at Jesus command showed Jesus' authority to those in the temple watching and listening to this confrontation. The question and answer dilemma illuminated Jesus' wit and mastery over the temple leaders. However, Jesus' imperatives and the temple leaders' responses were the more powerful lesson for those in the temple witnessing their interactions. Mt and Lk did not include imperatives comparable to Mk 11: 30 in their parallel narratives of Jesus' questions to the chief priests, scribes, and elders.

Mk 12: 15 But, knowing their hypocrisy, he said to them, "Why put me to the test? <u>Bring me a denarius and let me look at it</u> φέρετέ μοι δηνάριον ἵνα ἴδω." And they brought one. And he said to them, "Whose likeness and inscription is this?" They said to him, "Caesar's." Jesus said to them, "<u>Render to Caesar the things that are Caesar's, and to God the things that are God's</u> τὰ Καίσαρος ἀπόδοτε Καίσαρι καὶ τὰ τοῦ θεοῦ τῷ θεῷ." And they marveled at him.

    Jesus' did not have a denarius in his possession since he commanded the Pharisees and Herodians to bring a denarius to him. His imperative "bring'" was plural, not singular. He exposed their group hypocrisy. Jesus' had commanded them as a group to give to Caesar what was Caesar's. His command "render" or some translations "give" proved their worship to Caesar with Caesar's own money.

Jesus did not imply or teach to withhold taxes. Given time and context, Caesar would likely have appreciated that Jesus had commanded Caesars' subordinates to pay Caesar taxes. He commanded those who worked for and were paid by Caesar to pay what Caesar demanded through taxes. He magnified their employment and bondage contract with Caesar through Caesar's currency. They marveled at him as they had likely given little concern to their covenant bondage to Caesar. Jesus exposed their indebtedness to the superior they worshiped. Contrary to a covenant with Caesar, God covenants are not bound by tributes through taxation. Jesus' imperatives exposed their bondage to politics and governance. Mt 22: 21; Lk 20: 25

Mk 12: 28–30 And one of the scribes came up and heard them disputing with one another, and seeing that he answered them well, asked him, "Which commandment is the most important of all?" Jesus answered, "The most important is, '<u>Hear, O Israel: The Lord our God, the Lord is one</u> Ακουε Ἰσραήλ κύριος ὁ θεὸς ἡμῶν κύριος εἷς ἐστιν. And you shall love the Lord your God with all your heart and with all your soul and with all your mind and with all your strength.' The second is this: 'You shall love your neighbor as yourself.' There is no other commandment greater than these." And the scribe said to him, "You are right, Teacher. You have truly said that he is one, and there is no other besides him. And to love him with all the heart and with all the understanding and with all the strength, and to love one's neighbor as oneself, is much more than all whole burnt offerings and sacrifices." And when Jesus saw that he answered wisely, he said to him, "You are not far from the kingdom of God." And after that no one dared to ask him any more questions.

The only recorded imperative is, "Hear, O Israel" Jesus then repeated the Hebrew laws that God is one and is to be loved with heart, soul, mind, and strength. His imperative "Hear O Israel" commanded them to recall what they should have known. His present active singular imperative addressed Israel as a nation. To know the Lord is one God and to love God was a proclamation not to be questioned.

Note that Jesus did not use imperatives to describe the laws. He did not say "love the Lord" in the Greek imperative. He referenced Lv 19: 18; 1 Sm 15: 22; Hs 6: 6; Mc 6: 6 – 8; and Ps 40: 6. Jesus' imperative demanded that Israel should have understood the message.

Many interpret and summarize the two greatest commandments as love the Lord and neighbor. Jesus' imperative here certainly affirmed those Hebrew commands. But here Jesus' imperative was to those in his midst. Israel should have had no doubt. Jesus command was to the nation as one. Jesus' command "Hear O Israel" proved that those in his presence knew the law but that they had forsaken its understanding. Dt 6: 4

Mk 12: 35-36 And as Jesus taught in the temple, he said, "How can the scribes say that the Christ is the son of David? David himself, in the Holy Spirit, declared, "'The Lord said to my Lord, <u>Sit at my right hand</u> Κάθου ἐκ δεξιῶν μου, until I put your enemies under your feet.'
    Jesus quoted David's imperative from Ps 110: 1 which affirmed Jesus' Davidic lineage and messianic kingdom rule. Mt 22: 44; Lk 20: 42

Mk 12: 37–40 David himself calls him Lord. So how is he his son?" And the great throng heard him gladly. And in his teaching he said, "<u>Beware of the scribes</u> βλέπετε ἀπὸ τῶν γραμματέων τῶν, who like to walk around in long robes and like greetings in the marketplaces and have the best seats in the synagogues and the places of honor at feasts, who devour widows' houses and for a pretense make long prayers. They will receive the greater condemnation."
    Jesus' commanded "beware" because his disciples must go past simply being warned. They must consciously beware of the Scribes. Jesus knew it would be easy to listen to them given the Scribe's perceived authority. Jesus went beyond cautioning. He demanded vigilance in their dealings with Scribes.

    Luke used προσέχετε and Mark used βλέπετε and both are translated as "Beware." Mark's Greek indicated "see" whereas Luke's Greek indicated "keep watch, look out" demanding a caution. The English "beware" is a solid translation from both Mark and Luke. Both Luke and Mark agree that Jesus demanded watchfulness when dealing with the Scribes. Lk 20: 46

Mk 13: 1–5 And as he came out of the temple, one of his disciples said to him, "Look, Teacher, what wonderful stones and what wonderful buildings!" And Jesus said to him, "Do you see these great buildings? There will not be left here one stone upon another that will not be thrown down." And as he sat on the Mount of Olives opposite the temple, Peter and James and John and Andrew asked him privately, "Tell us, when will these things be, and what will be the sign when all these things are about to be accomplished?" And Jesus began to say to them, "See that no one leads you astray Βλέπετε μή τις ὑμᾶς πλανήσῃ.

>Jesus here commanded Peter, James, John, and Andrew as a group (second person plural) that they were not to be lead astray. This was not a suggestion or a caution from Jesus. Jesus' imperative was that they guard themselves as a group not to be deceived. Mark recorded Jesus command as plural, not singular to assure the continuity of their community. He instructed them as a group that no single person (no one) leads them astray. Jesus' imperative merged their protection for one another. Mt 24: 4; Lk 21: 8

Mk 13: 7-8 And when you hear of wars and rumors of wars, do not be alarmed μὴ θροεῖσθε. This must take place, but the end is not yet. For nation will rise against nation, and kingdom against kingdom. There will be earthquakes in various places; there will be famines. These are but the beginning of the birth pains.

>Jesus commanded Peter, James, John, and Andrew (present, passive, plural) not to be alarmed when they heard of wars and rumors of wars. Even if in the past they had been distressed at cataclysmic worldly events they were no longer as a group or individually to have fear. Jesus knew wars and rumors of wars caused two results: fear and expectation of an end. Jesus commanded the opposite. The imperative was given to Peter, James, John, and Andrew after they specifically asked about end times.

>They were not to fear. However, more importantly, alarm and fear were not to be brought to others. There are those who will be alarmed and fearful of wars and rumors of war, but Peter, James, John, and Andrew were commanded to be separate and different from those who fear. As Jesus' chosen disciples, after having heard news of wars and rumors of wars, peace was to be exemplified. Note that Jesus' imperative was given to his key disciples Peter, James, John, and Andrew. Those with weaker faith may have been unable at that time to exhibit such peace in the midst of catastrophe. Jesus' key leaders were commanded to exhibit harmony in a time of calamity and work amidst wars and rumors of war. Mt 24: 6; Lk 21: 10

Mk 13: 9 "But be on your guard Βλέπετε δὲ ὑμεῖς ἑαυτούς. For they will deliver you over to councils, and you will be beaten in synagogues, and you will stand before governors and kings for my sake, to bear witness before them.

>Jesus again commanded Peter, James, John, and Andrew in the plural as a group to be on their guard. Jesus affirmed that they would be turned over to counsels and beaten in synagogues. Thus, he commanded they beware. Jesus prepared them by command.

>Note: Some English translations (ESV, NAU, and NIV) did not translate the Greek reflexive masculine plural pronoun ἑαυτούς "yourselves." The KJV "but take heed to yourselves" and NKJV "but watch out for yourselves" are better translations for including the personal pronoun. Jesus' words to them as a group are emphatic. He specifically targeted them in plural as a group to be on guard. Lk 21: 14

Mk 13: 11 And when they bring you to trial and deliver you over, <u>do not be anxious beforehand what you are to say</u> μὴ προμεριμνᾶτε τί λαλήσητε, but <u>say whatever is given in that hour</u> ὃ ἐὰν δοθῇ ὑμῖν ἐν ἐκείνῃ τῇ ὥρᾳ τοῦτο λαλεῖτε, for it is not you who speak, but the Holy Spirit.

    Jesus' gave two imperatives to Peter, James, John, and Andrew. "Do not be anxious beforehand what you are to say." and "Say whatever is given in that hour." Support one another. Jesus here affirmed to them that the Spirit's working would deliver them in trial.

    Mark recorded Jesus' words for all to read yet Mark did not record these specific commands to all disciples or to those who heard them. They were given to Peter, James, John, and Andrew in preparation for their future as to what they would endure as believers. Yet, in both historical and contemporary context, all believers expect trials, are prepared and know words will be provided at their appointed hour of need. Lk 21: 14

Mk 13: 12–14 And brother will deliver brother over to death, and the father his child, and children will rise against parents and have them put to death. And you will be hated by all for my name's sake. But the one who endures to the end will be saved. "But when you see the abomination of desolation standing where he ought not to be (let the reader <u>understand</u>) νοείτω, then let those who are in Judea <u>flee to the mountains</u> φευγέτωσαν φευγέτωσαν εἰς τὰ ὄρη.

    Here Jesus referred to those who had read the apocalyptic destruction of the "abomination of desolation" in Dn 9: 27; 11: 31; 12: 11. Knowing the impending desolation they were commanded to flee from Judea to the mountains. The imperative command "flee" was absolute.

    Judea and mountains were real in both literal and metaphoric senses. That is, at seeing destruction, fleeing was not an option. Fleeing had been commanded. Similar to Lot's departure from Sodom and Gomorrah, they fled from the moral destruction of their town, a precursor to the eventual physical destruction. Mt 24: 15 – 16; Lk 21: 21

Mk 13: 15-18 <u>Let the one who is on the housetop not go down, nor enter his house, to take anything out</u>, ὁ ἐπὶ τοῦ δώματος μὴ καταβάτω μηδὲ εἰσελθάτω τι ἆραι ἐκ τῆς οἰκίας αὐτοῦ and <u>let the one who is in the field not turn back to take his cloak</u> ὁ εἰς τὸν ἀγρὸν μὴ ἐπιστρεψάτω εἰς τὰ ὀπίσω ἆραι τὸ ἱμάτιον αὐτοῦ. And alas for women who are pregnant and for those who are nursing infants in those days! <u>Pray that it may not happen in winter</u> προσεύχεσθε δὲ ἵνα μὴ γένηται χειμῶνος

    Mark continued recording Jesus' imperatives to Peter, James, John, and Andrew regarding end times. Jesus commands them that if they are not prepared their time for preparation had passed. His command was extremely descriptive providing an example that if someone was on the roof passing through his house to gather belongings on the way out was not an option. Even as a homeowner running past his personal belongings when fleeing, nothing was to be taken out.

    He emphasized the urgency of departure. Jesus made the point to Peter, James, John, and Andrew that there will come a time when for preparing for an end will have passed. Jesus commanded them to pray that the end they would experience "may not" (Greek Subjunctive) come in winter. His command made them realize that the devastation would, without doubt, be worse in winter. Their prayers were intended to bring mercy to those unaware of the sure ruin and changes to come. Mt 24: 17 - 20

Mk 13: 21 And then if anyone says to you, 'Look, here is the Christ!' or 'Look, there he is!' <u>do not believe it</u> μὴ πιστεύετε.

> Jesus commanded Peter, James, John, and Andrew that there was no belief in someone who proclaimed another Messiah's return. They would not believe a false message. There was one Messiah and Jesus' imperative gave them confidence that they would not believe a false return. Jesus' imperative to them assured them that it would be impossible for them to be fooled by a false message. Not everyone, however, would be able to identify deception. Mt 24: 23

Mk 13: 22–23 For false christs and false prophets will arise and perform signs and wonders, to lead astray, if possible, the elect. <u>But be on guard</u> ὑμεῖς δὲ βλέπετε; I have told you all things beforehand.

> Jesus concluded his imperatives regarding the end of age issues and commanded them to be on guard. Reminding them that he had told them beforehand what would happen, his command to be on guard came as a result of what had been revealed to them. His disciples had been warned and prepared. Jesus' imperative to be on guard was clear and they would be on guard. Mt 24: 26

Mk 13: 24–28 "But in those days, after that tribulation, the sun will be darkened, and the moon will not give its light, and the stars will be falling from heaven, and the powers in the heavens will be shaken. And then they will see the Son of Man coming in clouds with great power and glory. And then he will send out the angels and gather his elect from the four winds, from the ends of the earth to the ends of heaven. "<u>From the fig tree learn its lesson</u> Ἀπὸ δὲ τῆς συκῆς μάθετε τὴν παραβολήν: as soon as its branch becomes tender and puts out its leaves, you know that summer is near.

> Jesus commanded them to learn the lesson from the fig tree's foliage in predicting seasons. The fig tree was more than a fruit-bearing tree for Peter, James, John, and Andrew. It was a lesson that predicted the future, changing times, end of old things, and the beginning of new things Mt 24: 32; Lk 21: 29

Mk 13:29 So also, when you see these things taking place, you <u>know</u> γινώσκετε (imperative or indicative) that he is near, at the very gates.

> The Koine Greek for "know" in v29 may be indicative or imperative. The plural, "you" preceding "know" in some English translations somewhat reduced the imperative power. More definitive renderings may be "know," "be assured," or "be certain" he is near. Jesus' commanded them to know that the Lord would be near when these things take place. In the midst of desolation, fear and preparation would fill most people. So, Jesus commanded his key disciples that they must not succumb to fear. They were the ones Jesus had prepared. They were not to fear given their knowledge Jesus had taught them. Mt 24: 33; Lk 21: 31

Mk 13: 30–33 Truly, I say to you, this generation will not pass away until all these things take place. Heaven and earth will pass away, but my words will not pass away. "But concerning that day or that hour, no one knows, not even the angels in heaven, nor the Son, but only the Father. Be on guard Βλέπετε, keep awake ἀγρυπνεῖτε. For you do not know when the time will come.
> Mark recorded that Jesus used two consecutive imperatives both which emphasized vigilance. Jesus hammered the point. He demanded their preparation. Peter, James, John, and Andrew knew these imperatives were not Jesus' suggestions. He required their watchfulness because they would not know the time. Lk 21: 34

Mk 13: 34–35 It is like a man going on a journey, when he leaves home and puts his servants in charge, each with his work, and commands the doorkeeper to stay awake. Therefore stay awake γρηγορεῖτε for you do not know when the master of the house will come, in the evening, or at midnight, or when the rooster crows, or in the morning—
> Mark recorded the conjunction, "Therefore" with an imperative, "stay awake" which stressed that while they would not know, they were commanded to always be prepared. Time was irrelevant. Jesus' servants were always to be prepared. Mt 24: 42; Lk 21: 36

Mk 13: 36–37 lest he come suddenly and find you asleep. And what I say to you I say to all: Stay awake γρηγορεῖτε."
> Jesus imperatives regarding endings or changes about to occur were directed to Peter, James, John, and Andrew. However, in v37 Mark recorded Jesus' closing words that his command to "stay awake" was not solely to Peter, James, John, and Andrew, but to all. Watchfulness was not simply for a few. Return and judgment were inevitable. Mt 24: 44; Lk 21: 36

Mk 14: 3–6 And while he was at Bethany in the house of Simon the leper, as he was reclining at table, a woman came with an alabaster flask of ointment of pure nard, very costly, and she broke the flask and poured it over his head. There were some who said to themselves indignantly, "Why was the ointment wasted like that? For this ointment could have been sold for more than three hundred denarii and given to the poor." And they scolded her. But Jesus said, "Leave her alone ἄφετε αὐτήν. Why do you trouble her? She has done a beautiful thing to me. For you always have the poor with you, and whenever you want, you can do good for them. But you will not always have me. She has done what she could; she has anointed my body beforehand for burial. And truly, I say to you, wherever the gospel is proclaimed in the whole world, what she has done will be told in memory of her."
> At Bethany where Jesus was anointed by the woman, he demanded that the woman be left alone from the accusations that she had been wasteful anointing Jesus with expensive nard. By this time in Jesus' ministry, many in his company had seen his miracles, healings, and heard his parables and teachings. Following up his v6 imperative in v9 he declared that her actions would be a memorial to her for what she had done wherever the gospel would be proclaimed. Jn 12: 7

Mk 14: 13–15 And he sent two of his disciples and said to them, "Go into the city ὑπάγετε εἰς τὴν πόλιν, and a man carrying a jar of water will meet you. Follow him ἀκολουθήσατε αὐτῷ, and wherever he enters, say to the master of the house εἴπατε τῷ οἰκοδεσπότῃ ὅτι, 'The Teacher says,

'Where is my guest room, where I may eat the Passover with my disciples?' And he will show you a large upper room furnished and ready; there prepare for us ἑτοιμάσατε ἡμῖν."

    Mark recorded a series of four imperatives to Jesus' disciples, "go", "follow", "say", and "prepare." These obvious imperatives on the first read in English seem unnecessary. Considering that the disciples were unaware of what was about to happen, Jesus was precise and intentional with his chosen imperatives. He did not want questions or uncertainty about their responsibilities given what was about to happen.

    How would Jesus have known that a man carrying a jar of water would meet them? How would Jesus have known about the place already prepared for the Passover meal? Mark did not record that any of the disciples questioned Jesus. The disciples followed Jesus' imperatives. They had spent enough time with him, saw and experienced the results of his imperatives. They did not hesitate.
Mt 26:18; Lk 22: 10 - 12

Mk 14: 22-25 And as they were eating, he took bread, and after blessing it broke it and gave it to them, and said, "Take λάβετε; this is my body." And he took a cup, and when he had given thanks he gave it to them, and they all drank of it. And he said to them, "This is my blood of the covenant, which is poured out for many. Truly, I say to you, I will not drink again of the fruit of the vine until that day when I drink it new in the kingdom of God."

    Jesus' plural imperative "take" affirmed the communal Passover meal as a community. They took the bread following his imperative. The disciples after their time with Jesus were likely very aware that his imperatives had meanings greater than what they could grasp.

    By now they were mindful that his imperatives had future intentions. His imperatives, while often either not understood or misunderstood, had meanings beyond perhaps their present comprehension. What he demanded of them had greater meaning than what they could surmise. They were changing from followers to disciples especially through experiencing, responding and trusting his imperative commands. Mt 26: 26; Lk 22: 17

Mk 14: 32 And they went to a place called Gethsemane. And he said to his disciples, "Sit here καθίσατε ὧδε while I pray."

    Jesus' command to his disciples that they "sit here" while he prayed may have seemed odd to them. Prior to this, Jesus had taught them to pray, prayed with them, and prayed for them. But here Jesus commanded them to sit. He did not invite them to pray with him. They sat waiting for his next words. Luke, however, recorded that Jesus had commanded them to, "pray" rather than "sit" as Matthew and Mark recorded. Mt 26: 36; Lk 22: 40

Mk 14: 33–34 And he took with him Peter and James and John, and began to be greatly distressed and troubled. And he said to them, "My soul is very sorrowful, even to death. Remain here μείνατε ὧδε and watch καὶ γρηγορεῖτε."

Jesus explained the sorrowful state of his soul to Peter, James, and John, but not to the others. He then commanded Peter, James, and John only two imperatives, "remain" and "watch." Jesus did not tell them why they were to remain or for what they were to watch. After three years with Jesus having heard and experienced his imperatives, Peter, James, and John did not complain. Mt 26: 38

Mk 14: 35–36 And going a little farther, he fell on the ground and prayed that, if it were possible, the hour might pass from him. And he said, "Abba, Father, all things are possible for you. <u>Remove this cup from me</u> παρένεγκε τὸ ποτήριον τοῦτο ἀπ᾽ ἐμοῦ. Yet not what I will, but what you will."

In his prayer, Jesus commanded the Father to remove the cup and immediately conceded his will submitting to the Father's will. Jesus imperatives to his disciples were from the father and were to be followed for reasons that his disciples may not have understood. Here Jesus conceded that his Father's will overrode his will. Jesus followed the father's commands and will.

Trust was the fruit of obedience was what Jesus portrayed through his prayer to the Father. How perplexing for Jesus and soon his disciples to follow imperatives without question even unto death. Mt 26: 39

Mk 14: 37–38 And he came and found them sleeping, and he said to Peter, "Simon, are you asleep? Could you not watch one hour? <u>Watch</u> γρηγορεῖτε <u>and pray</u> καὶ προσεύχεσθε that you may not enter into temptation. The spirit indeed is willing, but the flesh is weak."

Jesus first questioned Peter in v37 and then commanded them in the plural as a group to "watch" and "pray." Jesus explained that watching and praying was intentioned to keep them from entering temptation. Though Peter was personally and solely addressed in v37, these commands were not only to Peter. These imperatives are plural. Both Mark and Matthew recorded that Jesus commanded to both "watch" and "pray." Luke recorded only a single imperative, "pray." Mt 26: 41; Lk 22: 46

Mk 14: 39–41 And again he went away and prayed, saying the same words. And again he came and found them sleeping, for their eyes were very heavy, and they did not know what to answer him. And he came the third time and said to them, "<u>Are you still sleeping</u> καθεύδετε τὸ λοιπὸν and <u>taking your rest</u> καὶ ἀναπαύεσθε? It is enough; the hour has come. The Son of Man is betrayed into the hands of sinners.

Some Greek tools identify "sleep" and "rest" as indicatives and/or imperatives resulting in various translations in the form of a question. Some translations render Jesus' imperatives into two questions, "Are you still sleeping and taking your rest?" which while acceptable in the contemporary context, such a translation, however, weakens the imperative. The Greek does not indicate that Jesus asked a double question.

Jesus' imperatives to them were sarcastic. He commanded them to sleep and rest because the hour had (aorist active) come. There was nothing they could do. It was too late. He commanded them to sleep and rest, perhaps derisively, but absolutely with intention. Those who heard Jesus' words would have perceived both the sarcasm and frustration. They certainly would have felt the weight of their weakness when Jesus affirmed that "the Son of Man is betrayed into the hands of sinners." His prior commands were "watch," "remain," "stay awake," and "pray." After betrayal he no longer commanded vigilance. He commanded them to sleep and rest. Their time for remaining awake had passed. Mt 26: 45

Mk 14: 42 <u>Rise</u> ἐγείρεσθε, let us be going; <u>see</u> ἰδοὺ, my betrayer is at hand."
After his imperatives to sleep and rest (v41), he immediately spoke a plural imperative to the group, "rise" or "get up" which is a hortatory imperative. They were likely sitting or lying down when the Judas approached with the temple guards. At Judas' approach, he commanded them to get up perhaps out of preparation, but more likely out of dignity and respect or to be without conveying shame. They were no longer to remain in the garden. They would depart. Everything had changed. Jesus' command to his disciples "get up" was his second to the last imperative to them until Mark 16: 15 where he commanded them to proclaim the gospel. Mt 26: 46

Mk 16: 14–15[13] Afterward he appeared to the eleven themselves as they were reclining at table, and he rebuked them for their unbelief and hardness of heart, because they had not believed those who saw him after he had risen. And he said to them, "Go into all the world and <u>proclaim the gospel to the whole creation</u> κηρύξατε τὸ εὐαγγέλιον πάσῃ τῇ κτίσει.
Similar to Mt 28: 19 – 20 the English word "Go" that starts the sentence gives the impression of an English command, but here the only imperative Mark recorded that Jesus said is "proclaim." The Greek word, Πορευθέντες which is an aorist passive deponent verb (deponent means the word is passive in form but active in meaning) is often rendered "go" to convey the act of going. The English word "Go" that starts the sentence however is perhaps an over translation because "Go" lacks the aorist (past) participle.

The YLT, "Having gone to all the world, proclaim the good news to all the creation." more clearly conveys the aorist passive participle. "Having gone" rather than "go" somewhat bridles the English sounding command. While "Having gone" may be strange to the English ear the past participle meaning is without question.

Mark recorded Jesus' final imperative as "proclaim the gospel to the whole creation." Matthew recorded Jesus' final imperative in Mt 28: 28 as "disciple all the nations." Both "proclaim" in Mark and "disciple" in Matthew are imperatives.

---

[13] Some manuscripts end the book [Mark] with 16:8; others include verses 9 – 20 immediately after verse 8. A few manuscripts insert additional material after verse 14; one Latin manuscript adds after verse 8 the following: *But they reported briefly to Peter and those with him all that they had been told. And after this, Jesus himself sent out by means of them, from east to west, the sacred and imperishable proclamation of eternal salvation.* Other manuscripts include this same wording after verse 8, then continue with verses 9 – 20 a. Ps 22:1 b. For 15: 39 – 41 see parallels Matt 27: 54 – 56; Luke 23: 47, 49 c. For 15: 42 – 47 see parallels Matt. 27: 57 – 61; Luke 23: 50 – 56; John 19: 38 – 42 d. For 16: 1 – 8 see parallels Matt 28; Luke 24: 1 – 10. *The Holy Bible, English Standard Version*, Thinline Edition, 853.

And he told them a parable: "Look at the fig tree, and all the trees. As soon as they come out in leaf, you see for yourselves and know that the summer is already near. So also, when you see these things taking place, you know that the kingdom of God is near. Truly, I say to you, this generation will not pass away until all has taken place. Heaven and earth will pass away, but my words will not pass away.

Lk 21: 29-33

# 11 Luke's Record of the Imperatives of Jesus

And he told them a parable: "Look at the fig tree, and all the trees. As soon as they come out in leaf, you see for yourselves and know that the summer is already near. So also, when you see these things taking place, you know that the kingdom of God is near. Truly, I say to you, this generation will not pass away until all has taken place. Lk 21: 29-32

## Luke

Matthew, Mark, and John personally knew and walked with Jesus. There is no biblical record that Luke met Jesus. Luke never conveyed in his gospel or book of Acts that he had heard Jesus speak. Some scholars stretch the point that Jesus may have spent time in Jerusalem or Galilee during Jesus' life. Most likely, however, Luke never met Jesus. Luke was not a Jew but a Gentile Greek doctor. His gospel does not indicate that he had lived or was ever in Jerusalem at the time of Jesus. Presuming Luke had never heard Jesus speak, why would Luke's gospel and the imperatives spoken by Jesus within Luke gospel be trustworthy?

Within his first four verses, Luke validated the exceptional authority with which he wrote. The English phrase, "to write an orderly account for you most excellent Theophilus" does not convey in English that Luke wrote a chronological or a sequence of accounts as they had happened.[1]. The English word "orderly" carries the idea of neat, tidy, organized, or systematized more so than chronological. Luke's narrative similar to Matthew and Mark is sequential.

More convincingly, however, because Luke depended on other written sources and personal testimonies, accuracy was paramount for his intended readers. In other words, Luke was resolute on the truthfulness of his message. Luke would not have recorded unsubstantiated claims, doubtful accounts, or obscure words. He likely knew of martyrdoms and the persecutions Paul, Peter, and others had experienced. Beyond his reputation alone, his life was at stake.

Luke focused on conveying truth to, "most excellent Theophilus" (Lk 1: 3; Ac 1: 1) with the assumption that Gentile readers would read his books in Rome and Greece. Luke's description "most excellent" to describe Theophilus is insightful. Brownrigg clarifies:

> 'Most excellent' indicates a specific person of some social prominence. The title would well have fitted a Roman official of equestrian rank. This man [Theophilus] had heard by repute about Jesus and his followers, and probably had requested further information. He received two scrolls, one about the birth, life, ministry, death and resurrection of Jesus, the other a selection of events connected with the society formed by the followers of this Jesus, particularly Peter and Paul.[2]

Not having been a disciple or eyewitness Luke was dependent on the writings of others but more importantly, relied on personal testimonies. Critical questioning and verifying the credibility

---

[1] Inasmuch as many have undertaken to compile a narrative of the things that have been accomplished among us, just as those who from the beginning were eyewitnesses and ministers of the word have delivered them to us, it seemed good to me also, having followed all things closely for some time past, to write an orderly account for you, most excellent Theophilus, that you may have certainty concerning the things you have been taught. Lk 1: 1-4

[2] Brownnrigg, Ronald, *Who's Who the New Testament*, 269.

of testimonies Luke heard, his written account and record of the imperative of Jesus are trustworthy. Luke having operated under the apostolic authority of Paul further credits Luke's record. Since Luke relied on other documents and witnesses, who provided their testimonies to Luke? Schreiner affirms:

> We should also not rule out that Luke may have received information from Mary the mother of Jesus, the disciples of John the Baptist, Manaen (an early disciple; cv. Acts 13: 2), Cleopas (Lk 24: 18), and others. Many New Testament scholars would doubt that Luke depended on any of these persons. But it is quite probable that Luke would have spoken to living persons about what they had heard and seen of Jesus when he came into contact with them. Any twentieth-century researcher would have done the same, and in the ancient world such a procedure would have been prized just as highly, as the early church father Papias in the second century made clear.[3]

Luke's first two chapters include extraordinary detail and read as if Luke's report is from Mary, mother of Jesus. Given the detail, it is likely Luke personally met with Mary and recorded her account which was affirmed by others such as Mary Magdalen, sisters Martha and Mary and possibly Lazarus. It is also possible Luke interviewed some of the disciples and followers of Jesus. Testimonies Luke heard would have vetted and corroborated before Luke recorded his gospel. Because of Luke's attention to detail, the imperatives Luke recorded were intentional. Schreiner clarified Luke's' intelligence, education, and writing skills:

> We do learn, however, that the author was not an eyewitness (Lk 1: 2), and thus anyone who observed Jesus in his public ministry can be eliminated. Furthermore, the writer of Luke clearly was intelligent and well educated, for he displays an ability to write in excellent Greek and is well acquainted with the Old Testament."[4]

Given that Luke made use of eyewitnesses, the timing of Luke's gospel is essential. Anyone who has written a biography understands the significance of interviewing living people closest to the person whose life story is the focus. Luke's gospel or biography of Jesus depended on those still living who had been with Jesus. In AD 40's, 50's and 60's the lives of those who had walked with Jesus were coming to an end. Given that Jesus was in his early 30's at the time of the crucifixion, Mary, his mother, and the lives of others perhaps 10, 20, or 30 years older than Jesus were ending. Luke had little time to waste. Timing mattered which is why Luke's gospel is dated before AD 70 most likely somewhere in late 50's or early 60's. Schreiner affirms:

> Since Luke was written before Acts, then the Gospel would be placed in the early 60's or late 50's. The same scholars would argue that the Gospel of Mark was written in the 50's. Other scholars date Luke between A.D. 65 – 70, arguing that it was probably written before the destruction of Jerusalem in A.D. 70. Certainty is impossible on such difficult matters, but a date before the destruction of Jerusalem in A.D. 70 seems probable.[5]

---

[3] Schreiner, Thomas R., "Luke" in Elwell, Walter A., Editor, *Baker Commentary on the Bible,* 802.
[4] Ibid. 799.
[5] Schreiner, Thomas R., "Luke" in Elwell, Walter A., Editor, *Baker Commentary on the Bible,* 801.

## Luke's Intellect

History writers are not playwrights. Effective historians record history in ways that establish foundations for future generations. Luke wrote as a historian. Luke's historical leanings as a writer and physician made his Gospel rich for readers then and today. Josephus similarly wrote with historical insight.[6] N. T. Wright compares Luke and Josephus:

> Though Luke's story thus focuses on Jesus' death as Josephus' does on the fall of Jerusalem, and hence forms a close parallel, Luke too is aware of Jerusalem's fall (whether as prophecy or as past event, we cannot here discuss). 'Unless you repent, you will all likewise perish': the words are those of Luke's Jesus (Lk 13: 3, 5). The fall of the Temple, seen as future from within Luke's narrative world is set in close parallel with the death of Jesus.[7]

The parallel of Jesus' death and the fall of the Jerusalem Temple is significant. Luke's intellect regarding history is noteworthy to his Gospel. History is evidence of divine interventions. N.T. Wright agrees:

> Luke was precisely a historian, not too unlike Josephus. For Luke, as for Josephus, history was the sphere of divine operation.[8]

Beyond a physician, Luke was an arduous, educated, reputable, historically astute, and skilled writer. The Greek imperatives of Jesus within Luke's gospel were deliberate. Luke's accuracy in having recorded Jesus' imperatives from eyewitness testimonies is reassuring. Beyond Luke's intellect is the scrutiny and validity from those who provided their accounts to him.

## Luke and Paul

As previously explained, Luke was not one of the twelve disciples. Most likely his initial and primary link to Jesus came through Paul. Paul knew Luke beyond Luke's profession as a physician. Paul likely had a close relationship with Luke sufficient enough to ask Luke to cross the Mediterranean Sea to meet the disciples and Mary. Perhaps Paul was familiar with Luke as Paul's physician. I. H. Marshal clarifies:

> Among the companions of Paul who send their greetings in his letter to Colossae there appears 'Luke (Gk. *Loukas*) the beloved physician' (Col 4:14); the way in which he is described suggests that he [Luke] had given medical care to Paul, no doubt during the latter's imprisonment. In Phm. 24, he [Luke] is described as a fellow-worker of Paul which suggests that his [Luke's] help in the work of the

---

[6] Flavius Josephus (A.D. 37-c. 100) is the author of what has become for Christianity perhaps the most significant extra-biblical writings of the first century. His works are principle sources for the history of the Jews from the reign of Antiochus Epiphanes (B.C. 175-160) to the fall of Masada in A.D. 73, and therefore, are of incomparable value for determining the setting of late inter-testamental and New Testament times.
Josephus, Flavius, *The Works of Josephus*, viii.
[7] Wright, N. T., *The New Testament and the People of God,* 373–374.
[8] Ibid. 378.

Gospel was not confined to his medical skill. There is a third reference to him [Luke] in what appears to have been one of Paul's last messages: 'Luke alone is with me' (2Ti 4: 11), and this confirms the close link between the two men.[9]

Luke was a friend, companion, and fellow worker with Saul (Paul).[10] Similar to Luke, there is no biblical record that Jesus and Saul had met during their earthly lives. Saul likely knew little about Jesus' life with his disciples. Neither Matthew, Mark, Luke nor John referenced Saul in their gospels. Before his Damascus conversion where Jesus confronted Saul, Saul had been overseeing and initiating the persecution of Jesus' followers in Jerusalem. Jewish leaders (particularly the Sanhedrin of which Saul was a member) in addition to persecuting followers of "the way" had denied Jesus as Messiah. Persecuting common Jews who gathered in communities (church) who saw Jesus as the Messiah was commonplace. Saul persecuted Christians for blasphemy in their believing Jesus as Messiah. Bruce clarifies:

> It is unlikely that the status, career, and teaching of Jesus conformed in any way with Paul's conception of the status, career, and teaching of the Messiah – but that was not the conclusive argument in Paul's mind. The conclusive argument was simply this: Jesus had been crucified. A crucified Messiah was a contradiction in terms. Whether his death by crucifixion was deserved or resulted from a miscarriage of justice was beside the Point: the point was that he was crucified, and therefore came with the meaning of the pronouncement in Deuteronomy 21: 23, "a hanged man is accursed by God."[11]

Saul focused on stopping the growing communities of Christians who were advocating Jesus as Messiah because in his mind and method of interpreting Hebrew Scriptures they were blaspheming and contradicting the law. After Saul's conversion at Damascus, he realized his interpretation was wrong. Jesus was Messiah. Given the relationship between Paul and Luke, Paul may have encouraged or even sent Luke to interview and record everything he could about the life of Jesus. Paul wrote epistles. Luke wrote the gospel or the biography of Jesus.

Both Luke and Paul relied on testimonies shared with them from the disciples and followers of Jesus. None of Paul's epistles offer anything by way of the chronology of Jesus' life. Certainly, Saul (Paul) given his persecution of Jesus' followers, was familiar with Jesus and the disciples of Jesus. Saul (Paul) was aware of what Jesus' teachings would bring to Jewish worship and Temple practices. He was also aware of what Jesus' disciples and followers could bring by spreading Jesus' teachings. In any event, during Jesus' life, neither Saul (Paul) nor Luke was part of Jesus' inner circle. Luke and Paul not being part of Jesus' inner circle meant that they (especially Luke) had to learn from personal testimonies of others.

Luke depended on talking with eyewitnesses. His accuracy as a physician carried into accuracy with his words. Whatever interviewees shared with Luke would have been highly scrutinized for precision. The book of Luke is trustworthy not because Luke was one of Jesus'

---

[9] Marshall, I. Howard, "Luke" in Douglas, J. D., ed., *The Illustrated Bible Dictionary*, 919.
[10] For clarity, Saul and Paul are the same person. Saul references Paul prior to his Damascus conversion. Paul references Saul after his Damascus conversion.
[11] Bruce, F. F., *Paul: Apostle of the Heart Set Free*, 70-71.

followers because he was not a follower. The book of Luke is trustworthy because Luke was not one of Jesus' followers. Luke depended on corroborated testimonies. Big difference.

The book of Acts is Luke's sequel to his gospel record. Luke recorded imperatives from Jesus to Ananias and Paul. Before delving into Acts, grasp the discipleship oriented imperatives of Jesus from Luke's record as a skilled writer and physician and friend of Paul.

## Luke's Record of the Imperatives of Jesus

Lk 4: 16–23 And he came to Nazareth, where he had been brought up. And as was his custom, he went to the synagogue on the Sabbath day, and he stood up to read. And the scroll of the prophet Isaiah was given to him. He unrolled the scroll and found the place where it was written, "The Spirit of the Lord is upon me, because he has anointed me to proclaim good news to the poor. He has sent me to proclaim liberty to the captives and recovering of sight to the blind, to set at liberty those who are oppressed, to proclaim the year of the Lord's favor." And he rolled up the scroll and gave it back to the attendant and sat down. And the eyes of all in the synagogue were fixed on him. And he began to say to them, "Today this Scripture has been fulfilled in your hearing." And all spoke well of him and marveled at the gracious words that were coming from his mouth. And they said, "Is not this Joseph's son?" And he said to them, "Doubtless you will quote to me this proverb, 'Physician, heal yourself θεράπευσον σεαυτόν.' What we have heard you did at Capernaum, do here in your hometown as well." ποίησον καὶ ὧδε ἐν τῇ πατρίδι σου

> Jesus quoted prior imperatives from a proverb. "Heal yourself" was a Jewish proverb more akin to meaning, "Take care of your own home before you come into ours." Jesus affirmed through quoting "do here in your hometown as well" from their proverbs that he knew exactly how they were attacking him.

Lk 4: 33-35 And in the synagogue there was a man who had the spirit of an unclean demon, and he cried out with a loud voice, "Ha! What have you to do with us, Jesus of Nazareth? Have you come to destroy us? I know who you are--the Holy One of God." But Jesus rebuked him, saying, "Be silent and come out of him Φιμώθητι καὶ ἔξελθε ἀπ αὐτοῦ!" And when the demon had thrown him down in their midst, he came out of him, having done him no harm.

There are two imperative here "be silent" and "come out" Mk 1: 25

Lk 5: 1-4 On one occasion, while the crowd was pressing in on him to hear the word of God, he was standing by the lake of Gennesaret, and he saw two boats by the lake, but the fishermen had gone out of them and were washing their nets. Getting into one of the boats, which was Simon's, he asked him to put out a little from the land. And he sat down and taught the people from the boat. And when he had finished speaking, he said to Simon, "Put out into the deep and let down your nets for a catch ἐπανάγαγε εἰς τὸ βάθος καὶ χαλάσατε τὰ δίκτυα ὑμῶν εἰς ἄγραν."

> Jesus' two imperatives "put out into the deep" and "let down your net for a catch" were not options for Peter. Jesus did not ask Peter, he told Peter to "put out" and "let down." Peter, knew that both the time and the proper depth for fishing which Jesus had commanded him were unlikely to net a catch. Nevertheless, Peter followed Jesus' imperatives. Luke did not record dialogue or an argument. Peter simply followed Jesus' imperatives as if he had no option to disobey.

Lk 5: 5-10 And Simon answered, "Master, we toiled all night and took nothing! But at your word I will let down the nets." And when they had done this, they enclosed a large number of fish, and their nets were breaking. They signaled to their partners in the other boat to come and help them. And they came and filled both the boats, so that they began to sink. But when Simon Peter saw it, he fell down at Jesus' knees, saying, "<u>Depart from me</u>, for I am a sinful man, O Lord." For he and all who were with him were astonished at the catch of fish that they had taken, and so also were James and John, sons of Zebedee, who were partners with Simon. And Jesus said to Simon, "<u>Do not be afraid</u> μὴ φοβοῦ from now on you will be catching men."

> Jesus' imperative "do not be afraid" was singular only to Peter. Peter, likely amazed at the catch was immediately commanded by Jesus not to be afraid. Peter had obeyed. He had cast the nets into the deep and the results from having obeyed Jesus' imperative were evident.
>
> After the catch, Peter heard another imperative from Jesus, "Do not fear." Peter likely thought, "When Jesus' gives a command, good things happen." Peter was not alone. Others in the boat also heard Jesus' imperatives to Peter and saw the results after having done what Jesus had commanded. Peter after having seen what had happened spoke an imperative to Jesus, "Depart from me."

Lk 5: 12-14 While he was in one of the cities, there came a man full of leprosy. And when he saw Jesus, he fell on his face and begged him, "Lord, if you will, you can make me clean." And Jesus stretched out his hand and touched him, saying, "I will; <u>be clean</u> καθαρίσθητι." And immediately the leprosy left him. And he charged him to tell no one, but go and <u>show yourself to the priest, and make an offering for your</u> cleansing δεῖξον σεαυτὸν τῷ ἱερεῖ καὶ προσένεγκε περὶ τοῦ καθαρισμοῦ σου, as Moses commanded, for a proof to them.

> Luke recorded in these passages that Jesus' spoke three imperatives, "be clean," "show," and "make an offering." While Mathew and Mark both included this story in their Gospels, they did not record Jesus' imperatives as Luke recorded.
> Mt 8: 3-4; Mk 1: 40-45

Lk 5: 18-23 And behold, some men were bringing on a bed a man who was paralyzed, and they were seeking to bring him in and lay him before Jesus, but finding no way to bring him in, because of the crowd, they went up on the roof and let him down with his bed through the tiles into the midst before Jesus. And when he saw their faith, he said, "Man, your sins are forgiven you." And the scribes and the Pharisees began to question, saying, "Who is this who speaks blasphemies? Who can forgive sins but God alone?" When Jesus perceived their thoughts, he answered them, "Why do you question in your hearts? Which is easier, to say, 'Your sins are forgiven you,' or to say, '<u>Rise and walk</u>' ἔγειρε καὶ περιπάτει?

> Here Jesus went beyond forgiving sins. His two imperatives "rise" and "walk" meant that beyond the healing there were things to do. The "rise" and "walk" imperatives were not simply affirmations of healing. They were commands that intended purpose beyond healing. Mt 2: 9; Mk 9: 5

Lk 5: 24 But that you may know that the Son of Man has authority on earth to forgive sins"--he said to the man who was paralyzed--"I say to you, <u>rise</u>, ἔγειρε pick up your bed and <u>go home</u>" πορεύου εἰς τὸν οἶκόν σου.

    In English, there seem to be three imperatives, "rise," "pick up your bed" and "go home." However, the only two imperatives are, "rise" and "go home." The English "pick up your bed" misses the aorist active participle which is better translated, "and having taken up your bed."
Mk 2: 11; Mt 9: 6-7

Lk 5: 25-27 And immediately he rose up before them and picked up what he had been lying on and went home, glorifying God. And amazement seized them all, and they glorified God and were filled with awe, saying, "We have seen extraordinary things today." After this he went out and saw a tax collector named Levi, sitting at the tax booth. And he said to him, "<u>Follow me</u> ἀκολούθει μοι." And leaving everything, he rose and followed him.

    Here Luke recorded the calling of Matthew. Similar to Matthew Luke recorded the imperative that Jesus spoke to Matthew, "follow me" as Mark also recorded.
 Mt 9: 9; Mk 2: 14

Lk 6: 6-8 On another Sabbath, he entered the synagogue and was teaching, and a man was there whose right hand was withered. And the scribes and the Pharisees watched him, to see whether he would heal on the Sabbath, so that they might find a reason to accuse him. But he knew their thoughts, and he said to the man with the withered hand, "<u>Come and stand here</u> ἔγειρε καὶ στῆθι εἰς τὸ μέσον." And he rose and stood there.

    These two imperatives "come" and "stand" were responded to by the man with the withered hand without delay. To the onlookers they may have presumed the man had no choice in his response. Immediately following Jesus' imperative, Luke recorded that he rose and stood.

Lk 6: 9-10 And Jesus said to them, "I ask you, is it lawful on the Sabbath to do good or to do harm, to save life or to destroy it?" And after looking around at them all he said to him, "<u>Stretch out your hand</u> ἔκτεινον τὴν χεῖρά σου." And he did so, and his hand was restored.

    Having hidden his withered hand under his cloak, Jesus commanded him to stretch out his hand for everyone to see. The text indicates that the healing may have occurred during the man's stretching of his own hand or it may have been healed before he stretched out his hand. Either way, Jesus issued an imperative to the man. He heard the imperative as did the scribes and Pharisees. Mk 3: 5; Mt 12: 13

Lk 6: 20-23 And he lifted up his eyes on his disciples, and said: "Blessed are you who are poor, for yours is the kingdom of God. Blessed are you who are hungry now, for you shall be satisfied. "Blessed are you who weep now, for you shall laugh. Blessed are you when people hate you and when they exclude you and revile you and spurn your name as evil, on account of the Son of Man! Rejoice in that day, and leap for joy, for behold, your reward is great in heaven; for so their fathers did to the prophets. <u>Rejoice in that day, and leap</u> χάρητε ἐν ἐκείνῃ τῇ ἡμέρᾳ καὶ σκιρτήσατε for joy, for behold, your reward is great in heaven; for so their fathers did to the prophets."

    The two imperatives Jesus spoke were "rejoice" and "leap." The words, "for joy" are not in Greek but are English amplifications. Jesus affirmed that responses to rewards in heaven through rejoicing to the point of uncontrollable leaping is acceptable. His command to rejoice "in that day" affirmed to them that their immediate response was acceptable. Jesus gave them no reasons to delay their rejoicing.

Lk 6: 24-27 "But woe to you who are rich, for you have received your consolation. "Woe to you who are full now, for you shall be hungry. "Woe to you who laugh now, for you shall mourn and weep. "Woe to you, when all people speak well of you, for so their fathers did to the false prophets. "But I say to you who hear, <u>Love your enemies</u> ἀγαπᾶτε τοὺς ἐχθροὺς ὑμῶν, <u>do good to those who hate you</u> καλῶς ποιεῖτε τοῖς μισοῦσιν ὑμᾶς,

"Love" and "do good" were the two imperatives Luke recorded. Those who heard Jesus speak or those who would eventually read Luke's Greek understood the command. The Greek offers deeper insight because of the language and culture of that time than what is possible in English. "Love" your enemies and "do good" to those who hate you were commands that identified both sides of a broken adversarial enmity filled relationship. Context indicated the separation was no small matter. Separation was highly confrontational.

The words, "enemies" and "hate" were two distinctly different Greek words in their context. The word, "enemies" τοὺς ἐχθροὺς Jesus spoke in the accusative case and Luke rightly recorded the direct object of who was to be loved. Enemies, those to whom they had something against, were to be the recipients of love. Those who "hate you" τοῖς μισοῦσιν ὑμᾶς Luke recorded in the dative case and the indirect object of who was to have good done to them. The broader context meant that both those to whom they had something against and those who had something against them applied.

More literally they were commanded to be active in the making a relationship toward those to whom they knew hated them. Luke recorded "well" as the adverb and "making" as the active verb. Enemies and those who hated them was plural, meaning that loving and doing good or making well were not singular one-time actions to only one person. Rather loving and making well were ongoing continuous actions toward numerous enemies and haters. Love here was an agape love, a sacrificial love, not brotherly, not natural affection, and not passion. "Do good" was literally "make well" and implied healing or helping sense.

Note the ESV begins this passage, "But I say to you who hear" an awkward construction particularly with the word, "hear" which conveys an English command to hear. Other translations are:

> "But I say to you that hear" (RSV)
> "But I say unto you which hear" (KJV)
> "But I tell you who hear me" (NIV) and
> "But I say to you who are hearing" (YLT).

Only the YLT conveys the present, active, dative, participle.

Lk 6: 28 <u>bless those who curse you</u> εὐλογεῖτε τοὺς καταρωμένους ὑμᾶς, <u>pray for those who abuse you</u> προσεύχεσθε περὶ τῶν ἐπηρεαζόντων ὑμᾶς.

    Immediately following the "love" and "make well" imperatives in v27, Jesus issued two more imperatives, "bless those who curse you" and "pray for those who abuse you" which on first hearing sounds strange. These two imperatives were followed by active participles which a clearer translation may be, "Bless those who are now cursing you and pray for those who are now abusing you." The active participle conveys the idea that others are now cursing and abusing you but the present active will change. Alternatively, more clearly, the imperatives "bless" and "pray" will bring an end to the cursing and abusing they were experiencing. The recipients of the blessings and prayers Luke recorded in plural form means that many people were cursing and abusing them.

Lk 6: 29 To one who strikes you on the cheek, <u>offer the other also</u> πάρεχε καὶ τὴν ἄλλην, and from one who takes away your cloak <u>do not withhold your tunic either</u>.

    Jesus here used an imperative "offer the other cheek." The English here reads as if the strike is singular. While "one who strikes you" is a good translation, the Greek is a participle, and a better rendering is "to the one who is striking you" indicating a present active ongoing striking. What sounds like an English command, "do not withhold your tunic either" Luke recorded as an aorist subjunctive with a negative. Both context and the negative aorist subjunctive applies which means that while Luke did not record an imperative, the tunic was to be made available to anyone who had first taken the cloak.

Lk 6: 30 <u>Give to everyone who begs from you</u> παντὶ αἰτοῦντί σε δίδου, and from one who takes away your goods <u>do not demand them back</u> σὰ μὴ ἀπαίτει.

    Jesus two imperatives were "give" and "do not demand" back what has been taken from you. Jesus' imperatives with present active participles asserted that there would always be people asking and taking their goods. Most English translations leave out the present participles. "Be giving to everyone who is begging from you" and "do not be asking back from those who are taking from you" convey more clearly the Greek. In other words, begging and stealing must always be addressed.

    Jesus's concern here was their response, not the fact that beggars may not need for all that they beg or thieves may not have a need for what they steal. Beggars beg, and stealers steal because they have a self-perceived need and have not learned how to obtain what they need outside of begging and stealing. He acknowledged the injustices of begging and stealing recognizing that those who beg and steal have ungodly motives and means. His imperatives were intentional because their normal responses would have been to withhold from beggars and attempt to get back the goods taken from them by thieves. His imperatives gave cause for seeing the broader issue.

Lk 6: 31 And as you wish that others would do to you, <u>do so to them</u> ποιεῖτε α ὐτοῖς ὁμοίως. This passage is often taken to be singular applying to a one to one relationship. Here, however, Jesus' spoke a plural imperative. As a group, they were commanded to do to others what they would have done to themselves as a group. They were to be see by others as a group doing to other groups what they would have done to themselves. Indeed an individual meaning is also applicable. However, the imperative is plural.

Lk 6: 33-35 And if you do good to those who do good to you, what benefit is that to you? For even sinners do the same. And if you lend to those from whom you expect to receive, what credit is that to you? Even sinners lend to sinners, to get back the same amount. <u>But love your enemies</u> πλὴν ἀγαπᾶτε τοὺς ἐχθροὺς ὑμῶν, <u>and do good</u> καὶ ἀγαθοποιεῖτε, <u>and lend</u> καὶ δανίζετε, expecting nothing in return, and your reward will be great, and you will be sons of the Most High, for he is kind <u>to</u> ἐπὶ the ungrateful and the evil.

    Jesus' three plural imperatives, "love," "do good," and "lend" were very clear. What may have been confusing to those hearing his words was his statement, "for he is kind to the ungrateful and evil." The words "'to' or 'toward' the ungrateful and evil" are fitting for English translations, yet conveys a horizontal relationship. The English words "to" or "toward" carries the meaning that God is next to or side by side with the ungrateful and evil whereas the Greek preposition epi ἐπὶ is better translated "upon" indicating his kindness is above and supreme over the ungrateful and the evil. A better translation is "for he is kind upon the ungrateful and evil" or "for he is kind over the ungrateful and evil." Big difference.

    His kindness, his goodness comes from above and is upon the ungrateful and the evil. In the sense that he is above and the ungrateful and evil are below a vertical (above / below) relationship exists. Jesus could have said, and Luke could have recorded other Greek prepositions such as toward πρὸς Lk 7:44, into εἰς Lk 9:53 to convey a horizontal relationship. Here the English word "to" which conveys a horizontal relationship is better replaced with the English word "upon" which conveys a vertical relationship. There is both horizontal (to) and vertical (upon) relationship Jesus conveyed that his disciples were to follow. However, here, Jesus emphasized the vertical relationship.

Lk 6: 36 <u>Be merciful</u> Γίνεσθε οἰκτίρμονες, even as your Father is merciful.
    Jesus' imperative "be merciful" was contrasted against the Father's mercy. Luke recorded a plural imperative meaning that Jesus addressed them as a group. Jesus commanded them as an assembly to be merciful.

Lk 6: 37-38 "<u>Judge not</u>, and you will not be judged; <u>condemn not</u>, and you will not be condemned; <u>forgive</u>, and you will be forgiven; <u>give</u>, δίδοτε and it will be given to you. Good measure, pressed down, shaken together, running over, will be put into your lap. For with the measure you use it will be measured back to you."
    The first two imperatives "judge not," and "condemn not," require contextual understanding. An extensive comment is provided in Chapter 9 Mt 7: 1-5

Lk 6: 39 - 42 He also told them a parable: "Can a blind man lead a blind man? Will they not both fall into a pit? A disciple is not above his teacher, but everyone when he is fully trained will be like his teacher. Why do you see the speck that is in your brother's eye, but do not notice the log that is in your own eye? How can you say to your brother, 'Brother, let me take out the speck that is in your eye,' when you yourself do not see the log that is in your own eye? You hypocrite, <u>first take the log out of your own eye</u> ἔκβαλε πρῶτον τὴν δοκὸν ἐκ τοῦ ὀφθαλμοῦ σοῦ, and then you will see clearly to take out the speck that is in your brother's eye.
    Mt 7: 3–5

Lk 7: 11–15 Soon afterward he went to a town called Nain, and his disciples and a great crowd went with him. As he drew near to the gate of the town, behold, a man who had died was being carried out, the only son of his mother, and she was a widow, and a considerable crowd from the town was with her. And when the Lord saw her, he had compassion on her and said to her, "<u>Do not weep</u> Μὴ κλαῖε." Then he came up and touched the bier, and the bearers stood still. And he said, "Young man, I say to you, <u>arise</u> ἐγέρθητι." And the dead man sat up and began to speak, and Jesus gave him to his mother.

> Jesus' imperative "do not weep" to the woman and "arise" to the young man were both singular. He spoke to each of them according to their needs. This miraculous raising of a dead young man from his coffin by Jesus simple one word imperative "arise" was a powerful testament to Jesus' authority. Jesus spoke the imperative to the young man who was in the bier or coffin. There was "a great crowd" and coffin "bearers" who heard Jesus' imperative. Common with many of Jesus' imperatives to individuals, there are other people nearby who heard them.

Lk 7: 22 And he answered them, "Go and <u>tell John what you have seen and heard</u> ἀπαγγείλατε Ἰωάννῃ ἃ εἴδετε καὶ ἠκούσατε: the blind receive their sight, the lame walk, lepers are cleansed, and the deaf hear, the dead are raised up, the poor have good news preached to them.

> On first look, the word "Go" appears in English to be an imperative but it is an aorist, passive, deponent, participle, verb which carries an active meaning. The English "Go" is acceptable, but the YLT is closest to Luke's Greek with, "Having gone on, report to John…" The plural imperative Jesus spoke was "tell John what you have seen and heard." Jesus through imperatives to John's disciples whom John had sent to Jesus, assured John through Jesus' imperative. Jesus imperative to John's disciples confirmed that he was the Messiah, the Lamb of God whom John had been proclaiming.

Lk 7: 41-50 "A certain moneylender had two debtors. One owed five hundred denarii, and the other fifty. When they could not pay, he canceled the debt of both. Now which of them will love him more?" Simon answered, "The one, I suppose, for whom he canceled the larger debt." And he said to him, "You have judged rightly." Then turning toward the woman he said to Simon, "Do you see this woman? I entered your house; you gave me no water for my feet, but she has wet my feet with her tears and wiped them with her hair. You gave me no kiss, but from the time I came in she has not ceased to kiss my feet. You did not anoint my head with oil, but she has anointed my feet with ointment. Therefore I tell you, her sins, which are many, are forgiven--for she loved much. But he who is forgiven little, loves little." And he said to her, "Your sins are forgiven." Then those who were at table with him began to say among themselves, "Who is this, who even forgives sins?" And he said to the woman, "Your faith has saved you; <u>go in peace πορεύου εἰς εἰρήνην</u>."

> Jesus imperative to the woman "go in peace" was singular. This imperative in English appears that the woman should go in or with peace, but the preposition εἰς means "into" more so than meaning that her faith will lead her into peace. Her faith in Greek is perfect and active meaning her faith had preceded her peace. Jesus' imperative "go in peace" affirmed her faith.
>
> The noun faith is feminine, singular, nominative. The verb "has saved you" has these characteristics of perfect and active. The result of the woman's faith was that she was saved in a perfect and active sense. Beyond her perfect and active salvation, she was commanded to walk in peace. The English rendering "go in peace" is acceptable, but lacks conveying to us the power of faith that precedes and ultimately leads into peace.

Lk 8: 4-8 And when a great crowd was gathering and people from town after town came to him, he said in a parable: "A sower went out to sow his seed. And as he sowed, some fell along the path and was trampled underfoot, and the birds of the air devoured it. And some fell on the rock, and as it grew up, it withered away, because it had no moisture. And some fell among thorns, and the thorns grew up with it and choked it. And some fell into good soil and grew and yielded a hundredfold." As he said these things, he called out, "He who has ears to hear, <u>let him hear ἀκουέτω</u>."

> Here the English word construction "let him hear" or "he must hear" is common, since in English all imperatives are second person. Mt 13: 9; Mk 4: 9

Lk 8: 16-18 "No one after lighting a lamp covers it with a jar or puts it under a bed, but puts it on a stand, so that those who enter may see the light. For nothing is hidden that will not be made manifest, nor is anything secret that will not be known and come to light. <u>Take care then how you hear βλέπετε οὖν πῶς ἀκούετε</u>, for to the one who has, more will be given, and from the one who has not, even what he thinks that he has will be taken away."
> Mk 4: 24

Lk 8: 36-39 And those who had seen it told them how the demon-possessed man had been healed. Then all the people of the surrounding country of the Gerasenes asked him to depart from them, for they were seized with great fear. So he got into the boat and returned. The man from whom the demons had gone begged that he might be with him, but Jesus sent him away, saying, "<u>Return to your home Ὑπόστρεφε εἰς τὸν οἶκόν σου</u>, and declare how much God has done for you." And he went away, proclaiming throughout the whole city how much Jesus had done for him.
> Mk 5: 19

Lk 8: 43-48 And there was a woman who had had a discharge of blood for twelve years, and though she had spent all her living on physicians, she could not be healed by anyone. She came up behind him and touched the fringe of his garment, and immediately her discharge of blood ceased. And Jesus said, "Who was it that touched me?" When all denied it, Peter said, "Master, the crowds surround you and are pressing in on you!" But Jesus said, "Someone touched me, for I perceive that power has gone out from me." And when the woman saw that she was not hidden, she came

trembling, and falling down before him declared in the presence of all the people why she had touched him, and how she had been immediately healed. And he said to her, "Daughter, your faith has made you well; <u>go in peace</u> πορεύου εἰς εἰρήνην."
 Luke here recorded the same imperative Jesus spoke in Lk 7: 50
 Mk 5: 34

Lk 8:49-50 While he was still speaking, someone from the ruler's house came and said, "Your daughter is dead; do not trouble the Teacher anymore." But Jesus on hearing this answered him, "<u>Do not fear; only believe</u> and she will be well Μὴ φοβοῦ μόνον πίστευσον καὶ σωθήσεται."
 Mk 5: 36

Lk 8: 51-52 And when he came to the house, he allowed no one to enter with him, except Peter and John and James, and the father and mother of the child. And all were weeping and mourning for her, but he said, "<u>Do not weep</u> Μὴ κλαίετε, for she is not dead but sleeping."
 In the parallel passage Mk 5:39, Mark did not record Jesus' use of an imperative
 but a question from Jesus, "Why all this commotion and wailing?"

Lk 8: 53-54 And they laughed at him, knowing that she was dead. But taking her by the hand he called, saying, "Child, <u>arise</u> Ἡ παῖς ἔγειρε."
 Mk 5: 41

Lk 9: 1-5 And he called the twelve together and gave them power and authority over all demons and to cure diseases, and he sent them out to proclaim the kingdom of God and to heal. And he said to them, "<u>Take nothing for your journey</u> Μηδὲν αἴρετε εἰς τὴν ὁδόν, no staff, nor bag, nor bread, nor money; and do not have two tunics. And whatever house you enter, <u>stay there</u> ἐκεῖ μένετε, and <u>from there depart</u> καὶ ἐκεῖθεν ἐξέρχεσθε. And wherever they do not receive you, when you leave that town <u>shake off the dust from your feet</u> τὸν κονιορτὸν ἀπὸ τῶν ποδῶν ὑμῶν ἀποτινάσσετε as a testimony against them."
 Mt 9: 9 - 14; Mk 6: 8-11

Lk 9: 12-13 Now the day began to wear away, and the twelve came and said to him, "<u>Send the crowd away</u> Ἀπόλυσον τὸν ὄχλον to go into the surrounding villages and countryside to find lodging and get provisions, for we are here in a desolate place." But he said to them, "<u>You give them something to eat</u> Δότε αὐτοῖς φαγεῖν ὑμεῖς." They said, "We have no more than five loaves and two fish--unless we are to go and buy food for all these people."
 "Send the crowd away" was an imperative that the twelve said to Jesus. "You give
 them something to eat" was an imperative Jesus spoke back to the twelve.
 Mt 14: 16; Mk 6: 37

Lk 9:14 For there were about five thousand men. And he said to his disciples, "<u>Have them sit down in groups of about fifty each</u> Κατακλίνατε αὐτοὺς κλισίας ὡσεὶ ἀνὰ πεντήκοντα."
 Mt 14: 18; Mk 6: 39-40

Lk 9:21-23 And he strictly charged and commanded them to tell this to no one, saying, "The Son of Man must suffer many things and be rejected by the elders and chief priests and scribes, and be killed, and on the third day be raised." And he said to all, "If anyone would come after me, <u>let him</u>

deny himself ἀρνησάσθω ἑαυτὸν and take up his cross daily καὶ ἀράτω τὸν σταυρὸν αὐτοῦ καθ ἡμέραν and follow me καὶ ἀκολουθείτω μοι.
> Jesus here spoke three imperatives in a sequence: deny, take up, and follow. Notice that "take up" and "follow" are preceded by the conjunction "and."
> Mk 8: 34; Mt 16: 24

Lk 9: 33-35 And as the men were parting from him, Peter said to Jesus, "Master, it is good that we are here. Let us make three tents, one for you and one for Moses and one for Elijah"--not knowing what he said. As he was saying these things, a cloud came and overshadowed them, and they were afraid as they entered the cloud. And a voice came out of the cloud, saying, "This is my Son, my Chosen One; listen to him ἀκούετε!"
> Jesus did not speak this imperative. The imperative they heard from "a voice out of the cloud" was "listen" which was plural. The plural imperative meant that from then on the three of them Peter, James, and John would go from beyond merely hearing to understanding what they had heard when Jesus spoke.
> Mt 17: 5; Mk 9: 7

Lk 9: 37-41 On the next day, when they had come down from the mountain, a great crowd met him. And behold, a man from the crowd cried out, "Teacher, I beg you to look at my son, for he is my only child. And behold, a spirit seizes him, and he suddenly cries out. It convulses him so that he foams at the mouth, and shatters him, and will hardly leave him. And I begged your disciples to cast it out, but they could not." Jesus answered, "O faithless and twisted generation, how long am I to be with you and bear with you? Bring your son here προσάγαγε ὧδε τὸν υἱόν σου."
> Mt 17: 17; Mk 9: 19

Lk 9: 41-44 Jesus answered, "O faithless and twisted generation, how long am I to be with you and bear with you? Bring your son here." While he was coming, the demon threw him to the ground and convulsed him. But Jesus rebuked the unclean spirit and healed the boy, and gave him back to his father. And all were astonished at the majesty of God. But while they were all marveling at everything he was doing, Jesus said to his disciples, "Let these words sink into your ears Θέσθε ὑμεῖς εἰς τὰ ὦτα ὑμῶν τοὺς λόγους τούτους: The Son of Man is about to be delivered into the hands of men."
> Jesus' second person plural imperative (you let these words sink) in English often eliminates "you" rendering "Let these words." Jesus' commanded them as a group to comprehend what was about to happen. His imperative was intentional. In both their individual and group immaturity at that time and place, they were unable to grasp what was about to happen. His imperatives develop faith and confidence.

Lk 9: 46-50 An argument arose among them as to which of them was the greatest. But Jesus, knowing the reasoning of their hearts, took a child and put him by his side and said to them, "Whoever receives this child in my name receives me, and whoever receives me receives him who sent me. For he who is least among you all is the one who is great." John answered, "Master, we saw someone casting out demons in your name, and we tried to stop him, because he does not follow with us." But Jesus said to him, "Do not stop him Μὴ κωλύετε, for the one who is not against you is for you."
> Mk 9: 39

Lk 9: 59-60 To another he said, "Follow me Ακολούθει μοι." But he said, "Lord, let me first go and bury my father." And Jesus said to him, "Leave the dead to bury their own dead Αφες τοὺς νεκροὺς θάψαι τοὺς ἑαυτῶν νεκρούς. But as for you, go and proclaim the kingdom of God διάγγελλε τὴν βασιλείαν τοῦ θεοῦ."

> Jesus' three sequential imperatives were "follow," "leave," and "proclaim." English usage conveys doubt if the man followed Jesus and proclaimed the Kingdom of God as Jesus commanded through his imperatives to the man. While the text does not affirm what the man did, Jesus' three Greek imperatives are compelling that the man did not return to bury his father, that he left those responsibilities to his family, that he followed Jesus and proclaimed the Kingdom of God. As much as we and first century readers of Luke's text would like to know, Luke did not record what the man did. Mt 8: 22

Lk 10: 1-11 After this the Lord appointed seventy-two others and sent them on ahead of him, two by two, into every town and place where he himself was about to go. And he said to them, "The harvest is plentiful, but the laborers are few. Therefore pray earnestly to the Lord of the harvest δεήθητε οὖν τοῦ κυρίου τοῦ θερισμοῦ to send out laborers into his harvest. Go your way ὑπάγετε; behold ἰδοὺ, I am sending you out as lambs in the midst of wolves. Carry no moneybag, no knapsack, no sandals μὴ βαστάζετε βαλλάντιον μὴ πήραν μὴ ὑποδήματα, and greet no one on the road. Whatever house you enter, first say, 'Peace be to this house!" πρῶτον λέγετε πρῶτον λέγετε Εἰρήνη τῷ οἴκῳ τούτῳ. And if a son of peace is there, your peace will rest upon him. But if not, it will return to you. And remain in the same house, eating and drinking what they provide, for the laborer deserves his wages. Do not go from house to house μὴ μεταβαίνετε ἐξ οἰκίας εἰς οἰκίαν. Whenever you enter a town and they receive you, eat what is set before you ἐσθίετε τὰ παρατιθέμενα ὑμῖν. Heal the sick in it θεραπεύετε τοὺς ἐν αὐτῇ ἀσθενεῖς and say to them καὶ λέγετε αὐτοῖς, 'The kingdom of God has come near to you.' But whenever you enter a town and they do not receive you, go into its streets and say εἴπατε, 'Even the dust of your town that clings to our feet we wipe off against you. Nevertheless know this, that the kingdom of God has come near τοῦτο γινώσκετε ὅτι ἤγγικεν ἡ βασιλεία τοῦ θεοῦ.'

> Jesus instructions to the 72 included 10 imperatives to those he sent out in pairs. He spoke these imperatives to all 72. Should one of the two falter, the other was available to fulfill Jesus' imperatives. Jesus' imperatives emphasized teamwork. Jesus' final imperative was that they also speak an imperative affirming that the Kingdom of God had come near. He had commanded them to know that the Kingdom of God has come near. This proclamation imperative to the 72 affirmed that with him and in him existed the Kingdom of God.

Lk 10: 17–20 The seventy-two returned with joy, saying, "Lord, even the demons are subject to us in your name!" And he said to them, "I saw Satan fall like lightning from heaven. Behold, I have given you authority to tread on serpents and scorpions, and over all the power of the enemy, and nothing shall hurt you. Nevertheless, do not rejoice in this, that the spirits are subject to you πλὴν ἐν τούτῳ μὴ χαίρετε ὅτι τὰ πνεύματα ὑμῖν ὑποτάσσεται, but rejoice that your names are written in heaven χαίρετε δὲ ὅτι τὰ ὀνόματα ὑμῶν ἐγγέγραπται ἐν τοῖς οὐρανοῖς."

> Jesus' two imperatives clarified the reasons for rejoicing. The 72 had returned amazed that demons were subject to them. They had experienced the power of their imperatives over the spirits, yet Jesus gave them a second imperative. Their having

power over spirits was not the reason for which they should rejoice. Jesus' second imperative clarified that even their power over demons was secondary to their salvation. Their names having been written in heaven was of greater value than the spirits being subject to them. They were commanded to rejoice at their salvation, not their authority over demons nor their safety. Jesus' imperatives in their ears left them gave a reason for their for rejoicing.

Lk 10: 25-28 And behold, a lawyer stood up to put him to the test, saying, "Teacher, what shall I do to inherit eternal life?" He said to him, "What is written in the Law? How do you read it?" And he answered, "You shall love the Lord your God with all your heart and with all your soul and with all your strength and with all your mind, and your neighbor as yourself." And he said to him, "You have answered correctly; <u>do this, and you will live</u> τοῦτο ποίει καὶ ζήσῃ."

> Jesus single imperative "do this" (love God with heart, soul, strength, and mind and your neighbor as yourself) left no doubt in the lawyer's mind. The lawyer heard, knew and was commanded to follow. Jesus' imperative was simple and clear. The lawyer had heard Jesus' imperative.

Lk 10: 29-37 But he, desiring to justify himself, said to Jesus, "And who is my neighbor?" Jesus replied, "A man was going down from Jerusalem to Jericho, and he fell among robbers, who stripped him and beat him and departed, leaving him half dead. Now by chance a priest was going down that road, and when he saw him he passed by on the other side. So likewise a Levite, when he came to the place and saw him, passed by on the other side. But a Samaritan, as he journeyed, came to where he was, and when he saw him, he had compassion. He went to him and bound up his wounds, pouring on oil and wine. Then he set him on his own animal and brought him to an inn and took care of him. And the next day he took out two denarii and gave them to the innkeeper, saying, '<u>Take care of him</u> Ἐπιμελήθητι αὐτοῦ, and whatever more you spend, I will repay you when I come back.' Which of these three, do you think, proved to be a neighbor to the man who fell among the robbers?" He said, "The one who showed him mercy." And Jesus said to him, "<u>You go</u> Πορεύου, <u>and do likewise</u> καὶ σὺ ποίει ὁμοίως."

> Jesus stated three imperatives in his Good Samaritan discourse. Here Jesus repeated the imperatives within the parable

> The Samaritan spoke an imperative to the innkeeper, "take care of him." Jesus' next two unmistakable imperatives were "go" and "do." The entire narrative was explication. Not until the end of the parable did Jesus speak two imperatives to the lawyer. Jesus' imperatives were first person singular to the lawyer.

> Those who heard Jesus' imperatives within the parable were also made aware of how those same imperatives applied to them. In English the tow Greek imperatives translated to English commands "You go and do likewise" do not equally convey the Greek in their historical context. In English we hear Jesus imperatives to the man without the depth of what Jesus also said to those who heard the parable then and Jesus says to us now by way of application. The English simply does not deeply convey the context of what they heard.

Lk 11: 1-4 Now Jesus was praying in a certain place, and when he finished, one of his disciples said to him, "Lord, teach us to pray Κύριε δίδαξον ἡμᾶς προσεύχεσθαι, as John taught his disciples." And he said to them, "When you pray, say λέγετε·: "Father, hallowed be your name Πάτερ, ἁγιασθήτω τὸ ὄνομά σου. Your kingdom come ἐλθέτω ἡ βασιλεία σου. Give us each day our daily bread τὸν ἄρτον ἡμῶν τὸν ἐπιούσιον δίδου ἡμῖν τὸ καθ ἡμέραν·, and forgive us our sins καὶ ἄφες ἡμῖν τὰς ἁμαρτίας ἡμῶν, for we ourselves forgive everyone who is indebted to us. And lead us not into temptation."

See Chapter 13 "The Imperatives of Jesus in the Lord's Prayer"

> Note, "lead us not into temptation" is conveyed in English as a command, but the Greek is an aorist subjunctive with a negative. The KJV and YLT respectively include "but deliver us from evil." and "but do thou deliver us from the evil."

Lk 11: 5-10 And he said to them, "Which of you who has a friend will go to him at midnight and say to him, 'Friend, lend me three loaves, for a friend of mine has arrived on a journey, and I have nothing to set before him'; and he will answer from within, 'Do not bother me Μή μοι κόπους πάρεχε; the door is now shut, and my children are with me in bed. I cannot get up and give you anything'? I tell you, though he will not get up and give him anything because he is his friend, yet because of his impudence he will rise and give him whatever he needs. And I tell you, ask, and it will be given to you αἰτεῖτε καὶ δοθήσεται ὑμῖν; seek, and you will find ζητεῖτε καὶ εὑρήσετε; knock, and it will be opened to you κρούετε καὶ ἀνοιγήσεται ὑμῖν. For everyone who asks receives, and the one who seeks finds, and to the one who knocks it will be opened.

> Jesus spoke four imperatives. The first, "Do not bother me" was within the narrative. The next three, "ask," "seek," and "knock" were for the hearers of the parable. Unique to these three imperatives was Jesus' assurances they would have after having followed his imperatives. Here Jesus comforted his listeners at the hearing of his imperatives. Asking resulted in receiving. Seeking resulted in finding. Knocking resulted in an open door.

Lk 11: 33-35 "No one after lighting a lamp puts it in a cellar or under a basket, but on a stand, so that those who enter may see the light. Your eye is the lamp of your body. When your eye is healthy, your whole body is full of light, but when it is bad, your body is full of darkness. Therefore be careful lest the light in you be darkness σκόπει οὖν μὴ τὸ φῶς τὸ ἐν σοὶ σκότος ἐστίν.

> The English phrase, "be careful" somewhat reduces the power of the Greek imperative which more accurately meant contemplate, observe, or prepare. This imperative was not merely a caution. This was not a suggestion as English conveys, but a command for vigilance to protect the eye and the light that it receives. This imperative is cautionary predicting what will happen. When the eye takes in darkness, the body suffers.

Lk 11: 37-41 While Jesus was speaking, a Pharisee asked him to dine with him, so he went in and reclined at table. The Pharisee was astonished to see that he did not first wash before dinner. And the Lord said to him, "Now you Pharisees cleanse the outside of the cup and of the dish, but inside you are full of greed and wickedness. You fools! Did not he who made the outside make the inside also? But give as alms those things that are within πλὴν τὰ ἐνόντα δότε ἐλεημοσύνην, and behold, everything is clean for you καὶ ἰδοὺ πάντα καθαρὰ ὑμῖν ἐστιν.

The English commands here are mild compared to what Luke recorded that Jesus said and what the Pharisees heard. The before meal washing in their context was not the same washing thought of today such as washing our hands for cleanliness before touching food. This washing in their context was a ceremonial practice more so than pre-meal wash your hands hygiene before you eat idea.

Jesus' imperative "give as alms those things that are within" was offensive to the Pharisees. Additionally striking was Jesus' imperative, "behold" meaning see, notice, or intentionally be aware that everything is clean if from within. English readers often read past pronouncement, greeting, or exclamatory imperatives like, "behold" in v37. This "behold" or "lo" (YLT) or "see" (NRS) offended the Pharisees. Jesus' imperative established that their ceremonial washings were not cleansing acts. Adding to the meaning that also angered the Pharisees is that Jesus' imperative was singular and spoken aloud. Those standing near Jesus close enough to hear his words heard him publically accuse the Pharisees as a group since he identified them in the singular. His imperatives revealed the hypocrisy of the Pharisees and everyone who heard Jesus knew of their deceitful way.

Lk 12: 1-7 In the meantime, when so many thousands of the people had gathered together that they were trampling one another, he began to say to his disciples first, "Beware of the leaven of the Pharisees Προσέχετε ἑαυτοῖς ἀπὸ τῆς ζύμης ἥτις ἐστὶν ὑπόκρισις τῶν Φαρισαίων, which is hypocrisy. Nothing is covered up that will not be revealed, or hidden that will not be known. Therefore whatever you have said in the dark shall be heard in the light, and what you have whispered in private rooms shall be proclaimed on the housetops. "I tell you, my friends, do not fear those who kill the body μὴ φοβηθῆτε ἀπὸ τῶν ἀποκτεινόντων τὸ σῶμα, and after that have nothing more that they can do. But I will warn you whom to fear: fear him who, after he has killed, has authority to cast into hell φοβήθητε τὸν μετὰ τὸ ἀποκτεῖναι ἔχοντα ἐξουσίαν ἐμβαλεῖν εἰς τὴν γέενναν. Yes, I tell you, fear him φοβήθητε! Are not five sparrows sold for two pennies? And not one of them is forgotten before God. Why, even the hairs of your head are all numbered. Fear not μὴ φοβεῖσθε; you are of more value than many sparrows.

> Jesus' numerous imperatives within this narrative about leavening required scrutiny by those who read Luke's words in the first-century context. Jesus made clear that death was not the ultimate fear but life after death. His first imperative "do not fear those who kill the body" regarded the Pharisees. His next imperative "fear him who, after he has killed, has authority to cast into hell" regarded bodily death as nothing to be feared. His third imperative "fear him" the one with earthly authority was quickly followed by a reassuring fourth imperative "fear not" the one with heavenly authority who is the protector. These Lukan passages were ripe with meaning to Luke's readers. Consider also the clarity with which his friends heard Jesus' imperatives. Mt 10: 29-31

Lk 12: 13-21 Someone in the crowd said to him, "Teacher, tell my brother to divide the inheritance with me." But he said to him, "Man, who made me a judge or arbitrator over you?" And he said to them, "Take care Ὁρᾶτε, and be on your guard against all covetousness καὶ φυλάσσεσθε ἀπὸ πάσης πλεονεξίας, for one's life does not consist in the abundance of his possessions." And he told them a parable, saying, "The land of a rich man produced plentifully, and he thought to himself, 'What shall I do, for I have nowhere to store my crops?' And he said, 'I will do this: I will tear down my barns and build larger ones, and there I will store all my grain and my goods. And I will say to my soul, Soul, you have ample goods laid up for many years; <u>relax</u> ἀναπαύου, <u>eat</u> φάγε, <u>drink</u> πίε, be merry εὐφραίνου.' But God said to him, 'Fool! This night your soul is required of you, and the things you have prepared, whose will they be?' So is the one who lays up treasure for himself and is not rich toward God."

> Here in the Parable of the Rich Fool Jesus stated two imperatives directed to the crowd and three imperatives within the parable. English words, "take care" can be more literally translated to "see," "catch sight," or "notice." The words, "take care" sound cautionary more so than commanding. The Greek is less ambiguous conveying a conscious awareness comprehensible after inspection.
>
> Jesus' second imperative "be on your guard against all covetousness" was more specific. Both his imperatives referred to vision, seeing, and watchfulness. English words, "be on your guard" accurately convey the visual warning. His audience and the man after having heard Jesus' imperatives likely looked at the Pharisees with distrust. The next three imperatives were within the narrative.

Lk 12: 22-34 And he said to his disciples, "Therefore I tell you, <u>do not be anxious about your life</u> μὴ μεριμνᾶτε, what you will eat, nor about your body, what you will put on. For life is more than food, and the body more than clothing. <u>Consider the ravens</u> κατανοήσατε τοὺς κόρακας: they neither sow nor reap, they have neither storehouse nor barn, and yet God feeds them. Of how much more value are you than the birds! And which of you by being anxious can add a single hour to his span of life? If then you are not able to do as small a thing as that, why are you anxious about the rest? <u>Consider the lilies</u> κατανοήσατε τὰ κρίνα, how they grow: they neither toil nor spin, yet I tell you, even Solomon in all his glory was not arrayed like one of these. But if God so clothes the grass, which is alive in the field today, and tomorrow is thrown into the oven, how much more will he clothe you, O you of little faith! <u>And do not seek what you are to eat and what you are to drink</u>, καὶ ὑμεῖς μὴ ζητεῖτε τί φάγητε καὶ τί πίητε <u>nor be worried</u> μὴ μετεωρίζεσθε. For all the nations of the world seek after these things, and your Father knows that you need them. <u>Instead, seek his kingdom, and these things will be added to you</u> ζητεῖτε τὴν βασιλείαν αὐτοῦ. "<u>Fear not, little flock</u> Μὴ φοβοῦ τὸ μικρὸν ποίμνιον, for it is your Father's good pleasure to give you the kingdom. <u>Sell your possessions</u> Πωλήσατε τὰ ὑπάρχοντα ὑμῶν, <u>and give to the needy</u> καὶ δότε ἐλεημοσύνην. <u>Provide yourselves with moneybags</u> ποιήσατε ἑαυτοῖς βαλλάντια that do not grow old, with a treasure in the heavens that does not fail, where no thief approaches and no moth destroys. For where your treasure is, there will your heart be also.

> Jesus' discourse about worry contained ten imperatives. Two imperatives, "consider the ravens" and "consider the lilies" directed his hearers to understand above and below heaven and earth concepts. Four imperatives were negative and four were positive. Do not be anxious. Do not be concerned about eating and drinking. Do not be worried. And do not be fearful as a small group. Jesus gave these imperatives to provide his disciples' assurance about how they would live after Jesus' crucifixion. These plural imperatives to his disciples as a group or community meant that they were to be seen by others as a community of people living without fear. They were to be sure and show confidence and trust that provisions would be provided to them from God.

Lk 12: 35-40 "Stay dressed for action Εστωσαν ὑμῶν αἱ ὀσφύες περιεζωσμένα and keep your lamps burning, and be like men who are waiting for their master to come home from the wedding feast, so that they may open the door to him at once when he comes and knocks. Blessed are those servants whom the master finds awake when he comes. Truly, I say to you, he will dress himself for service and have them recline at table, and he will come and serve them. If he comes in the second watch, or in the third, and finds them awake, blessed are those servants! But know this τοῦτο δὲ γινώσκετε, that if the master of the house had known at what hour the thief was coming, he would not have left his house to be broken into. You also must be ready καὶ ὑμεῖς γίνεσθε ἕτοιμοι, for the Son of Man is coming at an hour you do not expect."

    The translation of Jesus' imperative "Stay dressed for action" is a good translation. However, a more literal translation from the Greek that conveys what the disciples heard is "keep your loins girded" (KJV, YLT). In today's contemporary sports context a parallel would be "suit up, put your athletic supporters on, and get ready to compete." As disciples of Jesus they had to be ready to move with their lamps kept burning. Jesus spoke the imperative, to clarify and remind his hearers about the difference between master and thief.

    He followed up two more imperatives, "Know this" and "be ready." The imperatives regarding preparation heard by the disciples were clear. There was no doubt in their minds that Jesus' imperatives demanded that his disciples always be prepared. His story about the master returning home from the wedding feast affirmed that his disciples would not know the time of return.

Lk 12: 57-59 "And why do you not judge for yourselves what is right? As you go with your accuser before the magistrate, make an effort to settle with him on the way ἐν τῇ ὁδῷ δὸς ἐργασίαν ἀπηλλάχθαι [ἀπ] αὐτοῦ, lest he drag you to the judge, and the judge hand you over to the officer, and the officer put you in prison. I tell you, you will never get out until you have paid the very last penny."

    Here, think of the accuser as the plaintiff and the the one who heard Jesus' imperative "make an effort to settle with him on the way" as the accused or defendant. The English prepositional phrase "on the way" means before standing in front of a judge. Clearly Jesus demanded that the defendant make an effort before standing in front of the judge to protect the defendant from being handed over for punishment or prison. Notice that Jesus did not guarantee that the defendant would win a favorable response from the plaintiff before they stood in front of the judge. Jesus demanded that his disciples when accused as defendants, make an effort to settle with their accusers/plaintiffs before going to court regardless of the outcome. Jesus was silent about the outcome. The outcome good or bad toward the defendant was irrelevant.

    There is another reason Jesus demanded that a defendant make an effort to negotiate with an accuser/plaintiff before standing in front of a judge. In their context judgments by either Roman rulers or Jewish leaders may not be favorable to either a plaintiff or defendant. Jesus' imperative here intended that the accused / defendant make effort to avoid unfavorable consequences that may befall both themselves and their accusers the plaintiffs.

His imperative to negotiate before going to Roman or Jewish courts was not a suggestion. His command to his followers was to seek resolution before court. Making effort to settle a dispute could benefit both plaintiffs and defendants. Winning or losing was not the issue. Note that Jesus' imperative command had nothing to do with outcome, guilt, innocence, judgment, penalty, or prison. All of these are real possibilities. Making effort to settle before court was Jesus' imperative. Mt 5: 25

Lk 13: 1-10 There were some present at that very time who told him about the Galileans whose blood Pilate had mingled with their sacrifices. And he answered them, "Do you think that these Galileans were worse sinners than all the other Galileans, because they suffered in this way? No, I tell you; but unless you repent, you will all likewise perish. Or those eighteen on whom the tower in Siloam fell and killed them: do you think that they were worse offenders than all the others who lived in Jerusalem? No, I tell you; but unless you repent, you will all likewise perish." And he told this parable: "A man had a fig tree planted in his vineyard, and he came seeking fruit on it and found none. And he said to the vinedresser, '<u>Look</u> Ἰδοὺ, for three years now I have come seeking fruit on this fig tree, and I find none. <u>Cut it down</u> ἔκκοψον αὐτήν. Why should it use up the ground?' And he answered him, '<u>Sir, let it alone this year also</u> Κύριε ἄφες αὐτὴν καὶ τοῦτο τὸ ἔτος, until I dig around it and put on manure. Then if it should bear fruit next year, well and good; but if not, you can cut it down.'" Now he was teaching in one of the synagogues on the Sabbath.

    These imperatives can be confusing without context within v1–10 that focused on repentance to the point of repent or perish. Jesus' imperatives explained the situation. The first imperative "look" to the vinedresser described to the vinedresser that the owner wanted the tree removed because after three years there was no fruit. His second imperative to the vinedresser, "cut it down" was responded to by the vinedresser with his own imperative. The vinedresser said "Sir, let it alone this year also" since the vinedresser wanted more time for the tree to bear fruit.

Notice that the English translation of the vinedresser's words, "but if not, you can cut it down." Some English translations are "you can," "you shall," "then cut it down" or "cut it" and are all appropriate translations. The Greek however is an active, second person, singular, indicative, future verb. The previous English translations miss the future component in the Greek. The future element means that the tree without fruit will be cut down. These are metaphors meaning people who bear no fruit will be cut off. Those who will be cut down will have already proven that they were not part of the garden kingdom, because they had shown no fruit.

Lk 13: 23-35 And someone said to him, "Lord, will those who are saved be few?" And he said to them, "<u>Strive to enter through the narrow door</u> Ἀγωνίζεσθε εἰσελθεῖν διὰ τῆς στενῆς θύρας. For many, I tell you, will seek to enter and will not be able. When once the master of the house has risen and shut the door, and you begin to stand outside and to knock at the door, saying, '<u>Lord, open to us</u> Κύριε ἄνοιξον ἡμῖν,' then he will answer you, 'I do not know where you come from.' Then you will begin to say, 'We ate and drank in your presence, and you taught in our streets.' But he will say, 'I tell you, I do not know where you come from. <u>Depart from me</u> ἀπόστητε ἀπ ἐμοῦ, all you workers of evil!' In that place there will be weeping and gnashing of teeth, when you see Abraham and Isaac and Jacob and all the prophets in the kingdom of God but you yourselves cast out. And people will come from east and west, and from north and south, and recline at table in the kingdom of God. <u>And behold</u> καὶ ἰδοὺ, some are last who will be first, and some are first who will be last." At that very hour some Pharisees came and said to him, "Get away from here, for Herod wants to kill you." And he said to them, "Go and <u>tell that fox</u> εἴπατε τῇ ἀλώπεκι, '<u>Behold</u> Ἰδοὺ, I cast out demons and perform cures today and tomorrow, and the third day I finish my course.

> The first imperative "strive to enter through the narrow door" preceded the story. Jesus said the imperative, "Lord, open to us" within the parable. After lengthy narrative where the lost attempted to convince by stating reasons for entry Jesus gave the imperative "depart from me." This imperative was unambiguous and conveyed the power of the Lord's word. In other words, they did not depart on their own. They departed because they were commanded to depart. This departure was not voluntary. This departure could not be stopped. This departure had been commanded.
>
> The imperative, "And behold" which preceded "some are last who will be first, and some are first who will be last." was preparatory. "And behold" is demonstrative meaning much more than the English "behold." "Remember what will happen" or "think about what you are about to see" in place of "behold" convey the idea that there was no way to stop the last from becoming first and the first from becoming last.
>
> Jesus would finish his course in three days. The sentence, "And he said to them, "Go Πορευθέντες (v32) and tell that fox" in English sounds like two imperatives, "go" and "tell." But most English translations convey the "Go Πορευθέντες" as an imperative command to go when Luke recorded an aorist, passive, deponent, nominative, plural participle. Young's Literal Translated, "Having gone, say to this fox, lo I cast forth demons...." which accurately conveyed the aorist passive.
>
> In English it is difficult to grasp that Jesus' gave them an imperative to give Herod an imperative to "behold." The imperative "tell that fox" to "behold" meant that they were to speak an imperative to King Herod. Speaking an imperative to King Herod was their task.

Lk 14: 7-14 Now he told a parable to those who were invited, when he noticed how they chose the places of honor, saying to them, "When you are invited by someone to a wedding feast, do not sit down in a place of honor, lest someone more distinguished than you be invited by him, and he who invited you both will come and say to you, '<u>Give your place to this person</u> Δὸς τούτῳ τόπον,' and then you will begin with shame to take the lowest place. But when you are invited, <u>go and sit in the lowest place</u> ἀνάπεσε εἰς τὸν ἔσχατον τόπον, so that when your host comes he may say to you, 'Friend, move up higher.' Then you will be honored in the presence of all who sit at [the] table with you. For everyone who exalts himself will be humbled, and he who humbles himself will be exalted." He said also to the man who had invited him, "When you give a dinner or a banquet, <u>do not invite your friends or your brothers or your relatives or rich neighbors</u> μὴ φώνει τοὺς φίλους σου μηδὲ τοὺς ἀδελφούς σου μηδὲ τοὺς συγγενεῖς σου μηδὲ γείτονας πλουσίους, lest they also invite you in return and you be repaid. But when you give a feast, <u>invite the poor, the crippled, the</u>

lame, the blind κάλει πτωχούς ἀναπείρους χωλούς τυφλούς, and you will be blessed, because they cannot repay you. For you will be repaid at the resurrection of the just."

    In the parable of humility and hospitality, Jesus stated four imperatives. The first imperative was within the story. The next three imperatives were for hearers. Sit in the lowest place, don't invite rich friends and relatives, and invite the poor. His imperatives were the opposite of what would have been expected in their context then and our context today. Jesus taught humility and hospitality by his own life. Here he taught with imperatives. They were beginning to understand his spoken imperatives in their context. Humility and hospitality are applicable in both historical and contemporary contexts.

Lk 14: 17-23 And at the time for the banquet he sent his servant to say to those who had been invited, 'Come, for everything is now ready Ερχεσθε ὅτι ἤδη ἕτοιμά ἐστιν.' But they all alike began to make excuses. The first said to him, 'I have bought a field, and I must go out and see it. Please have me excused.' And another said, 'I have bought five yoke of oxen, and I go to examine them. Please have me excused.' And another said, 'I have married a wife, and therefore I cannot come.' So the servant came and reported these things to his master. Then the master of the house became angry and said to his servant, 'Go out quickly to the streets and lanes of the city Εξελθε ταχέως εἰς τὰς πλατείας καὶ ῥύμας τῆς πόλεως, and bring in the poor and crippled and blind and lame καὶ τοὺς πτωχοὺς καὶ ἀναπείρους καὶ τυφλοὺς καὶ χωλοὺς εἰσάγαγε ὧδε.' And the servant said, 'Sir, what you commanded has been done, and still there is room.' And the master said to the servant, 'Go out to the highways and hedges Εξελθε εἰς τὰς ὁδοὺς καὶ φραγμοὺς and compel people to come in καὶ ἀνάγκασον εἰσελθεῖν, that my house may be filled.

    In the parable of the great dinner, Jesus quoted imperatives within the parable which were not prescriptive in their historical context nor prescriptive in our contemporary context. His imperatives were prescriptive within the narrative. Jesus' imperatives gave rise to kingdom ethics.

Lk 14: 31-35 Or what king, going out to encounter another king in war, will not sit down first and deliberate whether he is able with ten thousand to meet him who comes against him with twenty thousand? And if not, while the other is yet a great way off, he sends a delegation and asks for terms of peace. So therefore, any one of you who does not renounce all that he has cannot be my disciple. It is of no use either for the soil or for the manure pile. It is thrown away. He who has ears to hear, let him hear αὐτό ὁ ἔχων ὦτα ἀκούειν ἀκουέτω."

    This imperative, "he who has ears to hear, let him hear" is one of Jesus' often used imperatives also found in Revelation. He often commanded listeners to go beyond just hearing. He demanded that they listen with the intent that his words were recognized, understood, and comprehended beyond just hearing. In Revelation John recorded the same imperative from Jesus' "He who has ears to hear, let him hear" in Rv 2: 7, 11, 17, 29; 3:6, 13, 22.

Lk 15: 6-9 "What man of you, having a hundred sheep, if he has lost one of them, does not leave the ninety-nine in the open country, and go after the one that is lost, until he finds it? And when he has found it, he lays it on his shoulders, rejoicing. And when he comes home, he calls together his friends and his neighbors, saying to them, 'Rejoice with me Συγχάρητέ μοι, for I have found my sheep that was lost.' Just so, I tell you, there will be more joy in heaven over one sinner who repents than over ninety-nine righteous persons who need no repentance. "Or what woman, having ten silver coins, if she loses one coin, does not light a lamp and sweep the house and seek diligently until she finds it? And when she has found it, she calls together her friends and neighbors, saying, 'Rejoice with me Συγχάρητέ μοι, for I have found the coin that I had lost.' Just so, I tell you, there is joy before the angels of God over one sinner who repents."

>In these two parables concerning the lost sheep and the lost coin, Jesus twice quoted the same imperative "rejoice" within the narrative. Each imperative conveyed an imperative to rejoice after having found something that had been lost.

>These two Greek imperatives appearing as English commands "rejoice" lessen the imperative in translation. However, in Greek, the imperative intent is not obscured. Note that Jesus explained the "joy before the angels of God" meaning that if the angels rejoiced, so too there must be and is rejoicing on earth.

Lk 15: 12-24 And the younger of them said to his father, 'Father, give me the share of property that is coming to me Πάτερ δός μοι τὸ ἐπιβάλλον μέρος τῆς οὐσίας.' And he divided his property between them. Not many days later, the younger son gathered all he had and took a journey into a far country, and there he squandered his property in reckless living. And when he had spent everything, a severe famine arose in that country, and he began to be in need. So he went and hired himself out to one of the citizens of that country, who sent him into his fields to feed pigs. And he was longing to be fed with the pods that the pigs ate, and no one gave him anything. "But when he came to himself, he said, 'How many of my father's hired servants have more than enough bread, but I perish here with hunger! I will arise and go to my father, and I will say to him, "Father, I have sinned against heaven and before you. I am no longer worthy to be called your son. Treat me as one of your hired servants ποίησόν με ὡς ἕνα τῶν μισθίων σου.'" And he arose and came to his father. But while he was still a long way off, his father saw him and felt compassion, and ran and embraced him and kissed him. And the son said to him, 'Father, I have sinned against heaven and before you. I am no longer worthy to be called your son.' But the father said to his servants, 'Bring quickly the best robe Ταχὺ ἐξενέγκατε στολὴν τὴν πρώτην and put it on him καὶ ἐνδύσατε αὐτόν and put a ring on his hand, and shoes on his feet καὶ δότε δακτύλιον εἰς τὴν χεῖρα αὐτοῦ καὶ ὑποδήματα εἰς τοὺς πόδας. And bring the fattened calf καὶ φέρετε τὸν μόσχον τὸν σιτευτὸν and kill it καὶ θύσατε, and let us eat and celebrate. For this my son was dead, and is alive again; he was lost, and is found.' And they began to celebrate.

>In the prodigal son parable, Jesus spoke seven imperatives. His imperatives are significant to the parable, and none are contemporarily prescriptive. That is, there is no need or imperative to kill a fattened calf for celebration, in today's context. The implied imperative is to celebrate the prodigal's return. The imperatives are from the son to his father and father to servants. Note the first two imperatives are both from the son to the father before the son left and after he returned. There are no imperatives to the son from the father, only from the father to the servants.

Lk 16: 2-9 He also said to the disciples, "There was a rich man who had a manager, and charges were brought to him that this man was wasting his possessions. And he called him and said to him, 'What is this that I hear about you? Turn in the account of your management ἀπόδος τὸν λόγον τῆς οἰκονομίας σου, for you can no longer be manager.' And the manager said to himself, 'What shall I do, since my master is taking the management away from me? I am not strong enough to dig, and

I am ashamed to beg. I have decided what to do, so that when I am removed from management, people may receive me into their houses.' So, summoning his master's debtors one by one, he said to the first, 'How much do you owe my master?' He said, 'A hundred measures of oil.' He said to him, 'Take your bill, and sit down quickly Δέξαι σου τὰ γράμματα καὶ καθίσας ταχέως and write fifty γράψον πεντήκοντα.' Then he said to another, 'And how much do you owe?' He said, 'A hundred measures of wheat.' He said to him, 'Take your bill Δέξαι σου τὰ γράμματα, and write eighty καὶ γράψον ὀγδοήκοντα.' The master commended the dishonest manager for his shrewdness. For the sons of this world are more shrewd in dealing with their own generation than the sons of light. And I tell you, make friends for yourselves by means of unrighteous wealth ἑαυτοῖς ποιήσατε φίλους ἐκ τοῦ μαμωνᾶ τῆς ἀδικίας, so that when it fails they may receive you into the eternal dwellings.

> While Jesus spoke seven imperatives in this parable of the shrewd manager, only one was prescriptive in their historical context which was "make friends for yourselves employing unrighteous wealth." This imperative was not given within the story, but after the story had been told to his disciples. Jesus imperative here was intended to contrast the worldly with the spiritual. He conveyed shrewdness of the earthly manager to prepare for his worldly future. Jesus was not commanding unrighteous wealth but demanded similar shrewdness, perception, understanding, and preparation such as the manager had exhibited through preparing for his future.

Lk 16: 22-31 The poor man died and was carried by the angels to Abraham's side. The rich man also died and was buried, and in Hades, being in torment, he lifted up his eyes and saw Abraham far off and Lazarus at his side. And he called out, 'Father Abraham, have mercy on me Πάτερ Ἀβραάμ ἐλέησόν με, and send Lazarus to dip the end of his finger in water and cool my tongue καὶ πέμψον Λάζαρον ἵνα βάψῃ τὸ ἄκρον τοῦ δακτύλου αὐτοῦ ὕδατος καὶ καταψύξῃ τὴν γλῶσσάν μου, for I am in anguish in this flame.' But Abraham said, 'Child, remember that you in your lifetime received your good things Τέκνον μνήσθητι ὅτι ἀπέλαβες τὰ ἀγαθά σου ἐν τῇ ζωῇ σου, and Lazarus in like manner bad things; but now he is comforted here, and you are in anguish. And besides all this, between us and you a great chasm has been fixed, in order that those who would pass from here to you may not be able, and none may cross from there to us.' And he said, 'Then I beg you, father, to send him to my father's house for I have five brothers--so that he may warn them, lest they also come into this place of torment.' But Abraham said, 'They have Moses and the Prophets; let them hear them ἀκουσάτωσαν αὐτῶν.' And he said, 'No, father Abraham, but if someone goes to them from the dead, they will repent.' He said to him, 'If they do not hear Moses and the Prophets, neither will they be convinced if someone should rise from the dead.'"

> Each imperative Jesus quoted was within the Rich Man and Lazarus narrative. These are not imperative by Jesus. Abraham's imperative, "Child, remember that you in your lifetime received good things" is a blunt reminder that in context then and context today, good things have been given by God received by all.

Lk 17: 3 Pay attention to yourselves προσέχετε ἑαυτοῖς! If your brother sins, rebuke him ἐὰν ἁμάρτῃ ὁ ἀδελφός σου ἐπιτίμησον αὐτῷ, and if he repents, forgive him καὶ ἐὰν μετανοήσῃ ἄφες αὐτῷ, and if he sins against you seven times in the day, and turns to you seven times, saying, 'I repent,' you must forgive him."

> Jesus spoke three imperatives in this verse. "Rebuke him" and "forgive him" were descriptive and prescriptive in their historical context. Today these imperatives are

prescriptive. In other words, Christians now and future Christians are to both "rebuke" a brother after his sin and "forgive" a brother after that brother repents. The disciples were not confused about Jesus' imperative to them. Note Jesus' use of the word "if" in both "if your brother sins" and "if he repents" before rebuke and forgiveness. Here Jesus did not say to forgive without repentance. He said, "if he repents, forgive him. The English words, "forgive him" are derived from the Greek words, ἄφες αὐτῷ where the idea of forgiving means to "let go" or "give up" or "cancel" or "let someone have something." The idea of loosening or freeing from a type of bondage or accountability is appropriate. In other words, if the sinning brother repents, to forgive the repentant brother means to no longer hold him accountable for his sin.

Lk 17: 6-10 And the Lord said, "If you had faith like a grain of mustard seed, you could say to this mulberry tree, 'Be uprooted and planted in the sea Ἐκριζώθητι καὶ φυτεύθητι ἐν τῇ θαλάσσῃ,' and it would obey you. "Will any one of you who has a servant plowing or keeping sheep say to him when he has come in from the field, 'Come at once and recline at table'? Will he not rather say to him, 'Prepare supper for me, and dress properly, and serve me Ἑτοίμασον τί δειπνήσω καὶ περιζωσάμενος διακόνει μοι while I eat and drink, and afterward you will eat and drink'? Does he thank the servant because he did what was commanded? So you also, when you have done all that you were commanded, say, 'We are unworthy servants λέγετε ὅτι Δοῦλοι ἀχρεῖοί ἐσμεν; we have only done what was our duty.'"

> These imperatives affirm that simply following imperatives does not guarantee a worthy servant. Jesus' statement, "So you also, when you have done all that you were commanded" conveys that completion of imperative commands is not an indication of worthy servanthood. Their duty was to fulfill commands, nothing more. These are both historically and contemporarily relevant teachings. The disciples were called to follow Jesus' imperatives as their duty. Salvation, however, was not dependent upon following imperatives. Salvation was not the issue. Kingdom workers were to implement commands from their King.

Lk 17: 11-19 On the way to Jerusalem he was passing along between Samaria and Galilee. And as he entered a village, he was met by ten lepers, who stood at a distance and lifted up their voices, saying, "Jesus, Master, have mercy on us." When he saw them he said to them, "Go and show yourselves to the priests ἐπιδείξατε ἑαυτοὺς τοῖς ἱερεῦσιν." And as they went they were cleansed. Then one of them, when he saw that he was healed, turned back, praising God with a loud voice; and he fell on his face at Jesus' feet, giving him thanks. Now he was a Samaritan. Then Jesus answered, "Were not ten cleansed? Where are the nine? Was no one found to return and give praise to God except this foreigner?" And he said to him, "Rise and go your way πορεύου; your faith has made you well."

> Only one leper of the 10 gave thanks. He was a Samaritan. Jesus' imperative "go your way" affirmed the thankful Samaritan's faith. The other nine did not receive the imperative given to this Samaritan who had given thanks. The English word "rise" sounds like a command, but Luke recorded as an aorist active participle more clearly "Having risen, go your own way" or "After you have gotten up, go your own way." The word rise is not imperative. "Go your way" is imperative.

Lk 17: 31-37 On that day, let the one who is on the housetop, with his goods in the house, <u>not come down to take them away</u> μὴ καταβάτω ἆραι αὐτά, and likewise let the one who is in the field <u>not turn back</u> μὴ ἐπιστρεψάτω εἰς τὰ ὀπίσω. <u>Remember Lot's wife</u> μνημονεύετε τῆς γυναικὸς Λώτ. Whoever seeks to preserve his life will lose it, but whoever loses his life will keep it. I tell you, in that night there will be two in one bed. One will be taken and the other left. There will be two women grinding together. One will be taken and the other left." And they said to him, "Where, Lord?" He said to them, "Where the corpse is, there the vultures will gather."

> Of Jesus' three imperatives, (two within the story) his imperative, "remember Lot's wife" was prescriptive to the disciples. Jesus was explaining the coming Kingdom of God. His use of Lot's wife reminded them of the destruction of evil Sodom similar to prior passages of Noah and salvation from the flood. Jesus' imperatives substantiated the absolute difference between those in the Kingdom and those not.

Lk 18: 1-6 And he told them a parable to the effect that they ought always to pray and not lose heart. He said, "In a certain city there was a judge who neither feared God nor respected man. And there was a widow in that city who kept coming to him and saying, '<u>Give me justice against my adversary</u> Ἐκδίκησόν με ἀπὸ τοῦ ἀντιδίκου μου.' For a while he refused, but afterward he said to himself, 'Though I neither fear God nor respect man, yet because this widow keeps bothering me, I will give her justice, so that she will not beat me down by her continual coming.'" And the Lord said, "<u>Hear what the unrighteous judge says</u> Ἀκούσατε τί ὁ κριτὴς τῆς ἀδικίας λέγει.

> The first imperative "Give me justice against my adversary" Jesus spoke within the narrative. Through the second imperative "Hear what the unrighteous judge says" Jesus communicated to his disciples that even an unjust judge is subject to repeated petition. They were expected to both know what the unrighteous judge said and what his words meant.

Lk 18: 13-14 "Two men went up into the temple to pray, one a Pharisee and the other a tax collector. The Pharisee, standing by himself, prayed thus: 'God, I thank you that I am not like other men, extortioners, unjust, adulterers, or even like this tax collector. I fast twice a week; I give tithes of all that I get.' But the tax collector, standing far off, would not even lift up his eyes to heaven, but beat his breast, saying, '<u>God, be merciful to me, a sinner</u> Ὁ θεός ἱλάσθητί μοι τῷ ἁμαρτωλῷ!' I tell you, this man went down to his house justified, rather than the other. For everyone who exalts himself will be humbled, but the one who humbles himself will be exalted."

> Jesus spoke this imperative within the story. He amplified the imperative spoken by the tax collector. The tax collector through his imperative indicated a Godly understanding compared to the Pharisee. The power of the tax collector's imperative that he spoke and that those around him heard differentiated the two groups. While in English this sounds somewhat insignificant, in the language of their day, the imperative mood carried power.

Lk 18: 16 But Jesus called them to him, saying, "<u>Let the children come to me, and do not hinder them</u> Ἄφετε τὰ παιδία ἔρχεσθαι πρός με καὶ μὴ κωλύετε αὐτά τῶν, for to such belongs the kingdom of God.

> There are two Greek imperatives here, "let the children come to me" and "do not hinder them." Jesus imperatives were centered less on the children or that they were hindered and more on the Kingdom of God. Mt 19:14; Mk 10: 14

Lk 18: 19-22 And a ruler asked him, "Good Teacher, what must I do to inherit eternal life?" And Jesus said to him, "Why do you call me good? No one is good except God alone. You know the commandments: 'Do not commit adultery, Do not murder, Do not steal, Do not bear false witness, Honor your father and mother Τίμα τὸν πατέρα σου καὶ τὴν μητέρα.'" And he said, "All these I have kept from my youth." When Jesus heard this, he said to him, "One thing you still lack. Sell all that you have πάντα ὅσα ἔχεις πώλησον and distribute to the poor αἰ διάδος πτωχοῖς, and you will have treasure in heaven; and come καὶ δεῦρο, follow me ἀκολούθει μοι."

> Jesus spoke four imperatives in this single verse. The Hebrew Scriptural commandments Jesus spoke, "Do not adulter," Do not murder," Do not steal"" and Do not bear false witness" were aorist subjunctives and imperative in meaning.
> Mt 19: 21; Mk 10: 21

Lk 18: 42 And Jesus said to him, "Recover your sight Ἀνάβλεψον; your faith has made you well." The Greek word Ἀνάβλεψον is composed of the prefix ἀνά and the root βλέπω. Where βλέπω without the prefix means "to see" or "to perceive," the word Ἀνάβλεψον is more descriptive beyond merely seeing or perceiving. The word more profoundly means "look up intentionally" or "regain sight by looking up" or "recover from your blindness." The point is that Jesus' imperative was intentional having told the man to look up not merely see or perceive.

Lk 19: 1-6 He [Jesus] entered Jericho and was passing through. And there was a man named Zacchaeus. He was a chief tax collector and was rich. And he was seeking to see who Jesus was, but on account of the crowd he could not, because he was small of stature. So he [Zacchaeus] ran on ahead and climbed up into a sycamore tree to see him, for he was about to pass that way. And when Jesus came to the place, he looked up and said to him, "Zacchaeus, hurry and come down Ζακχαῖε σπεύσας κατάβηθι, for I must stay at your house today." So he hurried and came down and received him joyfully.

> The English commands "hurry" and "come down" both sound like individual commands. But the only imperative here is "come down." Zacchaeus had previously run ahead and had already climbed the sycamore tree. Jesus said, "Hurry and come down." The English, "hurry" σπεύσας comes from an aorist active masculine singular particle verb more correctly translated as "having hurried." Jesus made the point that just as Zacchaeus had hurried to climb the sycamore tree, he was to come down in the same way. Zacchaeus came down in a hurrying way.

Lk 19: 19-27 And he said to him, 'And you are to be over five cities Καὶ σὺ ἐπάνω γίνου πέντε πόλεων.' Then another came, saying, 'Lord, here is your mina, which I kept laid away in a handkerchief; for I was afraid of you, because you are a severe man. You take what you did not deposit, and reap what you did not sow.' He said to him, 'I will condemn you with your own words, you wicked servant! You knew that I was a severe man, taking what I did not deposit and reaping what I did not sow? Why then did you not put my money in the bank, and at my coming I might have collected it with interest?' And he said to those who stood by, 'Take the mina from him Ἄρατε ἀπ αὐτοῦ τὴν μνᾶν, and give it to the one who has the ten minas καὶ δότε τῷ τὰς δέκα μνᾶς ἔχοντι.' And they said to him, 'Lord, he has ten minas!' 'I tell you that to everyone who has, more will be given, but from the one who has not, even what he has will be taken away. But as

for these enemies of mine, who did not want me to reign over them, <u>bring them here</u> ἀγάγετε ὧδε and <u>slaughter them before me</u> καὶ κατασφάξατε αὐτοὺς ἔμπροσθέν μου.'"
>These five imperatives were spoken within the narrative of the parable of the ten pounds. Matthew, Mark, and John did not include this parable.

Lk 19: 28-30 And when he had said these things, he went on ahead, going up to Jerusalem. When he drew near to Bethphage and Bethany, at the mount that is called Olivet, he sent two of the disciples, saying, "<u>Go into the village in front of you</u> Ὑπάγετε εἰς τὴν κατέναντι κώμην, where on entering you will find a colt tied, on which no one has ever yet sat. Untie it and <u>bring it here</u> ἀγάγετε.
>Jesus spoke clear imperatives in preparation for his entrance into Jerusalem. These imperatives were directed at his disciples to accomplish his purpose at that time and place. The English phrase "untie it" sounds like a command, but the Greek is an aorist active masculine plural participle verb, meaning "after you have loosened the colt" or "having loosened it (the colt)" bring it here. There is no conjunction "and" in the Greek. To reduce the English sounding command "untie" some more literal Greek reflective translations are "having loosened it, lead it" or "having loosed it, bring it" or "after you have untied it, bring it here." Mk 11: 2–3; Mt 21: 2

Lk 20: 1-4 One day, as Jesus was teaching the people in the temple and preaching the gospel, the chief priests and the scribes with the elders came up and said to him, "<u>Tell us</u> by what authority you do these things, or who it is that gave you this authority." He answered them, "I also will ask you a question. <u>Now tell me</u> καὶ εἴπατέ μοι was the baptism of John from heaven or from man?"
>The English word "now" is better translated "and." The imperative "tell me" is plural meaning to the chief priests and scribes and elders. As they were in unity against Jesus, Jesus likewise commanded them as a group. In v22 WHO identify the word they spoke to Jesus as an indicative. The NA27 identified the Greek as an imperative "Tell us" in v2. Note that Jesus responded to their imperative to him with his imperative back to them. Mk 11:29

Lk 20: 21-25 So they watched him and sent spies, who pretended to be sincere, that they might catch him in something he said, so as to deliver him up to the authority and jurisdiction of the governor. So they asked him, "Teacher, we know that you speak and teach rightly, and show no partiality, but truly teach the way of God. Is it lawful for us to give tribute to Caesar, or not?" But he perceived their craftiness, and said to them, "<u>Show me a denarius</u> Δείξατέ μοι δηνάριον. Whose likeness and inscription does it have?" They said, "Caesar's." He said to them, "<u>Then render</u> ἀπόδοτε to Caesar the things that are Caesar's, and to God the things that are God's."
>Mk 12: 15; Mt 22: 21

Lk 20: 42 For David himself says in the Book of Psalms, "'The Lord said to my Lord, Sit κάθου at my right hand,
>Mk 12: 36; Mt 22: 44

Lk 20: 44 And in the hearing of all the people he said to his disciples, "<u>Beware of the scribes</u> Προσέχετε ἀπὸ τῶν γραμματέων, who like to walk around in long robes, and love greetings in the marketplaces and the best seats in the synagogues and the places of honor at feasts,

Luke wrote προσέχετε, and Mark wrote βλέπετε. Both are translated as "Beware." Mark's Greek used, "see" which in English reads like a reasonable caution. Luke's Greek indicates "keep watch, look out" which demands a more emphatic caution than Mark. When contrasting Mark and Luke, we are wise to remember that Luke depended upon witnesses. Mark may have heard Jesus' words or Peter may have told Mark Jesus' words. In any case, his disciples were to beware of the scribes. Jesus' follow-up description of "long robes," "greetings in the marketplace," and "best seats" made the scribes easy to identify. Mk 12: 38

Lk 21: 7 - 8 And they asked him, "Teacher, when will these things be, and what will be the sign when these things are about to take place?" And he said, "<u>See that you are not led astray</u> βλέπετε μὴ πλανηθῆτε. For many will come in my name, saying, 'I am he!' and, 'The time is at hand!' Do not go after them.
    Mk 13: 5-7; Mt 24: 4-6

Lk 21: 9 And when you hear of wars and tumults, <u>do not be terrified</u> μὴ πτοηθῆτε (aorist, passive, subjunctive with a negative), for these things must first take place, but the end will not be at once."
    The English phrase "do not be terrified" conveys to the English ear a command. But the Greek morphology is an aorist passive second person plural subjunctive verb. While the English command is acceptable, the idea is when they hear of wars and tumults, their ability, capacity, or skill not to be terrified but to be at peace will come from God. Mk 13:9

Lk 21: 11-15 There will be great earthquakes, and in various places famines and pestilences. And there will be terrors and great signs from heaven. But before all this they will lay their hands on you and persecute you, delivering you up to the synagogues and prisons, and you will be brought before kings and governors for my name's sake. This will be your opportunity to bear witness. <u>Settle it therefore in your minds</u> θέτε οὖν ἐν ταῖς καρδίαις ὑμῶν not to meditate beforehand how to answer, for I will give you a mouth and wisdom, which none of your adversaries will be able to withstand or contradict.
    The English word "settle" derives from the Greek word θέτε from the root τίθημι meaning a place or location of agreement or an arrangement. In context, both parties are in agreement meaning that there is no confusion between the parties.

Following what was to be settled or agreed, some English translations chose the word "minds" others chose "hearts" to convey the idea that intellectual agreement alone is not sufficient. There must be an agreement or a settling of the mind that impacts the heart. The Greek word is "hearts" not "minds" as in many English translations. While agreement in mind or intellect is possible, an intellectual agreement must move the heart.

In short, their cerebral similitude or intellectual agreement was not sufficient. Their knowledge must be in agreement to such depths their hearts are impacted so as not to produce internal division. Same today. Our intellectual agreement must move to our hearts. Mk 13: 11

Lk 21: 16-20 You will be delivered up even by parents and brothers and relatives and friends, and some of you they will put to death. You will be hated by all for my name's sake. But not a hair of your head will perish. By your endurance you will gain your lives. "But when you see Jerusalem surrounded by armies, <u>then know that its desolation has come near</u> τότε γνῶτε ὅτι ἤγγικεν ἡ ἐρήμωσις αὐτῆς.

> The English word "know" γνῶτε (verb aorist active) somewhat lessons the Greek imperative the understood in their context. Knowledge alone was not the issue. A command to respond to knowing something that was previously unknown required a response.

Lk 21: 21 Then let those who are in Judea <u>flee to the mountains</u> φευγέτωσαν εἰς τὰ ὄρη, <u>and let those who are inside the city depart</u> καὶ οἱ ἐν μέσῳ αὐτῆς ἐκχωρείτωσαν, and <u>let not those who are out in the country enter it</u> καὶ οἱ ἐν ταῖς χώραις μὴ εἰσερχέσθωσαν εἰς αὐτήν.

> The Greek present active imperative to English "flee to the mountains" is clear. The following two commands "let those" and "let not those" are derived from Greek third person imperatives. Here the English use of the word "let" softens the Greek imperative.

> Some translations that emphasize the Greek imperative are "make sure those inside the city depart from the city" and "don't let those out in the country come into the city." The English phrase "make sure" and "don't let" more clearly convey the Greek imperatives. Mk 13: 14; Mt 24: 15

Lk 21:28-29 Now when these things begin to take place, <u>straighten up</u> ἀνακύψατε <u>and raise your heads</u> καὶ ἐπάρατε τὰς κεφαλὰς ὑμῶν, because your redemption is drawing near." And he told them a parable: "<u>Look at the fig tree and all the trees</u> ἴδετε τὴν συκῆν καὶ πάντα τὰ δένδρα.

> Parallel passages in Matthew and Mark recorded that Jesus had commanded the disciples to "learn" from the fig tree. Luke did not use the imperative "lean" but recorded the imperative "look." In all contexts, the meaning is the same. Understanding a warning is imperative. Mk 13: 28; Mt 24: 32

Lk 21: 30-31 As soon as they come out in leaf, you see for yourselves and know that the summer is already near. So also, when you see these things taking place, <u>you know that the kingdom of God is near</u> γινώσκετε (imperative or indicative present active second person plural) ὅτι ἐγγύς ἐστιν ἡ βασιλεία τοῦ θεοῦ.
> Mk 13: 29; Mt 24: 33

Lk 21: 32-34 Truly, I say to you, this generation will not pass away until all has taken place. Heaven and earth will pass away, but my words will not pass away. "<u>But watch yourselves</u> Προσέχετε δὲ ἑαυτοῖς lest your hearts be weighed down with dissipation and drunkenness and cares of this life, and that day come upon you suddenly like a trap.
> Mk 13: 33

Lk 21: 35-36 For it will come upon all who dwell on the face of the whole earth. But <u>stay awake at all times</u> ἀγρυπνεῖτε δὲ ἐν παντὶ καιρῷ, praying that you may have strength to escape all these things that are going to take place, and to stand before the Son of Man."

The English "Stay awake" is acceptable, but the Greek word ἀγρυπνεῖτε is not solely a reference to staying awake from sleep. While being awake from sleep is appropriate the Greek word in their context meant to be watchful, alert, aware, and attentive. The English "stay awake" limits the imperative to be watchful. Staying awake from sleep is not sufficient. Further, Jesus explanation "at all times" was not about "stay awake" from sleep. The imperative is plural, meaning that their watchfulness and alertness was to benefit and protect all in the community. Mk 13: 35; Mt 24: 42

Lk 22: 7-8 Then came the day of Unleavened Bread, on which the Passover lamb had to be sacrificed. So Jesus sent Peter and John, saying, "Go and <u>prepare the Passover for us that we may eat it</u> ἑτοιμάσατε ἡμῖν τὸ πάσχα ἵνα φάγωμεν."

> The word "go" found in most English translations conveys an English command. However, the Greek is an aorist passive deponent participle which is better translated "having proceeded" or "having gone" rather than "go." The YLT provides a translation that more accurately conveys Jesus' words to Peter and John, "and he sent Peter and John, saying, 'Having gone on, prepare to us the Passover that we may eat." Luke did not use the conjunction "and" common in English translations that produce the words "Go and prepare" sounding as if there are two commands. Jesus here gave one plural imperative to Peter and John, "prepare the Passover for us that we may eat it." Peter and John

Lk 22: 9–12 They [Peter and John] said to him, "Where will you have us prepare it?" He said to them, "<u>Behold</u> Ἰδοὺ, when you have entered the city, a man carrying a jar of water will meet you. <u>Follow him into the house that he enters</u> ἀκολουθήσατε αὐτῷ εἰς τὴν οἰκίαν εἰς ἣν εἰσπορεύεται and tell the master of the house, 'The Teacher says to you, 'Where is the guest room, where I may eat the Passover with my disciples?' And he will show you a large upper room furnished; <u>prepare it there</u> ἐκεῖ ἑτοιμάσατε."

> Luke recorded three imperatives, "behold," follow him into the house," and "prepare it [the Passover meal] there." The English phrase "tell the master of the house" in many English Bibles sounds like an English command "tell." The Greek καὶ ἐρεῖτε τῷ οἰκοδεσπότῃ τῆς οἰκίας is a second person plural future indicative verb more accurately, "and you will tell the master of the house." The English "tell" obscures the Greek future indicative. Mk 14: 13–15; Mt 26: 18

Lk 22: 17-19 And he took a cup, and when he had given thanks he said, "<u>Take this</u> λάβετε τοῦτο and <u>divide it among yourselves</u> καὶ διαμερίσατε εἰς ἑαυτούς. For I tell you that from now on I will not drink of the fruit of the vine until the kingdom of God comes." And he took bread, and when he had given thanks, he broke it and gave it to them, saying, "This is my body, which is given for you. <u>Do this in remembrance of me</u> τοῦτο ποιεῖτε εἰς τὴν ἐμὴν ἀνάμνησιν."

> Jesus' most followed words in both historical and contemporary context were his imperatives to his disciples. His imperative "Do this in remembrance of me." Through The Lord's Supper or Communion or Eucharist or whatever the rite is called by various churches, continues to be a practice by all Christian churches, assemblies, or communities.

Denominational and non-denominational church interpretations and meanings of the Lord's Supper vary. Transubstantiation, Consubstantiation, Spiritual Presence, or Memorial Views regarding the elements, what they mean before, during, and after are subjective. However, the objective distribution and consumption of both bread and wine/grape juice are Christian practices regardless of church or denomination name.

The two imperatives "take this" and "divide it among yourselves" have been subject to interpretation throughout church history. Methodologies, of communion element distribution, vary. Distribution of the elements varies as does meaning by various leaders of churches and leadership groups of churches. There is no agreement. Some church bodies require participants to leave their seats and approach the communion table at the front of a church where they may be handed or take the elements. Others, pass plates that hold the elements down the pews or chair rows. However, regardless of actual methodology, Jesus' words "Do this in remembrance of me" have been historically followed by Christians since the day he spoke them to those in the house where Peter and John had been directed.
Mk 14: 22; Mt 26: 26; 22: 17

Lk 22: 24-26 A dispute also arose among them, as to which of them was to be regarded as the greatest. And he said to them, "The kings of the Gentiles exercise lordship over them, and those in authority over them are called benefactors. But not so with you. Rather, <u>let the greatest among you become as the youngest</u> ὁ μείζων ἐν ὑμῖν γινέσθω ὡς ὁ νεώτερος, and the leader as one who serves.

As a refresher, all imperatives in English are second person (you). Here the Greek imperative is third person (he/she and they) not typical to English. To make sense of the Greek / English person conflict "let" and "must" are English words often used to precede the pronoun. "Let the greatest among you become as the youngest" is an acceptable translation.

A translation, however, that reflects the power Jesus' imperative is, "The greatest among you must become as the youngest." The English translation "Let the greatest among you become as the youngest" conveys in English that a suggestion or permission is needed to let the "greatest" become like the "youngest."

The Greek, however, conveys the full power of Jesus' imperative. Those who heard Jesus speak realized that he had commanded them that size μείζων, age νεώτερος, those leading ἡγούμενος, or those serving διακονῶν (leading and serving are participles) were secondary to their working together. Others would see Their cooperation and collaboration with one another. His words, "But not so with you." preceded his imperative establishing that his followers were different. Jesus' followers are not like others.

Lk 22: 31-32 "Simon, Simon, behold, Satan demanded to have you, that he might sift you like wheat, but I have prayed for you that your faith may not fail. And when you have turned again, strengthen your brothers στήρισον τοὺς ἀδελφούς σου."

> Jesus' imperative here was singular only to Peter. Jesus knew the temptations from Satan that Peter would soon encounter. Given the time that Peter had spent with Jesus and having had experienced Jesus' imperatives, Peter likely would have received Jesus' imperative with a sigh of relief. His imperative was purposed to both provide comfort and place responsibility upon Peter.

Lk 22: 35-37 And he said to them, "When I sent you out with no moneybag or knapsack or sandals, did you lack anything?" They said, "Nothing." He said to them, "But now let the one who has a moneybag take it Ἀλλὰ νῦν ὁ ἔχων βαλλάντιον ἀράτω ὁμοίως, and likewise a knapsack. And let the one who has no sword sell his cloak καὶ ὁ μὴ ἔχων πωλησάτω τὸ ἱμάτιον αὐτοῦ and buy one (sword) καὶ ἀγορασάτω μάχαιραν. For I tell you that this Scripture must be fulfilled in me: 'And he was numbered with the transgressors.' For what is written about me has its fulfillment."

> Jesus' three imperatives directly pertained to what they had carried with them after Jesus had sent them out to clarify the Kingdom of God. In Lk 9: 1-6 Jesus had forbidden them to carry things ensuring their dependence on God to provide.

> Jesus' imperatives here, however, were intended to prepare them for what was about to happen. A literal interpretation is acceptable. Here sword, money bag, and knapsack were permitted. Times had changed. Before, they had gone out with nothing. Now they had to prepare for a different mission. Preparation mattered. Jesus' words, "but now" spoken before his imperatives assured them that there had been a change. His imperatives affirmed that they were to furnish and prepare themselves.

Lk 22: 40 And when he came to the place, he said to them, "Pray that you may not enter into temptation." προσεύχεσθε μὴ εἰσελθεῖν εἰς πειρασμόν.

> In parallel passages, Matthew and Mark quoted Jesus' imperative that they "sit."
> Luke recorded Jesus imperative that they "pray." Mt 26:36; Mk 14:32

Lk 22: 42-46 And he withdrew from them about a stone's throw, and knelt down and prayed, saying, "Father, if you are willing, remove this cup from me παρένεγκε τοῦτο τὸ ποτήριον ἀπ ἐμοῦ. Nevertheless, not my will, but yours, be done πλὴν μὴ τὸ θέλημά μου ἀλλὰ τὸ σὸν γινέσθω." And there appeared to him an angel from heaven, strengthening him. And being in an agony he prayed more earnestly; and his sweat became like great drops of blood falling down to the ground. And when he rose from prayer, he came to the disciples and found them sleeping for sorrow, and he said to them, "Why are you sleeping? Rise and pray προσεύχεσθε that you may not enter into temptation."

> Jesus' first two imperatives were to his Father. The first "remove this cup from me" preceded by "Father, if you are willing" demanded from his Father removal of the bitterness he would endure. This imperative mirrored the desire of any person about to experience certain death on the cross.

The second demanded the Father fulfill the Father's will. Immediately after Jesus' imperative that the Father fulfill the Father's will, there appeared an angel.

Although "rise" appears in English as a command, it is an active aorist participle. Luke recorded "pray" as the imperative Jesus gave to his disciples after Jesus' imperatives to his Father. Pray is the imperative, not Mk 14: 32-42; Mt 26: 36-41

Lk 22: 49–51 And when those who were around him saw what would follow, they said, "Lord, shall we strike with the sword?" And one of them struck the servant of the high priest and cut off his right ear. But Jesus said, "No more of this Εᾶτε ἕως τούτου!" And he touched his ear and healed him.

> The English reads, "No more of this" but Luke did not record a literal "no." The literal Greek word order is "allow unto this" or "permit as far as this" but here the Greek word order is not as significant as the Greek morphology. Enhanced English translations that eliminate the word "no" and conveys the Greek are "This has gone far enough." or "Everything has been permitted up to this point of cutting off this man's ear" or "Enough of this!" Jesus' imperative "permit" or "allow" followed by "until now" or "as far as this" was his instructions that going forward his followers would not harm anyone as a consequence for his crucifixion. None of the gospel writers recorded Jesus' views about the Roman soldier's use of the sword or about the Temple guard's use of the sword. This imperative is not about the Roman soldiers nor Temple guards use of the sword. Jesus' imperative here indicated that he was aware of the anger and motives that would follow his crucifixion. His imperative intended to stop further bloodshed following his crucifixion. "Until this" or "as far as this" in English sounds insignificant yet holds solid teaching to all Christians. Evangelism does not come by the sword or by shedding blood as some religions promulgate. What Jesus imperative meant to those who heard him was that his followers were not to shed blood as a response to what was about to happen, the crucifixion of an innocent man. Mt 26:52, Jn 10:11

Lk 23: 27-31 And there followed him a great multitude of the people and of women who were mourning and lamenting for him But turning to them Jesus said, "Daughters of Jerusalem, do not weep for me Θυγατέρες Ἰερουσαλήμ μὴ κλαίετε ἐπ ἐμέ, but weep for yourselves and for your children πλὴν ἐφ ἑαυτὰς κλαίετε καὶ ἐπὶ τὰ τέκνα ὑμῶν. For behold, the days are coming when they will say, 'Blessed are the barren and the wombs that never bore and the breasts that never nursed!' Then they will begin to say to the mountains, 'Fall on us Πέσετε ἐφ ἡμᾶς,' and to the hills, 'Cover us καὶ τοῖς βουνοῖς Καλύψατε ἡμᾶς.' For if they do these things when the wood is green, what will happen when it is dry?"

> Jesus' first two imperatives were "Don't weep" and "Weep" which affirmed to them that Jesus knew what he was doing. He knew what was about to come upon their children. After his imperatives, he explained their future including two more imperatives regarding judgment that was to come upon Jerusalem. Jesus knew the judgment to come upon Jerusalem and the daughters of Jerusalem. He warned the daughters of Jerusalem through imperatives. He told them not to weep for him. He told them to weep for their children. Then he prophesied the imperatives the

daughters of Jerusalem would speak in their sufferings at the soon coming destruction of their city.

The green wood compared to dry wood may be from Ez 20: 47 or a metaphorical reference to what once was green and healthy has become dry and ready for burning and destruction. This may be Jesus' prophesy regarding the Temple destroyed in AD 70 or what happens to any faith community unwilling to recognize the Messiah.

Lk 23: 32-34 Two others, who were criminals, were led away to be put to death with him. And when they came to the place that is called The Skull, there they crucified him, and the criminals, one on his right and one on his left. And Jesus said, "<u>Father, forgive them</u>, Πάτερ, ἄφες αὐτοῖς for they know not what they do." And they cast lots to divide his garments.

Matthew, Mark, and John did not record this imperative. Luke relied on witnesses who had seen and heard Jesus speak, which means, one or more persons at the cross had to have told Luke what Jesus had said. There are three issues: 1. Luke 23: 34 was not part of original texts 2. Greek word definition, and 3. Greek Grammar.

1.   Many English Bibles surround v34a with brackets indicating that the words in v34a were not recorded in earlier texts but were later additions. Textual critics are not agreeably convinced on authenticity and textual traditions. It is not problematic that Lk 23: 34a is not found in earlier manuscripts. Those preaching this text must consider the text's origin and complexity.

2.   Here the Greek word ἄφες, is often rendered "forgive" in English. However, because ἄφες carries a broader meaning in Greek in addition to context the English rendered "forgive" is not the only possibility. Perhaps "forgive" in contemporary English was not the meaning Jesus nor Luke intended to be rendered from the Greek in their context. Note four Greek lexicon references Friberg, Danker, Brown, and Mounce:

Friberg: 1. send off or away, let go 2. divorce 3. abandon, leave behind 4. set aside, neglect 5 let go, leave in peace, allow 6. forgive, pardon, cancel.

Danker: 1. to dismiss or release someone or someth. [ing] from a place or one's presence 2. to release from legal or moral obligation or consequence, cancel, remit, pardon 3. To move away, w. implication of causing a separation, leave, depart from 4. Leave standing/lying 5. Leave it to someone to do something, let, let go, allow, tolerate

Brown: let go, cancel, remit, leave, forgive; release, pardon, cancellation, forgiveness; letting pass, passing over.

Mounce: Depending on particular context, *aphiemi* means to "forgive, leave, abandon."

Note that Friberg, Brown, and Mounce record the word "forgive" latter in their definitions. Danker does not render the English word "forgive" in any of his six listings. If those at the cross heard Jesus tell the Father to "let them go" perhaps they did not perceive Jesus' words to be beneficial to those crucifying him.

Depending on word meaning and context, Jesus' imperative command to the Father to "let them go" or "abandon them" or "leave them behind" or "release them" or "divorce them" they may have been understood as judgment more so than forgiveness. In short, contemporary English readers interpret forgiveness meaning a universality of salvation regardless of sin even upon the crucifixion perpetrators. However, hearers of Jesus may have understood the crucifiers as being out of God's hands. Why? Because context, word meaning, and grammar effect interpretation.

3. Much of the Greek grammar is not clearly rendered into English due to complexity of conveying what was contextually understood in their day. What we read today may not be equivalent to what they understood then. Following the imperative, Luke recorded the reason for Jesus' command often rendered through the English as, "for they know not what they do" which weakly conveys the Greek <u>perfect active indicative</u> οὐ γὰρ οἴδασιν and the <u>present active indicative</u> τί ποιοῦσιν. The indicative mood describes a fact. English rendering conveys to readers that those who crucified Jesus were innocent and forgiven because they did not know what they were doing. Jesus' use of the indicative affirmed the facts. They were guilty of not knowing what they should have known.

The YLT comes close to conveying the Greek <u>perfect active indicative</u> and <u>present active indicative</u> with, a) "for they have not known (perfect active indicative) what they do (present active indicative)." A more detailed rendering is, b) "for they have not known (perfect active indicative) what they are doing (present active indicative)." Another is, c) "for after having not known (perfect active indicative) what they are doing (present active indicative)." C is a bit wordy and jumbled in English but conveys the Greek grammar.

What those at the cross may have heard and understood was, "Father, let them go because they (those crucifying me) are still doing what they have not known." and is understood by English readers as judgmental not a universalism salvation mindset. Big difference. Grasping forgiveness was and is not simple.

To review, Jesus' Greek imperative πάτερ, ἄφες αὐτοῖς, rendered as an English command, "Father, forgive them" sounds comforting and theologically sound to the English ear because our ears and our mindset of grace and mercy dominate. So, "Father, forgive them" makes sense whereas, "Father, let them go" sounds to the English ear as judgmental. Luke likely interviewed John, Mary, and others who had been at the cross which means Luke's Greek sourced from numerous people who were there is not problematic.

If Luke's Greek word choice and grammar were exactly what Jesus said, Jesus had commanded his Father to, "let them go" not in a non-judgmental (forgiving), inclusion ideal, as we understand in English, but in a judgmental, exclusion from God's presence. To be "let go" from God's presence is distinctly different than forgiving. Why? Because they (those who crucified) were still doing wrong after having not known what was wrong. In other words, they should have known better. Rendering, "Father, forgive them for they know not what they do." even lacking the Greek word meaning is an acceptable rendering emphasizing Jesus' grace. However, lack of rendering rich Greek word meaning and grammar in historical context has provided English readers meaning that may have differed from what those at the cross heard and understood.

While today's English readers interpret forgiveness, perhaps what John, Mary, others at the cross and certainly those crucified with Jesus heard and understood was judgment such as, "Father, let them go out of your hand into judgment because they should have known not to do what they are doing."

In any event, this brief study is not a dogmatic teaching but a study highlighting the complexities of Greek grammar, word meaning, the indicatives and the imperatives. The Greek to English text is not simple and requires in-depth study.

Lk 24: 39 <u>See my hands and my feet</u> ἴδετε τὰς χεῖράς μου καὶ τοὺς πόδας μου, that it is I myself. <u>Touch me, and see</u> ψηλαφήσατέ με καὶ ἴδετε. For a spirit does not have flesh and bones as you see that I have."

Jesus' three imperatives, "see," "touch" and "see" provided assurance to the disciples that Jesus had been (and is) resurrected from the dead. His spoken imperatives were intentional said to convict more than convince them. After having witnessed Jesus' death by crucifixion and his lifeless crucified body sealed in the tomb, his imperatives were calculated and purposeful. Those who heard him speak had no reason to doubt. These imperatives would have been told to Luke by those who had heard Jesus speak. They would have corroborated with one another to verify Jesus' words. Their joint affirmations of what Jesus had said is what Luke recorded. Their validations affirm the accuracy of Luke's gospel.

Lk 24: 45-53 Then he opened their minds to understand the Scriptures, and said to them, "Thus it is written, that the Christ should suffer and on the third day rise from the dead, and that repentance and forgiveness of sins should be proclaimed in his name to all nations, beginning from Jerusalem. You are witnesses of these things. <u>And behold</u> καὶ ἰδοὺ, I am sending the promise of my Father upon you. <u>But stay in the city until you are clothed with power from on high</u> δὲ καθίσατε ἐν τῇ πόλει ἕως οὗ ἐνδύσησθε ἐξ ὕψους δύναμιν." Then he led them out as far as Bethany, and lifting up his hands he blessed them. While he blessed them, he parted from them and was carried up into heaven. And they worshiped him and returned to Jerusalem with great joy, and were continually in the temple blessing God.

Jesus' final two imperatives recorded by Luke were "Behold" a greeting imperative, and an imperative properly translated into an English command "stay in the city until you are clothed with power from on high." They were to stay in the city because the city was where Jesus would send the promise of his Father to them. The city is where they would receive the power. The power from on high would take them out of the city. Until that power arrived they were to stay in the city.

Immediately after Jesus' final imperative Luke recorded that Jesus led them to Bethany where "while he blessed them, he parted from them and was carried up into heaven." Here Luke recorded heaven as singular, not plural.

Whatever you ask in my name, this I will do, that the Father may be glorified in the Son. If you ask me anything in my name, I will do it. "If you love me, you will keep my commandments. And I will ask the Father, and he will give you another Helper, to be with you forever, even the Spirit of truth, whom the world cannot receive, because it neither sees him nor knows him. You know him, for he dwells with you and will be in you.

Jn 14: 13-17

# 12 John's Record of the Imperatives of Jesus

Whatever you ask in my name, this I will do, that the Father may be glorified in the Son. If you ask me anything in my name, I will do it. If you love me, you will keep my commandments. And I will ask the Father, and he will give you another Helper, to be with you forever, even the Spirit of truth, whom the world cannot receive, because it neither sees him nor knows him. You know him, for he dwells with you and will be in you. Jn 14: 13-17

## John

Many Christians have been taught that Jesus' disciples were poor, uneducated, simple men without status or influence. While none of the twelve documented by Matthew, Mark, Luke, and John were Pharisees, Sadducees, Temple aristocrats, Herodians, Zealots, Essenes or Sanhedrin members, to presume the disciples were not men of means is a mistake. Along with Zebedee (the Father of James and John and wife Salome) Peter, Andrew, James, and John were successful entrepreneurs. They partnered in business, employed people and were well connected. Brownrigg affirms John and his brother James as having been successful and influential:

> John and his brother James were fishermen, whom Luke describes as partners with Peter and Andrew. John, his brother James, and Peter formed the inner circle of the disciples of Jesus. Jesus called John and his brother while they were in their boat mending their nets. They promptly left their father Zebedee in the boat with the men he employed. Salome [wife of Zebedee, mother of James and John] is listed as one of the women who 'looked after' Jesus in Galilee. It seems, therefore, that Zebedee's family was of some substance. John appears to have been sufficiently acquainted with the high priest's palace in Jerusalem to know the girl portress and to be able to persuade her to admit Peter at the time of the trial of Jesus. It is not impossible that they might have been purveyors of Galilean fish to the high priest's household. Certainly, the disciples of Jesus were men of varying means.[1]

For Zebedee and Salome, to have the means to support their businesses while losing Peter, Andrew, James, and John during the years, they followed Jesus meant that Zebedee and Salome were people of means. Matthew, Mark, Luke, and John each recorded events that did not occur on the north side of the Sea of Galilee where their fishing businesses were located. This meant that John along with Peter, Andrew and his brother James spent considerable time away from their fishing businesses. However, given the numerous references to fishing and Jesus crossing the Sea of Galilee, most likely the brothers and partners, at least in some measure continued their fishing when near Galilee. Zebedee and Salome likely managed their businesses during their absence.

John was very close to Jesus in presence and confidence. Jesus while on the cross gave John responsibility for Mary is sufficiently proves Jesus' trust in John. Surprisingly John never identifies himself as the author of his gospel. Comfort clarifies why:

---

[1] Brownrigg, Ronald, "John, son of Zebedee" in *Who's Who the New Testament*, 119.

John wanted his readers to know that he had a special relationship with Jesus - not for the sake of boasting, but for the sake of affirming the trustworthiness of his testimony. He [John] attempted to retain some humility by referring to himself in the third person; at the same time, he probably expected the immediate circle of readers to identify him as the apostle John and to believe in the validity of his written account.[2]

Agreeing with Comfort the validity of John's testimony means Jesus' imperatives within John's book are trustworthy. Given their existing business partnership before flowing Jesus, the relationship between John and Peter was already strong. Peter is often mentioned throughout John's gospel. A significant insight affirming the relationship between John and Peter is that John referred to himself in his gospel four times as someone, "Jesus loved" but every time he presents his status with Jesus, Peter is also part of the narrative.[3]

## John's Theology

Scholars do not include John's gospel with the synoptic gospels (Synoptics) of Matthew, Mark, and Luke. The Synoptics reflect a similar chronology of Jesus' life. John's gospel is not as inclusive of numerous events found in the Synoptics. For example, John recorded Jesus' temple table turning event early in Jesus' ministry in Chapter 2. Matthew, Mark, and Luke recorded the event later in Jesus life in Mt 12, Mk 11, and Lk 19 respectively. While John's book provides certain events found in the Synoptics, John in 20: 30-31 specifically described why he wrote what he wrote. Chronology was less critical to John because John was more concerned with Jesus having fulfilled the messianic prophecy for the Jews. John selected narratives significant to his intended readers, the Jews to recognize Jesus as their prophesied Messiah, the Christ.

---

[2] Comfort, Philip Wesley, Wendell C. Hawley, *Opening the Gospel of John*, xii.
[3] The four of the five narratives where John referenced himself as one whom "Jesus loved" John also referenced Peter, (Jn 19: 26 John referenced Mary):
    One of his disciples, whom Jesus loved, was reclining at table close to Jesus, so Simon Peter motioned to him to ask Jesus of whom he was speaking. Jn 13: 23-24
    Now on the first day of the week Mary Magdalene came to the tomb early, while it was still dark, and saw that the stone had been taken away from the tomb. So she ran and went to Simon Peter and the other disciple, the one whom Jesus loved, and said to them, "They have taken the Lord out of the tomb, and we do not know where they have laid him." So Peter went out with the other disciple, and they were going toward the tomb. Jn 20: 1-3
    Just as day was breaking, Jesus stood on the shore; yet the disciples did not know that it was Jesus. Jesus said to them, "Children, do you have any fish?" They answered him, "No." He said to them, "Cast the net on the right side of the boat, and you will find some." So they cast it, and now they were not able to haul it in, because of the quantity of fish. That disciple whom Jesus loved therefore said to Peter, "It is the Lord!" When Simon Peter heard that it was the Lord, he put on his outer garment, for he was stripped for work, and threw himself into the sea. Jn 21: 4-7
    Peter turned and saw the disciple whom Jesus loved following them, the one who had been reclining at table close to him and had said, "Lord, who is it that is going to betray you?" When Peter saw him, he said to Jesus, "Lord, what about this man?" Jesus said to him, "If it is my will that he remain until I come, what is that to you? You follow me!" Jn 21: 20-22

> Now Jesus did many other signs in the presence of the disciples, which are not written in this book; but these are written so that you may believe that Jesus is the Christ, the Son of God, and that by believing you may have life in his name.
> Jn 20: 30-31

John wrote to the Jews specifically for them to know Jesus as their awaited Messiah, their Christ and believing, they will have life in his name. John' book is deeply theological which means the imperatives within John's book point to Jesus as Messiah. John also differs from the Synoptics in that John did not include the "Olivet Discourse" where within the Synoptics Jesus prophesied the fall of the Jerusalem Temple that occurred in AD 70. The "Olivet Discourse" is found in Mt 24 – 15; Mk 13 and Lk 21. Matthew, Mark, and Luke each included the parable of the fig tree. There is no "Olivet Discourse" in John nor parable of the fig tree. Rather than write a prophecy similar to the "Olivet Discourse" in his gospel as Matthew, Mark, and Luke had done, John wrote another book of prophecy, Revelation. Because John was specific to record the signs that Jesus had done in the presence of the disciples the imperatives John recorded have strategic meaning.

As with all letters, words, sentences, paragraphs, chapters, and books, both historical and cultural conditioning is ever present. Before wrestling with English texts, Raymond Brown identifies the need to wrestle with the history and culture of the Greek text:

> But one must recognize that every word of the Gospel [Gospel of John] is historically and culturally conditioned. The fact that it is written in Koine Greek is prima facie evidence of this truth. There is inevitably something "strange" and "foreign" about the biblical text which demands that we wrestle with it. First-century history and culture must play a part in interpretation. The Fourth Gospel, like all biblical texts handed down to us by Jewish and Christian tradition, is a difficult text, and a great deal of this difficulty comes from its strangeness when read in our present cultural context. The original readers of the Gospel are an important point of reference in following the interplay between author and reader in the text.[4]

John's primary theological point to the Jews, that Jesus is the Christ / Messiah, is embedded within the historically and culturally conditioned Greek of his day. John's Greek and more specifically the imperatives within John's Greek conveyed John's main point that Jesus is the Christ / Messiah to the Jews. Perhaps one reason for reading John in English is standard practice for new Christians is that John's message in Greek to the Jews is irrefutable and straightforward. As you study Jesus' imperatives from John, keep in mind John's message to the Jews: Jesus is the Messiah.

## John's Greek

Luke in Ac 4: 5-13 recorded that the Jerusalem rulers, elders, scribes, Annas the high priest, Caiaphas, John and Alexander affirmed that John and Peter were illiterate and unskilled. Peter and John operating fishing businesses on the northern shores of the Galilean Sea and not skilled in reading or writing Greek is not surprising. John's illiteracy does not mean the biblical writings attributed to him are suspect. To the contrary, John's illiteracy contributed to the accuracy and

---

[4] Brown, Raymond E., *An Introduction to the Gospel of John*, 36.

supportability of John's authorship. John depended on scribes and editors for accuracy. All the more reason to trust John's words.[5]

In spite of John's limited reading or writing skills compared to others of his day or John's lack of disciplined or formal training that Sanhedrin, Pharisees, Scribes or Temple leaders most likely had received, John's authorship lead by the Holy Spirit produced precisely what God intended. John was one of Jesus' closest disciples and had received Jesus teachings in rabbinical tradition. John's scribes and editors would not have had the flexibility to interpret John's words. They translated John's words. They did not interpret John's words. John would not have misquoted Jesus' words. Gospel of John scholar Phillip Comfort affirms:

> In John's day, it was the customary practice for an author to dictate the words to a scribe and then read over the manuscripts to make editorial adjustments.[6]

John and Peter's illiteracy, rather than give doubt to their record, provides credibility to the accuracy of John's book. The process of scribing, dictating and editing was extensive. What scribes recorded from either John's verbalized dictation or his sophomoric self-written Greek would have been edited numerous times for clarity and truth. Without a doubt, before any of John's writings were distributed, John's Gospel, John 1, 2, and 3, and Revelation were extensively edited for grammatical accuracy and precision.

The Greek imperatives John recorded were deliberate. He could have used different Greek moods, but he did not. He made sure the imperatives of Jesus were clear. Had Jesus not spoken imperatives, John would not have recorded imperatives. John made sure that what the scribes recorded was precisely what he wanted to be written. The editing process warranted that whatever imperatives Jesus spoke, John was confident of their correct recording. Some scholars have proposed that John's original writings were written in Aramaic, the vernacular of the Palestinian Jews and then translated to Greek. F.F. Bruce negated this proposition:

> This [The book of John originally in Aramaic] is quite improbable. The Gospel of John as such was a Greek composition from the beginning.[7]

---

[5] See Chapter Four regarding John and Peter's literacy. Luke recorded two words in Acts 4:13 that described the assessment of John and Peter:
>ἀγράμματοί εἰσιν which meant their grammar abilities (reading and writing) were lacking. Illiteracy meant they were unable to read and write Greek. Illiteracy, however, did not mean that they were unable to hear and speak comprehensible Greek of their day.
>καὶ ἰδιῶται which meant they lacked professional or intentional training for a specific craft or skill. Many English translations inaccurately convey that they were uneducated, ignorant, unsophisticated, or unlearned which is misleading. They merely lacked deeper advanced higher learning, particularly in reading, writing or professional or recognized literary skills. However, John, James, Peter, and Andrew were fishermen on the Sea of Galilee affirming that these men were sufficiently educated to profitably and successfully operate an ongoing business partnership. Their hearing, speaking, reading and writing skills may have been limited (especially reading and writing), but their language skills were sufficient to the point of being recognized as successful and productive members in their communities. John and Peter though illiterate at least in part were smart men astute at their professions.

[6] Comfort, Philip Wesley, Wendell C. Hawley, *Opening the Gospel of John*, xv.

[7] Bruce, F. F., *The Gospel of John*, 2. (Bruce expounded that there are no Aramaisms in the Greek form. The Greek John authored inclusive of the imperative spoken by Jesus is reliable.)

Greek students are commonly assigned John's gospel and his three epistles John One, Two, and Three for Greek study because John's Greek is both theologically steeped and helpful for study. The Greek in John's Gospel is good Greek, not likely solely written by someone illiterate. John's Greek in his Gospel and three epistles is useful with meaning because it is simple. Wilson affirms the similar Greek in John's Gospel and his first epistle:

> The sentence structure in both is simple and the style repetitious. Moreover, the gospel and epistle share certain grammatical features.[8]

John's unpretentious Greek style was intended for the readers of his time. John's simple and accurate Greek provided his early readers with comprehensible theology steeped in soteriology (salvation) and Kingdom affirmation. John's Greek was precise and clear. In other words, John wrote with the intention that his words would be read not by scholars of his day, but by people of everyday Greek. Raymond Brown on John's Gospel affirmed that John knew well his intended audience and their Greek:

> Much more than a knowledge of the syntactically correct and straightforward Greek of the text of the Fourth Gospel is presupposed of its reader."[9]

The Greek in the Gospel of John was useful for John's readers. John likely heard and spoke Greek on a conversant level and wrote Greek on a rudimentary but not literary level. Scribes and editors fine-tuned John's words John intended for his immediate readers. There are differences between those who speak to audiences and those who write to readers. First-time readers of the book of John in English is relatively simple because John's Greek was straightforward in his day. John's theology, however, is steep.

Given the presence of the Holy Spirit, we have the assurance that the words (for our purpose, the imperatives) John recorded were those of Jesus. Because of John's illiteracy, he was dependent on dictation and editing. What John recorded by the power of the Holy Spirit was what Jesus said. Jesus words were recorded as John would have heard them. John was thorough with what he had recorded, especially Jesus' imperatives.

## John's Record of the Imperatives of Jesus

Jn 1: 35-39 The next day again John was standing with two of his disciples, and he looked at Jesus as he walked by and said, "Behold, the Lamb of God!" The two disciples heard him say this, and they followed Jesus. Jesus turned and saw them following and said to them, "What are you seeking?" And they said to him, "Rabbi" (which means Teacher), "where are you staying?" He said to them, "<u>Come and you will see</u> ερχεσθε καὶ ὄψεσθε ἦλθαν." So they came and saw where he was staying, and they stayed with him that day, for it was about the tenth hour.

> Jesus commanded that they "come" with the assurance that they would see where Jesus was staying. They immediately were obedient. There was no hesitation, no discussion, and no doubt. They went with Jesus. Jesus' imperative "come" was present middle or passive deponent meaning the Greek form (morphology) was

---

[8] Wilson, Marvin R., Chris Alex Vlachos, *A Workbook for New Testament Greek*, 1-2.
[9] Brown, Raymond E., *An Introduction to the Gospel of John*, 36.

passive but the meaning was active. Hence, they came and saw (past tense) where Jesus was staying exactly as Jesus had commanded them through his imperative. He said, "Come and you will see." And they went and saw. John did not, however, record where they went and what they say. Where they went and what they saw was less important than following Jesus' imperatives.

During the early stages of Jesus' time with his disciples, he did not require them to 'do' things. His initial methodology was more like, "watch me." Often those trying to make disciples of others jump too quickly to commanding others to be or do what they have never seen or experienced. Jesus did not teach that way. This early imperative command at the beginning of John's gospel, "Come and you will see" affirmed his methods. They would see him work certainly through his miracles, healings, and casting out demons principally done through spoken imperatives.

Jn 1: 40-43 One of the two who heard John speak and followed Jesus was Andrew, Simon Peter's brother. He first found his brother Simon and said to him, "We have found the Messiah" (which means Christ). He brought him to Jesus. Jesus looked at him and said, "So you are Simon the son of John? You shall be called Cephas" (which means Peter). The next day Jesus decided to go to Galilee. He found Philip and said to him, "Follow me" Ἀκολούθει μοι Now Philip was from Bethsaida, the city of Andrew and Peter. Philip found Nathanael and said to him, "We have found him of whom Moses in the Law and also the prophets wrote, Jesus of Nazareth, the son of Joseph." Nathanael said to him, "Can anything good come out of Nazareth?" Philip said to him, "Come and see."

>Jesus' words to Philip paralleled his words to other disciples. Jesus simply gave an imperative command "Follow me." His imperative was not negotiated or refuted. Later in v45 John recorded that Andrew had said: "We have found the Messiah." Given Jesus' imperatives and as time with Jesus progressed Philip realized that Jesus had found him, that Philip had found Jesus. Jesus questioned Philip in 14:9, "Have I been with you so long, and you still do not know me, Philip? Whoever has seen me has seen the Father. How can you say, 'Show us the Father'?" The first imperative to Philip "Follow me" initiated Jesus' imperatives to the other disciples. Jesus' imperatives were central to teaching Philip and the others.

>John's recording of Jesus' "follow me" imperative to Peter here in the first chapter is found again at the end of John's gospel in Jn 21: 19, 22. John started his gospel with Jesus' imperatives to Peter "follow me" and ended his gospel with the same imperatives to Peter, "follow me." With this in mind, the relationship John and Peter shared was close from their fishing businesses on the northern side of the Sea of Galilee before they met Jesus to their last days after having heard Jesus' numerous imperatives.

Jn 2: 1-7 On the third day there was a wedding at Cana in Galilee, and the mother of Jesus was there. Jesus also was invited to the wedding with his disciples. When the wine ran out, the mother of Jesus said to him, "They have no wine." And Jesus said to her, "Woman, what does this have to do with me? My hour has not yet come." His mother said to the servants, "Do whatever he tells you." Now there were six stone water jars there for the Jewish rites of purification, each holding twenty or thirty gallons. Jesus said to the servants, "Fill the jars with water." And they filled them up to the brim. And he said to them, "Now draw some out and take it to the master of the feast." So they took it. Jesus said to the servants, "<u>Fill</u> γεμίσατε the jars with water." And they filled them up to the brim.

> The servants flawlessly followed Jesus' imperative. The supporting text, "and they filled them up to the brim" affirmed that the jars were precisely filled as Jesus had commanded. John's narrative taught early readers that Jesus' imperatives were not violable. When Jesus commanded "fill" he did not mean near to the top but to the brim. John insightfully recorded that the servants followed Jesus' imperatives to perfection. The jars were not simply filled. They were filled to the brim. John's detail is no mistake.

Jn 2: 8 And he said to them, "<u>Now draw some out</u> ἀντλήσατε νῦν and <u>take it to the master of the feast</u> φέρετε φέρετε τῷ ἀρχιτρικλίνῳ· οἱ δὲ ἤνεγκαν" So they took it.

> Jesus' two imperatives, "draw" and "take" were followed without delay just as his prior imperatives that the jars be filled were followed. Note that John again conveyed their response fulfilling the imperatives through his words, "So they took it."

Jn 2: 16-17 And he told those who sold the pigeons, "<u>Take</u> ἄρατε these things away; <u>do not make my Father's house a house of trade</u>."μὴ ποιεῖτε τὸν οἶκον τοῦ πατρός μου οἶκον ἐμπορίου His disciples remembered that it was written, "Zeal for your house will consume me."

> Here, Jesus' imperatives on the first read seem to command Temple marketers that they were not to make Jesus' Father's house a house of trade. That is true, but there is more. His imperative also affirmed that the Temple was never able to be made into a house of trade.

> The Temple overseers thought that they had made the Temple a house of trade. Try as they might to make a market in the Temple, it was not possible. A true Temple, a Temple where God was intended to reside, the house of Jesus' Father could never be a market. God never resides in a market.

> Jesus' imperatives conveyed to them in the context of their day that the Temple was no longer where God resided. It was not possible that the place where God resides with his people could be a market. A market in the Temple affirmed that God was no longer in residence. The house of Jesus' father, the Temple was still God's but he no longer resided in a formerly holy the place of prayer that had become a market. Jesus' command, "do not make" was true then and is true today true. The place where God resides, be that a physical bodily temple or gathering of faithful believers in community housed in a physical building, no matter where God resides, he does not reside where goods must be marketed to be in his presences.

Jn 2: 18-22 So the Jews said to him, "What sign do you show us for doing these things?" Jesus answered them, "<u>Destroy this temple</u> λύσατε τὸν ναὸν τοῦτον, and in three days I will raise it up." The Jews then said, "It has taken forty-six years to build this temple, and will you raise it up in three days?" But he was speaking about the temple of his body. When therefore he was raised from the dead, his disciples remembered that he had said this, and they believed the Scripture and the word that Jesus had spoken.

The Greek morphology affirms that the imperative "destroy this temple" was a command to the Jews to put Jesus to death. The imperative "destroy" is second person plural. A clarifying meaning is, "You as a group destroy this singular temple of my body." Jesus affirmed that after they would destroy him at his command, he would raise in three days.

Jesus did not say, "If you destroy this temple." He did not say, "When you destroy this temple." He was not speaking about the Jerusalem Temple. Jesus commanded the Jews as a group to destroy his temple, his body. That is what they heard although denied. The English pronoun "this" is derived from a Greek accusative masculine singular demonstrative pronoun. The demonstrative pronoun here functioned as an adjective. There was no audible (heard) or textual (written) confusion that Jesus was talking about his own body.

Both the definite article and noun "this Temple" τὸν ναὸν are masculine singular. In v20 John recorded that the Jews used a definite article and a demonstrative pronoun that identified "the Temple." In v20 the ESV has translated ὁ ναὸς as "this Temple" but a more accurate translation agreeing with the Greek nominative masculine singular article and the nominative masculine singular noun should be "the Temple." While in English the difference between "this" and "the" sound and seem insignificant. The distinction in both audible and written Greek is more profound than in English.

John further affirmed in v21 that Jesus was speaking of his own body. Intentional contemporary and historical eisegesis (compared to literal, contextual exegesis) has caused confusion regarding the Jewish Temple's structure or Jesus' bodily temple. The Jews had heard him correctly yet referenced "the Temple." As a result, the physical temple structure or Jesus bodily temple became a hermeneutical or interpretive point of contention for them.

As each gospel records, Jesus' bodily temple was destroyed on the cross and raised in three days. Jesus' imperative that he gave to the Jews was completed. They precisely did as he commanded. He had given them a command to destroy his bodily temple, and they did. Wallace agrees:

> The sense of the imperative here is, minimally, "If you destroy….."But if λύσατε [destroy] follows the normal semantic pattern of conditional imperative, the force is even stronger: "If you destroy this temple – and I command you to – in three days I will raise it up." Though this may seem farfetched at first glance, it is in fact likely.[10]

---

[10] Wallace, Daniel, B., *Greek Grammar Beyond the Basics: An Exegetical Syntax of the New Testament,* 490.

Jn 4: 7-8 A woman from Samaria came to draw water. Jesus said to her, "Give me a drink." δός μοι πεῖν (For his disciples had gone away into the city to buy food.)

Jesus' imperative "Give me a drink" initiated conversation with the Samaritan woman. John recorded Jesus' first words not as conversant or cordial, but as commanding her. After having heard Jesus' imperative "give me a drink" the woman asked Jesus a question in response to his command v10. John did not record that the woman drew water or that Jesus drank from the well. John did not record if she followed Jesus' command.

The NIV dynamic equivalent Bible took liberty with Jesus' command. Rather than translate the imperative as a command, the NIV eliminated the command and substituted a question: "When a Samaritan woman came to draw water, Jesus said to her, "Will you give me a drink?" Jn 4:7 NIV, The difference in translation accuracy, may seem insignificant. But John did not record that the Samaritan woman heard a question. John recorded that Jesus said and she heard an imperative. The difference between the ESV and NIV may seem trite, but John recorded a Greek imperative, not a question.

Jn 4: 9-10 The Samaritan woman said to him, "How is it that you, a Jew, ask for a drink from me, a woman of Samaria?" (For Jews have no dealings with Samaritans.) Jesus answered her, "If you knew the gift of God, and who it is that is saying to you, 'Give me a drink δός μοι πεῖν,' you would have asked him, and he would have given you living water."

Jesus clarified that the woman did not know him. In this verse, for a second time, he quoted to her his initial imperative "Give me a drink." He affirmed that if she had given him an imperative command to give her a drink, he would have given her living water. In context, Jesus had told the woman to command Jesus to give her living water. Just as Jesus did not ask, but commanded a drink, he affirmed that had the woman commanded him he would have given her living water.

Asking implies doubt. Begging the question, "Will you give me drink?" in English creates an option with either a negative or a positive response. Commanding implied certainty. God's desire was to be known so well, so intimately, so relationally, so respectfully and so trusted for what he provides that those who truly know him do not ask, they command him to give them his will. Just as Jesus' commanded the woman to give him drink, he commanded his faithful followers to command him to give his will to them.

The English phrase, "you would have asked him" σὺ ἂν ᾔτησας αὐτὸν sounds simple enough. In English Jesus' words sound like Jesus conveyed to the woman something like, "you should have asked me." But the Greek word ᾔτησας meaning "to ask" is an aorist active indicative second person singular verb. The Greek aorist indicative conveyed in their context that she understood Jesus as being able to provide the living water. English wording does not so clearly convey the Greek indicative. In short, the Samaritan woman knew or trusted that Jesus could provide the living water that was his to provide.

Those who command God that his will be given to them, rather than asking, affirm their knowledge of God's sovereignty. Same with asking or demanding living water from Jesus. Only Jesus provides the living water. Jesus did not command her to command him for living water. Instead he conveyed that living water is available. Jesus challenged her to ask or more deeply with boldness and confidence to demand the living water. The issue here is less about the imperative or the question and more about the living water only available through Jesus.

Jn 4: 16-19 Jesus said to her, "Go, ὕπαγε call your husband φώνησον σου τὸν ἄνδρα and come here ἐλθὲ ἐνθάδε." The woman answered him, "I have no husband." Jesus said to her, "You are right in saying, 'I have no husband'; for you have had five husbands, and the one you now have is not your husband. What you have said is true." The woman said to him, "Sir, I perceive that you are a prophet.

Jesus' three imperatives, "go," "call," and "come" provided no options for the woman at the well. Jesus commanded her to go away from him, to leave the well. He next commanded her to call her husband, and then he commanded her to return to where Jesus would be, at the well. Answering his three imperatives with, "I have no husband." affirmed that she believed she was unable to fulfill Jesus' imperatives.

The ESV and most English translations correctly render "for you have had five husbands" from πέντε γὰρ ἄνδρας ἔσχες rather than "for you had five husbands" appropriately conveying the aorist active indicative verb ἔσχες. Had Jesus said, or John recorded "for you had five husbands" or "for you had had five husbands" the lack of the perfect or pluperfect would have conveyed a different relationship with her former husbands. John record an aorist active indicative verb, not a perfect active or pluperfect active. The aorist is undefined and indefinite.

In other words, Jesus conveyed to the woman in her understanding something like, "the fact that you have married five husbands is not going away." Jesus quickly confronted her opinion and desire to deny her past with "I have no husband." Jesus did not let her opinion that she had no husband continue. While the English struggles to convey the depth of Jesus' confrontation with the woman in what she erroneously tried to convey to Jesus, the Greek John recorded would have deeply resonated with his original hearers and readers.

Her incorrect definition of a husband which conflicted with Jesus' definition of a husband is exposed. Having realized she had been confronted about her previous five husbands as well as the man with whom she was living was not her husband triggering her response, "Sir I perceive that you are a prophet." is no surprise.

Jn 4: 21-30 Jesus said to her, "Woman, believe me πίστευέ μοι, the hour is coming when neither on this mountain nor in Jerusalem will you worship the Father. You worship what you do not know; we worship what we know, for salvation is from the Jews. But the hour is coming, and is now here, when the true worshipers will worship the Father in spirit and truth, for the Father is seeking such people to worship him. God is spirit, and those who worship him must worship in spirit and truth." The woman said to him, "I know that Messiah is coming (he who is called Christ).

When he comes, he will tell us all things." Jesus said to her, "I who speak to you am he." Just then his disciples came back. They marveled that he was talking with a woman, but no one said, "What do you seek?" or, "Why are you talking with her?" So the woman left her water jar and went away into town and said to the people, "Come Δεῦτε, see ἴδετε a man who told me all that I ever did. Can this be the Christ?" They went out of the town and were coming to him.

> The woman had first called Jesus a prophet but realized that Jesus was more than what she had presumed. Jesus had first commanded her to give him drink. He had also commanded her to believe. The Samaritan woman experienced first-hand the power of Jesus' imperatives and as a result, returned to her village and told others about the man she had met at the well who knew all that she had done.

> In v29 John recorded that the woman gave two imperative commands "come" and "see" to the people. John did not write that the woman said to the people, "Let me tell you what happened to me at the well." John recorded the woman's spoken imperatives to the town people. Not surprisingly John also recorded that her imperatives were followed as she had commanded. She said, "come" and "see" and John recorded, "They went out of town and were coming to him." The power of the Greek imperative is evident in these texts but challenging to comprehend in English.

Jn 4: 35 Do you not say, 'There are yet four months, then comes the harvest'? Look, I tell you, ἰδοὺ λέγω ὑμῖν lift up your eyes ἐπάρατε τοὺς ὀφθαλμοὺς ὑμῶν, and see θεάσασθε that the fields are white for harvest. Already the one who reaps is receiving wages and gathering fruit for eternal life, so that sower and reaper may rejoice together.

> Jesus did not merely command his disciples to see. He spoke three imperatives here. After commanding, "Look" or "Behold" he next commanded them to "lift up" their eyes and then commanded them to "see" that fields white for harvest.

> His three imperatives here clarified that they must make an effort. Without exertion, without intentionally looking up they would not see that the fields ripened and ready for harvest.

Jn 4: 46-49 So he came again to Cana in Galilee, where he had made the water wine. And at Capernaum there was an official whose son was ill. When this man heard that Jesus had come from Judea to Galilee, he went to him and asked him to come down and heal his son, for he was at the point of death. So Jesus said to him, "Unless you see signs and wonders you will not believe." The official said to him, "Sir, come down before my child dies." Κύριε κατάβηθι πρὶν ἀποθανεῖν τὸ παιδίον μου. Jesus said to him, "Go. πορεύου Your son will live." The man believed the word that Jesus spoke to him and went on his way.

> In v49 the official gave an imperative to Jesus and said, "Sir, come down before my child dies." This is not an imperative from Jesus, but an imperative from the official to Jesus.

> Openly issuing a command to Jesus in public, the official exhibited total faith in Jesus. Jesus immediately responded with an imperative to the man "go." Jesus' responded to the official's imperative command. The official's imperative affirmed

to all those who heard his imperative to Jesus, the faith of the official. Later the official's servants verified the time of the healing. The official and his whole household believed. Jesus quickly responded to this official who had faith enough to speak imperative to Jesus.

Understanding the depth of the imperative usage of Jesus and others, there is much to learn in this exchange of imperatives between Jesus and the official. Essential to the narrative is the presence of those who heard the exchange of imperatives and learned of the healing that followed the imperative.

Jn 5: 1-9 After this there was a feast of the Jews, and Jesus went up to Jerusalem. Now there is in Jerusalem by the Sheep Gate a pool, in Aramaic called Bethesda, which has five roofed colonnades. In these lay a multitude of invalids--blind, lame, and paralyzed. One man was there who had been an invalid for thirty-eight years. When Jesus saw him lying there and knew that he had already been there a long time, he said to him, "Do you want to be healed?" The sick man answered him, "Sir, I have no one to put me into the pool when the water is stirred up, and while I am going another steps down before me." Jesus said to him, "<u>Get up</u> ἔγειρε, <u>take up your bed</u> ἆρον τὸν κράβαττόν σου, and <u>walk</u> περιπάτει." And at once the man was healed, and he took up his bed and walked. Now that day was the Sabbath.
    This is an example of a faith-inspired imperative. The pool was not needed for healing the invalid. Note that John did not expound with additional words from Jesus or the former invalid after the invalid had taken up his bed and walked.
    Mk 2: 9

Jn 5: 10-14 So the Jews said to the man who had been healed, "It is the Sabbath, and it is not lawful for you to take up your bed." But he answered them, "The man who healed me, that man said to me, '<u>Take up your bed, and walk</u>.'" They asked him, "Who is the man who said to you, '<u>Take up your bed and walk</u>'?" Now the man who had been healed did not know who it was, for Jesus had withdrawn, as there was a crowd in the place. Afterward Jesus found him in the temple and said to him, "<u>See, you are well</u>! Ἴδε ὑγιὴς γέγονας. <u>Sin no more</u>, μηκέτι ἁμάρτανε that nothing worse may happen to you."
    Note John recorded that both the healed man and the Jew's repeated Jesus' imperative, "Take up your bed and walk."

Jesus' two imperatives, "see you are well" and "sin no more," were followed by an explanation of consequences "that nothing worse may happen to you" for disobedience to his imperative. As a consequence to sin, Jesus' imperatives were purposed to stop continuance of the illness.

Here Jesus affirmed that unrepented ongoing sin could result in illnesses that can get worse, or result in something worse than an illness. His words, "that nothing worse may happen to you" might mean the same illness can get worse, or a different disorder, tragedy, or death might occur. Here Jesus taught the consequences of sin.

Jn 5: 25-28 "Truly, truly, I say to you, an hour is coming, and is now here, when the dead will hear the voice of the Son of God, and those who hear will live. For as the Father has life in himself, so he has granted the Son also to have life in himself. And he has given him authority to execute judgment, because he is the Son of Man. <u>Do not marvel at this</u> μὴ θαυμάζετε τοῦτο ὅτι, for an hour is coming when all who are in the tombs will hear his voice

>Some Jews sought to kill Jesus. Jesus commanded them that they were not to marvel at Jesus' authority from the Father to judge sin. They were not to be surprised by the authority he would receive as the Son of Man, to judge.

Jn 5: 41-47 I do not receive glory from people. But I know that you do not have the love of God within you. I have come in my Father's name, and you do not receive me. If another comes in his own name, you will receive him. How can you believe, when you receive glory from one another and do not seek the glory that comes from the only God? <u>Do not think that I will accuse you to the Father</u> μὴ δοκεῖτε ὅτι ἐγὼ κατηγορήσω ὑμῶν πρὸς τὸν πατέρα. There is one who accuses you: Moses, on whom you have set your hope. For if you believed Moses, you would believe me; for he wrote of me. But if you do not believe his writings, how will you believe my words?"

>Jesus continued giving imperatives to the Jews who sought to kill him. His imperative, "<u>Do not think that I will accuse you to the Father</u>" affirmed to the Jews that he would not accuse them to the Father. Moses would accuse them for wrongly interpreting Moses' words. They had set their hopes on Moses' words. Their defective interpretation would bring Moses' accusation and condemnation upon them.

>Those interpreting Scripture today are cautioned by this biblical historical example. Interpretation mistakes were just as much a possibility in Jesus' day then as in our day now. In God's view, far beyond making a mistake, intentional subjective interpretation to advocate a biased or self-serving agenda was egregious and consequential.

Jn 6: 4-10 Now the Passover, the feast of the Jews, was at hand. Lifting up his eyes, then, and seeing that a large crowd was coming toward him, Jesus said to Philip, "Where are we to buy bread, so that these people may eat?" He said this to test him, for he himself knew what he would do. Philip answered him, "Two hundred denarii would not buy enough bread for each of them to get a little." One of his disciples, Andrew, Simon Peter's brother, said to him, "There is a boy here who has five barley loaves and two fish, but what are they for so many?" Jesus said, "<u>Have the people sit down</u> ποιήσατε τοὺς ἀνθρώπους ἀναπεσεῖν." Now there was much grass in the place. So the men sat down, about five thousand in number.

>Jesus commanded his disciples to "have the people sit down. Two minor English anomalies are found. The Greek is "make the men sit down." English translates "men" to "people" which is not problematic and common because ἀνθρώπους is perfectly translatable to "people."

>The second anomaly concerns the imperative. The English word "have" does not convey the imperative as strongly as "make." The YLT translation, "make the men sit down" conveys the Greek imperative and the gender distinction. Jesus' imperative to his disciples left no doubt that the disciples were responsible for

crowd control of the men, their families, and the entire five thousand. Jesus knew family values in that when the men sat down, so too would the wives and children. Jesus' imperative placed responsibility upon the disciples to make the people sit. Jesus did not make the people sit. That responsibility Jesus gave to his disciples.

Jn 6: 12-13 And when they had eaten their fill, he told his disciples, "<u>Gather up the leftover fragments</u> συναγάγετε τὰ περισσεύσαντα κλάσματα, that nothing may be lost." So they gathered them up and filled twelve baskets with fragments from the five barley loaves left by those who had eaten.

> In addition to crowd control, Jesus commanded his disciples to pick up the leftovers. His imperative "gather up the leftover fragments" intended to make sure nothing was to be lost or wasted. Note that immediately after Jesus' imperative to his disciples to gather the leftovers, they did exactly as he had told them. There was no hesitation nor argument after having heard Jesus' imperative. John went further and recorded exactly how much was gathered which affirmed the response by the disciples to Jesus' imperative.

Jn 6: 16-20 When evening came, his disciples went down to the sea, got into a boat, and started across the sea to Capernaum. It was now dark, and Jesus had not yet come to them. The sea became rough because a strong wind was blowing. When they had rowed about three or four miles, they saw Jesus walking on the sea and coming near the boat, and they were frightened. But he said to them, "It is I; <u>do not be afraid</u>."
Mt 14: 24–33; Mk 6: 47–52

Jn 6: 23-27 Other boats from Tiberias came near the place where they had eaten the bread after the Lord had given thanks. So when the crowd saw that Jesus was not there, nor his disciples, they themselves got into the boats and went to Capernaum, seeking Jesus. When they found him on the other side of the sea, they said to him, "Rabbi, when did you come here?" Jesus answered them, "Truly, truly, I say to you, you are seeking me, not because you saw signs, but because you ate your fill of the loaves. <u>Do not labor for the food that perishes</u> ἐργάζεσθε μὴ τὴν βρῶσιν τὴν ἀπολλυμένην, but for the food that endures to eternal life, which the Son of Man will give to you. For on him God the Father has set his seal."

> Jesus addressed the crowd and commanded them not to labor for perishing food. The present middle imperative continues commanding that their labor must be for the food that endures to eternal life. The deponent, Koine Greek imperative, meant that while the verb has a middle voice, the verb conveyed an active voice in meaning to them in their context.

> Jesus had commanded the crowd to be active in working for food that endured to eternal life given by the Son of Man. Jesus used the term Son of Man when he referred to himself. He told them that he Jesus himself would provide eternal food for life.

Jn 6: 41-43 So the Jews grumbled about him, because he said, "I am the bread that came down from heaven." They said, "Is not this Jesus, the son of Joseph, whose father and mother we know? How does he now say, 'I have come down from heaven'?" Jesus answered them, "<u>Do not grumble among yourselves</u> Μὴ γογγύζετε μετ ἀλλήλων. No one can come to me unless the Father who sent me draws him. And I will raise him up on the last day.

> Jesus specifically gave an imperative to the Jews in the crowd who were grumbling. They complained and murmured among themselves about Jesus' referenced to himself as the bread from heaven. They supported and approved one another at their disagreement with Jesus. His command to them "Do not grumble among yourselves." was for their future wellbeing.
>
> Their grumbling would not benefit them nor the Kingdom. Further, their grumbling would not benefit them in their futures. Jesus' imperative was intentional and beneficial for them as well as for the crowd who heard this imperative to them. His imperative was not solely for the grumbling Jewish group. His imperative was intended to benefit the crowd through Jesus' purpose for the Kingdom.

Jn 7: 5-8 Now the Jews' Feast of Booths was at hand. So his brothers said to him, "Leave here and go to Judea, that your disciples also may see the works you are doing. For no one works in secret if he seeks to be known openly. If you do these things, show yourself to the world." For not even his brothers believed in him. Jesus said to them, "My time has not yet come, but your time is always here. The world cannot hate you, but it hates me because I testify about it that its works are evil. <u>You go up to the feast</u> ὑμεῖς ἀνάβητε ὑμεῖς ἀνάβητε εἰς τὴν ἑορτήν. I am not going up to this feast, for my time has not yet fully come." After saying this, he remained in Galilee.

> Jesus imperative to his brothers "you go up to the feast" without him confirmed that Jesus knew of the deep hatred toward him. Jesus' imperative was purposed to save them from harm which they may have been unaware. He knew their association with him would hurt them if they remained with him and did not go to the feast.
>
> Jesus in following the father's will was master of his own time and the timing of those who encouraged him to show his works. His work with his disciples was not yet finished. At the time he spoke these words, the crucifixion was in the future. Jesus was not motivated by fame or popularity to promote his cause, but by His father's assignments to him.

Jn 7: 19-24 Has not Moses given you the law? Yet none of you keeps the law. Why do you seek to kill me?" The crowd answered, "You have a demon! Who is seeking to kill you?" Jesus answered them, "I did one work, and you all marvel at it. Moses gave you circumcision (not that it is from Moses, but from the fathers), and you circumcise a man on the Sabbath. If on the Sabbath a man receives circumcision, so that the law of Moses may not be broken, are you angry with me because on the Sabbath I made a man's whole body well? <u>Do not judge by appearances</u> μὴ κρίνετε μὴ κρίνετε κατ ὄψιν, <u>but judge with right judgment</u> ἀλλὰ τὴν δικαίαν κρίσιν κρίνετε."

> To the crowd that accused Jesus of having a demon he gave two imperatives, "do not judge" and "judge." His imperatives were purposed to teach that they must discern wrong judgments from right judgments. He commanded them not to judge by what they had seen, but to judge by what they knew was right. On the surface,

in English, these imperatives appear as if they were intended to save Jesus from harm while in the Temple. It first appears that he implored them not to judge him for his benefit wrongly.

His imperatives had nothing to do with his protection His imperatives here were for their future, for their profit and their benefit. Jesus taught them that their judgments, no matter right or wrong, would be known regardless if they judged by appearances or by right judgments. More important than their judgments was that others would observe, see, critique, and tell others about their judgments. Jesus' followers would be judged for how they judged. Those who observed their judgments would make their judgments about them.

Having exposed their double standard in breaking the Sabbath themselves through their own 'religious activity' (i.e., circumcision), Jesus foiled their growing conspiracy that Jesus should be killed for healing on the Sabbath. He had exposed their refusal to abide by the spirit of the law. Their superficial judgments condemned them.

Jn 7: 37-38 On the last day of the feast, the great day, Jesus stood up and cried out, "If anyone thirsts, let him <u>come to me</u> ἐρχέσθω πρός με <u>and drink</u> καὶ πινέτω. Whoever believes in me, as the Scripture has said, 'Out of his heart will flow rivers of living water.'"

Jesus stood and cried to the crowd two imperatives which were both third person singular. He commanded individuals from the crowd to come and drink. He supported his imperatives prophesying that for those who believed in Jesus as the Scriptures testified, living waters would flow out of a person's heart.

Jn 7: 53 - 8: 11 The two imperatives found within the narrative of the woman caught in adultery must be considered with the following insight. John may or may not have recorded this narrative nor the two imperatives by Jesus within the narrative. Phillip Comfort and Wendell C. Hawley are worth quoting at length:

> This passage about the adulterous woman is not included in any of the earliest manuscripts. Its first appearance in a Greek manuscript is in the fifth century, but it is not contained in any other Greek manuscript until the ninth century. No Greek church father comments on the passage prior to the twelfth century-and then Euthymius Zigabenus declares that the accurate copies do not contain it. When this story is inserted in later manuscripts, it appears in different places: after John 7:52, at the end of John's Gospel, or after Luke 21: 38. And when it does appear, it is often marked of by asterisks or obeli to signal its probable spuriousness. The story is part of an oral tradition that was included in the Syriac Peshitta, circulated in the Western church, eventually finding its way into the Latin Vulgate, and from there into later Greek manuscripts, the like of which were used in formulating the Textus Receptus (Metzer).[11]

---

[11] Comfort, Philip Wesley, Wendell C. Hawley, *Opening the Gospel of John*, 134-135.

Jn 8: 2-11 Early in the morning he came again to the temple. All the people came to him, and he sat down and taught them. The scribes and the Pharisees brought a woman who had been caught in adultery, and placing her in the midst they said to him, "Teacher, this woman has been caught in the act of adultery. Now in the Law Moses commanded us to stone such women. So what do you say?" This they said to test him that they might have some charge to bring against him. Jesus bent down and wrote with his finger on the ground. And as they continued to ask him, he stood up and said to them, "Let him who is without sin among you be the first to <u>throw a stone at her</u> ἐπ αὐτὴν βαλέτω λίθον." And once more he bent down and wrote on the ground. But when they heard it, they went away one by one, beginning with the older ones, and Jesus was left alone with the woman standing before him. Jesus stood up and said to her, "Woman, where are they? Has no one condemned you?" She said, "No one, Lord." And Jesus said, "Neither do I condemn you; <u>go</u> πορεύου, and from now on <u>sin no more</u> μηκέτι ἁμάρτανε."

    Jesus' first imperative in this narrative "throw a stone at her" is third person singular aorist active with the condition that the one who threw a stone would have judged himself to have been without sin. One or many were commanded to throw individually. To throw a stone one at a time meant that everyone could see those who presumed themselves sinless. They were not commanded to throw as a group, Jesus commanded one man to be the first to throw.

A more lucid rendering is "Whoever in this group is without sin must throw the first stone." or "If you are without sin, throw the first stone." Those who had condemned the woman caught in adultery were commanded to throw if they had no sin. Jesus' imperative demanded self-assessment. His imperative made it impossible for them to throw the first stone. If a stone was thrown, the thrower would have been assessed by others as to the thrower's self-presumed sinless life. The only person who could have thrown a stone was Jesus. Jesus' imperative went beyond the command to throw. Not acting on Jesus' imperative defined them as being unable to throw. His imperative affirmed their sin, perhaps their adulteries or perhaps their complicities having set up the woman to catch her in the adultery to question Jesus.

Jesus spoke three imperatives. His first imperative was to any person who was without sin. His next two imperatives "go" and "sin no more." were to the woman. Interesting that Jesus did not say to the woman or anyone there, "Follow me." Rather than ask her or anyone to follow him, he commanded her to "go" and "sin no more." The only place where she could have gone where she would sin no more would have been to return to her husband. Had she gone with her adulterous partner she would have continued in sin. Only in a restored sexually trusting marital relationship could she have fulfilled Jesus' two imperatives "go" and "sin no more."

When she publically called Jesus, "Lord" she openly identified and confessed Jesus as her savior certainly from the stoning and also for her future life. Jesus two imperatives "go" and "sin no more" identified Jesus as her savior beyond stoning to a savior for eternal life. He commanded her to be sinless going forward through his words, "and from now on."

Readers of this text, regardless of if John did or did not write the text, do not know what happened to her after Jesus had commanded her. There is no record that she returned to her husband. We know what happened to the accusers, but we do not know what happened to her. Given the power of Jesus' two imperatives, "go" and "sin no more" we might presume she returned to her husband and marital faithfulness following her encounter with Jesus. But the wherever this narrative developed there is no record that the woman complied with Jesus' imperatives. We only know that Jesus had commanded her to "go" and "sin no more" through the imperatives within the text.

Jn 9: 1-11 As he passed by, he saw a man blind from birth. And his disciples asked him, "Rabbi, who sinned, this man or his parents, that he was born blind?" Jesus answered, "It was not that this man sinned, or his parents, but that the works of God might be displayed in him. We must work the works of him who sent me while it is day; night is coming, when no one can work. As long as I am in the world, I am the light of the world." Having said these things, he spat on the ground and made mud with the saliva. Then he anointed the man's eyes with the mud and said to him, "<u>Go</u> ὕπαγε <u>wash in the pool of Siloam</u>" νίψαι εἰς τὴν κολυμβήθραν τοῦ Σιλωάμ (which means Sent). So he went and washed and came back seeing. The neighbors and those who had seen him before as a beggar were saying, "Is this not the man who used to sit and beg?" Some said, "It is he." Others said, "No, but he is like him." He kept saying, "I am the man." So they said to him, "Then how were your eyes opened?" He answered, "The man called Jesus made mud and anointed my eyes and said to me, '<u>Go</u> ὕπαγε to Siloam and <u>wash</u> νίψαι.' So I went and washed and received my sight."

> Jesus gave two present active imperatives "go" and "wash" to the blind man. The blind man after being questioned by others as to what had happened repeated the same imperatives "go" and "wash" that Jesus had given them. He also added past tense of each of Jesus imperatives. In addition to the blind man, two groups of people became aware of Jesus' imperatives: people who saw and people who later would hear what happened. We only know what Jesus and the blind man said. Jesus spoke the imperatives, and the blind man responded precisely as Jesus had commanded and was healed. Jesus said, "Go" and the blind man "went." Jesus said, "Wash" and the blind man "washed."

Jn 10: 33-37 The Jews answered him, "It is not for a good work that we are going to stone you but for blasphemy, because you, being a man, make yourself God." Jesus answered them, "Is it not written in your Law, 'I said, you are gods'? If he called them gods to whom the word of God came--and Scripture cannot be broken--do you say of him whom the Father consecrated and sent into the world, 'You are blaspheming,' because I said, 'I am the Son of God'? If I am not doing the works of my Father, then <u>do not believe me</u> μὴ πιστεύετέ μοι;

> Jesus' spoke this imperative to the Jewish leaders in the Temple. He commanded them not to believe if he was not doing works of his father. His imperative to them affirmed that he was doing works of his Father. Jesus' imperatives placed the responsibility to believe upon those who had heard his commands and seen the results of Jesus imperatives. Because the Jewish leaders in the Temple saw that he was doing the work of the Father, they had no options other than to believe. Because they had no options having seen Jesus do works of the Father, they became angry.

Jn 10: 38 but if I do them, even though you do not believe me, <u>believe the works</u> τοῖς ἔργοις πιστεύετε that you may know and understand that the Father is in me and I am in the Father."

> Jesus' plural imperative "believe the works" commanded them as a group. They as a group would not be able to deny Jesus' miraculous works which they also had seen a group. Jesus purposely spoke an imperative which commanded them to believe what they had seen. They had no options but to believe. Their collective unbelief in his works proved their unbelief in him. They denied Jesus' miracles because they valued their community and their interpretations more than Jesus and the proof he displayed.

Jn 11: 34-42 And he said, "Where have you laid him?" They said to him, "Lord, come and see." Jesus wept. So the Jews said, "See how he loved him!" But some of them said, "Could not he who opened the eyes of the blind man also have kept this man from dying?" Then Jesus, deeply moved again, came to the tomb. It was a cave, and a stone lay against it. Jesus said, "<u>Take away the stone.</u>" ἄρατε ἄρατε τὸν λίθον. Martha, the sister of the dead man, said to him, "Lord, by this time there will be an odor, for he has been dead four days." Jesus said to her, "Did I not tell you that if you believed you would see the glory of God?" So they took away the stone. And Jesus lifted up his eyes and said, "Father, I thank you that you have heard me. I knew that you always hear me, but I said this on account of the people standing around, that they may believe that you sent me."

> Jesus imperative "take away the stone" to those standing near the tome opened the tomb where Lazarus had been entombed. Jesus' plural imperative affirmed the stone required more than one person to move it. He did not command the stone to move. He did not move the stone himself. He commanded others to move the stone.

Jn 11: 43-44 When he had said these things, he cried out with a loud voice, "<u>Lazarus, come out.</u>" Λάζαρε δεῦρο ἔξω. The man who had died came out, his hands and feet bound with linen strips, and his face wrapped with a cloth. Jesus said to them, "<u>Unbind him</u> λύσατε αὐτὸν, and <u>let him go.</u>" ἄφετε αὐτὸν ὑπάγειν.

> Jesus' two plural imperatives "unbind him" and "let him go" affirmed that Lazarus could walk in response to Jesus' imperative, "Lazarus, come out." but the hands and feet of Lazarus were still bound. Lazarus, "the man who died came out" needing no additional help beyond being freed from his burial wrappings. Lazarus stood and walked proving that Jesus' imperatives were not partial but complete.

Jn 12: 3-8 Mary therefore took a pound of expensive ointment made from pure nard, and anointed the feet of Jesus and wiped his feet with her hair. The house was filled with the fragrance of the perfume. But Judas Iscariot, one of his disciples (he who was about to betray him), said, "Why was this ointment not sold for three hundred denarii and given to the poor?" He said this, not because he cared about the poor, but because he was a thief, and having charge of the moneybag he used to help himself to what was put into it. Jesus said, "<u>Leave her alone</u> ἄφες αὐτήν, so that she may keep it for the day of my burial. For the poor you always have with you, but you do not always have me."

> The imperative here "Leave her alone" derives from the Greek word ἄφες translated in other places within the New Testament as "let go," "divorce," and "forgive." Danker: 1 the act of freeing and liberating from something that confines, release. 2 the act of freeing from an obligation, guilt, or punishment,

pardon, cancellation.[12] 155. Brown: *aphiemi* (derived from *apo*, from, and *heimei*, to put in motion, send), attested since Homer, means the voluntary release of a person or thing over which one has legal or actual control.[13]

Regarding Jesus anointment with oil, here John recorded Jesus' imperative to Judas in the singular person. Mark recorded the imperative in the plural, not to Judas, but to a group. Matthew did not record an imperative, but Jesus referenced the disciples in the plural, not just Judas. Luke referred to the Pharisees and Simon but without any imperatives. There is more than one anointing with oil in the four Gospels. Matthew, Mark, and John mention Bethany. Luke does not mention Bethany.
Mk 14: 6

Jn 12: 24-26 Truly, truly, I say to you, unless a grain of wheat falls into the earth and dies, it remains alone; but if it dies, it bears much fruit. Whoever loves his life loses it, and whoever hates his life in this world will keep it for eternal life. If anyone serves me, he must follow me ἐμοὶ ἀκολουθείτω; and where I am, there will my servant be also. If anyone serves me, the Father will honor him.

Jesus' imperative "he must follow me" did not permit wavering. Serving was ineffectual without first following. Following, required adherence. Following was a prerequisite to service. The father would not honor those who thought they were serving, yet did not first follow.

Some English translations record "let him follow me" in agreement translation methodology in that there is no third person in English.

Jn 12: 27 "Now is my soul troubled. And what shall I say? 'Father, save me from this hour Πάτερ σῶσόν με ἐκ τῆς ὥρας ταύτης?' But for this purpose I have come to this hour.

John recorded Jesus' imperative "Father save me from this hour." with a prerequisite question, "And what shall I say"? Jesus' imperative affirmed Jesus' relationship with the Father and the purpose for the hour.

This imperative is couched in a rhetorical question "And what shall I say"? The answer is an understood "no" because Jesus knew his purpose and had agreed to it long before the hour approached. The imperative acknowledged the relationship between father and son and their purpose. Jesus submitted to and obeyed the father even unto death. Those who heard Jesus' imperative would have known that the relationship between the Father and Jesus was reciprocal. The Father and Son were one in their mission.

---

[12] Danker, Frederick William, ed. Walter Bauer, *A Greek-English Lexicon of the New Testament and other Early Christian Literature*. 155.
[13] Brown, Colin, ed., *New International Dictionary of New Testament Theology*. Volume 1, 697.

Jn 12: 28 Father, <u>glorify your name</u> δόξασόν σου τὸ ὄνομα." Then a voice came from heaven: "I have glorified it, and I will glorify it again." The crowd that stood there and heard it said that it had thundered. Others said, "An angel has spoken to him." Jesus answered, "This voice has come for your sake, not mine.

> Jesus' made a command imperative to the Father that the Father glorify his name. Immediately after Jesus' imperative, the voice from heaven affirmed past and future glory. The responsive and confirming words, "I have glorified it, and I will glorify it again." left no doubt. Commanding the Father with an imperative would have been confusing to them. Telling God what to do in their context would have seemed disrespectful to God's sovereignty. The relationship between Jesus and the Father affirms that the imperative has been and would be met. The Father has done in the past and will do in the future what Jesus commanded.
>
> To those who heard Jesus speak, to those who would read Johns words in their language and context then, Jesus imperative and the Father's response affirmed their oneness. Their singleness of will to glorify the Father was equal.
>
> Those who heard the voice regardless if they thought it thunder or an angel could not deny the message. Jesus then counseled them that the words they heard were for them, not him. Jesus' knew that the Father had and would glorify his name. To those who heard his words, Jesus affirmed that the Father's glorification, past, present, and future were impossible to stop.

Jn 12: 29-35 The crowd that stood there and heard it said that it had thundered. Others said, "An angel has spoken to him." Jesus answered, "This voice has come for your sake, not mine. Now is the judgment of this world; now will the ruler of this world be cast out. And I, when I am lifted up from the earth, will draw all people to myself." He said this to show by what kind of death he was going to die. So the crowd answered him, "We have heard from the Law that the Christ remains forever. How can you say that the Son of Man must be lifted up? Who is this Son of Man?" So Jesus said to them, "The light is among you for a little while longer. <u>Walk while you have the light</u> περιπατεῖτε ὡς τὸ φῶς ἔχετε, lest darkness overtake you. The one who walks in the darkness does not know where he is going.

> Jesus' imperative to the crowd who heard the Father's words, "I have glorified it, and I will glorify it again." instructed them to walk while in the light. The imperative "Walk" implied an urgency because time was short. He spoke in metaphor. Darkness would overtake them if they remained unmoved.

Jn 12: 36 While you have the light, <u>believe in the light</u> πιστεύετε εἰς τὸ φῶς, that you may become sons of light." When Jesus had said these things, he departed and hid himself from them.

> Jesus' imperative "believe" was not a metaphor as was "in the light." Immediately after this imperative Jesus (the light) departed and hid from them. At Jesus' absence, their belief would be central to their faith. His physical presence would no longer be required. Only with faith would they become "sons of light."

Jn 13: 21-30 After saying these things, Jesus was troubled in his spirit, and testified, "Truly, truly, I say to you, one of you will betray me." The disciples looked at one another, uncertain of whom he spoke. One of his disciples, whom Jesus loved, was reclining at table close to Jesus, so Simon Peter motioned to him to ask Jesus of whom he was speaking. So that disciple, leaning back against Jesus, said to him, "Lord, who is it?" Jesus answered, "It is he to whom I will give this morsel of bread when I have dipped it." So when he had dipped the morsel, he gave it to Judas, the son of Simon Iscariot. Then after he had taken the morsel, Satan entered into him. <u>Jesus said to him, "What you are going to do, do quickly</u> λέγει οὖν αὐτῷ Ἰησοῦς ὁ ποιεῖς ποίησον τάχιον." Now no one at the table knew why he said this to him. Some thought that, because Judas had the moneybag, Jesus was telling him, "Buy what we need for the feast," or that he should give something to the poor. So, after receiving the morsel of bread, he immediately went out. And it was night.

> Judas followed Jesus' imperative "what you are going to do, do quickly" just as Judas was commanded. In the last verse of the above narrative John recorded, "he immediately went out. And it was night." Even at betrayal, Jesus issued this imperative to Judas and Judas followed. Without hesitation, Judas "immediately went out."

Jn 14: 1-5 "<u>Let not your hearts be troubled</u> Μὴ ταρασσέσθω ὑμῶν ἡ καρδία. Believe in God; believe also in me. In my father's house are many rooms. If it were not so, would I have told you that I go to prepare a place for you? And if I go and prepare a place for you, I will come again and will take you to myself, that where I am you may be also. And you know the way to where I am going."

> These passages are sometimes understood out of context due to translation from Greek to English. English wording makes the passage read and sound to the ear as if there are two imperatives, "believe in God" and "believe in me." However, the only imperative John recorded that Jesus said was "let not your hearts be troubled." While "believe in God" and "believe also in me" read as commands in English, John recorded those two phrases as Greek present active plural indicatives, not imperatives as English conveys in many translations.

> Indicatives can be continuous (I am believing.) or undefined (I believe.) Some translators have chosen the undefined action which when read in English reads and sounds like Greek imperatives rendered to English commands, "Believe in God; believe also in me." Most English translations convey an imperative. However, the Greek morphology is without question. These English command word "believe" is not a Greek imperative.

> Here, John's use of the indicative mood in Jesus words described what was true for them, not something that might be true for them in the future. Rather than command them to believe in God and Jesus, Jesus affirmed to them that they did believe in God and Jesus. His imperative "let not your hearts be troubled" affirmed that they would be persecuted for their belief in both God and Jesus.

> A clarifying way to understand these passages is that their hearts were not to be troubled believing in both God and Jesus. Hearts that are not troubled (the imperative) are indicated by believing in God and Jesus. The balance of v 2-4 validates the truth of Jesus' imperative in v1.

A healthier translation that does not create an English command from a Greek present active indicative verb is, "Do not let the heart (singular) of you (plural) be troubled that you believe in God and me." English translations convey that Jesus commanded that they believe in God and believe in him. While believing both in God and Jesus sounds orthodox today, Jesus assured them that there was no need to fear believing in both God and Jesus in their day. Big difference.

In the Jewish context belief in anyone but Yahweh would have been blasphemous. Here Jesus affirmed that he and the father are one. They were not to have troubled hearts believing in both God and Jesus as they would face persecution from Jews who would not accept Jesus as both Messiah and Lord.

Jn 14: 8-11 Jesus said to him, "I am the way, and the truth, and the life. No one comes to the Father except through me. If you had known me, you would have known my Father also. From now on you do know him and have seen him." Philip said to him, "Lord, show us the Father, and it is enough for us." Jesus said to him, "Have I been with you so long, and you still do not know me, Philip? Whoever has seen me has seen the Father. How can you say, 'Show us the Father' Δεῖξον ἡμῖν τὸν πατέρα? Do you not believe that I am in the Father and the Father is in me? The words that I say to you I do not speak on my own authority, but the Father who dwells in me does his works. Believe me that I am in the Father and the Father is in me, or else believe on account of the works themselves.

> Here Jesus repeated Philip's imperative, "Lord, show us the Father." Jesus asked Philip, "How can you say, 'Show us the Father'" affirming that they had seen the Father in Jesus and that Philip's imperative was misplaced.

Jn 14: 27-31 Peace I leave with you; my peace I give to you. Not as the world gives do I give to you. Let not your hearts be troubled, neither let them be afraid μὴ ταρασσέσθω ὑμῶν ἡ καρδία μηδὲ δειλιάτω. You heard me say to you, 'I am going away, and I will come to you.' If you loved me, you would have rejoiced, because I am going to the Father, for the Father is greater than I. And now I have told you before it takes place, so that when it does take place you may believe. I will no longer talk much with you, for the ruler of this world is coming. He has no claim on me, but I do as the Father has commanded me, so that the world may know that I love the Father. Rise, let us go from here Ἐγείρεσθε ἄγωμεν ἐντεῦθεν.

> They had been commanded to keep their hearts from being both troubled and fearful. After Jesus affirmed that the ruler of this world had no claim on him, but rather Jesus did what the Father commanded him so the world might know his love for the father, After Jesus' clarification, he then commanded them to rise. Note that Jesus first affirmed them and then commanded them.

Note: The following passages in John 15 include Jesus' use of vine and branches, abiding and keeping his commandments.

Jn 15: 1-4 "I am the true vine, and my Father is the vinedresser. Every branch in me that does not bear fruit he takes away, and every branch that does bear fruit he prunes, that it may bear more fruit. Already you are clean because of the word that I have spoken to you. Abide in me, and I in you μείνατε ἐν ἐμοί κἀγὼ ἐν ὑμῖν καθὼς. As the branch cannot bear fruit by itself, unless it abides in the vine, neither can you, unless you abide in me.

> The imperative word "Abide" meant to them the idea to remain, continue, or endure. Jesus assured them that he would abide in them. He prepared them with confidence that he would abide in them because his impending crucifixion was about to occur. He prepared them for the uncertainty that his death would bring them. Note that Jesus again used the word "abide" with branches, vine, and fruit.

Jn 15: 5-9 I am the vine; you are the branches. Whoever abides in me and I in him, he it is that bears much fruit, for apart from me you can do nothing. If anyone does not abide in me he is thrown away like a branch and withers; and the branches are gathered, thrown into the fire, and burned. If you abide in me, and my words abide in you, ask whatever you wish, and it will be done for you. By this my Father is glorified, that you bear much fruit and so prove to be my disciples. As the Father has loved me, so have I loved you. <u>Abide in my love</u> μείνατε ἐν ἐμοί κἀγὼ ἐν ὑμῖν καθὼς.

> His imperative, "abide in my love" meant to them to stay, remain, or endure in his love. Jesus contrasted the love of the father for him with his love for those who head had commanded to abide in him.

Jn 16: 21-28 When a woman is giving birth, she has sorrow because her hour has come, but when she has delivered the baby, she no longer remembers the anguish, for joy that a human being has been born into the world. So also you have sorrow now, but I will see you again, and your hearts will rejoice, and no one will take your joy from you. In that day you will ask nothing of me. Truly, truly, I say to you, whatever you ask of the Father in my name, he will give it to you. Until now you have asked nothing in my name. <u>Ask, and you will receive that your joy may be full</u> αἰτεῖτε καὶ λήμψεσθε ἵνα ἡ χαρὰ ὑμῶν ᾖ πεπληρωμένη. "I have said these things to you in figures of speech. The hour is coming when I will no longer speak to you in figures of speech but will tell you plainly about the Father. In that day you will ask in my name, and I do not say to you that I will ask the Father on your behalf; for the Father himself loves you, because you have loved me and have believed that I came from God. I came from the Father and have come into the world, and now I am leaving the world and going to the Father."

> The imperative "ask" was followed by the assurance of receiving a reward of full joy. To eliminate any confusion, John immediately conveyed Jesus' clarification regarding Jesus use of figures of speech. Jesus affirmed that his use of figures of speech would be replaced by his speaking plainly about the Father. Jesus then referred to asking in his name. The English command word, "ask" is a single powerful word not encumbered with surrounding words.

> Just before Jesus' command "Ask" he stated, "Until now you have asked nothing in my name." to assure them. This assurance that preceded his imperative was premeditated and intentional.

Jn 16: 32–33 Behold, the hour is coming, indeed it has come, when you will be scattered, each to his own home, and will leave me alone. Yet I am not alone, for the Father is with me. I have said these things to you, that in me you may have peace. In the world you will have tribulation. <u>But take heart; I have overcome the world</u> ἀλλὰ θαρσεῖτε ἐγὼ νενίκηκα τὸν κόσμον.

> The imperative John recorded, "Take heart" has been translated, "be of good courage" (DBY), "be of good cheer" (KJV), or "take courage" (NRS, YLT). John recorded "Take heart" as a second person plural present active imperative verb. Jesus had commanded them as a group that they were no longer to have fear. Jesus enabled them to be active, meaning that fear was not to hold them back. He warned them of the tribulation they would experience. John recorded the tribulation as singular not plural. The tribulation was not to be feared.
>
> Jesus words "that in me you may have peace" guaranteed the peace was available to them through him. In context, he first affirmed the peace available to them and then commanded them to "take heart" or embrace the peace. Also significant to this imperative is the ending statement, "I have overcome the world." The English reads and sounds somewhat staid. John recorded the Greek inflection that would be read and heard as a perfect active. The English "I have overcome" conveys a sound translation, but does not convey the power of the first person singular perfect active indicative in Greek. To include the perfect active indicative verb, "I have overcome and continue to overcome the world, and that will never change." is more in line with what Jesus' listeners heard and what John's early readers understood when they read or heard the Greek texts. Given that deep affirmation, Jesus' imperative, "Take heart" provided certainty.

Jn 17: 1-5 When Jesus had spoken these words, [Jesus words in 16: 32-33] he lifted up his eyes to heaven, and said, "Father, the hour has come; <u>glorify your Son</u> δόξασόν σου τὸν υἱόν that the Son may glorify you, since you have given him authority over all flesh, to give eternal life to all whom you have given him. And this is eternal life, that they know you the only true God, and Jesus Christ whom you have sent. I glorified you on earth, having accomplished the work that you gave me to do. <u>And now, Father, glorify me</u> καὶ νῦν δόξασόν με σύ, πάτερ in your own presence with the glory that I had with you before the world existed.

> Here Jesus' two imperatives "glorify your son" and "glorify me" linked his oneness with the father. Jesus intended his prayer and imperatives to the father be heard by his disciples and read by others just as John had recorded. These imperatives interpreted by his disciples conveyed Jesus' relationship with the Father beyond a relationship that the disciples had with the Father. That Jesus was crucified for blasphemy is one issue. These imperatives heard by the disciples brought their understanding of Jesus and the father to a deeper level. Even more compelling to those who heard Jesus' two imperatives was Jesus' affirmation that he held glory with the Father before the world existed. To grasp the context seek to understand what it was the disciples learned when they heard Jesus' imperatives. Consider what the early readers understood after having read these text within years of Jesus crucifixion, resurrection, and promise of his soon return.

Jesus' statement "And now, Father, glorify me in your own presence with the glory that I had with you before the world existed." involves the theological word, Kenosis which "refers to the self-emptying of Christ in the incarnation."[14]

Jn 17: 7-11 Now they know that everything that you have given me is from you. For I have given them the words that you gave me, and they have received them and have come to know in truth that I came from you; and they have believed that you sent me. I am praying for them. I am not praying for the world but for those whom you have given me, for they are yours. All mine are yours, and yours are mine, and I am glorified in them. And I am no longer in the world, but they are in the world, and I am coming to you. Holy Father, <u>keep them in your name which you have given me</u> τήρησον αὐτοὺς ἐν τῷ ὀνόματί σου ᾧ δέδωκάς μοι, that they may be one, even as we are one.

> The disciples, after having heard Jesus' prior imperative would have been relieved at Jesus' next imperative to the Father, that the Father would keep the disciples. The disciples would have perceived that their relationship with one another must be like that of Jesus and the Father. They must be one.

> More specifically, the Father's fulfilling of this imperative prayer, would produce the disciple's oneness. The relief they would have felt at hearing Jesus' imperatives and their relationship with one another through Jesus, and the Father would take on a new experience of truly being one with one another through Jesus. Jesus in front of them had commanded the Father to keep them in the Father's name. He established a relationship as sons of God for the family of God. When the disciples heard Jesus command to the father, "Keep them in your name which you have given me that they may be one even as we are one." they would have realized their new relationship with one another, Jesus, and the father. Big change.

Jn 17: 12-17 While I was with them, I kept them in your name, which you have given me. I have guarded them, and not one of them has been lost except the son of destruction, that the Scripture might be fulfilled. But now I am coming to you, and these things I speak in the world, that they may have my joy fulfilled in themselves. I have given them your word, and the world has hated them because they are not of the world, just as I am not of the world. I do not ask that you take them out of the world, but that you keep them from the evil one. They are not of the world, just as I am not of the world. <u>Sanctify them in the truth</u> ἁγίασον αὐτοὺς ἐν τῇ ἀληθείᾳ; your word is truth.

> The disciples, after having heard Jesus' imperative to the Father about them "Sanctify them in the truth." provided confidence. At the time of Jesus' imperatives here, they had not yet received Jesus' imperative to make disciples nor experienced the Holy Spirit. Their commissioning and Pentecost were yet in the future.

> Thus, Jesus' imperative here was preparatory. Whether it was Jesus' spoken word at that moment or the written words after John had recorded them, the words of Jesus had set them apart. The importance of God's word in the disciples' lives is further emphasized that in v19 Jesus sanctified himself for the same purpose.

---

[14] Grenz, Stanley, J., David Guretzki, and Cherith Fee Nordling, *Pocket Dictionary of Theological Terms*, 70.

Jesus had been sanctified in the truth, and they too would be sanctified in the truth. The importance of Jesus' example cannot be understated. Truth would be their tool. They may not have understood Jesus' first utterings. they came to know the truth of Jesus' words as evidenced by how they spread the Gospel. Truth held power.

Jn 18: 3-9 So Judas, having procured a band of soldiers and some officers from the chief priests and the Pharisees, went there with lanterns and torches and weapons. Then Jesus, knowing all that would happen to him, came forward and said to them, "Whom do you seek?" They answered him, "Jesus of Nazareth." Jesus said to them, "I am he." Judas, who betrayed him, was standing with them. When Jesus said to them, "I am he," they drew back and fell to the ground. So he asked them again, "Whom do you seek?" And they said, "Jesus of Nazareth." Jesus answered, "I told you that I am he. So, if you seek me, <u>let these men go</u> ἄφετε τούτους ὑπάγειν." This was to fulfill the word that he had spoken: "Of those whom you gave me I have lost not one."

> The disciples after having seen Judas, numerous soldiers, officers of the chief priests and Pharisees in the garden and then after having heard Jesus' imperative "let these men go" may have known that Jesus' imperatives were impossible to disobey. Neither Matthew, Mark, Luke nor John recorded that any of the disciples with Jesus in the garden had any harm come to them. They were let go just as Jesus had commanded.

Jn 18: 10-11 Then Simon Peter, having a sword, drew it and struck the high priest's servant and cut off his right ear. (The servant's name was Malchus.) So Jesus said to Peter, "<u>Put your sword into its sheath</u> Βάλε τὴν μάχαιραν εἰς τὴν θήκην; shall I not drink the cup that the Father has given me?"

> Given Jesus' imperative "put your sword into its sheath" it is safe to presume that Peter sheathed his sword. There is no record that Peter ever again carried a sword much less unsheathed one. Nowhere throughout John's gospel did John record that Peter had ever had a sword. Jesus did not tell Peter to let go of his sword and never use it again. Jesus did not command Peter to take the sword from his belt. Jesus did not command Peter to drop the sword to the ground. Jesus commanded Peter to put the sword in its sheath.

Jn18: 19-21 The high priest then questioned Jesus about his disciples and his teaching. Jesus answered him, "I have spoken openly to the world. I have always taught in synagogues and in the temple, where all Jews come together. I have said nothing in secret. Why do you ask me? <u>Ask those who have heard me what I said to them</u> ἀκηκοότας τί ἐλάλησα αὐτοῖς; they know what I said."

> Jesus' imperative condemned the high priest who questioned him. The high priest knew that their plot to kill Jesus was fabricated. The high priest also knew that Jesus' teachings, as well as the teachings of Jesus' disciples, were not an affront to God. The high priest knew both the conspiracy and the truth of Jesus' and his disciples' teachings. Even the high priest would come to know the truth. Jesus' imperatives were from God. Here Jesus gave a command to the high priest that required the high priest to know the mockery and the guilt. Likely the high priest had already asked some and would ask more. In any event, the high priest was saddled with knowing the testimonies of those who heard Jesus.

Jn 18: 22-23 When he had said these things, one of the officers standing by struck Jesus with his hand, saying, "Is that how you answer the high priest?" Jesus answered him, "If what I said is wrong, <u>bear witness about the wrong</u> μαρτύρησον περὶ τοῦ κακοῦ; but if what I said is right, why do you strike me?" Annas then sent him bound to Caiaphas the high priest.

    The officer who struck Jesus, had asked him the question, "Is that how you answer the high priest"? Jesus responded with the imperative "bear witness about the wrong." The officer who struck Jesus had no choice but to bear witness about the wrong. Jesus' imperatives are unmovable. The officer had struck Jesus and asked him a question. Jesus responded with an imperative to bear witness to the truth.

    Notices that immediately after Jesus' imperative to the officer, Annas sent Jesus bound to Caiaphas, the high priest. John makes the text appear as if Annas had nothing to do with the officer who would have to bear witness to the wrong. John provided no further dialogue or narrative after Jesus imperative. John directly recorded that Annas immediately had Jesus bound and sent to Caiaphas.

Jn 19: 26-27 When Jesus saw his mother and the disciple whom he loved standing nearby, he said to his mother, "Woman, <u>behold, your son</u> ἴδε ὁ υἱός σου!" Then he said to the disciple, "<u>Behold, your mother</u> ἴδε ἡ μήτηρ σου." And from that hour the disciple took her to his own home.

    Jesus' two imperatives to his mother Mary "behold, you son" and his disciple whom Jesus loved (likely John) "Behold your mother" are interjection imperatives meaning to see, look, behold or affirm. With these imperatives, Jesus left no doubt as to Mary's and John's responsibilities toward each other. Jesus' imperatives even from the cross are without ambiguity.

    The word, "behold" is a pronouncement or performance imperative indicating future responsibilities. With Jesus' imperatives, both Mary and John knew their new accountabilities to one another. Others also heard Jesus' imperatives to both of them near the cross.

    These were the last two imperatives of Jesus' earthly life that John recorded.

Jn 20: 11-18 But Mary stood weeping outside the tomb, and as she wept she stooped to look into the tomb. And she saw two angels in white, sitting where the body of Jesus had lain, one at the head and one at the feet. They said to her, "Woman, why are you weeping?" She said to them, "They have taken away my Lord, and I do not know where they have laid him." Having said this, she turned around and saw Jesus standing, but she did not know that it was Jesus. Jesus said to her, "Woman, why are you weeping? Whom are you seeking?" Supposing him to be the gardener, she said to him, "Sir, if you have carried him away, tell me where you have laid him, and I will take him away." Jesus said to her, "Mary." She turned and said to him in Aramaic, "Rabboni!" (which means Teacher). Jesus said to her, "<u>Do not cling to me</u> μή μου ἅπτου, for I have not yet ascended to the Father; but <u>go to my brothers</u> πορεύου δὲ πρὸς τοὺς ἀδελφούς and <u>say to them</u> εἰπὲ αὐτοῖς, 'I am ascending to my Father and your Father, to my God and your God.'" Mary Magdalene went and announced to the disciples, "I have seen the Lord"--and that he had said these things to her.

    Jesus' imperative to Mary Magdalene "Do not cling to me." was clear. She was not to embrace him. The Greek word ἅπτου may mean "touch." However, the words, "cling" or "hold" or "embrace" are more suitable. In the contemporary context, a high five is less relational than a firm handshake or an embrace. Here John recorded that Jesus spoke of a stronger context than just touch. While context conveyed clinging or embracing, Jesus' imperative to Mary was immediately obeyed as v18 John recorded "Mary Magdalen went" which affirmed her speedy departure.

In any context touching or clinging via an embrace, Jesus' command was because he would be ascending to the father. The next two imperatives he spoke to Mary Magdalene, "go" and "say" affirmed his relationship with her to be his messenger. In short, she was sent by Jesus as an apostle with a message to the disciples. She was commanded not to touch or embrace him by way of acknowledging him. She was given a higher calling by Jesus' imperatives, "Go to my brothers" and "say to them." Beyond acknowledging and worshipping him, she was commanded to bring news as his messenger.

Early readers of John's gospel would have recognized these imperatives from Jesus to Mary that in English today are challenging to grasp. These three imperatives were the first imperatives John recorded that Jesus spoke after the resurrection. Jesus' imperatives to the woman, Mary Magdalene as a sent apostle with a message to the disciples, would have been understood by early Greek readers whereas English readers might struggle with the depth of Jesus' imperatives in today's contemporary context.

Notice in v18 that John recorded no hesitation from Mary Magdalene after she had heard Jesus' imperatives. She did not vacillate. She did not engage Jesus in conversation. She did not ask him questions. John recorded, "Mary Magdalene went and announced to the disciples, 'I have seen the Lord'--and that he had said these things to her."

John did not waver. The power of Jesus' imperatives was then and is now obvious.

Jn 20: 21-22 Jesus said to them again, "Peace be with you. As the Father has sent me, even so I am sending you." And when he had said this, he breathed on them and said to them, "<u>Receive the Holy Spirit</u> λάβετε πνεῦμα ἅγιον.
> Given all that the disciples had experienced during their time with Jesus but mainly having heard Jesus' numerous imperatives, when they heard his imperative to them "Receive the Holy Spirit" they were certain that they had received the Holy Spirit.

There was no contemplation of rejection. By his breath and his imperative, the Holy Spirit was received by them. They were confident of the Holy Spirit's indwelling. By now, after their time with Jesus and all the imperatives they had heard, experienced, and seen fulfilled, in their minds, Jesus' imperatives were unassailable.

Jn 20: 26-28 Eight days later, his disciples were inside again, and Thomas was with them. Although the doors were locked, Jesus came and stood among them and said, "Peace be with you." Then he said to Thomas, "<u>Put your finger here</u> φέρε τὸν δάκτυλόν σου ὧδε, <u>and see my hands</u> καὶ ἴδε τὰς χεῖράς μου; <u>and put out your hand</u> καὶ φέρε τὴν χεῖρά σου, <u>and place it in my side</u> καὶ βάλε εἰς τὴν πλευράν μου. <u>Do not disbelieve</u> καὶ μὴ γίνου ἄπιστος, but believe." Thomas answered him, "My Lord and my God!"

> Thomas was likely familiarity with Jesus' imperatives during their time together. He likely heard Jesus' imperatives to Peter and others as saw the responses of those who had been given an imperative by Jesus. Thomas having received five imperatives "Put your finger" "See my hands" "Put out your hand" "Place it in my side" and "Do not disbelieve" in one sentence, resulted in Thomas' response, "My Lord and my God!"
>
> Jesus' imperatives to Thomas were also for others in the room. Jesus did not hesitate to begin his imperatives to Thomas. The other disciples heard Jesus imperatives. They too were convicted at Jesus' resurrection and Jesus' imperatives to Thomas.

Jn 21: 1-7 After this Jesus revealed himself again to the disciples by the Sea of Tiberias, and he revealed himself in this way. Simon Peter, Thomas (called the Twin), Nathanael of Cana in Galilee, the sons of Zebedee, and two others of his disciples were together. Simon Peter said to them, "I am going fishing." They said to him, "We will go with you." They went out and got into the boat, but that night they caught nothing. Just as day was breaking, Jesus stood on the shore; yet the disciples did not know that it was Jesus. Jesus said to them, "Children, do you have any fish?" They answered him, "No." He said to them, "<u>Cast the net on the right side of the boat</u> βάλετε εἰς τὰ δεξιὰ μέρη τοῦ πλοίου τὸ δίκτυον, and you will find some." So they cast it, and now they were not able to haul it in, because of the quantity of fish. That disciple whom Jesus loved therefore said to Peter, "It is the Lord!" When Simon Peter heard that it was the Lord, he put on his outer garment, for he was stripped for work, and threw himself into the sea.

> This command to Peter came at a time after Peter had experienced many of Jesus' imperatives. Peter's response affirmed his growing understanding of Jesus and certainly Jesus' spoken imperatives. Peter had heard and experienced Jesus' imperatives during their time together.
>
> Jesus spoken an imperative in his post-resurrection life indicated the inviolability of his imperatives. His imperatives held sacred power when he walked with Peter before in his earthly life and after his post-death resurrected life. Peter and John knew the power of Jesus' imperatives.
>
> There was no time hesitation in the narrative. Immediately after having heard Jesus' imperative "Cast the net on the right side of the boat." They complied, and the response was immediate. Immediately after John said to Peter, "It is the Lord?" John did not record any delay on Peter's part. Peter threw himself into the sea.
>
> After no less than three years of walking and talking with Jesus, his imperatives meant more to his disciples.

Jn 21: 8-14 The other disciples came in the boat, dragging the net full of fish, for they were not far from the land, but about a hundred yards off. When they got out on land, they saw a charcoal fire in place, with fish laid out on it, and bread. Jesus said to them, "<u>Bring some of the fish that you have just caught</u> ἐνέγκατε ἀπὸ τῶν ὀψαρίων ὧν ἐπιάσατε νῦν." So Simon Peter went aboard and hauled the net ashore, full of large fish, 153 of them. And although there were so many, the net was not torn. Jesus said to them, "<u>Come and have breakfast</u> δεῦτε ἀριστήσατε." Now none of the disciples dared ask him, "Who are you?" They knew it was the Lord. Jesus came and took the bread and gave it to them, and so with the fish. This was now the third time that Jesus was revealed to the disciples after he was raised from the dead.

    John recorded Jesus' third appearance after Jesus' resurrection. At each appearance Jesus' spoke imperatives. Here Jesus began at breakfast. He had commanded them to "Bring some of the fish that you have just caught." The disciples rather than fear Jesus' imperatives anticipated them. He commanded an invitation and they went.

Jn 21: 15-19 When they had finished breakfast, Jesus said to Simon Peter, "Simon, son of John, do you love me more than these?" He said to him, "Yes, Lord; you know that I love you." He said to him, "<u>Feed my lambs</u> βόσκε τὰ ἀρνία μου." He said to him a second time, "Simon, son of John, do you love me?" He said to him, "Yes, Lord; you know that I love you." He said to him, "<u>Tend my sheep</u> ποίμαινε τὰ πρόβατά μου." He said to him the third time, "Simon, son of John, do you love me?" Peter was grieved because he said to him the third time, "Do you love me?" and he said to him, "Lord, you know everything; you know that I love you." Jesus said to him, "<u>Feed my sheep</u> βόσκε τὰ πρόβατά μου. Truly, truly, I say to you, when you were young, you used to dress yourself and walk wherever you wanted, but when you are old, you will stretch out your hands, and another will dress you and carry you where you do not want to go." (This he said to show by what kind of death he was to glorify God.) And after saying this he said to him, "<u>Follow me</u> ἀκολούθει μοι."

    Jesus spoke four imperatives to Peter. Each was within earshot of Thomas, Nathanael, James, John, and two others. Pastorally both agape and brotherly love were the focus, but here Jesus' imperatives took priority. Feed my lambs, tend my sheep, and feed my sheep were three imperatives that identified feeding and tending to both immature young lambs and mature elder sheep. John who was listening to Peter and Jesus' conversation knew Peter's responsibilities after having heard Jesus' four imperatives to Peter:

| | |
|---|---|
| Feed my lambs | βόσκε τὰ ἀρνία μου. |
| Tend my sheep | ποίμαινε τὰ πρόβατά μου. |
| Feed my sheep | βόσκε τὰ πρόβατά μου |
| Follow me | ἀκολούθει μοι |

Both Peter and John understood what Jesus had said to Peter. Peter's words in his books First and Second Peter affirmed that he had followed of Jesus imperatives. Peter's two letters include narratives with instructions for Jesus' followers that fed and tended them. Through Jesus' imperative "follow me" and Jesus's description, "you will stretch out your hands" Peter and John knew Peter's eventual death would be on the cross. Peter and John knew three things. Peter would follow Jesus, in his aged years he would be dressed by others, and he would die on a cross. His cross would glorify God.

Jn 21: 20-25 Peter turned and saw the disciple whom Jesus loved following them, the one who had been reclining at table close to him and had said, "Lord, who is it that is going to betray you?" When Peter saw him, he said to Jesus, "Lord, what about this man?" Jesus said to him, "If it is my will that he remain until I come, what is that to you? <u>You follow me</u> σύ μοι ἀκολούθει!" So the saying spread abroad among the brothers that this disciple was not to die; yet Jesus did not say to him that he was not to die, but, "If it is my will that he remain until I come, what is that to you?" This is the disciple who is bearing witness about these things, and who has written these things, and we know that his testimony is true. Now there are also many other things that Jesus did. Were every one of them to be written, I suppose that the world itself could not contain the books that would be written.

    John recorded Jesus' last two spoken imperatives to Peter, "Follow me" in v19 and "You follow me" in v22. After having heard these imperatives, Peter likely had no doubt about his future. Jesus' imperatives were clear. And Peter knew Jesus' imperatives were inviolable.

This final command to Peter recorded by John is a lesson about following Jesus to all Christians. Peter and those on the beach with him knew their tasks. They did not know and did not need to know the details. They had been commanded to remain in Jesus, listen, and move with the Spirit that had indwelled them.

Same is true of believers, past, present, and future who remain in Jesus, listen, and move with the indwelling Spirit.

So they called them and charged them not to speak or teach at all in the name of Jesus. But Peter and John answered them, "Whether it is right in the sight of God to listen to you rather than to God, you must judge, for we cannot but speak of what we have seen and heard."

Ac 4: 18-20

# 13 The Imperatives of Jesus in Acts

So they called them and charged them not to speak or teach at all in the name of Jesus. But Peter and John answered them, "Whether it is right in the sight of God to listen to you rather than to God, you must judge, for we cannot but speak of what we have seen and heard." Ac 4: 18-20

## Reliability of Luke

Luke never heard Jesus speak nor saw Jesus walk or perform miracles. He was not at the cross. Luke did not see the resurrected Jesus. There is no record that he had experienced a Christophany. There is no record that Luke had a "Damascus Road" experience like Paul or that he was blinded and saw again. Luke's Gospel depended on what Peter and John and others had seen and heard. Luke's book of Acts included Paul's experiences. His Gospel and Acts, like Matthew, Mark, and John would have been critically edited for accuracy. Remembering that Luke was limited to interviewing those who had heard and seen Jesus, Luke's relationships of trust and truth contributed to the accuracy of his Gospel. Luke's close association with Paul was fundamental to Luke's meticulousness within his writing of Acts. Luke's attention to detail so clearly evident in his Gospel carried into Acts. Most textual scholars attribute Luke as the author of Acts. Litfin agrees:

> Since we know Paul definitely had a fellow-worker named Luke (Philem, 24), and we also have the universal attestation of the early church that the gospel was written by the same man, the preponderance of evidence is on the side of Lukan authorship for the two-volume work of Luke-Acts.[1]

Russel identifies Luke's use of the personal pronoun, "we" in Acts to affirm authorship:

> By writing "we" instead of "they" in recounting events when he was present, the author indicates that he was a companion of Paul. If a later writer had incorporated these "we" sections, he would have named their author to enhance their authority. But the style of the "we" passages cannot be distinguished from the style of the rest of Acts or from that of Luke's Gospel. The author Luke and Acts is the author of the "we" sections of acts and a companion of Paul.[2]

Central to understanding Jesus' ten imperatives to Paul and five imperatives to Ananias that Luke recorded in Acts is Luke's relationship with Paul. Paul most probably told Luke what Ananias had told Paul in Damascus. Given Luke and Paul's relationship, Paul would have been certain that Luke precisely recorded what had been said. Further, Luke would have made certain that Paul was accurate. There are no biblical nor extra-biblical writings indicating that Luke had a relationship or spoke with Ananias to affirm what Jesus had said to Ananias. Thus, more likely Paul's words about what Ananias had said to Paul were what Luke recorded.

---

[1] Litfin, Bryan, *After Acts: Exploring the Lives and Legends of the Apostles*, 61.
[2] Emmet Russell, "Acts of the Apostles" in Douglas, J. D. and Tenney, Merrill C., *The New International Dictionary of the Bible*, 13.

## Luke and Paul

Significant to the book of Acts is the relationship between Luke and Paul. Luke, a physician, and Paul a tent maker and likely former member of the Jerusalem Temple Sanhedrin were both men of means and influence. In Acts, Luke affirmed Paul's employment and Paul's regular visits to synagogues to persuade both Jews and Greeks.[3] Bruce affirms Paul's status:

> Paul is said by Luke to have been a "tent-maker" (*skenopoios*), by which we may understand that he was engaged in the manufacture of wares from local *cilicium*, but he appears to have belonged to a well-to-do family.[4]

During Paul's imprisonment Paul wrote to Timothy, "Luke is with me." 2 Tim 4:11. That Luke and Paul knew each other well, contributes to the trustworthiness of Jesus' imperatives to Paul. McRay supports that Luke's research and writing involved Paul's personal recollections:

> During this time Luke surely did some of his research and writing, based on Paul's personal recollection. It would be unreasonable to assume otherwise.[5]

Any time where Luke and Paul were together provided sufficient opportunity for Luke to get Paul's message right. Comparing hundreds of imperatives spoken by Jesus in the Gospels, there is a significant difference in Jesus' ten imperatives to Paul in Acts. Repeatedly in the Gospels, those who heard Jesus' speak struggled to understand his imperatives. Luke does not convey any doubt from Paul. That Paul responded without question to Jesus' first two imperatives to him is a noticeable difference from the disciples. Jesus' disciples and followers heard hundreds of imperatives from him and slowly trusted and then followed. Paul heard ten imperatives and followed immediately. The Disciples had been with Jesus for years during his ministry. They had seen his miracles. They had heard Jesus' numerous healing imperatives. They had heard imperatives that caused demons to depart. They had heard Jesus imperatives to them. Paul, on the other hand, had one single encounter with Jesus and after having heard Jesus' imperatives, followed straight away. These powerful ten imperatives are the only ones Luke recorded in Acts to Paul.

## Imperatives Relocated Paul in Asia

The Disciples had heard hundreds of Jesus' imperatives. Luke only recorded that Paul had heard ten. These imperatives conveyed to early followers that the church would spread the Gospels, heal, do miracles, and grow the church. Jesus' imperatives to Paul seem to be significant to Paul's effectiveness. This study does not include a study of Paul's imperatives to the churches.

Paul as a likely member of the Sanhedrin in Jerusalem, a significant leader there would have spoken imperatives as well. Paul knew the intention and power of the imperative. Thus when Paul heard Jesus' imperatives to him, Paul knew the Lord's power and expectation. The miraculous

---

[3] After this Paul left Athens and went to Corinth. And he found a Jew named Aquila, a native of Pontus, recently come from Italy with his wife Priscilla, because Claudius had commanded all the Jews to leave Rome. And he went to see them, and because he was of the same trade he stayed with them and worked, for they were tentmakers by trade. And he reasoned in the synagogue every Sabbath and tried to persuade Jews and Greeks. Act 18:1-4
[4] Bruce, F. F., *Paul: Apostle of the Heart Set Free*, 36.
[5] McRay, John, *Paul: His Life and Teaching*, 81.

restoration of his sight would have been a significant proof of Jesus' power. Moreover, so too would Jesus' imperatives be significant directives to Paul.

Paul's epistles to individuals Titus, Timothy, Philemon, and those in Rome, Galatia, Ephesus, Philippi, Corinth, and Thessalonica are packed with imperatives. His letters were loving and compassionate. Perhaps more significantly Paul's letters included Paul's imperatives. Early readers would have discerned the power of the Greek imperatives as Paul intended. Similar to the gospels recorded by Matthew, Mark, Luke and John, the imperatives in Paul's letters are sometimes less clear in English than in Koine Greek. That for future study. Below is Luke's record of the imperatives spoken by Jesus to Paul and Ananias in Acts.

## The Imperatives of Jesus in Acts

To Saul (Paul)
Ac 9: 1-6 But Saul, still breathing threats and murder against the disciples of the Lord, went to the high priest and asked him for letters to the synagogues at Damascus, so that if he found any belonging to the Way, men or women, he might bring them bound to Jerusalem. Now as he went on his way, he approached Damascus, and suddenly a light from heaven flashed around him. And falling to the ground he heard a voice saying to him, "Saul, Saul, why are you persecuting me?" And he said, "Who are you, Lord?" And he said, "I am Jesus, whom you are persecuting. But rise ἀλλὰ ἀνάστηθ and enter the city καὶ εἴσελθε εἰς τὴν πόλιν, and you will be told what you are to do."

> After Luke recorded Saul's experiences he then recorded Jesus two imperatives to Saul (Paul), "rise" and "enter." Paul immediately followed Jesus' first two imperatives. And Jesus followed with more imperatives and instructions. Paul proclaimed in the synagogues, "Jesus is the son of God." Paul's synagogue messages affirmed that Paul was doing what he had been told to do. Paul rose and went into the city, just as Jesus had commanded him. Also, Jesus gave him further instructions. Paul's immediate recognition of Jesus as Lord here bore itself out later when Paul publicly proclaimed Jesus as Lord.

To Ananias
Ac 9:10-12 Now there was a disciple at Damascus named Ananias. The Lord said to him in a vision, "Ananias." And he said, "Here I am, Lord." And the Lord said to him, "Rise ἀνάστα and go to the street called Straight πορεύθητι ἐπὶ τὴν ῥύμην τὴν καλουμένην Εὐθεῖαν, and at the house of Judas look for a man of Tarsus named Saul καὶ ζήτησον ἐν οἰκίᾳ Ἰούδα Σαῦλον ὀνόματι Ταρσέα, for behold, he is praying ἰδοὺ γὰρ προσεύχεται and he has seen in a vision a man named Ananias come in and lay his hands on him so that he might regain his sight."

> Ananias received four imperatives from Jesus: rise, go, look, and behold. The greeting imperative, "behold" affirmed to Ananias that he would enter and lay hands on Saul and Saul's sight would be restored. This imperative demanded Ananias' reverence for the Lord and Saul's prayer and preceded Ananias to lay hands on Saul. The behold imperatives serves as a ground or reason for why Ananias should go. It is the preparation done by the Lord for accomplishing his work.

To Ananias
Ac 9:13-16 But Ananias answered, "Lord, I have heard from many about this man, how much evil he has done to your saints at Jerusalem. And here he has authority from the chief priests to bind all who call on your name." But the Lord said to him, "<u>Go</u>, Πορεύου for he is a chosen instrument of mine to carry my name before the Gentiles and kings and the children of Israel. For I will show him how much he must suffer for the sake of my name."

> Jesus' gave a singular imperative, "go" which may sound simple. The English wording is not sufficient to convey the power of the Greek imperative. Ananias attempted to dissuade the Lord from the imperatives he had initially heard in v 10 – 12. Ananias explained that he knew Saul's (Paul's) reputation that Saul had persecuted followers of "the way," later to be called Christians. Jesus spoke a command that clarified Saul as a chosen instrument of God. Despite Ananias' fear, Jesus' one imperative, "go" left Ananias without an option. Ananias went. His challenge or more factually his desire and effort to disobey Jesus' imperatives were ineffective.

To Paul
Ac 18:8-11 Crispus, the ruler of the synagogue, believed in the Lord, together with his entire household. And many of the Corinthians hearing Paul believed and were baptized. And the Lord said to Paul one night in a vision, "<u>Do not be afraid</u> Μὴ φοβοῦ, <u>but go on speaking</u> ἀλλὰ λάλει and do not be silent, for I am with you, and no one will attack you to harm you, for I have many in this city who are my people." And he stayed a year and six months, teaching the word of God among them.

> Jesus' imperatives to Paul in a dream "do not be afraid" and "keep speaking." were affirming to Paul. The phrase "and do not be silent" was written as an aorist subjunctive which complimented the imperative. Paul was to keep speaking. These two imperatives to Paul, the first not to fear and the second to keep speaking affirmed to Paul that he had been chosen by Jesus. Note that there were two audiences for these two imperatives. These two imperatives were intended for both Paul and those who would eventually read Jesus' imperatives to Paul. Paul had been chosen. Those who read them were assured that Jesus had called Paul in spite of his former persecutions against people of "the way."

To Paul
Ac 22: 6-10 "As I was on my way and drew near to Damascus, about noon a great light from heaven suddenly shone around me. And I fell to the ground and heard a voice saying to me, 'Saul, Saul, why are you persecuting me?' And I answered, 'Who are you, Lord?' And he said to me, 'I am Jesus of Nazareth, whom you are persecuting.' Now those who were with me saw the light but did not understand the voice of the one who was speaking to me. And I said, 'What shall I do, Lord?' And the Lord said to me, 'Rise, and <u>go into Damascus</u> πορεύου εἰς Δαμασκόν, and there you will be told all that is appointed for you to do.' And since I could not see because of the brightness of that light, I was led by the hand by those who were with me, and came into Damascus. "And one Ananias, a devout man according to the law, well spoken of by all the Jews who lived there, came to me, and standing by me said to me, 'Brother Saul, <u>receive your sight</u>.' And at that very hour I received my sight and saw him. And he said, 'The God of our fathers appointed you to know his will, to see the Righteous One and to hear a voice from his mouth; for you will be a

witness for him to everyone of what you have seen and heard. And now why do you wait? Rise and be baptized and wash away your sins, calling on his name.'

> Paul repeated the imperatives that Jesus spoke at his conversion in Damascus. "Rise" appears in English as a command. The Greek, however, is not in the imperative mood form but an aorist active participle. "Go" is acceptable, but Young's Literal Translation is "having risen." The context was clear. Paul was to get up and go to Damascus, which was precisely what Paul did. Paul rose and went to Damascus.
>
> Note: In v11–16 Ananias spoke three imperatives to Paul which mirrored the imperatives Ananias had received from Jesus: "receive your sight," "be baptized" and "wash away your sins."

To Paul
Ac 22: 17-21 "When I had returned to Jerusalem and was praying in the temple, I fell into a trance and saw him saying to me, 'Make haste Σπεῦσον and get out of Jerusalem quickly καὶ ἔξελθε ἐν τάχει ἐξ Ἱερουσαλήμ, because they will not accept your testimony about me.' And I said, 'Lord, they themselves know that in one synagogue after another I imprisoned and beat those who believed in you. And when the blood of Stephen your witness was being shed, I myself was standing by and approving and watching over the garments of those who killed him.' And he said to me, 'Go Πορεύου, for I will send you far away to the Gentiles.'"

> Paul repeated the imperatives that Jesus had given him after Paul had started to pray and had fallen into a trance while in the Temple. Paul was commanded to hurry and leave Jerusalem. After Paul explained to the Lord what Paul had done against Stephen, Jesus did not deny or criticize Paul's actions. Jesus did not say, "Yes, Paul I know you have persecuted my followers." Jesus did not say, "Paul, you need to repent for those you persecuted." Jesus just gave imperatives to Paul, powerfully confirming that Jesus would send Paul to the Gentiles.

Faithful followers of Jesus are able to identify their past sins and acknowledge a changed life. Saul, a former persecutor of Christians, had been commanded by Jesus to quickly get out of Jerusalem and go to where Jesus would send him, far away to the Gentiles.

Note: Given that the Jews considered the Temple the place where God resided, the dwelling where heaven and earth met, and the residence where God spoke to his priests his people, the imperatives spoken by Jesus to Paul within the Temple are profound. Jesus did not tell Paul to stay in the Jerusalem Temple. Jesus' imperatives to Paul was the last time that any communication would come from God in Jesus from within the Temple. Jesus' imperatives to Paul to get out of the Jerusalem Temple conveyed to Paul and those who read Luke's record that God would no longer indwell the Temple.

The last command from within the Temple heard only by Paul was that he "quickly get out of Jerusalem" or in short, leave the city soon. Clearly, God had left the building. Jesus had spoken to Paul while in Paul was in the Temple. Paul was moved because he knew the importance of the Jewish Temple. The Jerusalem Temple was destroyed in AD 70. God had brought an end to the possibility of restoring Jewish Temple practices. First century Jews who read Luke's record of Jesus' imperatives to Paul spoken within in the Temple should have realized that Judaism had so severely abused the Temple that God was bringing Judaism to an end. In AD 70, the end of the age of Judaism and Temple practices had come. Jesus' imperatives to Paul from within the Temple from the resurrected Christ the Lord Jesus Immanuel that the Jews should have recognized. In English, this passage is easy to overlook. In Greek and in their context the meaning is much more profound.

To Paul
Ac 23: 11 The following night the Lord stood by him and said, "Take courage Θάρσει, for as you have testified to the facts about me in Jerusalem, so you must testify also in Rome."

> This imperative accompanied by a promise of continued mission assured Paul that he would survive his current situation. In the end, Paul ultimately testified in Rome. Paul perhaps aware that Jesus' imperatives were inviolable was not fearful of his shipwreck to come. That Paul assured all ship passengers of their safety is no surprise. In Ac 27:22, 34 Paul expressed with absolute certainty to those in the ship during a storm that no one would perish. He did not fear because he had the experience of Jesus' prior imperatives. He knew he would testify in Rome. Paul trusted Jesus' imperatives because Paul first trusted Jesus.

To Paul
Ac 26:14–18 And when we had all fallen to the ground, I heard a voice saying to me in the Hebrew language, 'Saul, Saul, why are you persecuting me? It is hard for you to kick against the goads.' And I said, 'Who are you, Lord?' And the Lord said, 'I am Jesus whom you are persecuting. But rise ἀλλὰ ἀνάστηθι and stand upon your feet καὶ στῆθι ἐπὶ τοὺς πόδας σου, for I have appeared to you for this purpose, to appoint you as a servant and witness to the things in which you have seen me and to those in which I will appear to you, delivering you from your people and from the Gentiles--to whom I am sending you to open their eyes, so that they may turn from darkness to light and from the power of Satan to God, that they may receive forgiveness of sins and a place among those who are sanctified by faith in me.'

> Paul repeated his conversion experience to Agrippa, just as Jesus' promise predicted he would. Paul after having had this experience was likely without doubt or fear or he was moving quickly toward absolute trust and faith in Jesus.

Paul had experienced Jesus' imperatives. What Jesus had said came true. What Jesus had commanded had been fulfilled. Just as Jesus' disciples understood Jesus words particularly his imperatives, Paul just like Jesus' disciples began to understand the unbreakable words of Jesus, especially Jesus' imperatives.

Luke who heard and recorded Jesus' words from the testimonies of others is a person to whom we give little thought about his conversion experience. Remembering that Luke had never met Jesus, Luke's careful record of the imperatives of Jesus found in his Gospel and Acts is noteworthy and a testimony of Luke's faith as well as his authorship.

Blessed is the one who reads aloud the words of this prophecy, and blessed are those who hear, and who keep what is written in it, for the time is near.

Rv 1: 3

# 14 The Imperatives of Jesus in Revelation

Blessed is the one who reads aloud the words of this prophecy, and blessed are those who hear, and who keep what is written in it, for the time is near. Rv 1: 3

## John's Record of Jesus' Imperatives during the Revelation

John in Revelation recorded 33 imperatives spoken by Jesus. Some of Jesus' imperatives were directly addressed to John. Others specifically were to seven individual churches or groups of churches. In the final chapter, John quoted both an angel and Jesus, but John did not record any final imperatives from Jesus. Jesus' quotes from chapter 22 focused on the nearness of his coming. Jesus' final words in v20 were, "Surely, I come quickly" and immediately John followed with his own words, "Amen. Even so, come, Lord Jesus" which affirmed that Jesus would soon return.

Jesus as "the lamb" in Revelation, particularly "the slain lamb" is a trustworthy title. However, John never recorded that "the lamb" spoke. "Lamb" served as a metaphoric (one word which describes another) title for Jesus. John wrote "lamb" which described Jesus and what he had done as the lamb, more correctly, the suffered, slain, sacrificed, slaughtered, bloodied, and innocent lamb.

In John's context before writing the Revelation, Jesus had validated many titles. He had been titled and even titled himself affirmations of the Christ, the Messiah, the lamb, the bread, the door, the way, the truth, the life, the son of man, and other numerous titles, but his given name was and still is Jesus.

In Revelation, Jesus spoke, but John did not record that the lamb spoke imperatives. In Revelation John wrote the Greek word "lamb" 28 times. Some English translations insert "lamb" in place of the personal pronoun "he" for clarity. When English translators made that addition, the number of times the word "lamb" is found increases in English, but in Greek John wrote 'lamb' 28 times. 26 times John included an article, "the lamb." Only twice did John record (v 5: 6; v 13: 11) "lamb" without an article. When John employed an article, both the article and the noun were neuter singular. Either with or without the article, John always recorded that "lamb" was a neuter singular noun.

Of the 28 lamb recordings in their Greek cases, 15 were genitive (of), five were dative (to), eight were nominative (subject/predicate), and none recorded in the accusative (direct object). In John's gospel, Jesus' imperatives are easily recognizable because John consistently recorded Jesus' name as masculine gender, single case, not neuter, not feminine nor plural. In Revelation, John recorded imperatives spoken by speakers such as the angel accompanying John, but nowhere did John record that the "lamb" or "the lamb" spoke an imperative.

## Interpreting Insight

Revelation is an apocalyptic book. It is not a Gospel. It was recorded by John who wrote with a future orientation for John's intended readers, particularly the seven churches. Beyond study, its interpretation requires understanding and appropriate application of literalism, metaphors, and symbolic language. Interpreting the Revelation given to John is not for beginners. While the authorship attributed to John by most scholars is seldom contested, the writing and distribution date is not settled.

Most scholars agree that a significant window exists for both John's authoring and distribution of Revelation. Few believe John received or wrote Revelation before AD 60 or after AD 90. Thus, Revelation's genre, the timing of John's writing, the timing of the letter's distribution, and methods of interpretation is central to understanding the book. Two timing proponents exist. One view is that the Revelation was written and distributed after AD 70 more likely around AD 90. Another view is that the Revelation occurred before AD 70 before the Temple in Jerusalem fell to the Romans which brought Jewish Temple practices to a close.

The critical historical event of the destruction of Jerusalem and the Temple in AD 70 is significant to determine the timing of when John authored his received Revelation. Matthew, Mark, and Luke each recorded Jesus' "Olivet Discourse," Jesus prophetic destruction the Temple and Jewish practices and his return. John's gospel is different from Matthew, Mark, and Luke, the Synoptics. The most evident difference is that John did not record the "Olivet Discourse" from Jesus not matter that John was in attendance.

Johns' book Revelation, however, parallels many of the images of Jesus' Olivet Discourse by Matthew, Mark, and Luke. If John were a similar age to Jesus, authorship of AD 90 would have meant that John would have been in his 90's, an age few men would have reached in that day. John may have lived beyond 90, and if so later authorship is possible. Jesus' Olivet Discourse recorded by Matthew, Mark, and Luke was prophetic of Jerusalem's destruction. Revelation is similar.

Nevertheless, the intention is not to debate the timing of the writing, copying and eventual distribution of the revelation to John. The intention is to highlight Jesus' imperatives that John recorded in the Revelation that he had received regardless of when John recorded them or when the book came to be distributed. Our primary goal is to understand, "what" Jesus said rather than when Jesus spoke, when John authored, when editing ensued, and when the book was distributed.

Similar to the methodology which John employed for authoring his New Testament gospel and his three epistles, what John recorded is clear. Despite his limited reading and writing ability previously presented, his finished work guided by the Spirit was precisely as intended. While he may have penned some or all of the Revelation himself, scribes or editors under his direction most likely ultimately produced to his exact approval. Copies likewise would have been highly scrutinized. His words were intentional. John's recording of Jesus' imperatives to him and the seven churches are central to the Revelation given to John. Jesus' imperatives were rich with meaning to John's early readers then as much as they are rich in meaning for those reading John's written words today.

Understanding Revelation is no small undertaking. An apocalyptic book, John's words are filled with meaning. While symbolism and figurative imaging are rampant, John's Greek particularly the imperative mood form is not confusing. Klein clarifies the apocalyptic genre:

> Most importantly, we must recognize that Revelation employs highly symbolic and figurative imagery that we dare not interpret too literally.[1]

Finding meaning in Jesus' imperatives within John's Revelation can illuminate past, present, or future apocalyptical insight. More importantly, however, is how Jesus' imperatives found in John's Revelation established and anticipated the absolute sovereignty, reign, and presence of Jesus Immanuel, son of Man. Below are 33 Greek imperatives John recorded as having been spoken by Jesus. Some imperatives Jesus spoke directly to John. Others Jesus gave to the seven churches through John.

---

[1] Klein, William, Craig L. Blomberg, and Robert L. Hubbard, Jr., *Introduction to Biblical Interpretation*, 445.

# The Imperatives of Jesus in Revelation

To John
Rv 1: 11 I was in the Spirit on the Lord's day, and I heard behind me a loud voice like a trumpet saying, "<u>Write what you see in a book</u> Ὃ βλέπεις γράψον εἰς βιβλίον and <u>send it to the seven churches</u> πέμψον ταῖς ἑπτὰ ἐκκλησίαις, to Ephesus and to Smyrna and to Pergamum and to Thyatira and to Sardis and to Philadelphia and to Laodicea."

    Jesus' two imperatives to John were "write" and "send." The fact that we have John's recorded Revelation from Jesus proved that John followed Jesus' imperatives. John wrote this letter and sent it. Following these two imperatives write and send, Jesus' continued with imperatives to John specifically to write to the seven churches, especially Jesus' plural imperatives to them. While each of the seven churches received an individual warning, each church was aware of their warnings and Jesus' warnings to the other churches. Each church had its failings, yet all seven could fall to any of the sins Jesus had warned against. The seven churches were not independent, autonomous or left only to themselves. Each church was both subject to its warnings and subject to the warnings Jesus had given other churches.

To John
Rv 1: 17-18 When I saw him, I fell at his feet as though dead. But he laid his right hand on me, saying, "<u>Fear not</u> Μὴ φοβοῦ, I am the first and the last, and the living one. I died, and behold I am alive forevermore, and I have the keys of Death and Hades.

    After Jesus' commanded John not to fear, Jesus' next imperative in v19 to John was "write." Jesus prepared John with his command, "Do not fear." The revelation John was about to receive would impart fear to John, hence Jesus' command imperative, "Fear not" or "Do not fear." Throughout the revelation, John recorded no indication that he exhibited fear at what the angel and Jesus revealed to him. As readers were then and may still be moved by the fearful imagery in the revelation, John never recorded or exhibited fear at what Jesus had revealed to him. In contemporary context today, Jesus' followers likewise are not to fear at what was or is or will be revealed.

To John
Rv 1: 19 <u>Write therefore the things that you have seen, those that are and those that are to take place after this</u>, γράψον οὖν ἃ εἶδες καὶ ἃ εἰσὶν καὶ ἃ μέλλει γινέσθαι μετὰ ταῦτα.

    Jesus limited John to writing only what he saw, past, present, and future. What John saw were past ("what you have seen"), present and future revelations. John recorded Jesus' words, "those that are and those that are to take place after this" as present and future truths. Jesus commanded John to write correctly to an angel of a named church.

    In Rv 2: 1 John had been commanded to write to the angel of the church of Ephesus. This messenger angel was to carry Jesus' revelation that had been given to John and on to church leadership in Ephesus. Each of the seven churches, Ephesus, Smyrna, Pergamum, Thyatira, Sardis, Philadelphia, and Laodicea had its own angel to whom John had been commanded to write. Each messenger angel was to convey Jesus' specific imperatives to them. Through the entire book of Revelation, each church first became aware of their own faults. As they read the entire Revelation each church also became aware of the faults of the other six churches.

Each greeting and salutation to the seven churches that Jesus had given John was the same. Each greeting began with an imperative, "write" and each salutation ended with an imperative, "hear." Write to the angel (singular) of the church (singular) and hear what the Spirit says to the churches, (plural).

To the Angel of the Ephesus Church
Rv 2: 1-7 "<u>To the angel of the church in Ephesus write</u> Τῷ ἀγγέλῳ Τῷ ἐν Ἐφέσῳ ἐκκλησίας γράψον: 'The words of him who holds the seven stars in his right hand, who walks among the seven golden lampstands. "'I know your works, your toil and your patient endurance, and how you cannot bear with those who are evil, but have tested those who call themselves apostles and are not, and found them to be false. I know you are enduring patiently and bearing up for my name's sake, and you have not grown weary. But I have this against you, that you have abandoned the love you had at first. <u>Remember therefore from where you have fallen</u>   μνημόνευε οὖν πόθεν πέπτωκας; <u>repent</u> μετανόησον, <u>and do the works you did at first</u> καὶ τὰ πρῶτα ἔργα ποίησον. If not, I will come to you and remove your lampstand from its place, unless you repent. Yet this you have: you hate the works of the Nicolaitans, which I also hate. He who has an ear, let him <u>hear what the Spirit says to the churches</u> ὁ ἔχων οὖς ἀκουσάτω τί τὸ πνεῦμα λέγει ταῖς ἐκκλησίαις. To the one who conquers I will grant to eat of the tree of life, which is in the paradise of God.'

> Jesus' three imperatives were, "remember from where you have fallen," "repent," and "do the works you did at first." The church in Ephesus here had been commanded to return to where they had been. Similar to Jewish Temple practices, apostasy, heresy, and failure to identify Yeshua Ha' Mashiach, (Messiah Jesus) and ethics of the Kingdom, the church in Ephesus had gone off course. Jesus warned Ephesus and the other six churches to be aware of their theology. Doctrines and practices were no small matter. His imperatives affirmed both the love they had lost and Jesus' revulsion regarding the works of the Nicolaitans. The morphological form of "the Nicolaitans" τῶν Νικολαϊτῶν, is a compound word "nike" meaning conquer and the "laos" meaning people. The Nicolaitans had physically or spiritually conquered people. Regardless if the conquering was physical or spiritual, Jesus hated what they had done. From context, the Nicolaitans had conquered with false faith. Jesus commanded to conquer not as the Nicolaitans had conquered. Conquering was to be done through repentance, and the work of their first love. Jesus was pleased with their work and endurance to test false apostles. Another view is that Jesus affirmed those at Ephesus in their hatred of the Nicolaitans. Jesus excoriated their lack of love. He commanded them to remember the devotion and deeds they had once done and their priority of love they had at the beginning. The Ephesians were not to conquer as the Nicolaitans had conquered.

To Angel of the Smyrna Church
Rv 2: 8–11 "And to the angel of the church in Smyrna write Καὶ τῷ ἀγγέλῳ τῷ ἐν Σμύρνῃ ἐκκλησίας γράψον: 'The words of the first and the last, who died and came to life. "'I know your tribulation and your poverty (but you are rich) and the slander of those who say that they are Jews and are not, but are a synagogue of Satan. Do not fear what you are about to suffer μή φοβοῦ ἃ μέλλεις πάσχειν. Behold, the devil is about to throw some of you into prison, that you may be tested, and for ten days you will have tribulation. Be faithful unto death γίνου πιστὸς ἄχρι θανάτου, and I will give you the crown of life. He who has an ear, let him hear what the Spirit says to the churches ἀκουσάτω τί τὸ πνεῦμα λέγει. The one who conquers will not be hurt by the second death.'

> Jesus' two imperatives, "do not fear" and "be faithful unto death" addressed what the suffering church in Smyrna was about to experience. Jesus quickly followed up affirming that the crown of life awaited them. These imperatives were not only for Smyrna. The closing imperative phrase, "hear what the Spirit says to the churches" was for all seven churches, not just Smyrna.

To the Angel of the Pergamum Church
Rv 2: 12-17 "And to the angel of the church in Pergamum write Καὶ τῷ ἀγγέλῳ τῆς ἐν Περγάμῳ ἐκκλησίας γράψον: 'The words of him who has the sharp two-edged sword. "'I know where you dwell, where Satan's throne is. Yet you hold fast my name, and you did not deny my faith even in the days of Antipas my faithful witness, who was killed among you, where Satan dwells. But I have a few things against you: you have some there who hold the teaching of Balaam, who taught Balak to put a stumbling block before the sons of Israel, so that they might eat food sacrificed to idols and practice sexual immorality. So also you have some who hold the teaching of the Nicolaitans. Therefore repent μετανόησον οὖν. If not, I will come to you soon and war against them with the sword of my mouth. He who has an ear, let him hear what the Spirit says to the churches ἀκουσάτω τί τὸ πνεῦμα λέγει ταῖς ἐκκλησίαις. To the one who conquers I will give some of the hidden manna, and I will give him a white stone, with a new name written on the stone that no one knows except the one who receives it.'

> Jesus' gave only one imperative to Pergamum, repent. Teachings of Balaam, sexual immorality and teachings of the Nicolaitans were problems for Pergamum. The Nicolaitan Christian sect was known for sexual immorality, extreme unrestrained indulgences, antinomianism, and dominating people in the church. Jesus followed his imperative with a stern warning of what would happen without their repentance.

To the Angel of the Thyatira Church
Rv 2: 18-29 "And to the angel of the church in Thyatira write Καὶ τῷ ἀγγέλῳ τῷ ἐν Θυατείροις ἐκκλησίας γράψον: 'The words of the Son of God, who has eyes like a flame of fire, and whose feet are like burnished bronze. "'I know your works, your love and faith and service and patient endurance, and that your latter works exceed the first. But I have this against you, that you tolerate that woman Jezebel, who calls herself a prophetess and is teaching and seducing my servants to practice sexual immorality and to eat food sacrificed to idols. I gave her time to repent, but she refuses to repent of her sexual immorality. Behold, I will throw her onto a sickbed, and those who commit adultery with her I will throw into great tribulation, unless they repent of her works, and I will strike her children dead. And all the churches will know that I am he who searches mind and heart, and I will give to each of you according to your works. But to the rest of you in Thyatira,

who do not hold this teaching, who have not learned what some call the deep things of Satan, to you I say, I do not lay on you any other burden. Only hold fast what you have until I come πλὴν ὃ ἔχετε κρατήσατε ἄχρις οὗ ἂν ἥξω. The one who conquers and who keeps my works until the end, to him I will give authority over the nations, and he will rule them with a rod of iron, as when earthen pots are broken in pieces, even as I myself have received authority from my Father. And I will give him the morning star. He who has an ear, let him hear what the Spirit says to the churches ἀκουσάτω τί τὸ πνεῦμα λέγει ταῖς ἐκκλησίαις.

> Toleration of immorality to the likes of Jezebel brings judgment. Judgment would arrive after a merciful time awaiting repentance. Not all in Thyatira were subject to judgment as not all held to Jezebel's teachings. There were some in Thyatira who had conquered and kept their works pure who had given their faithfulness and would have authority over nations.

> Although some within the Thyatira church had adopted immoral teachings, some had not fallen to false teachings. Jesus affirmed that he was fully aware of their burdens. He also warned the other six churches of a similar fate should they fall to Jezebel's teachings. "Hold fast" and "hear" were the two imperatives John recorded in this text to the Angel of the Thyatira Church.

To the Angel of the Sardis Church
Rv 3: 1-6 "And to the angel of the church in Sardis write Καὶ τῷ ἀγγέλῳ τῆς ἐν Σάρδεσιν ἐκκλησίας γράψον: 'The words of him who has the seven spirits of God and the seven stars. "'I know your works. You have the reputation of being alive, but you are dead. Wake up γίνου γρηγορῶν, and strengthen what remains and is about to die καὶ στήρισον τὰ λοιπὰ ἃ ἔμελλον ἀποθανεῖν, for I have not found your works complete in the sight of my God. Remember, then, what you received and heard μνημόνευε οὖν πῶς εἴληφας καὶ ἤκουσας. Keep it καὶ τήρει, and repent καὶ μετανόησον. If you will not wake up, I will come like a thief, and you will not know at what hour I will come against you. Yet you have still a few names in Sardis, people who have not soiled their garments, and they will walk with me in white, for they are worthy. The one who conquers will be clothed thus in white garments, and I will never blot his name out of the book of life. I will confess his name before my Father and before his angels. He who has an ear, let him hear what the Spirit says to the churches ἀκουσάτω τί τὸ πνεῦμα λέγει ταῖς ἐκκλησίαις.'

> Sardis received more imperatives than any of the other six churches. Jesus' five imperatives were: "wake up," "strengthen," "remember," "keep," and "repent." Similar to Thyatira there were people within Sardis who did not need an awakening. That means that some were still strong. Some remembered what they had heard. Some were repentant. But not all. Even as bad as those in Sardis were, those within the faithful remnant were worthy. They would walk with Jesus in white garments. Their names would remain in the book of life. Through this message to Sardis, the other six churches also were reminded that there might be some faithful within their church body.

To the Angel of the Philadelphia Church
Rv 3: 7-13 "And to the angel of the church in Philadelphia write Καὶ τῷ ἀγγέλῳ τῆς ἐν Φιλαδελφείᾳ ἐκκλησίας γράψον: 'The words of the holy one, the true one, who has the key of David, who opens and no one will shut, who shuts and no one opens. "'I know your works. Behold, I have set before

you an open door, which no one is able to shut. I know that you have but little power, and yet you have kept my word and have not denied my name. Behold, I will make those of the synagogue of Satan who say that they are Jews and are not, but lie--behold, I will make them come and bow down before your feet and they will learn that I have loved you. Because you have kept my word about patient endurance, I will keep you from the hour of trial that is coming on the whole world, to try those who dwell on the earth. I am coming soon. <u>Hold fast what you have</u> κράτει ὃ ἔχεις, so that no one may seize your crown. The one who conquers, I will make him a pillar in the temple of my God. Never shall he go out of it, and I will write on him the name of my God, and the name of the city of my God, the new Jerusalem, which comes down from my God out of heaven, and my own new name. He who has an ear, <u>let him hear what the Spirit says to the churches</u> ἀκουσάτω τί τὸ πνεῦμα λέγει ταῖς ἐκκλησίαις.

> Philadelphia received only one imperative: "hold fast to what you have." The question is begged, what was it that the church in Philadelphia held that they were to keep? Jesus listed their works. They had kept his word. They had not denied Jesus' name. Jesus identified those masquerading as Jews who were not covenanted faithful Jews. Here the term Jews was more likely a reference to the truly faithful rather than nationality or temple practicing Jews who were unfaithful Jews. These false Jews who deferred to Satan's synagogue would eventually bow to the faithful Jews. The false Jews would realize that the faithful had been and are loved. Jesus warned that if Philadelphia did not hold fast, their crown could be seized. The other six churches were equally warned.

To the Angel of the Laodicea Church
Rv 3: 14-22 "<u>And to the angel of the church in Laodicea write</u> Καὶ τῷ ἀγγέλῳ τῆς ἐν Λαοδικείᾳ ἐκκλησίας γράψον: 'The words of the Amen, the faithful and true witness, the beginning of God's creation. "'I know your works: you are neither cold nor hot. Would that you were either cold or hot! So, because you are lukewarm, and neither hot nor cold, I will spit you out of my mouth. For you say, I am rich, I have prospered, and I need nothing, not realizing that you are wretched, pitiable, poor, blind, and naked. I counsel you to buy from me gold refined by fire, so that you may be rich, and white garments so that you may clothe yourself and the shame of your nakedness may not be seen, and salve to anoint your eyes, so that you may see. Those whom I love, I reprove and discipline, <u>so be zealous</u> ζήλευε οὖν <u>and repent</u> καὶ μετανόησον. Behold, I stand at the door and knock. If anyone hears my voice and opens the door, I will come in to him and eat with him, and he with me. The one who conquers, I will grant him to sit with me on my throne, as I also conquered and sat down with my Father on his throne. He who has an ear, let him <u>hear what the Spirit says to the churches</u> ἀκουσάτω τί τὸ πνεῦμα λέγει ταῖς ἐκκλησίαις.'"

> Jesus only gave two imperatives to the Laodicea Church, "be zealous" and "repent." Jesus corrected their lukewarm attitude. Both his present active imperative to always "be zealous" and Jesus' aorist active imperative, "repent" for falling into their mediocre mindset of the church were clear. Jesus commanded them to always be zealous, a continuous present active mindset. Repentance was purposed to return them to continuous zealousness so as not to become lukewarm again. That they were not zealous affirmed their timidity or perhaps fearfulness or diffidence. The other six churches were likewise warned. Avoid timidity and remain zealous having received Jesus' full revelation given John to pass to them.

To John
Rv 4: 1 After this I looked, and behold, a door standing open in heaven! And the first voice, which I had heard speaking to me like a trumpet, said, "<u>Come up here, and I will show you what must take place after this.</u>"Ἀνάβα ὧδε καὶ δείξω σοι ἃ δεῖ γενέσθαι μετὰ ταῦτα.

> Jesus commanded John to enter the open door in heaven. Only after having entered the open door would John receive a greater revelation. "Come up here" was Jesus' last imperative to John. Although John recorded that Jesus spoke again in Rv 16: 15; 22: 7, 12, 13, 16, and 20, John did not record any additional imperatives. John's record of Jesus' imperatives within the Revelation had finished with Jesus' final imperative to John, "come up here" at which John was rewarded by knowing what would take place after this.
>
> As with Jesus' imperatives throughout the Gospels, whether recorded by Matthew, Mark, Luke, or John, obedience to an imperative by Jesus always produced a consequence.

## Summary of Jesus' Imperatives to the Seven Churches

Each church identified in Revelation was warned of blessings and curses. Jesus both commended and cautioned with impending judgment. His imperatives were purposeful because consequences upon those churches were unavoidable without change if having strayed from God's will. His grace provided mercy for a limited time awaiting repentance for knowingly advocating a false church and return to orthodoxy (right belief) and orthopraxy (right practice).

His words to these seven churches affirm that Jesus' church and his churches were his then. Jesus' church and his churches are his now. His imperatives were operative then and are operative now. His repeated imperatives, "hear what the Spirit says to the churches" recorded by John were intentional then and intentional now. His warnings through his spoken imperatives recorded by John had purpose then and have purpose now.

The impending destruction of the Temple in AD 70 would have been inconceivable to those in John's time. John's letter heralded what was to happen in their day. The abuses that the Temple system placed on God's people and the destruction that occurred would have been meaningful to anyone reading the Revelation to John either before or after the Temple destruction. Those with ears to hear in their day heard the impending destruction that was about to occur in AD 70. Those with ears to hear who read and heard about the Revelation shortly after AD 70 would have understood Jesus' words to those who heard the Revelation before AD 70 as an affirmation or a confirmation or a verification on judgement past, present, and future.

Those who read John's revelation before AD 70 were warned of what was to come. Those who read John's revelation after AD 70 were reminded of what John had warned. Before AD 70 the warnings to the seven churches mattered because the Temple and Jerusalem were about to be destroyed. After AD 70 those reading the warnings to the churches would have realized why the church that belongs to Jesus Immanuel (God with us) was important following the destruction of the Temple and Jerusalem by the Romans.

The imperatives in Revelation can be past, present and future in past, present, and future contexts. There is wisdom knowing both the mercy and the judgement God has shown throughout the Bible to individuals, communities, nations, and churches both gone astray and in his will.

Jesus is King of his Kingdom and Lord of his church.

Pray then like this: "Our Father in heaven, hallowed be your name. Your kingdom come, your will be done, on earth as it is in heaven.

Mt 6: 9-10

# 15 The Imperatives of Jesus in the Lord's Prayer

Pray then like this: "Our Father in heaven, hallowed be your name. Mt 6: 9

## The Setting of the Lord's Prayer

Jesus taught the disciples how to pray in response to their prior imperative to him that he teach them to pray.[1] Both Matthew and Luke provided an account of Jesus' instructions to his disciples on prayer. Matthew's record of the Lord's Prayer is found in the Sermon on the Mount Mt 5–6. Matthew, however, did not record any imperatives from the disciples to Jesus as Luke had recorded to start the prayer. Luke conveyed that the disciples had asked or entreated or commanded Jesus to teach them to pray. Beyond an entreaty imperative, however, they did not merely ask and hope that Jesus would teach them as is conveyed in English. Their imperative that Luke recorded expected Jesus' response that he would teach them to pray. Luke's record conveyed that their imperative command initiated Jesus' response.

Jesus answer to their imperative came quickly. He was not ambiguous. His teaching presented a challenge to them. Jesus commanded his disciples to pray. More specifically he commanded them to pray to their Father imperatively. They were not to ask God. Had Jesus taught Scribes, Pharisees, Sadducees, or Temple leaders to pray as he taught his disciples, his crucifixion may have come sooner. Religious leaders had they heard Jesus' imperatives to God within the prayer would have immediately accused him of blasphemy. Matthew recorded Jesus' prayer instructions with imperatives to God the Father which in their time and their context was offensive.

Similarly, today as the disciples heard, commanding God as a mindset seems offensive. Moreover, the Lord's Prayer holds seven imperatives from Jesus on how to pray. Because Greek is a more specific language, English translations struggle to express the verbal imperative vein in Jesus' words within this prayer. The spoken or written imperative conveyed an order or a command, such as, "You do this or that!" or "Do this or that now!"

Historical and contemporary Greek scholars sometimes term Jesus' imperatives within this prayer as 'entreaty imperatives' softening the perception of commanding or offending God. Entreaty imperatives can be challenging to translate from Greek to English because imperatives to God from man appear at the very least, arrogant and prideful. Entreaty imperatives in English convey a request or a plea rather than a command. While entreaty imperatives temper the imperatival intent, the Greek morphological imperative form Matthew recorded is without question. Matthew recorded the Greek formed imperatives in the Lord's Prayer because Jesus spoke an imperative in the Lord's Prayer. Regardless of if Jesus spoke Hebrew, Aramaic, or Greek, Matthew recorded a Greek imperative.

## Greek to English

The Lord's Prayer in English is difficult to convey what Jesus said, what the disciples heard and what Matthew wrote in Greek grammar and context. Had you been there listening to Jesus

---

[1] Now Jesus was praying in a certain place, and when he finished, one of his disciples said to him, "Lord, teach us to pray, as John taught his disciples." Lk 11: 1 (See Chapter 16: Imperatives to Jesus. The phrase from one of his disciples "Lord, teach us to pray" includes a Greek imperative to Jesus.)

speak or had you been an early first-century reader of Matthew's record, you might find the prayer today to be quite different from what they thought. Unlearning is the hardest form of learning.

In the context of the disciples, this prayer was no simple prayer. This prayer was revolutionary. This prayer countered what they had previously been taught to believe about prayer. This prayer challenged what they believed. Jesus started his prayer with an imperative, "pray this way" because what followed was difficult for his listeners to swallow. The imperatives and aorist subjunctive within Lord's Prayer can be problematic which is why entreaty imperatives are termed to soften the Greek command imperatives. No one in Jesus' day would dare have thought to command God what to do, especially religious leaders. Jesus commanded his disciples to pray imperatives to the Father. Big difference.

Today the prayer in English renders a far different prayer than how Jesus' disciples may have heard the prayer in their time and context in Aramaic or Greek. Today we recite the Lord's Prayer from memory perhaps without considering what the prayer meant in the time and context of Jesus' listeners. How profound it was for the disciples who heard Jesus teach prayer through imperatives. Hearing Jesus' instructions his disciples likely realized two truths. There was a risk for Jesus in how he was teaching them. There was a risk for them in what he commanded them. He clarified the Kingdom and those in the Kingdom through the Lord's Prayer. Interpreters often classify Jesus' imperatives as entreaty imperatives. Mounce clarifies entreaty imperatives:

> From a pastoral perspective, isn't it arrogant to issue a command imperative to God?" In the imperatives of Jesus in the Lord's Prayer (Mt 6:11; Lk 11:3), he stated an unquestionable imperative aorist active second person singular verb translated as "Give us this day, our daily bread." While "Give" is in the imperative mood form, most scholars classify it as an entreaty imperative "used to encourage or ask someone to do something.

Mounce continues:

> You do not command God to do something; you 'entreat' him, both in English and in Greek.[2]

While entreaty (request) imperatives are correct, the Greek imperatives recorded by Matthew and Luke in the Lord's Prayer are morphologically written imperatives. Syntactically they first conveyed an imperative idea. Matthew could have recorded that Jesus said, "Ask your father…" But Matthew did not record that Jesus told his disciples to ask, seek, or knock on a door as a means to petition God.[3] Matthew could have recorded that Jesus said, "Ask God to feed you." Or "Seek God for your daily needs." Or "Knock on God's door and he will open it and meet your needs." Here in this prayer, Matthew was intentional to record that Jesus spoke an imperative. While an entreaty intent is appropriate and viable, the Greek imperative idea is not to be negated.

---

[2] Mounce, William D., *Basics of Biblical Greek, Second Edition,* 315.
[3] "Ask, and it will be given to you; seek, and you will find; knock, and it will be opened to you. Αἰτεῖτε καὶ δοθήσεται ὑμῖν ζητεῖτε καὶ εὑρήσετε κρούετε καὶ ἀνοιγήσεται ὑμῖν·" Mt 7: 7 Matthew recorded that Jesus spoke the imperatives, "ask," "seek," and "knock." While each of these words is an imperative similar to the imperative "give," in their context "give" did not convey an entreaty impression similar to "ask," "seek," and "knock." The three words carried entreaty context. The word "give" did not carry an entreaty context.

His disciples likely realized that his prayer was not a prayer religious leaders of their day would have accepted. Even with entreaty imperatives that soften the idea of a command, grammatically and morphologically the Greek imperatives were what Matthew recorded. Today's English recitation or reading of the Lord's Prayer vary from what the Disciples heard and were taught. What Jesus commanded, what they heard, and what Matthew recorded in the Lord's Prayer are perhaps the most profound of all imperatives given to the disciples.

Understanding the prayer with its imperative context, we recognize that Jesus' commands were not gentle petitions. What they heard and what Matthew recorded was, "Your name must be kept holy. Your reign must come, and your will must be done and fulfilled here on earth as it is in heaven."

Both Mt 6:9-13 and Lk 11:2-4 documented that Jesus taught disciples how to pray. Matthew recorded that Jesus said seven imperatives and one aorist subjunctive with a negative. Luke recorded four imperatives and one aorist subjunctive with a negative. (Refresher: aorist subjunctives with a negative convey imperative intent.) How the Lord's Prayer could be more understandably translated into English, the following may be helpful.

## The Imperatives of Jesus in the Lord's Prayer

Mt 6: 9 <u>Pray then like this</u> Οὕτως οὖν προσεύχεσθε ὑμεῖς: "Our Father in heaven, <u>hallowed be your name</u> ἁγιασθήτω τὸ ὄνομά σου.

Lk 11: 2a And he said to them, "When you pray, <u>say: "Father, hallowed be your name</u>. λέγετε Πάτερ ἁγιασθήτω τὸ ὄνομά σου

> Jesus spoke two imperatives at the beginning of the prayer. His first imperative was plural. A more clarifying amplified translation might be, "To my disciples hearing my words then, all of you pray the way I am about to command you and keep praying the way I am about to command you." Matthew recorded that the disciples heard Jesus address them in the plural, not singular. Christians have traditionally memorized this prayer and have both privately recited it and publicly voiced it unison. Pastors often lead congregations in this prayer as a group paralleling Jesus' imperatives to his disciples (in plural) as a group.
> 
> Matthew recorded Jesus' first command "Pray" as a present middle or passive deponent imperative which conveyed to them that they were to start praying as he taught and continue praying in future as he would now teach them. Jesus began his instructions with an imperative "pray then like this" is logical because his imperatives that followed within the prayer instructions were uncharacteristic in their context. His disciples would not have expected the type of prayer that he taught. Luke did not use the imperative, "pray" as Matthew recorded. Luke used the imperative, "say" preceded by "when you pray."
> 
> Matthew recorded in v9 that Jesus stated heavens (plural), not heaven (singular) as English translations commonly render. Matthew's word, "heavens" agree with the Greek plural article that preceded heavens. An amplified translation is, "The father of us in the heavens." While many churched Christians have been taught a singular heaven not heavens in this prayer, the Greek form Matthew recorded that quoted

Jesus was without question plural, heavens. Luke, however, did mentioned neither "heaven" nor "heavens" in his recording of Jesus' instructions.

Jesus was not ambiguous. He had commanded his disciples to pray in a given way. More specifically he had commanded them to imperatively pray to the Father. The Lord's Prayer from both Matthew and Luke contains many morphologically formed Greek imperative mood formed words. The first imperative was that the Father would make his name holy. The English translation, "Hallowed be thy name" somewhat obscures the power of Jesus' imperative. The English rendering conveys that the person praying is acknowledging more than commanding. The Greek is unambiguous. Jesus here commanded his disciples to command God that his name would be made holy. The imperative was aorist passive third person singular which amplified may be, "Make your name holy because you have made and are making your name holy." This translation sounds strange to an
English ear, but the point is that God is in the business of making his name holy. That is what Jesus' wanted his disciples to know.

The aorist passive imperative affirmed that Jesus made the point that his disciples were passive in that his disciples had no control over God's holiness. Jesus commanded his disciples to demand that their father, more specifically their father in the heavens (plural), make his holiness known. Jesus' first imperative "Pray like this" is simple enough, but to pray with an imperative that God makes his name holy would have been difficult for Jesus' hearers and certainly contemptible to religious leaders of that time. Jesus' prayer instructions in their minds were like no other instructions.

Jesus taught his disciples to command God to make his name holy. Jesus wanted his disciples to grasp that God both had and would continue to make his name holy on earth as in the heavens. The aorist passive imperative is significant because the disciples were to command God a task that they (the disciples) fully expected God to complete. Hyperbole or not, Greek imperatives come with the expectation that the imperatives be completed. What that meant to them was that the disciples expected the Holiness of God to be in their presence and time. Moreover, Jesus, the very holiness of God was in their midst.

Mt 6: 10 <u>Your kingdom come</u> (make your kingdom come) ἐλθέτω ἡ βασιλεία σου, <u>your will be done</u> (make your will be done) γενηθήτω τὸ θέλημά σου, on earth γῆς as it is in heaven.
Lk 11: 2b <u>Your kingdom come</u>. ἐλθέτω ἡ βασιλεία σου·
    Note Luke did not include "your will be done" following "your kingdom come" as Matthew had recorded. Jesus taught that with the coming of God's Kingdom, God's will had come and God's will, would be done. God's will is inherent in God's Kingdom, hence "your kingdom come, your will be done" are both imperatives. There was no option. Within God's Kingdom is God's will.

Jesus' aorist imperatives to the Father were first that God's Kingdom would come and second that his will would be done here on earth just as in heaven. English translations have removed the imperative command idea to the Father and replaced with "your (thy) kingdom come, your (thy) will be done." These two aorist imperatives are commonly translated to English using "let," i.e. "Let your kingdom come, and "Let your will be done." Softening the command imperatives to the Father in today's translations does not convey the Kingdom as entirely having come in Jesus birth, life, death, and resurrection. To the contrary, Jesus' imperatives acknowledged the coming of the Kingdom. That is how the disciples understood Jesus' imperatives. Today because of the fragile translation of the aorist imperatives from Greek to English, readers of English Bibles are unable to comprehend what the disciples comprehended.

Critical to these two imperatives is that "your kingdom come" is an imperative aorist active verb while "your will be done" is an aorist passive deponent imperative. The deponent verb is passive in form but active in meaning. What that meant then and means now is significant. Jesus taught that with the coming of God's Kingdom, God's will had come and God's will, was then and is now being done. God's will is inherent in the Kingdom. There was no option. Within God's Kingdom, his will was and continues to be active. English renderings do not convey the depth of God's Kingdom. English renderings do a poor job not conveying God's will then and there, nor God's will here and now.

Here Jesus stated both earth and heaven in singular, not plural and confirmed to his disciples that the Kingdom of heaven had come to the earth. The word for earth is γῆς (ges) meaning land, firma, not kosmos meaning world. What Jesus conveyed to his disciples was that the Kingdom had come to earth. Their understanding was irrelevant to the fact that the Kingdom of God had arrived.

Mt 6: 11 <u>Give us this day our daily bread</u> τὸν ἄρτον ἡμῶν τὸν ἐπιούσιον δὸς ἡμῖν σήμερον
Lk 11: 3 <u>Give us each day our daily bread</u> τὸν ἄρτον ἡμῶν τὸν ἐπιούσιον δίδου ἡμῖν τὸ καθ ἡμέραν
Note the different Greek constructions between Matthew and Luke. Also note the different English word, "this" and "each" within the ESV. YLT translation reads "our appointed bread be giving us daily."

The entreaty imperative that God gave them that same day, (the day of their prayer) affirmed that their daily sustenance, would always be with them. This entreaty imperative confirmed that God had in the past, was then in the present, and would in the future provide their needs.

Regardless of time, amount or sufficiency, their needs would be met. Their anxiety was removed because meeting their needs was never-ending. This imperative gave the disciples great comfort. If we understand today as they understood then, great comfort could abound today. The imperative from Jesus to those who heard him affirmed God's provision to them within the Kingdom. Those who would read Jesus' imperatives within the prayer were affirmed that in the Kingdom of God their provisions were and would be secure. The disciples had security having heard Jesus imperatives about the Kingdom.

Mt 6: 12 and <u>forgive us our debts as we also have forgiven our debtors</u> ἄφες ἡμῖν τὰ ὀφειλήματα ἡμῶν ὡς καὶ ἡμεῖς ἀφήκαμεν τοῖς ὀφειλέταις ἡμῶν
Lk 11: 4a and <u>forgive us our sins, for we ourselves forgive everyone who is indebted to us</u> ἄφες ἡμῖν τὰς ἁμαρτίας ἡμῶν καὶ γὰρ αὐτοὶ ἀφίομεν παντὶ ὀφείλοντι ἡμῖν·

The English commands "forgive" or "let go" or "permit" derives from the Greek imperative ἄφες. Note the different Greek constructions between Matthew and Luke. Matthew recorded "our debt" τὰ ὀφειλήματα ἡμῶν and "our debtors" τοῖς ὀφειλέταις ἡμῶν. Hence, rightly, within Mt 6: 12, the ESV, KJV, NAS, NRS, NIV, and YLT recorded "debts" and "debtors."

Luke recorded "our sins" τὰς ἁμαρτίας ἡμῶν and "indebted to us" ὀφείλοντι ἡμῖν which differ from Matthew. Hence, most English translations rightly recorded Luke's "sins" and "indebted to us" with the exception of the NIV which did not translate the Greek word for "indebted to us" but chose "who sins against us."

In short, Matthew recorded "debt" and "debtors" and Luke recorded, "sin" and "indebted to us" two different recordings. The NIV translators used one English word to accommodate two different Greek words found in Luke. This anomaly within the NIV is not overly problematic. For this book, we are concerned with the imperatives.

God's Kingdom rule of forgiveness of debts and judgment had arrived. Jesus intended that his disciples reflect on how they had forgiven in the past and begin forgiving as God forgives. Repentance and a changed view of forgiveness was Jesus' message to them which was why he spoke the aorist active imperative "forgive us our debts" and then the aorist active indicative "as we have forgiven our debtors." Here Jesus' imperatives told them to command God to forgive them as they had forgiven those who had sinned against them.

Some English translations miss the aorist active and convey a present tense in the translation, "and forgive us our debts, as we forgive our debtors" in the present active. An amplified aorist active is more reflective, "as we also have forgiven those who sinned against us and continue forgiving those who sin against us."

This imperative was comparable to asking God to judge them just as they had already judged others and would judge others in their future. Their judgments were to parallel the judgments of God. As they had learned through their Jewish history God's judgments allowed time for repentance. His merciful judgments were not hasty. They were expected to be judged by others as they had judged which would have made them aware of their own shortcomings at forgiveness. This imperative confirmed the Spirit within the Kingdom. Jesus' prayer instructions were purposed to transform them. Their transformation did not mean abdication or abandonment of forgiving and judging. Their transformation meant forgiving and judging as God had forgiven and judged in the past and would forgive and judge in the future. God's Kingdom rule of forgiveness of debts and judgment had arrived.

Both Matthew and Luke recorded words Jesus spoke regarding the Lord's Supper. Matthew and Luke are similar, but not precisely these same. Note that Matthew recorded Jesus' focus on debts and debtors. Luke focused on sins and debts owed:

> and forgive us our sins, for we ourselves forgive everyone who is indebted to us. καὶ ἄφες ἡμῖν τὰς ἁμαρτίας ἡμῶν καὶ γὰρ αὐτοὶ ἀφίομεν παντὶ ὀφείλοντι ἡμῖν· Lk 11: 4a

While differences in word choice by Matthew and Luke are evident, the context linking sins, debts, and forgiveness are similar. Matthew's word choice was appropriate to his Jewish readers, and Luke's word choice was appropriate to his Gentile reader (Theophilus in Lk 1: 3). Luke as a Gentile Greek and Matthew as a Hebrew Jew in Palestine would not have employed the same words for their intended readers. The variances are insignificant to context.

Mt 6: 13 'And do not lead us into temptation καὶ μὴ εἰσενέγκῃς ἡμᾶς εἰς πειρασμόν, but deliver us from evil ἀλλὰ ῥῦσαι ἡμᾶς ἀπὸ τοῦ πονηροῦ.
Lk 11: 4b And lead us not into temptation καὶ μὴ εἰσενέγκῃς ἡμᾶς εἰς πειρασμόν

On the first read of 6:13A the English translation "and do not lead us into temptation" from the Greek aorist subjunctive with a negative seems to imply that God can lead them into temptation. The English word formations in both Matthew and Mark sound like a command to God for God not to lead them into temptation.

If we are asking God not to lead us into temptation, then can or will God lead us into temptation? The aorist subjunctive in both Matthew and Luke were intentional to avoid using an imperative. Of course, the translation from Greek to English is difficult making the aorist subjunctive sound like an English command when no imperative is present from Matthew or Luke. This Greek word formation about temptation does not include a Greek imperative. Most English translations convey a command which is not overly problematic but does not convey the aorist subjunctive with a negative. The YLT comes close with "and mayest thou not bring us into temptation" but is a strange English construction. James 1: 13 affirmed that God does not tempt.[4]

Luke stopped with "and lead us not into temptation." Matthew continued with "but deliver us from evil." The imperative in Matthew is found in "deliver us from evil" or more specifically "deliver us from the evil one" rightly from the NIV and NRSV. Some English translations do not translate "the evil one" preferring "evil" softening the idea of Satan as a God created yet fallen angel, a singular being.

What they heard, what Matthew recorded, and what readers of Matthew's book read from Jesus was without question "the evil one" identified by a singular masculine gender, not neuter. Further confirmation is the masculine singular article "the" which affirmed that "the evil one" not "evil" was what Matthew recorded that

---

[4] Let no one say when he is tempted, "I am being tempted by God," for God cannot be tempted with evil, and he himself tempts no one. Ja 1: 13

Jesus said. Some English translations miss this insight in the text and provide footnotes for clarity.

This imperative in some translations is written as an affirmation that God will deliver them from evil similarly to an entreaty imperative, which does not identify Satan as a singular person in gender, but evil as a non-being. Greek morphological forms and articles however likely were not confusing to hearers or readers of Greek. When they heard Jesus say, "the evil one" they identified Satan as a being or at the very least real in power to deceive. English translations sometimes do not convey what the Greek conveyed to earliest hearers and readers.

Initially the imperative, "deliver us" would have been unusual to their idea of praying to the Father. Jesus conveyed that their relationship was to be so close to the Father that his will and their will would be the same. Jesus taught them that the Kingdom of God was the Kingdom for them.

In short, Jesus had commanded them to command God that God himself deliver them from the evil one. With this type of prayer, filled with imperatives, following his instructions his disciples began to understand that Jesus was preparing his disciples for apostolic power. They too would taste what it is to know and do the will of the Father.

Comprehending the depth of the prayer in historical context is challenging through English without understanding the Greek or Greek imperatives within the prayer.

This was no ordinary pray in the language of their day.

# Section 4

# Beyond His Commands

He is not here, for he has risen, as he said. Come, see the place where he lay. Then go quickly and tell his disciples that he has risen from the dead, and behold, he is going before you to Galilee; there you will see him. See, I have told you." So they departed quickly from the tomb with fear and great joy, and ran to tell his disciples. And behold, Jesus met them and said, "Greetings!" And they came up and took hold of his feet and worshiped him. Then Jesus said to them, "Do not be afraid; go and tell my brothers to go to Galilee, and there they will see me."

Mt 28: 6-10

What is your judgment?" They answered, "He deserves death." Then they spit in his face and struck him. And some slapped him, saying, "Prophesy to us you, Christ! Who is it that struck you?"

Mt 26: 66 - 68

# 16 Imperatives to the Christ

So the Jews gathered around him and said to him, "How long will you keep us in suspense? If you are the Christ, tell us plainly." Jesus answered them, "I told you, and you do not believe. Jn 10: 24–25a

## How to Salt a Steak

It is Saturday night. You are at your favorite fine dining restaurant. A perfectly cooked steak, exactly as you have ordered from the menu, has been placed before you. The salt shaker stands next to the pepper on the far side of the table. You have some options. You can pose a question and ask someone at the far side of the table seated near the salt, "Would you please pass me the salt?" Or, you can disregard a question and tell someone, "Please pass me the salt." Maybe you will salt your steak. Maybe you won't. Much depends on how you ask or how you tell. Salting your steak depends on what the hearer perceives. Of course, you can stand up, walk around the table and get the salt yourself. You don't need their help.

Your steak is getting cold. You want the salt. Maybe no one will recall if you verbally asked for the salt or if you told somebody to give you the salt. Maybe no one cares about your words or how you went about getting the salt from the other end of the table to your steak. Maybe either posing a question or voicing a command is irrelevant to the situation. It is a fine dining restaurant. Maybe a verbal question is more appropriate.

Not so with Jesus. His words were recorded. His Greek imperatives demanded much more than salt for a steak. Hungry? Below are the imperatives spoken to Jesus recorded by Matthew, Mark, Luke, and John.

## Greek Imperatives / English Commands Spoken to Jesus

The Gospel writers recorded Jesus' conversations. Some people asked him questions, and others demanded answers. Some spoke as superiors to him, some requested the blessings of him, and others commanded answers from him. How Jesus responded to the Greek imperatives spoken to him revealed much about Jesus to those who had commanded him, those who heard his responses and early readers of what the Gospel writers recorded. Did he do what they told him to do?

All four Gospel writers documented numerous people who had commanded Jesus to do or say something. Each Gospel writer recorded that Satan and demons commanded Jesus through spoken Greek imperatives. His disciples both as individuals and as a group had commanded him. A Canaanite woman, Roman soldiers, Chief Priests, temple leaders, religious leaders, Pharisees, Sadducees, lepers, the blind, and parents of sick children commanded Jesus what to do.

Not often does a private tell a general what to do. Not often does an employee tell an employer what to do. Not often does a player tell a coach what to do. Not often does a child tell a parent what to do. Not often does a disciple tell a rabbi what to do. You get the picture. We have all experienced the consequences of a misplaced command to a superior. Challenging authority by telling a boss what to do can be cause for immediate dismissal. So what happened when sinners told sinless Jesus, the paramount redeemer, the commander in chief, what to do?

People of different ranks, unique needs, demons, and Satan commanded him. His response to their commands revealed to them three truths. One, his humanity and divinity, second, his purpose, and third, his Kingdom. This chapter identifies each Greek morphological imperative recorded by Matthew, Mark, Luke, and John addressed to Jesus.

## Imperatives to Jesus in Matthew's Gospel

Satan Demanded a Miracle from Jesus
Mt 4: 1-6 Then Jesus was led up by the Spirit into the wilderness to be tempted by the devil. And after fasting forty days and forty nights, he was hungry. And the tempter came and said to him, "If you are the Son of God, command these stones to become loaves of bread." εἶπον ἵνα οἱ λίθοι οὗτοι ἄρτοι γένωνται. Then the devil took him to the holy city and set him on the pinnacle of the temple and said to him, "If you are the Son of God, throw yourself down βάλε σεαυτὸν κάτω, for it is written, "'He will command his angels concerning you,' and" 'On their hands they will bear you up, lest you strike your foot against a stone.'"

Satan's two imperatives are often referred to as "temptations." Satan's imperatives were beyond mere temptations. Satan expected Jesus to follow them. The Greek imperative carries a volition, an expectation that the imperative will be followed. Thus, Jesus knew that Satan expected Jesus to follow Satan's imperative.

Satan was fully aware that Jesus could turn stones into bread. He knew Jesus' power. Satan would not have commanded Jesus to turn stones into bread had Satan not known that Jesus, in fact, could turn stones into bread. He also knew angels would save Jesus if Jesus followed Satan's imperative to throw himself off the Temple peak. Satan's imperatives affirmed his knowledge of Jesus' sovereignty. In other words, Satan fully knew Jesus' power. Jesus was in control of all things and Satan knew it. While Jesus had the option of positively responding to Satan's commands, he did not. Jesus could have commanded the stones and he could have thrown himself off the Temple.

The Centurion's Imperative to Jesus
Mt 8: 5-10 When he entered Capernaum, a centurion came forward to him, appealing to him, "Lord, my servant is lying paralyzed at home, suffering terribly." And he said to him, "I will come and heal him." But the centurion replied, "Lord, I am not worthy to have you come under my roof, but only say the word, and my servant will be healed ἀλλὰ μόνον εἰπὲ λόγῳ καὶ ἰαθήσεται ὁ παῖς μου. For I too am a man under authority, with soldiers under me. And I say to one, 'Go,' and he goes, and to another, 'Come,' and he comes, and to my servant, 'Do this,' and he does it." When Jesus heard this, he marveled and said to those who followed him, "Truly, I tell you, with no one in Israel have I found such faith.

In the later narrative of Mt 8: 5-13, Jesus had been moved by the centurion's imperatives. Matthew affirmed Jesus emotions having recorded, "When Jesus heard this, he marveled." The centurion was accustomed to commanding his troops by direct orders. If the centurion spoke Greek his orders, his commands would have been formed with the imperative Greek form. More likely, however, is that the centurion spoke Latin (see Jn 19: 20). The centurion, like Jesus, knew the power of imperatives, his own and others. The centurion described three commands, "Go,"

"Come," and "Do this." Regardless of if the centurion spoke Latin or Greek, Matthew recorded each of the centurion's words as Greek imperatives.

There was no ambiguity within their conversation about the imperative commands from the centurion or imperative commands from Jesus. Latin imperative commands to Roman soldiers by the centurion or Greek imperative commands to disciples by Jesus were expected to be followed.

Jesus affirmed in v10 that the centurion's faith was beyond all in Israel. The dialogue between Jesus and the centurion included imperatives from both the centurion and Jesus. Jesus acknowledged the centurion's faith by confirming that the centurion understood the power of imperatives.

The most essential point of Matthew's record was that the centurion had first conveyed to Jesus that he knew the power and trustworthiness of Jesus' imperatives. Given that Jesus spoke of the centurion's commands, because of the centurion's faith in both Jesus and Jesus' imperatives, Jesus identified him as a man of great faith.

Imperatives from people of faith carry great power.

A Disciple's Imperative for Permission to Bury His Father
Mt 8: 21-22 Another of the disciples said to him, "Lord, let me first go and bury my father Κύριε ἐπίτρεψόν μοι πρῶτον ἀπελθεῖν καὶ θάψαι τὸν πατέρα μου." And Jesus said to him, "Follow me, and leave the dead to bury their own dead."
> One disciple spoke the imperative "let me go" to Jesus. The English format conveys that the phase, "and bury my father" is also a command. However, there is only one imperative from this particular disciple. Jesus responded with two imperatives.
>
> Jesus' first imperative was that the man follows Jesus and the second that the man leaves the dead bury the dead. Jesus did not positively respond to the disciple's imperative. Jesus did not grant this disciple his permission to go. Instead, Jesus was silent until he returned two spoken imperatives, "Follow me" and "leave the dead." Mt 8: 21–22

Disciples' Imperative for Salvation
Mt 8: 24-27 And behold, there arose a great storm on the sea, so that the boat was being swamped by the waves; but he was asleep. And they went and woke him, saying, "Save us, Lord; we are perishing Κύριε σῶσον ἀπολλύμεθα. And he said to them, "Why are you afraid, O you of little faith?" Then he rose and rebuked the winds and the sea, and there was a great calm. And the men marveled, saying, "What sort of man is this, that even winds and sea obey him?"
> The disciples in the boat were so afraid that they did not ask. They demanded that Jesus save them. Notice that before he calmed the wind and sea, he first asked them why they were afraid. His question to them chastised them for their fear which was the result of having little of faith. Not until after he had disciplined them did he rebuke the winds and sea. Here Jesus linked faith and lack of fear, a lesson that his

disciples linked in the future affirmed at the spreading of the Gospel. They spread the Gospel and performed miracles because not primarily because they were unafraid, but because their faith was strong enough to disregard fear.

Demon's Imperative to Jesus Regarding Pigs
Mt 8: 28–31 And when he came to the other side, to the country of the Gadarenes, two demon-possessed men met him, coming out of the tombs, so fierce that no one could pass that way. And behold, they cried out, "What have you to do with us, O Son of God? Have you come here to torment us before the time?" Now a herd of many pigs was feeding at some distance from them. And the demons begged him, saying, "If you cast us out, <u>send us away into the herd of pigs</u> ἀπόστειλον ἡμᾶς εἰς τὴν ἀγέλην τῶν χοίρων.

> Matthew recorded an imperative in that the demons had commanded Jesus to send them into the herd of pigs. Some translations (NKJ, YLT) use the word "permit" instead of "send" which does not convey the clear Greek imperative spoken by the demons to Jesus. The ESV unnecessarily included the word "away" where the English from the Greek is more accurately, simply and understandably translated, "send us into the pigs." Lk 8: 26-34; Mk 5: 12

Two Blind Men's Imperative to Jesus for Mercy
Mt 9: 27 And as Jesus passed on from there, two blind men followed him, crying aloud, "<u>Have mercy on us, Son of David</u> Ἐλέησον ἡμᾶς υἱὲ Δαυίδ."

> Here the two blind men loudly cried and demanded mercy from Jesus. There is no biblical evidence that these two men had any prior relationship with Jesus. Matthew recorded that they had cried aloud, likely to make their commands known to others in earshot of Jesus. In addition to their command, "Have mercy on us," they said, "Son of David" as leverage publically affirming that they knew Jesus without having previously met him. See Mt 8: 28 for Jesus' imperative answer to them.

Pharisees Imperative That Jesus Take Notice
Mt 12: 1-6 At that time Jesus went through the grain fields on the Sabbath. His disciples were hungry, and they began to pluck heads of grain and to eat. But when the Pharisees saw it, they said to him, "<u>Look</u> Ἰδοὺ, your disciples are doing what is not lawful to do on the Sabbath." He said to them, "Have you not read what David did when he was hungry, and those who were with him: how he entered the house of God and ate the bread of the Presence, which it was not lawful for him to eat nor for those who were with him, but only for the priests? Or have you not read in the Law how on the Sabbath the priests in the temple profane the Sabbath and are guiltless? I tell you, something greater μεῖζόν than the temple is here.

> The Pharisees stated a one word imperative, "Look" which had commanded that Jesus must see for himself the failures of his disciples. Their imperative could have been a literal "Look" as well as a metaphorical, more like, "You, Jesus need to understand." Their imperative also conveyed that the Pharisees knew the law as well.

Their imperative was their attempt to expose that Jesus did not know the law. Matthew did not record that Jesus looked nor conceded their claim. Jesus initially responded with questions. His ending sentence conveyed that he, the Messiah, who is greater than the temple, had arrived. Jesus had told them in Mt 12: 6 "something greater than the Temple is here." Jesus clarified beyond merely seeing via a visual command. His greatness surpasses that of the Temple.

Most English translation use "something greater is coming" or "one greater is coming." But Matthew did not record "something" or "one." The YLT is more accurate with the translation, "that a greater than temple is here." The English word "greater" is derived from the Greek word μεῖζόν a comparative, neuter, singular, nominative adjective.

Disciples' Demanded Jesus to Explain a Parable
Mt 13: 36 Then he left the crowds and went into the house. And his disciples came to him, saying, "Explain to us the parable of the weeds of the field Διασάφησον ἡμῖν τὴν παραβολὴν τῶν ζιζανίων τοῦ ἀγροῦ." He answered, "The one who sows the good seed is the Son of Man. The field is the world, and the good seed is the sons of the kingdom. The weeds are the sons of the evil one, and the enemy who sowed them is the devil. The harvest is the close of the age, and the reapers are angels.

> Matthew did not record the name of a person or persons stating the imperative. He recorded the imperative in plural form. One or two of the disciples likely posed the question and the others agreed. A group demanded an explanation of the parable, and Jesus quickly responded by clarifying the parable. In context, it appears as if the disciples were so wanting clarification that posing a question was a waste of time. Matthew likely in the group who recorded their words, wanted clarification as well. Their perceived urgency left no time to ask, only time to demand from Jesus the clarity they sought.

Disciples' Imperative to Send Crowds Away
Mt 14: 15 Now when it was evening, the disciples came to him and said, "This is a desolate place, and the day is now over; send the crowds away to go into the villages and buy food for themselves ἀπόλυσον τοὺς ὄχλους ἵνα ἀπελθόντες εἰς τὰς κώμας ἀγοράσωσιν ἑαυτοῖς βρώματα." But Jesus said, "They need not go away; you give them something to eat."

> Perhaps due to their exhaustion, the disciples did not engage Jesus in dialogue. Matthew recorded that they as a group had chosen the imperative "send." Jesus, however, did not comply nor fulfill their imperative. He did not send the crowds away. Instead he responded with an imperative that his disciples, the one who had commanded Jesus to send the crowd away give the people something to eat.
> Lk 9: 12–14; Mk 6: 36

Peter's Imperative to Jesus
Mt 14: 25-29 And in the fourth watch of the night he came to them, walking on the sea. But when the disciples saw him walking on the sea, they were terrified, and said, "It is a ghost!" and they cried out in fear. But immediately Jesus spoke to them, saying, "Take heart it is I Θαρσεῖτε ἐγώ εἰμι. Do not be afraid μὴ φοβεῖσθε." And Peter answered him, "Lord, if it is you, command me to come to you κέλευσόν με ἐλθεῖν πρός σε on the water." He said, "Come ἐλθέ." So Peter got out of the boat and walked on the water and came to Jesus.

> Jesus had initially stated two imperatives, the first was "Take heart." The second imperative was "Do not be afraid." Jesus said these two imperatives before Peter replied to Jesus with his imperative. Hearing Peter's imperative Jesus quickly

answered with his third imperative, "come." Peter after having heard the Lord's words and after having seen Jesus walk on water spoke an imperative to Jesus. What is often absent in the English is clarification that Peter had first commanded Jesus to command Peter. Matthew recorded four spoken imperatives within this dialogue. Three were from Jesus, 'Take heart." "Do not be afraid." and "Come." One was from Peter, "Command me to come to you."

Effectively, Peter with his growing faith told Jesus what to do. Jesus after having heard Peter's imperative did what Peter had commanded. Without hesitation as soon as Jesus heard Peter's imperative, Jesus responded to Peter with his own imperative, "Come." There was power in both Peter's and Jesus' commands. Peter had intentionally commanded Jesus for an imperative command.

Beyond Peter walking on water, there was another miracle in process. Peter and the disciples in the boat who saw and heard the verbal exchange between Peter and Jesus would no longer doubt the power of Jesus' imperatives. Those in the boat having heard Jesus' imperative to Peter, knew the authority of Jesus' imperative. They were learning the power of Jesus' imperatives. They were also learning the power of their own imperatives through Jesus.

Peter's imperative, "Command me to come to you." And Jesus' responsive imperative in return, "Come." Followed by Peter walking on water in fulfillment of both imperatives taught a lesson to those in the boat as well as to Peter.

Peter's Imperative for Clarification
Mt 15: 15 But Peter said to him, "Explain the parable to us Φράσον ἡμῖν τὴν παραβολήν." And he said, "Are you also still without understanding? Do you not see that whatever goes into the mouth passes into the stomach and is expelled? But what comes out of the mouth proceeds from the heart, and this defiles a person. For out of the heart come evil thoughts, murder, adultery, sexual immorality, theft, false witness, slander. These are what defile a person. But to eat with unwashed hands does not defile anyone."

    Following Peter's imperative, Jesus straightaway explained the parable. He asked a series of questions and followed up with more explanation. Here it may be that Peter was exercising his imperatives. Perhaps Matthew recorded that Peter was thinking his relationship was so close to Jesus, that Peter was exercising his imperative power through Jesus. An entreaty imperative as a means of asking rather than commanding is appropriate. Mk 7: 17

Canaanite Woman's Imperative to Jesus
Mt 15: 21-28 And Jesus went away from there and withdrew to the district of Tyre and Sidon. And behold, a Canaanite woman from that region came out and was crying, "Have mercy on me, O Lord, Son of David Ἐλέησόν με κύριε υἱὸς Δαυίδ; my daughter is severely oppressed by a demon." But he did not answer her a word. And his disciples came and begged him, saying, "Send her away, for she is crying out after us Ἀπόλυσον αὐτήν ὅτι κράζει ὄπισθεν ἡμῶν." He answered, "I was sent only to the lost sheep of the house of Israel." But she came and knelt before him, saying, "Lord, help me Κύριε βοήθει μοι." And he answered, "It is not right to take the children's bread and throw

it to the dogs." She said, "Yes, Lord, yet even the dogs eat the crumbs that fall from their masters' table." Then Jesus answered her, "O woman, great is your faith! Be it done for you as you desire." And her daughter was healed instantly.

>Matthew recorded that Jesus heard three imperatives. The first imperative was from the woman, the second from the disciples, and the third was again from the woman. Matthew recorded that Jesus completely ignored the disciples' command to Jesus that he must send her away. Rather Jesus responded to the woman's imperatives. He acknowledged her faith and then commanded that what she desired would be done as she had demanded.

>The healing of her daughter immediately followed Jesus' imperative which followed both imperatives from the woman, "Have mercy on me" and "help me." What is easily often overlooked in English is Jesus' unresponsiveness to the disciple's imperative. The disciples should have perceived the woman's demands for mercy and help. The disciples perhaps missed the insight that her faith had preceded her commands. Jesus ignored his disciple's imperative to send her away.

A Man with an Epileptic Son and the Weakness of Disciples
Mt 17: 14-20 And when they came to the crowd, a man came up to him and, kneeling before him, said, "Lord, have mercy on my son Κύριε ἐλέησόν μου τὸν υἱόν, for he is an epileptic and he suffers terribly. For often he falls into the fire, and often into the water. And I brought him to your disciples, and they could not heal him." And Jesus answered, "O faithless and twisted generation, how long am I to be with you? How long am I to bear with you? Bring him here to me." And Jesus rebuked the demon, and it came out of him, and the boy was healed instantly. Then the disciples came to Jesus privately and said, "Why could we not cast it out?" He said to them, "Because of your little faith. For truly, I say to you, if you have faith like a grain of mustard seed, you will say to this mountain, 'Move from here to there,' and it will move, and nothing will be impossible for you."

>The father of the epilepsy son had spoken an imperative to Jesus that explained that Jesus' disciples were unable to heal the man's son. Jesus responded with two imperatives, the first one to the father, "Bring him here to me." His next imperative second to his disciples was, "Move from here to there" by way of commanding a mountain to move. Jesus' was teaching his disciples the power of imperatives to both heal and move mountains. However, at this point, his disciples were unable to heal the epileptic son much less move a mountain with imperatives. Jesus' lesson on their imperatives to move mountains was a primer lesson showing them that nothing would be impossible for them.

The Pharisees as a Group Demanded Insight from Jesus
Mt 22: 17 Tell us, then, what you think εἶπον οὖν ἡμῖν τί σοι δοκεῖ. Is it lawful to pay taxes to Caesar, or not?"

>The Pharisees were more than exasperated with Jesus' ability with words. Their imperative, "Tell us then, what you think," affirmed their desire to entrap him. Jesus knew their method of using an imperative to him that was heard by those near them.

Disciples Demanded to Know When
Mt 24: 3 As he sat on the Mount of Olives, the disciples came to him privately, saying, "Tell us, when will these things be εἶπον ἡμῖν πότε ταῦτα ἔσται, and what will be the sign of your coming and of the close of the age?" And Jesus answered them, "See that no one leads you astray Βλέπετε μή τις ὑμᾶς πλανήσῃ·

> Jesus answered their imperative "Tell us," by giving them an imperative "See that no one leads you astray." The rest of the verses in Mt 24 provided details. Jesus more than answered their imperative. He explained the end of the age both when and how.

Virgins without Oil Demanding the Lord Open the Door to Them
Mt 25: 1–13 "Then the kingdom of heaven will be like ten virgins who took their lamps and went to meet the bridegroom. Five of them were foolish, and five were wise. For when the foolish took their lamps, they took no oil with them, but the wise took flasks of oil with their lamps. As the bridegroom was delayed, they all became drowsy and slept. But at midnight there was a cry, 'Here is the bridegroom! Come out to meet him.' Then all those virgins rose and trimmed their lamps. And the foolish said to the wise, 'Give us some of your oil, for our lamps are going out.' But the wise answered, saying, 'Since there will not be enough for us and for you, go rather to the dealers and buy for yourselves.' And while they were going to buy, the bridegroom came, and those who were ready went in with him to the marriage feast, and the door was shut. Afterward the other virgins came also, saying, 'Lord, lord, open to us.' But he answered, 'Truly, I say to you, I do not know you.' Watch therefore, for you know neither the day nor the hour.

> Here Jesus requoted the imperative from the virgins without oil for their lamps, "Lord, lord, open to us." After Jesus conveyed that the Lord did not know those without the oil, Jesus immediately spoke an imperative to those listening to the parable, "Watch therefore, for you know neither the day nor the hour."

Chief Priests and the Whole Council Demanded that Jesus Prophesy to Them
Mt 26: 66–68 What is your judgment?" They answered, "He deserves death." Then they spit in his face and struck him. And some slapped him, saying, "Prophesy to us you, Christ! προφήτευσον ἡμῖν, χριστέ Who is it that struck you?"

> Here some from the Chief Priests and the whole council gave Jesus an imperative to prophesy that he is the Christ. The sardonic irony is easier to grasp in Greek than English. Their admission had fulfilled their imperative. They called him the Christ, which was true. They commanded him to prophesy to them, and by their admission, they had verbally affirmed Jesus as their Messiah. What they thought was mockery was true to the core. Jesus was their Messiah. Their contemptuous words affirmed reality, yet they refused to accept the truth in their words. The irony either heard or read in Greek would have been clear to those who heard their words or those who read their words in the first-century context. Insight and satire are nearly impossible to glean in English given that ultimately he had prophesied to them that he was, in fact, the Messiah, the Christ. The Greek imperative used by those who persecuted Jesus illuminated then what is not so easy to translate into English today. Their demand that Jesus should prophesy that he was whom he said he was had been affirmed in their own words. Readers and hearers of the Greek text likely grasped the wisdom and irony of Matthew's record which is difficult to glean in English.

# Imperatives to Jesus in Mark's Gospel

Demons Demanded that Jesus Send Them into the Pigs
Mk 5: 12 and they begged him, saying, "<u>Send us to the pigs</u> Πέμψον ἡμᾶς εἰς τοὺς χοίρους; let us enter them." So he gave them permission. And the unclean spirits came out, and entered the pigs, and the herd, numbering about two thousand, rushed down the steep bank into the sea and were drowned in the sea.

> Demons gave Jesus an imperative, "Send us to the pigs" and Jesus complied as they had demanded. The immediate consequence following their command was that the pigs, having been invaded by demons, drowned in the sea. Only Mark recorded that the demons gave Jesus an imperative to send them into the pigs. Parallel passages casting out demons from a demoniac man into swine are Mt 8: 28-32 and Lk 8: 26-34. Only Matthew and Mark recorded an imperative to Jesus from the demons. Luke did not record any imperatives from the demons perhaps because Luke was not an eyewitness or hearer of Jesus' words. In Lk 8: 32 Luke recorded, "Now a large herd of pigs was feeding there on the hillside, and they begged him to let them enter these. So he gave them permission." While Luke recorded the event, he did not use imperatives nor quoted the demons. Luke described the situation. Matthew and Mark likely were present with Jesus and the demonic man when this event occurred.

Disciples Demanded Jesus Send Crowd Away
Mk 6: 35-39 And when it grew late, his disciples came to him and said, "This is a desolate place, and the hour is now late. <u>Send them away</u> ἀπόλυσον αὐτούς to go into the surrounding countryside and villages and buy themselves something to eat." But he answered them, "<u>You give them something to eat</u> Δότε αὐτοῖς ὑμεῖς φαγεῖν." And they said to him, "Shall we go and buy two hundred denarii worth of bread and give it to them to eat?" And he said to them, "How many loaves do you have? Go and see." And when they had found out, they said, "Five, and two fish." Then he commanded them all to sit down in groups on the green grass.

> The disciples had commanded Jesus to send the crowd away, but Jesus' answered with an imperative to them to give the people something to eat. Jesus did not follow their imperative. Instead, Jesus gave them an imperative that he expected and knew would be followed. The crowd was eventually fed just as Jesus had commanded.
> Lk 9: 12–13; Mt 14: 15

Father of Epileptic Son
Mk 9: 20-27 And they brought the boy to him. And when the spirit saw him, immediately it convulsed the boy, and he fell on the ground and rolled about, foaming at the mouth. And Jesus asked his father, "How long has this been happening to him?" And he said, "From childhood. And it has often cast him into fire and into water, to destroy him. But if you can do anything, have compassion on us and <u>help us</u> βοήθησον ἡμῖν σπλαγχνισθεὶς ἐφ ἡμᾶς." And Jesus said to him, "'If you can'! All things are possible for one who believes." Immediately the father of the child cried out and said, "I believe; <u>help my unbelief</u> βοήθει μου τῇ ἀπιστίᾳ!" And Jesus said to him, "'If you can'! All things are possible for one who believes." And when Jesus saw that a crowd came running together, he rebuked the unclean spirit, saying to it, "You mute and deaf spirit, I command you, <u>come out of him and never enter him again</u>." And after crying out and convulsing him terribly, it

came out, and the boy was like a corpse, so that most of them said, "He is dead." But Jesus took him by the hand and lifted him up, and he arose.

>The father's first imperative to Jesus demanded that Jesus help them by having compassion on them. The English translation, "have compassion on us and help us" sound like two imperatives, "have compassion" and "help us" but there is only one imperative, "help." The father's second imperative found later in the text was that Jesus would help the father's unbelief. Notice the exchange of imperatives. Jesus then spoke an imperative to the mute and deaf spirit. Here Jesus linked belief with imperatives to heal and cast out a demon. Jesus did not dialogue with the demon. He first criticized the demon for being mute and deaf. Then Jesus spoke an imperative that commanded the demon to come out of him.

James and John Demanded Special Recognition
Mk 10: 35-27 And James and John, the sons of Zebedee, came up to him and said to him, "Teacher, we want you to do for us whatever we ask of you." And he said to them, "What do you want me to do for you?" And they said to him, "Grant us to sit, one at your right hand and one at your left, in your glory Δὸς ἡμῖν ἵνα εἷς σου ἐκ δεξιῶν καὶ εἷς ἐξ ἀριστερῶν καθίσωμεν ἐν τῇ δόξῃ σου." Jesus said to them, "You do not know what you are asking. Are you able to drink the cup that I drink, or to be baptized with the baptism with which I am baptized?" And they said to him, "We are able." And Jesus said to them, "The cup that I drink you will drink, and with the baptism with which I am baptized, you will be baptized, but to sit at my right hand or at my left is not mine to grant, but it is for those for whom it has been prepared." And when the ten heard it, they began to be indignant at James and John.

>James and John in earshot of the other disciples had ordered Jesus to give them special recognition. They did not ask. They demanded. Mark recorded that they spoke an imperative which disgruntled the other disciples. They could have asked in private, but Mark conveyed that James and John directed Jesus in earshot of the others. The disciples were offended by the both the arrogance and request from James and John. Further, the disciples were disgruntled with the way James and John had verbalized their command through their imperatives to Jesus.

Blind Man Demanded Mercy
Mk 10: 46–52 And they came to Jericho. And as he was leaving Jericho with his disciples and a great crowd, Bartimaeus, a blind beggar, the son of Timaeus, was sitting by the roadside. And when he heard that it was Jesus of Nazareth, he began to cry out and say, "Jesus, Son of David, have mercy on me Υἱὲ Δαυὶδ Ἰησοῦ ἐλέησόν με!" And many rebuked him, telling him to be silent. But he cried out all the more, "Son of David, have mercy on me ὁ δὲ πολλῷ μᾶλλον ἔκραζεν Υἱὲ Δαυὶδ ἐλέησόν με!" And Jesus stopped and said, "Call him." And they called the blind man, saying to him, "Take heart. Get up; he is calling you." And throwing off his cloak, he sprang up and came to Jesus. And Jesus said to him, "What do you want me to do for you?" And the blind man said to him, "Rabbi, let me recover my sight." And Jesus said to him, "Go your way; your faith has made you well." And immediately he recovered his sight and followed him on the way.

>Mark recorded six imperatives in this narrative. The first two imperatives were from the blind beggar. He twice demanded mercy. The third was from Jesus to the others to, "call him." The group then said two more imperatives to the blind beggar, "Take heart," and "get up." Mark recorded the sixth imperative from Jesus, "go your own

way" and then recorded that Bartimaeus had recovered his sight and went on his way as Jesus had commanded. Mark's recording of successive imperatives is no mistake.

Note that immediately after the large crowd had commanded Bartimaeus to "take heart" and "get up," he responded as they had commanded. Then Jesus issued his final command with a sixth imperative that the formerly blind beggar "go your way." Jesus had heard the imperatives of Bartimaeus. The blind beggar highlighted the power of Jesus' imperatives. The blind beggar also uncovered the power of his own imperatives to Jesus for mercy.

Peter and the Dead Fig Tree
Mk 11: 20-22 As they passed by in the morning, they saw the fig tree withered away to its roots. And Peter remembered and said to him, "Rabbi, look Ραββί ἴδε! The fig tree that you cursed has withered." And Jesus answered them, "Have faith in God."

    First, Peter had exhorted Jesus with an imperative. Then Jesus replied to Peter with the imperative, "Have faith in God." Peter's imperative to Jesus sounds simple enough. But Mark had previously clarified that Peter had, "remembered" before Peter gave the imperative, "look" to Jesus. Mt 21: 20 – 22

Peter, James, John and Andrew Demanded to Know the End
Mk 13: 3-4 And as he sat on the Mount of Olives opposite the temple, Peter and James and John and Andrew asked him privately, "Tell us Εἰπὸν ἡμῖν, when will these things be, and what will be the sign when all these things are about to be accomplished?"

    Peter, James, John, and Andrew did not make their imperative to Jesus in public but in private. Their imperative in private conveyed their sincere desire to know as soon as possible what was soon to happen.

Some Chief Priests, Elders, and Scribes Demanded Jesus Prophesy
Mk 14: 60–65 And the high priest stood up in the midst and asked Jesus, "Have you no answer to make? What is it that these men testify against you?" But he remained silent and made no answer. Again the high priest asked him, "Are you the Christ, the Son of the Blessed?" And Jesus said, "I am, and you will see the Son of Man seated at the right hand of Power, and coming with the clouds of heaven." And the high priest tore his garments and said, "What further witnesses do we need? You have heard his blasphemy. What is your decision?" And they all condemned him as deserving death. And some began to spit on him and to cover his face and to strike him, saying to him, "Prophesy Προφήτευσον!" And the guards received him with blows.

    Here, after questioning intended to support their charges of blasphemy, the Chief Priests, Elders, and Scribes demanded that Jesus prophecy to them. Their imperatives Prophesy" by some showed that they had forgotten that just minutes before Jesus had already prophesied his death and resurrection to them (v58). Mt 26: 66 – 68 this chapter.

Pilate Demanded Jesus Know the Charges from Jewish Leaders
Mk 15: 4 And Pilate asked him, "Are you the King of the Jews?" And he answered him, "You have said so." And the chief priests accused him of many things. And Pilate again asked him,

"Have you no answer to make? <u>See how many charges they bring against you</u> ἴδε πόσα σου κατηγοροῦσιν."

> Mark recorded Pilate's imperative to Jesus, "See how many charges they bring against you." to assert that the Jewish leaders, Pilate, and Jesus knew the charges. Pilate did not ask Jesus if he knew the charges. Pilate had commanded Jesus to know the charges. English sometimes conveys emotion at the expense of the reality. Greek conveys the certainty.

Soldiers Saluted and Mocked With Imperative to Him and Listeners
Mk 15: 16–18 And the soldiers led him away inside the palace (that is, the governor's headquarters), and they called together the whole battalion. And they clothed him in a purple cloak, and twisting together a crown of thorns, they put it on him. And they began to salute him, "<u>Hail, King of the Jews</u> Χαῖρε βασιλεῦ τῶν Ἰουδαίων·

> Note Mark's inclusion of the whole battalion. Mark made sure that the readers of his Gospel record were aware that they sardonically and mockingly hailed Jesus as King of the Jews. The soldiers were unaware that their cynical words were true.

Passersby Demanded Jesus Save Himself
Mk 15: 29-30 And those who passed by derided him, wagging their heads and saying, "Aha! You who would destroy the temple and rebuild it in three days, <u>save yourself, and come down from the cross</u> σῶσον σεαυτὸν, καταβὰς ἀπὸ τοῦ σταυροῦ.

> The English text reads as if there are two imperatives, "save yourself" and "come down" but there is only one imperative, "save yourself." A more literal translation conveying the Greek participle "coming" may be, "Save yourself coming down from the cross." Both are acceptable. The context conveys mockery in one sense. Ironically their exhortation that Jesus come off the cross to save himself, unbeknownst to them, was true. In one sense, Jesus did not follow their imperatives. He could have, but he did not. In another sense, Jesus saved himself from the cross by overcoming it. He is no longer on the cross.

## Imperatives to Jesus in Luke's Gospel

Satan Commanded Jesus to Turn Stone into Bread
Lk 4: 1–4 And Jesus, full of the Holy Spirit, returned from the Jordan and was led by the Spirit in the wilderness for forty days, being tempted by the devil. And he ate nothing during those days. And when they were ended, he was hungry. The devil said to him, "If you are the Son of God, <u>command this stone to become bread</u> εἰπὲ τῷ λίθῳ τούτῳ ἵνα γένηται ἄρτος." And Jesus answered him, "It is written, 'Man shall not live by bread alone.'"

> The ESV chose the English word, "command" but the Greek word that Mark recorded was, "say" or "speak." Note Luke's chronology. Satan's imperative here came after Jesus had been filled with the Holy Spirit from v1. The devil knew the power of Jesus' spoken words. Rather than Jesus fulfill the devil's imperative, Jesus denied his imperative and cited Dt 8: 3. See Mt 4: 1–4; Mk 1: 13: Note that Mark did not record the conversation of Jesus and Satan. Mark only provided a brief affirmation of Jesus' 40 days in the wilderness, nothing more. Luke not having been present and relying on testimonies from others, likely is more accurate in detail.

Satan Commanded Jesus to Throw Himself from the Temple[1]
Lk 4: 9–12 And he took him to Jerusalem and set him on the pinnacle of the temple and said to him, "If you are the Son of God, <u>throw yourself down from here</u> βάλε σεαυτὸν ἐντεῦθεν κάτω for it is written, "'He will command his angels concerning you, to guard you,' and "'On their hands they will bear you up, lest you strike your foot against a stone.'" And Jesus answered him, "It is said, 'You shall not put the Lord your God to the test.'"

> The English command, "throw" is appropriate which conveys that Satan knew Jesus, now filled with the Holy Spirit and intentional on following the father's will, was in control of his body. Jesus had the power to remain or throw himself from the temple peak. Taking this further, Jesus was also in control of his mission which included the cross, his death, resurrection, ascension, reception of all authority that would be given to him, and his ever presence with his followers. Mt 4:6

Peter Demanded Jesus to Depart From Him
Lk 5: 8 But when Simon Peter saw it, he fell down at Jesus' knees, saying, "<u>Depart from me</u> Εξελθε ἀπ ἐμοῦ, for I am a sinful man, O Lord."

> Upon Peter's awareness of his sins following a great catch of fish from the deep, Peter's imperative, "depart from me," is understandable. Peter realized that he and Jesus were not equals. Peter's sins and Jesus' purity are opposition.

Centurion Commanded Jesus, not to Trouble Himself
Lk 7: 1–7 After he had finished all his sayings in the hearing of the people, he entered Capernaum. Now a centurion had a servant who was sick and at the point of death, who was highly valued by him. When the centurion heard about Jesus, he sent to him elders of the Jews, asking him to come and heal his servant. And when they came to Jesus, they pleaded with him earnestly, saying, "He is worthy to have you do this for him, for he loves our nation, and he is the one who built us our synagogue." And Jesus went with them. When he was not far from the house, the centurion sent friends, saying to him, "<u>Lord, do not trouble yourself</u> Κύριε μὴ σκύλλου οὐ, for I am not worthy to have you come under my roof. Therefore I did not presume to come to you. But say the word, and let my servant be healed.

> The English word, "trouble" could also be, "annoy" or "bother" which meant to them that the centurion knew his rank was below Jesus in authority. The centurion's phrase, "but say the word" went beyond his knowledge about rank. He conveyed his knowledge, faith, and trust in Jesus' words. His trust showed his both his faith and his knowledge of Jesus and the power of Jesus' imperatives. Mt 8: 8

---

[1] Within this dialogue between Satan and Jesus, we are wise to remember that this verbal exchange would have been taught by Jesus to his disciples after it had happened. Neither Matthew, Mark, Luke, nor John was standing on the Temple ridge listening to their dialogue. Jesus shared this encounter with Satan with his disciples.

Simon Commanded Jesus to Tell Simon What Jesus Had to Say
Lk 7: 36-40 One of the Pharisees asked him to eat with him, and he went into the Pharisee's house and took his place at the table. And behold, a woman of the city, who was a sinner, when she learned that he was reclining at table in the Pharisee's house, brought an alabaster flask of ointment, and standing behind him at his feet, weeping, she began to wet his feet with her tears and wiped them with the hair of her head and kissed his feet and anointed them with the ointment. Now when the Pharisee who had invited him saw this, he said to himself, "If this man were a prophet, he would have known who and what sort of woman this is who is touching him, for she is a sinner." And Jesus answering said to him, "Simon, I have something to say to you." And he answered, "Say it, Teacher Διδάσκαλε εἰπέ φησίν."

> Simon the Pharisee whose home Jesus had entered was bold enough to demand that Jesus tell Simon of his error. Jesus then told a parable. From Simon's criticism of the woman and the ointment, Jesus chose not to castigate Simon directly.

Disciples Demanded Jesus to Send the Crowd Away
Lk 9: 12-13 Now the day began to wear away, and the twelve came and said to him, "Send the crowd away Ἀπόλυσον τὸν ὄχλον to go into the surrounding villages and countryside to find lodging and get provisions, for we are here in a desolate place." But he said to them, "You give them something to eat." They said, "We have no more than five loaves and two fish--unless we are to go and buy food for all these people."

> The intensity of the imperative conveyed the disciples' resolve. They could have asked a question, but Luke recorded that they chose an imperative. The twelve were in agreement on the imperative to send the crowd away. Nevertheless, Jesus responded with an imperative. Those who gave Jesus the imperative to send the crowd away were commanded to feed the crowd with his imperative command to them. Mt 14: 15; Mk 6: 36

Two Men Told Jesus to Give Them More Time
Lk 9: 59-61 To another he said, "Follow me." But he said, "Lord, let me first go and bury my father ἐπίτρεψόν μοι πρῶτον ἀπελθόντι θάψαι τὸν πατέρα μου." And Jesus said to him, "Leave the dead to bury their own dead. But as for you, go and proclaim the kingdom of God." Yet another said, "I will follow you, Lord, but let me first say farewell to those at my home πρῶτον δὲ ἐπίτρεψόν μοι ἀποτάξασθαι τοῖς εἰς τὸν οἶκόν μου." Jesus said to him, "No one who puts his hand to the plow and looks back is fit for the kingdom of God."

> The men's two imperatives to Jesus, "let me go" and "let me bury" for permission to delay with what may have appeared as a reasonable excuse were ineffective. Jesus responded with a series of imperatives and with a visual story. Looking back on the dead is without value in the Kingdom of God.

Disciples Demanded Jesus to Teach Them to Pray
Lk 11: 1 Now Jesus was praying in a certain place, and when he finished, one of his disciples said to him, "Lord, teach us to pray Κύριε δίδαξον ἡμᾶς προσεύχεσθαι, as John taught his disciples."

> Here his disciples commanded Jesus to teach them. Their imperative holds an urgency. They were not interested in discussion. They wanted to be taught. Within Jesus teaching them he included many imperatives within the Lord's Prayer. Chapter 15: "The Imperatives of Jesus in the Lord's Prayer"

Brother Demanded Jesus to Force an Inheritance
Lk 12: 13-15 Someone in the crowd said to him, "Teacher, tell my brother to divide the inheritance with me Διδάσκαλε εἰπὲ τῷ ἀδελφῷ μου μερίσασθαι μετ ἐμοῦ τὴν κληρονομίαν." But he said to him, "Man, who made me a judge or arbitrator over you?" And he said to them, "Take care, and be on your guard against all covetousness, for one's life does not consist in the abundance of his possessions."

> An imperative from an individual in a crowd that Jesus secures his inheritance did not stop Jesus from responding with an imperative. Jesus' imperative "Take care, and be on your guard against all covetousness" exposed the coveted heart of the person who demanded Jesus to intercede with the man's brother for his inheritance.

Pharisees Told Jesus to Leave for His own Safety
Lk 13: 31-32 At that very hour some Pharisees came and said to him, "Get away from here Ἐξελθε καὶ πορεύου ἐντεῦθεν, for Herod wants to kill you." And he said to them, "Go and tell that fox, 'Behold, I cast out demons and perform cures today and tomorrow, and the third day I finish my course.

> In the Greek text there are two imperatives. While the ESV, "Get away from here" is acceptable, perhaps more aligning with the Greek imperative in context is, "get out" and "keep going." As critical as Jesus often was of the Pharisees, here the Pharisees intended to protect Jesus from Herod's hatred and wrath toward Jesus. Jesus responded with two more imperatives with his statement, "Go and tell that fox." Jesus' imperatives assured that Jesus' words would get back to Herod through the Pharisees.

Apostles Demanded Jesus to Increase Their Faith
Lk 17: 5-6 The apostles said to the Lord, "Increase our faith Πρόσθες ἡμῖν πίστιν!" And the Lord said, "If you had faith like a grain of mustard seed, you could say to this mulberry tree, 'Be uprooted and planted in the sea,' and it would obey you.

> The apostles through an imperative to Jesus demanded their faith increase. Jesus immediately responded with an imperative within of a story about faith. The apostles did not ask. Instead, they demanded that Jesus increase their faith. Jesus did not respond with a direct imperative to them. Instead Jesus used an example of imperatives to the tree.

> He taught power that went beyond merely uprooting a tree to having it planted in the sea. Jesus' imperatives exemplified a more profound consequence as a result of increased faith. Here Jesus affirmed that with faith their words and their spoken imperatives held power and authority.

Ten Lepers Demanded that Jesus give them Mercy
Lk 17: 12-14 And as he entered a village, he was met by ten lepers, who stood at a distance and lifted up their voices, saying, "Jesus, Master, have mercy on us Ἰησοῦ ἐπιστάτα ἐλέησον ἡμᾶς." When he saw them he said to them, "Go and show yourselves to the priests." And as they went they were cleansed.

> Preceding their imperative they had called Jesus by name and had publically affirmed Jesus by the title, "Master." The Lepers did not ask. They demanded that

Jesus have mercy on them. Luke did not record that Jesus responded with their immediate healing. Rather Jesus demanded through an imperative that they go and show themselves to the priests (note plural priests, not singular). They were not instantaneously healed but were healed before arriving in front of the priests. The English word, "go" by Jesus to English ears sounds like an imperative, but the verb is aorist, passive, nominative, masculine, plural, participle. The YLT more accurately translates as, "having gone" which conveys the idea that after they arrive something will have happened.

The word, "go" is not an incorrect translation but does not convey the Greek aorist participle. Jesus' imperative was "show" or "prove" or "affirm" a second person plural imperative. They as a group were to "show themselves to the priests" as an affirmation of the healing that had occurred while they were in transit or "as they went" to see the priests. Here their healing was not instantaneous, but occurred over time while they were in transit. The text itself, "and as they went they were cleansed" affirms that healing had happened at a specific time in their travel or during the time of their travels.

Blind Beggar Demanded Jesus to give him Mercy
Lk 18: 35-43 As he drew near to Jericho, a blind man was sitting by the roadside begging. And hearing a crowd going by, he inquired what this meant. They told him, "Jesus of Nazareth is passing by." And he cried out, <u>Jesus, Son of David, have mercy on me</u> Ιησοῦ υἱὲ Δαυίδ ἐλέησόν με!" And those who were in front rebuked him, telling him to be silent. But he cried out all the more, "<u>Son of David, have mercy on me</u> Υἱὲ Δαυίδ ἐλέησόν με!" And Jesus stopped and commanded him to be brought to him. And when he came near, he asked him, "What do you want me to do for you?" He said, "Lord, let me recover my sight." And Jesus said to him, "<u>Recover your sight</u>; your faith has made you well." And immediately he recovered his sight and followed him, glorifying God. And all the people, when they saw it, gave praise to God.
 The blind beggar stated two imperatives, both demands. He twice named, Jesus, "Son of David" as well as publically identified Jesus as "Lord" in v41. Luke recorded the blind man's words as an aorist subjunctive and is correctly translated "let me recover my sight." Jesus responded with an imperative "Recover your sight." Without delay, the blind man's sight was restored.

The blind man's dual affirmation of Jesus as Son of David, his having identified and affirmed Jesus as Lord, his two imperatives that Jesus have mercy on him, and his aorist subjunctive to recover his sight, each contributes to Mark's narrative. Mark then concluded that all the people saw and praised God. What the crowd saw and heard was the fulfillment of imperatives.

Men Held Jesus and Demanded that He Prophesy to Them
Lk 22: 63-71 Now the men who were holding Jesus in custody were mocking him as they beat him. They also blindfolded him and kept asking him, "<u>Prophesy! Who is it that struck you?</u>" Προφήτευσον τίς ἐστιν ὁ παίσας σε?" And they said many other things against him, blaspheming him. When day came, the assembly of the elders of the people gathered together, both chief priests and scribes. And they led him away to their council, and they said, "<u>If you are the Christ, tell us</u> Εἰ

σὺ εἶ ὁ Χριστός εἰπὸν ἡμῖν." But he said to them, "If I tell you, you will not believe, and if I ask you, you will not answer. But from now on the Son of Man shall be seated at the right hand of the power of God." So they all said, "Are you the Son of God, then?" And he said to them, "You say that I am." Then they said, "What further testimony do we need? We have heard it ourselves from his own lips."
    See Mk 14: 60-65; Mt 26: 66–68 this chapter

Rulers Mocked With Imperatives That Jesus Save Himself
Lk 23: 35 And the people stood by, watching, but the rulers scoffed at him, saying, "He saved others; let him save himself Αλλους ἔσωσεν σωσάτω ἑαυτόν, if he is the Christ of God, his Chosen One!"

> The English "let him save himself" while an acceptable translation somewhat diminishes the Greek imperative. The imperative spoken by the rulers conveyed their mockery. As with the Chief Priests, in time the rulers would know that Jesus had saved others, saved himself, and would save others following him.

Two Demands from a Criminal
Lk 23: 39-43 One of the criminals who were hanged railed at him, saying, "Are you not the Christ? Save yourself and us σῶσον σεαυτὸν καὶ ἡμᾶς!" But the other rebuked him, saying, "Do you not fear God, since you are under the same sentence of condemnation? And we indeed justly, for we are receiving the due reward of our deeds; but this man has done nothing wrong." And he said, "Jesus, remember me when you come into your kingdom Ιησοῦ μνήσθητί μου ὅταν ἔλθῃς εἰς τὴν βασιλείαν σου." And he said to him, "Truly, I say to you, today you will be with me in Paradise."

> The criminal made two demands. The first was that Jesus would save himself. The second was that the criminal would be remembered after Jesus has entered (aorist active) his Kingdom. Jesus assured the criminal of his second imperative that the criminal would be with Jesus in paradise. Assuring the criminal's salvation also assured the criminal that Jesus also would be saved.

In this passage, the word, "today" combined with the comma placement in English can be challenging. "I say to you today,…" or "I say to you, today…" produce different time elements as to exactly when the criminal would enter the Kingdom. In English the "I say to you, today…" conveyed to the thief, readers and hearers of the text that on the very same day the criminal was in paradise with Jesus. The phrase, "I say to you today…" conveyed to the thief, readers, and hearers of the text that Jesus affirmed on that day that eventually in the future the criminal would be in paradise, but not necessarily on that same day.

Most translations consider context and choose the, "I tell you, today…" version conveying that on that day the thief entered into paradise with Jesus. However, codex scriptures were recorded in Greek uncials which are all capital Greek letters without punctuation. Also, translators must contend with where Jesus went immediately after his death before his resurrection. While the conundrum of the thief's salvation timing is eschatologically crucial to the thief, readers, and hearers of the text, there is a more critical issue. William C. Kaiser, Jr. affirms:

When Jesus makes this promise to the thief, it does more than simply comfort the dying man and promise him the reward of faith. What it does is to announce the completion of salvation.[2]

Cleopas and His Friend Demanded Jesus Stay with Them
Lk 24: 28-31 So they drew near to the village to which they were going. He acted as if he were going farther, but they urged him strongly, saying, "<u>Stay with us</u> Μεῖνον μεθ ἡμῶν, for it is toward evening and the day is now far spent." So he went in to stay with them. When he was at table with them, he took the bread and blessed and broke it and gave it to them. And their eyes were opened, and they recognized him. And he vanished from their sight.

> Cleopas and his friend did not merely urge Jesus. Those around them and Jesus heard an imperative. Moreover, Jesus immediately accepted their imperative invitation affirmed by the phrase, "So he went in to stay with them." Cleopas and his friend did not invite Jesus by saying, "We invite you to stay with us." Nor did they ask Jesus, "Would you like to stay with us?" Note Luke's modifier phrase, "but they urged him strongly, saying..." The imperative held power.

## Imperatives to Jesus in John's Gospel

The woman at the Well Demanded Living Water
Jn 4: 13-19 Jesus said to her, "Everyone who drinks of this water will be thirsty again, but whoever drinks of the water that I will give him will never be thirsty again. The water that I will give him will become in him a spring of water welling up to eternal life." The woman said to him, "<u>Sir, give me this water</u> Κύριε δός μοι τοῦτο τὸ ὕδωρ, so that I will not be thirsty or have to come here to draw water." Jesus said to her, "<u>Go, call your husband, and come here</u>." The woman answered him, "I have no husband." Jesus said to her, "You are right in saying, 'I have no husband'; for you have had five husbands, and the one you now have is not your husband. What you have said is true." The woman said to him, "Sir, I perceive that you are a prophet.

> The woman had spoken a single imperative to Jesus, "give me this water." Jesus responded with three consecutive imperatives, "go," "call your husband" and "come here." The woman's imperative conveyed her sincerity. She demanded the eternal life that he could give. Jesus' responsive imperative conveyed his knowledge of the truth of her marital life. Note that Jesus did not immediately meet her demand. He revealed her numerous husbands and current marital situation. Her ultimate repentance preceded her receiving the living water. Her response, "Sir, I perceive that you are a prophet." was her confession that Jesus was right.

Disciples Demanded Jesus Eat
Jn 4: 31 Meanwhile the disciples were urging him, saying, "<u>Rabbi, eat</u> Ραββί φάγε." But he said to them, "I have food to eat that you do not know about."

> The imperative "Rabi, eat/" from the disciples seems simple enough and appropriate. However, John did not record any passages that established that Jesus had listened to their imperative to him "eat" or that he did eat. John is silent on if Jesus responded to their imperative.

---

[2] Kaiser, Jr., Walter C., Peter H. Davids, F.F. Bruce, Manfred T. Brauch, *Hard Sayings of the Bible,* 489.

## An Official Demanded a Visit from Jesus

Jn 4: 45-49 So when he came to Galilee, the Galileans welcomed him, having seen all that he had done in Jerusalem at the feast. For they too had gone to the feast. So he came again to Cana in Galilee, where he had made the water wine. And at Capernaum there was an official whose son was ill. When this man heard that Jesus had come from Judea to Galilee, he went to him and asked him to come down and heal his son, for he was at the point of death. So Jesus said to him, "Unless you see signs and wonders you will not believe." The official said to him, "<u>Sir, come down before my child dies</u> Κύριε κατάβηθι πρὶν ἀποθανεῖν τὸ παιδίον μου." Jesus said to him, "<u>Go</u>; your son will live." The man believed the word that Jesus spoke to him and went on his way.

> As is often the case with imperatives to Jesus, he responded with an imperative, "go." to the official's imperative to him, "Sir, come down before my child dies." with an imperative. Here Jesus' followed up his imperative, "go" with "Your son will live." Jesus' phrase following the imperative affirmed to the official that his son would live.

## A Crowd Demanded Bread from Heaven

Jn 6: 30-35 So they said to him, "Then what sign do you do, that we may see and believe you? What work do you perform? Our fathers ate the manna in the wilderness; as it is written, 'He gave them bread from heaven to eat.'" Jesus then said to them, "Truly, truly, I say to you, it was not Moses who gave you the bread from heaven, but my Father gives you the true bread from heaven. For the bread of God is he who comes down from heaven and gives life to the world." They said to him, "<u>Sir, give us this bread always</u> Κύριε πάντοτε δὸς ἡμῖν τὸν ἄρτον τοῦτον." Jesus said to them, "I am the bread of life; whoever comes to me shall not hunger, and whoever believes in me shall never thirst.

> In context, the crowd demanded bread from heaven. Jesus fulfilled their imperative but in a way that the crowd had not have anticipated. Jesus responded that he is the bread of life and that whoever comes and believes will never hunger or thirst. The crowd and Jesus both understood their imperative to him. Their imperative, "give us 'this' bread" conveyed their faith that Jesus would provide not bread for eating but the metaphorical bread equivalent to what sustained the Hebrews in the desert.

## Jesus' Brothers Demanded that He Leave Galilee for Judea

Jn 7: 1-5 After this Jesus went about in Galilee. He would not go about in Judea, because the Jews were seeking to kill him. Now the Jews' Feast of Booths was at hand. So his brothers said to him, "<u>Leave here and go to Judea</u> Μετάβηθι ἐντεῦθεν καὶ ὕπαγε εἰς τὴν Ἰουδαίαν, that your disciples also may see the works you are doing. For no one works in secret if he seeks to be known openly. If you do these things, <u>show yourself to the world</u> φανέρωσον σεαυτὸν τῷ κόσμῳ." For not even his brothers believed in him.

> "Leave" and "go" were Jesus' brothers' first two imperatives. The English translation of the second part of the sentence, "that your disciples also may see the works you are doing" could be improved. A more accurate translation is, "that your disciples also will see the works you are doing." The brothers gave Jesus imperatives because they were not certain that Jesus' works would be seen by using an indicative future active verb.

The English word, "may" in place of "will" or "shall" leaves speculation such as maybe, maybe not, might, and might not. The English word "may" in the phrase "'may' see the words you are doing" is acceptable. However, the words, "will" or "shall" more accurately convey the future, active, third person plural indicative verb. As a general rule, futures are more accurately translated with, "will" or "shall" implying an assurance in time over "may" or "might" which in English allow for assumption. Jesus' brothers were certain that Jesus' works would be seen. Their lack of assurance however, that his works would be effective, confirmed their imperative. They simply wanted proof.

Temple Jews Demanded Affirmation
Jn 10: 22-26 At that time the Feast of Dedication took place at Jerusalem. It was winter, and Jesus was walking in the temple, in the colonnade of Solomon. So the Jews gathered around him and said to him, "How long will you keep us in suspense? If you are the Christ, <u>tell us plainly</u> εἶπον ἡμῖν παρρησίᾳ. Jesus answered them, "I told you, and you do not believe. The works that I do in my Father's name bear witness about me, but you do not believe because you are not part of my flock.

    Jews in the Temple gave Jesus a clear imperative, "tell us plainly." However, the English word "plainly" weakens the Greek word which more accurately means, "boldly" or "confidently" or "with certainty." Jesus answered their imperative that he had already told them. Regardless of Jesus' affirmation, "I told you, and you do not believe." they did not believe. He answered in a way that ridiculed their imperative to him that he must tell them who he is.

Jews Responded to Jesus' Question
Jn 11: 33-34 When Jesus saw her weeping, and the Jews who had come with her also weeping, he was deeply moved in his spirit and greatly troubled. And he said, "Where have you laid him?" They said to him, "<u>Lord, come and see</u> Κύριε ἔρχου καὶ ἴδε." Jesus wept.

    Their two imperatives to Jesus, "come" and "see" affirmed their answer to Jesus' question, "Where have you laid him?" Their imperatives revealed lack of faith that Jesus could bring Lazarus back to life. He followed their imperatives. He went to the tomb and saw where they had laid Lazarus.

Phillip Demanded Jesus to Show Them the Father
Jn 14: 8-11 Philip said to him, "<u>Lord, show us the Father</u> Κύριε δεῖξον ἡμῖν τὸν πατέρα, and it is enough for us." Jesus said to him, "Have I been with you so long, and you still do not know me, Philip? Whoever has seen me has seen the Father. <u>How can you say, 'Show us the Father'</u> πῶς σὺ λέγεις Δεῖξον ἡμῖν τὸν πατέρα? Do you not believe that I am in the Father and the Father is in me? The words that I say to you I do not speak on my own authority, but the Father who dwells in me does his works. Believe me that I am in the Father and the Father is in me, or else believe on account of the works themselves.

    Phillip in the presence of the disciples gave Jesus an imperative that Jesus shows the Father to the disciples. First, Jesus affirmed that whoever has seen Jesus has seen the Father. Then Jesus asked Phillip in a questioning manner how Phillip could demand from Jesus an imperative to show the father. Jesus then clarified that he and the Father are one.

Soldiers' Imperatives to Jesus
Jn 19: 1-3 Then Pilate took Jesus and flogged him. And the soldiers twisted together a crown of thorns and put it on his head and arrayed him in a purple robe. They came up to him, saying, "<u>Hail, King of the Jews</u> χαῖρε ὁ βασιλεὺς τῶν Ἰουδαίων!" and struck him with their hands.

    The English word, "hail" is used for the word, "rejoice" also sometimes translated "greetings." In a literal sense, by their imperative, "hail" the soldiers affirmed that Jesus was, in fact, King of the Jews. Also termed a "greeting imperative" the power of the Greek imperative is reduced when conveyed in English to an emotive exclamation. The English emotive exclamation is correct but also somewhat obscures the Greek imperative.

Mary Magdalene's Imperative to Jesus
Jn 20: 15 Jesus said to her, "Woman, why are you weeping? Whom are you seeking?" Supposing him to be the gardener, she said to him, "Sir, if you have carried him away, <u>tell me where you have laid him</u> εἰπέ μοι ποῦ ἔθηκας αὐτόν, and I will take him away." Jesus said to her, "Mary." She turned and said to him in Aramaic, "Rabboni!" which means teacher.

    John recorded that Mary, not knowing to whom she spoke, gave an imperative to Jesus. Mary's imperative, "tell me where you have laid him" to the man that she supposed as a gardener affirmed her determination. She did not kindly ask. John recorded that she commanded to know. There are numerous propositions about why Mary did not recognize Jesus. Reasons for her inability to recognize him are irrelevant to her resolve. John did not record that she asked but that she gave an imperative to Jesus whom she thought was a gardener. Jesus did not hesitate in responding to her imperative.

    John recorded that Jesus immediately called Mary by name and then she recognized him. She did not ask. She had commanded the gardener who she then recognized as her teacher, her "Rabboni" in Aramaic. John's record of Mary's use of Aramaic affirms the multi-lingual abilities of Mary Magdalene, Jesus, and John, the author.

# Summary

Given the importance of the Greek imperative, the Gospel writers were unbiased in having recorded both imperatives from Jesus and imperatives to Jesus. Had the Gospel writers recorded something different than what was said, the editing process would have corrected those oversights. The Greek imperatives to Jesus within the Greek text are not mistakes or additions. When anyone gave Jesus imperatives, the Gospel writers were intentional to record them as imperatives which we often read as English commands.

Supplementing the imperatives given to Jesus in the comments are Jesus' responses to those imperatives. He and his listeners heard the imperatives given to Jesus. Commands to him were heard by those in earshot of Jesus' presence. Jesus considered how his responses were received by two groups of people: those who gave him imperatives, the speaker(s) and those who heard the imperatives.

For English readers, we must return to the days of Jesus and first hear what he heard in their context and second understand what they understood in their context. Assessing how Jesus responded, we find that he did not always follow the imperatives given to him. Often, however, after having heard an imperative to him, he responded with one or more imperatives. In some narratives, Jesus was silent, and in others, he did not respond with imperatives but merely gave a defense for why he would not be following the imperatives given to him. (See the narratives of the dialogue with the devil after Jesus had left the desert.)

Sometimes grasping the Greek imperative from English commands difficult because of the translation challenges. The morphology, however, the word form that identifies a Greek imperative is elementary. Words and meaning are essential. Iotas and dots or letters, strokes, of the written word mattered to Jesus.

> For truly, I say to you, until heaven and earth pass away, not an iota, not a dot,
> will pass from the Law until all is accomplished. Mt 5: 18

Minutiae, in the sense of literal, metaphorical, or allegorical dotted i's and crossed t's, was important to Jesus. Minutiae was necessary to Matthew, Mark, Luke, and John for their every letter and word. Minutiae is no less needed today. Iotas and dots matter.

He who has an ear, let him hear what the Spirit says to the churches.

Rv 2: 7, 2: 11, 2: 17, 2: 29, 3: 6, 3: 13, 3: 22

# 17 Spirit's Power, Father's Will, and Trinity in Jesus' Commands

*For I have come down from heaven, not to do my own will but the will of him who sent me. Jn 6: 38.*

## Titles and Names

In John's Gospel, the words, "Holy Spirit" are quoted by Jesus in Jn 14: 26[1] Jn 20: 22.[2] In Revelation, however, Jesus did not use the adjective, "holy" to describe the Spirit. In Rv 1: 13 John recorded that, "one like the Son of Man" (Jesus) repeated the words, "he who has an ear, let him hear what the Spirit says to the churches." In Rv 2: 7, 11, 17, 29; 3: 6, 3, 13, and 22 Jesus repeated this phrase. Clearly, Jesus was intentional to reiterate the imperative, "let him hear."

Inclusion or exclusion of the adjective "holy" to describe the Spirit in John's Gospels or Revelation is not problematic. The repetitive English word, "hear" derives from the Greek third person singular aorist active imperative verb ἀκουσάτω. Most English Bibles correctly render "let him hear" instead of only "hear." Readers and hearers of John's Revelation likely understood the same Holy Spirit without the adjective. Through Greek imperatives, John recorded that Jesus had commanded both early readers and listeners not to disregard what the Spirit says "to the churches." Understanding what the spirit says applies today. Today, many Christians and Churches principally focus on evangelism, missions, and church growth with little attention given to what the spirit says to the churches. Why?

What the Spirit had said and meant were to be understood, not merely heard. In their context, both the Spirit and the Spirit's message were not intended to be mysteries. Same today. The Spirit and the Spirits' message should not be mysteries thousands of years after John's record. Neither John nor Jesus was confused about the Spirit. Further, John wrote as if his readers also were not confused. John's Revelation in their context was written as if there was both clarity and understanding of the Father's will and the Spirit's power. That same clarity and understanding were imparted to those who heard Jesus and those who read John's words in their day. That availability of that same clarity and understanding has not abated today, even though many individuals, faith communities, churches, and denominations do not believe that same clarity is possible.

The power and clarity of John's words were neither magical nor mystical to them in their day. Experiencing and being moved by that same power today is not so simple for today's Christians. Our challenge today is believing and employing that power toward Kingdom use.

As mentioned in previous chapters, today's Bibles have numerous titles and names for both Spirit and Holy Spirit. For our purposes regarding Jesus' words, we center our attention on what John recorded, more specifically what Jesus commanded. In John 14 Jesus spoke about the promise of the Holy Spirit. In John 16 Jesus spoke about the work or power of the Spirit. The promise, power, presence, and work of the Holy Spirit are central to Jesus' imperatives.

---

[1] But the Helper, the Holy Spirit, whom the Father will send in my name, he will teach you all things and bring to your remembrance all that I have said to you. Jn 14: 26

[2] And when he had said this, he breathed on them and said to them, "Receive the Holy Spirit." Jn 20: 22

The Paraclete (transliteration of ὁ παράκλητος *parakletos*), Comforter, Counselor, Helper, and Advocate are contemporary English words or names or titles found in many English bibles describing the Holy Spirit. Comparing what these words may have meant to them in their day compared to us in our day can be helpful.

## Paraclete

The Greek word or more specific the title, Paraclete ὁ παράκλητος (*parakletos*) is not often literally translated or transliterated into English in English Bibles. While words like, counselor, helper, advocate, or comforter are commonly found, these English words can miss the deeper meaning of the Greek word and title Paraclete. After Jesus' promise to them of the Holy Spirit, and his ascension, the disciples were not left alone. Citing Goodrick-Kohlenberger #4156 Mounce upholds that the Holy Spirit compensate for the departure of Jesus:

> [4156] παράκλητος, *parakletos 5x one called or sent for to assist another; an advocate, one who pleads the cause of another; an advocate, one who leads the cause of another;* 1 Jn 2: 1; genr. *one present to render various beneficial service,* and thus *the Paraclete*, whose influence and operation were to compensate for the departure of Christ himself, Jn. 14: 16, 26; 15: 26; 16: 7.[3]

Considering the morphological word formation for Paraclete ὁ παράκλητος (*parakletos*) can be helpful. In historical context, the prefix, "para" conveyed the ideas of alongside, next to, near to, or together with. The root, "kaleo" conveyed in historical context the idea of calling, saying, speaking, or addressing with an affirmation of support. Combining the prefix and root, the Greek word "Paraclete" conveyed in their context not merely consolation or encouragement, but power and authority through to completion. Mounce affirms a summation of terms and Pre-Christian Greek in his definition of counselor:

> The Greek word [Paraclete] literally means "one who is called to someone's aid." Various translations have been given to summarize the term: "counselor, helper, advocate," or simply transliterated as "Paraclete." *parakletos* was used in pre-Christian Greek literature to mean "one who appears in another's behalf ("mediator, inter-cessor").[4]

Below is a chart identifying the different English words translated from the Greek word παράκλητος, *parakletos*. Note the consistencies from each translation and note the historical development. Remembering that the ESV, KJV, and NAS are considered "essentially literal translations" while the NIV is a "dynamic equivalent paraphrase."

---

[3] Mounce, William D., *Mounce's Complete Expository Dictionary of Old & New Testament Words*, Goodrick-Kohlenberger #4156, 1,234.

[4] Mounce, William D., *Mounce's Complete Expository Dictionary of Old & New Testament Words*, 139.

Greek: παράκλητος, *parakletos*

| Published:<br>English Bible | 1611<br>KJV | 1971<br>NAS | 1978<br>NIV | 2001<br>ESV |
|---|---|---|---|---|
| Jn 14: 16 | comforter | helper | counselor | helper |
| Jn 14: 26 | comforter | helper | counselor | helper |
| Jn 15: 26 | comforter | helper | counselor | helper |
| Jn 16: 7 | comforter | helper | counselor | helper |
| 1 Jn 2: 1 | advocate | advocate | one who speaks to | advocate |

Given no equivalent English word for παράκλητος *parakletos,* translators must find English words that convey meaning equivalent or similar to those who first wrote and spoke those words. Finding meaningful words requires an understanding of some terms: Etymology, Etymological Fallacy, and Illegitimate Totality Transfer: Demoss expounds:

Etymology: The study of the derivation of words, both their forms and meaning.[5]

Etymological Fallacy: The mistaken notion that the true meaning of a term lies in its primitive meaning (etymology), that the earliest historical occurrence of a term yields, the correct definition. It is a fallacy because the meanings of words evolve over time so that some words are quite detached from their origins.[6]

Illegitimate Totality Transfer: The error of taking the conclusions of a word study – observing the various meanings of a word over time and in different contexts – and assuming them all to be present in a single contextual usage of that word.[7]

Etymology matters because differences between historical meaning context and contemporary meaning effects interpretation. In short, if we want to know what something means, we are wise to know what something meant. Also, both the Etymological Fallacy (total dependence on original meaning) and Illegitimate Totality Transfer (total dependence on contemporary meaning only) must be considered. Focus must first be on meaning then, rather than meaning now.

## Paraclete Then, Paraclete Now

How today's Christians perceive the Holy Spirit, is shaped by the English words used to describe the Holy Spirit in their Bibles and from pulpits in their churches. Church leaders in the United States often tread lightly on teaching about the Holy Spirit because of the differences in what the Holy Spirit has meant to their particular communities or more specifically their churches. What did the Paraclete mean to first-century hearers of John's writings? How did they interpret Paraclete in their context? What does Paraclete mean today? How have we come to believe what the Paraclete does or does not do today? To follow are present-day meanings of four English words or titles: Comforter, Counselor, Helper, and Advocate each rendered from a single Greek

---

[5] Demoss, Matthew S., *Pocket Dictionary for the Study of New Testament Greek*. 53.
[6] Ibid. 53.
[7] Ibid. 70.

παράκλητος *parakletos*. To follow are brief overviews describing perhaps weakness in some English words today compared to power in historical context of the single word, Paraclete ὁ παράκλητος (*parakletos*).

## Comforter

The English word, comforter derived from Greek, Paraclete today conveys a sense of ease or relief that someone arrives to comfort another person in distress. Our contemporary English idea of comforting however, may be a much weaker meaning compared to early Christian thought. The English word, comfort originally conveyed the meaning of power or meaning of coming with power. The prefix, "com" means with, thru, by, nearby, or alongside. The root, "fort" means power, strength, protection, or means. Hence, a coming alongside with supremacy and power provides a bit more accuracy to historical context. In short, God's work is only through the Spirit that has come alongside a person.

The word, comfort in today's contemporary English carries a passive, relaxing, restful idea. However, a passive, somewhat mild power that comes alongside the believer is not what Jesus had in mind when he spoke to them or when the earliest readers read the Gospel writers' narratives.

Indeed, the Holy Spirit brings comfort, however, the Holy Spirit provides power beyond comfort alone. A comforter in English contemporized context was not what John intended his readers to comprehend. Today our perception of real power from the Holy Spirit is weakened by the way we interpret the word or title Comforter. When they heard or read the word, "Paraclete" ὁ παράκλητος (*parakletos*) they did not hear or interpret a type of restful, secure assistance to their life challenges. Yes, the Spirit brings comfort in English understanding, but Paraclete brought more than just comfort as Jesus earliest followers knew. Much can be lost in translation.

## Counselor

The contemporary English word, counselor similar to comforter derived from Greek, Paraclete today implies a less involved person such as a school counselor or guidance counselor, or mental health counselor, you the idea. The word, counselor brings to mind perhaps a therapist, analyst, psychologist, social worker, pastor, cleric, or lawyer. A counselor is generally thought to be someone providing emotional, mental, social, legal or even spiritual insight such as a therapist who attempts to bring understanding. A counselor, in a legal sense, presents, declares and brings before all witnesses the force and truth of the law on behalf of the one on trial. Beyond revealing light and truth counselors can empower persons to bear the light and accept the truth. In today's context, a counselor both reveals and enables.

When the Holy Spirit in contemporary English seems relegated to only a counselor the power that the Spirit can provide becomes reduced. The Holy Spirit as a counselor is demoted to a person who provides us with "Ah ha!" insights but little more. The English word counselor similar to comforter often seems to be one facet of the Holy Spirit that gives counseling perhaps that brings understanding, but little power.

Much can be lost in translation.

## Helper

The English word, helper derived from Greek, Paraclete similarly tends to soften the Holy Spirit's power. Indeed, the Holy Spirit helps as in the concept of a helper, but the word leaves the responsibility for the person needing the help. When the Holy Spirit comes to be viewed only as a type of helper, there is a tendency to believe that we are the ones who are doing the real work. The words, help and helper often convey meaning that the help or helper is optional, something helpful, but not essential. Today we think that while the Holy Spirit helps, we are the ones doing the heavy lifting.

When the Holy Spirit is considered to be just our helper, our self-power pride to solve our sin problems becomes our responsibility. Life-saving and soul-saving help from the Holy Spirit appears miraculous rather than expected when we perceive the Holy Spirit only to be a helper. The Holy Spirit is much more than just a helper which is why for some today the English word helper conveys a weakness. Much can be lost in translation.

## Advocate

The English word, advocate derived from Greek, Paraclete tends to suggest a lawyer, a representative, or a person who stands next to a defendant advocating a case before a judge. Because the word, advocate brings to mind a judicial setting, advocate certainly conveys a more powerful active meaning than a comforter, counselor, or helper. However, the Spirit is more than a judicial advocate in a courtroom setting.

In a contemporary context, there is no doubt that advocates or lawyers do not always win. They can lose before judges and juries. In legal context, an advocate brings to mind a public setting or someone speaking for another. While the word, advocate is helpful, advocate does not convey the same meaning Jesus' hearers of John's readers would have understood. The Holy Spirit is not just and an advocate or a lawyer with power. The Holy Spirit never lost a case. That is an advocate of power. Big difference. Much can be lost in translation.

## Jesus and the Holy Spirit

Below are selected verses recorded by Matthew, Mark, and Luke after John baptized Jesus in the Jordan River. These verses provide insight into the relationship between the incarnate Jesus and the Holy Spirit:

> And when Jesus was baptized, immediately he went up from the water, and behold, the heavens were opened to him, and he saw <u>the Spirit of God descending</u> like a dove and <u>coming to rest</u> on him; and behold, a voice from heaven said, "This is my beloved Son, with whom I am well pleased." Then Jesus was <u>led up by the Spirit</u> into the wilderness to be tempted by the devil. Mt 3: 16-4:1

> And when he came up out of the water, immediately he saw the heavens being torn open and <u>the Spirit descending on</u> him like a dove. And a voice came from heaven, "You are my beloved Son; with you I am well pleased." <u>The Spirit immediately drove him out</u> into the wilderness. Mk 1: 10-12

And Jesus, full of the Holy Spirit, returned from the Jordan and was led by the Spirit in the wilderness for forty days, being tempted by the devil. Lk 4: 1-2a

Notice the verbs and phrases linked to the Holy Spirit: descending, coming to rest, led up, descending on, drove him out, returned and led by. These verbs in Greek are all active. The Holy Spirit's initiative within Jesus at the Father's will was clear to first-century readers because of Greek and context. English readers, however, might have trouble gleaning that link in English.

Matthew, Mark, and Luke each recorded that after his baptism Jesus was under direction from the Spirit, the Spirit which led (Mt and Lk) or drove (Mk) Jesus into the wilderness. Jesus did not enter the wilderness on his own. Neither Matthew, Mark, Luke, nor John recorded that Jesus had performed miracles before the Spirit came upon Jesus at baptism by John or during his time in the wilderness and temptation by Satan. Jesus' power of miracles and healing only occurred after Jesus' had returned from the desert and had been with the Holy Spirit.

## Roman Dove Power

A peaceful descending dove from heaven that brought the power that healed, freed the demonized, calmed seas, and raised the dead was not what the crowd expected. Power from heaven would seem more appropriate to have arrived with lightning bolts, thunder, earthquakes or anything that exhibited natural power that the Hebrews had experienced in their history.

Within the Hebrew, Hellenistic and Roman cultic mindsets Godly power came with a boom of sound, a flash of light, or something experiential. For the Hebrews, power exhibited in the horrific, dramatic ten plagues upon Egypt would have been familiar. A descending dove different from all other powers arrived with a spirit that was holy. Why a dove? R. Alan Streett offers historical insight regarding birds, kingship, and power:

> Rome chose nearly all of its kings by observing the flight of birds, a form of divination known as augury. According to Cicero (106 – 46BC), Romulus, the legendary founder and first king of Rome, was named to his royal post through this method. Augurs were trained to read avian signs and confirm whom the gods had chosen to be the next emperor. They watched to see upon whose shoulder a bird landed, and that man became the new emperor. Avian signs accompanied the selection and confirmation of all Roman rulers from Octavian to Domitian except one.[8]
>
> When the senate confirmed Octavian as Rome's emperor in 27 BC, it bestowed upon him the title Augustus, which is linked etymologically to the word "augury," possibly because he was confirmed and consecrated through the art of augury. The term "augur" found in our English word "in*augur*ation," which refers to the coronation of a king. Roman kings were in*augur*ated to kingship.
>
> To the first-century believers, the descent of the Holy Spirit on Jesus "in bodily form" as a dove is a sign that Jesus is God's choice to be his earthly King, just as the Roman gods send birds to confirm their choice of the Roman emperor.

---

[8] Cicero, De Divination, trans. By W.A. Galconer, Loeb Classical Library series, no. 154 (Cambridge: Harvard University Press, 1923). Streett, R. Alan., *Heaven on Earth: Experiencing The Kingdom Of God In The Here And Now*, 77.

The Voice from heaven speaks once again and announces, "This is My beloved Son, in whom I am well pleased" (Matthew 3: 17). The first part of this sentence is a quoted from Psalm 2: 7, an enthronement psalm that describes David's installation as king. Whenever a new king of Israel took the throne, he was anointed by a prophet and declared to be God's son or his representative on earth (see 2 Samuel 7: 12 – 16). In the Gospels, Jesus is portrayed as God's final king, the end-time Messiah. At Jesus's baptism, the Voice confirms that the Kingdom rests on Jesus's shoulders.

The last part of the declaration ("in who I am well pleased") is a paraphrase of Isaiah 42: 1-2: "Behold! My Servant, who I uphold, My Elect One in whom my soul delights! I have put My Spirit upon Him."[9]

Beyond Streett's historical insights on augury, the power that came with a descending dove would have seemed contrary to the power of a King as the Jews saw power. Per Streett, augury as divination was a Roman concept. Jesus' inauguration came with power. Each of the ten plagues upon Egypt was destructive.[10] Jesus imperatives in contrast to the ten plagues were productive.[11]

## Blasphemy against the Holy Spirit

Both the presence and power of the Holy Spirit were central to Jesus' teachings and mission. The Holy Spirit's power was so essential that forgiveness was available for those who blasphemed Jesus as the Son of Man, but there was no forgiveness for those who blasphemed the Holy Spirit. Matthew, Mark, and Luke each quoted warnings from Jesus about blasphemy against the Holy Spirit:

> And whoever speaks a word against the Son of Man will be forgiven, but whoever speaks against the Holy Spirit will not be forgiven, either in this age or in the age to come. Mt 12: 32

> Truly, I say to you, all sins will be forgiven the children of man, and whatever blasphemies they utter, but whoever blasphemes against the Holy Spirit never has forgiveness, but is guilty of an eternal sin"-- for they were saying, "He has an unclean spirit." Mk 3: 28-30

> And everyone who speaks a word against the Son of Man will be forgiven, but the one who blasphemes against the Holy Spirit will not be forgiven. Lk 12: 10

---

[9] Streett, Alan R., *Heaven on Earth: Experiencing The Kingdom Of God In The Here And Now*, 77 – 78.
[10]: 1. Water turned to blood Ex 7: 14–25, 2. Plague of frogs Ex 8: 1–15, 3. Plague of gnats/lice Ex 8:16-19, 4. Plague of flies Ex 8: 20–32, 5. Plague against livestock Ex 9: 1–7, 6. Plague of boils Ex 9: 8–12, 7. Plague of hail Ex 9: 13–35, 8. Plague of locusts Ex 10: 1–20, 9. Plague of darkness Ex 10: 21–29, 10. Death of the firstborn Ex 11: 1–10, 12: 29–32.
[11] It appears from the English that Jesus commanded the demons to enter the pigs was destructive. See Mt 8: 32; Lk 8: 32; Mk 5: 11–13. In a deeper study of the Greek, Jesus permitted them to enter the pigs at their spoken imperative to him. Here Jesus did not command the destruction of the swine. John did not record a Greek imperative. Jesus permitted their destruction after the demons had entered the swine.

These passages affirmed both the objective presence of the Holy Spirit within Jesus and the subjective work of the Holy Spirit through Jesus. Because the Holy Spirit is both the objective presence and the subjective work, there is no surprise that Jesus declared blasphemy for anyone speaking against the Holy Spirit. Jesus knew that anyone denying the presence and the power of the Holy Spirit in him would also deny the presence and power of the Holy Spirit in his followers. Scott McKnight affirms:

> While the Spirit is the object, however, it is the Spirit's work in Jesus Christ that is the focus of the passage.[12]

Stephen Motyer agrees about the seriousness of blasphemy against the Holy Spirit:

> Jesus teaches that the blasphemy for which there is not forgiveness is that against the Holy Spirit; all other blasphemies, particularly those against "the Son of Man," may be forgiven. Insults toward the Son of Man" may be forgiven because they are committed in ignorance of who he is: his heavenly glory does not appear on earth. However, to ascribe obvious manifestations of the Spirit to the devil's agency is a much more serious offense not committed in ignorance.[13]

## Beyond Jesus, Toward His Imperatives

To reemphasize, the person of the Holy Spirit, both in presence and power working through the imperative commands of Jesus is without question. Contextually in their time and culture, what about the presence and power of the Holy Spirit in Jesus' followers in his day? And in contemporary context, what about the presence and power of the Holy Spirit in Jesus' followers today?

Regardless of church type or doctrinal beliefs, publicly or privately repudiating the power of the Holy Spirit is not without consequences. It is no small matter to deny the presence and power of the working Holy Spirit. Scott McKnight clarifies Luke's insight:

> Luke puts this same saying in a slightly different context: the public acknowledgment of Jesus Christ. Jesus says it is one thing to deny him publicly; it is quite another thing to repudiate the power of the Holy Spirit Lk 12: 8–10. Thus, the unforgivable sin here seems to be the public repudiation of the power of the Spirit in the ministry of the apostles of Jesus.[14]

Given McKnight's insight, if the unforgivable sin was a public repudiation of the power of the Spirit in the ministry of the apostles of Jesus, how does that unforgivable sin apply to repudiate the power of the Spirit to work today in whomever God chooses?

The role of the Holy Spirit in Jesus' commands went beyond him alone. The role of the Holy Spirit was not limited to only Jesus but continued through his apostles and his followers.

---

[12] McKnight, Scott, "Blasphemy Against the Holy Spirit" in Elwell, Walter A., *Baker Theological Dictionary of the Bible*, 68.
[13] Motyer, Stephen, "Blasphemy" in Elwell, Walter A., *Baker Theological Dictionary of the Bible*, 67.
[14] McKnight, Scott, "Blasphemy Against the Holy Spirit" in Elwell, Walter A., *Baker Theological Dictionary of the Bible*, 68.

Unforgivable blasphemy occurred when there was denial of the presence and power of the Holy Spirit in Jesus. Unforgivable blasphemy also occurred when there was a denial of the presence and power of the Holy Spirit working through his followers. The presence and power of the Holy Spirit was affirmed when Jesus told his followers that they would do greater works:

> Truly, truly, I say to you, whoever believes in me will also do the works that I do; and greater works than these will he do, because I am going to the Father. Jn 14: 12

Greater works were impossible without the presence and power of the Holy Spirit within Jesus' early followers. So, what were these greater works then and what are they today? Are they only spiritual works? Are they only physical works? Were they only for a past time? Are they both spiritual and physical for our time? George Ladd simplifies that these works are first spiritual, that then produce that ultimately transformed lives:

> These greater works are surely in the spiritual realm and not the in physical realm. The 'greater works' consist of the transformation of lives wrought by the Holy Spirit as a result of the preaching of the gospel.[15]

The presence and power of the Holy Spirit within Jesus would be available to others, with the beginning indwelling with his immediate disciples and in future believers, the ones sent. McNight continues:

> What we see here is probably an application: since it is blasphemous to reject the Spirit in the ministry of Jesus, so it is also blasphemous to reject the Spirit in the ministry of the Twelve (since they are personal agents of Jesus). After all, the Spirit purifies and enables holiness (Ps 51: 11–13; Ezek. 36: 25–27). In summary, we may confidently conclude that "blasphemy against the Spirit" is overt, even verbal, repudiation of the presence of God's Spirit in the ministry of Jesus and those whom he has sent.[16]

The Holy Spirit's presence and power indwelt Jesus. The same presence and power were present through his words, particularly his spoken imperatives. His imperatives and the fulfillment of his imperatives validated his warning against blasphemy. Further, the Holy Spirit's presence and power were present and within Peter and Paul as they healed the sick at the utterances of their own spoken imperatives.

In short, when those who saw what happened after Jesus spoke imperatives or those who read what happened after Jesus spoke imperatives, those fulfilled imperatives indicated and validated the Holy Spirit's presence, power and Trinitarian work through them.

---

[15] Ladd, George Eldon, *A Theology of the New Testament*, 333.
[16] McKnight, Scott, "Blasphemy Against the Holy Spirit" in Elwell, Walter A., *Baker Theological Dictionary of the Bible*, 68.

# Holy Spirit through the Spoken Imperatives of Peter and Paul

Following are passages that include Greek imperatives spoken by Peter and Paul recorded by Luke in Acts. Commentary follows each passage.

Peter's Imperative to the Crippled Beggar
Ac 3: 1–8 Now Peter and John were going up to the temple at the hour of prayer, the ninth hour. And a man lame from birth was being carried, whom they laid daily at the gate of the temple that is called the Beautiful Gate to ask alms of those entering the temple. Seeing Peter and John about to go into the temple, he asked to receive alms. And Peter directed his gaze at him, as did John, and said, "Look at us" εἶπεν Βλέψον εἰς ἡμᾶς. And he fixed his attention on them, expecting to receive something from them. But Peter said, "I have no silver and gold, but what I do have I give to you. In the name of Jesus Christ of Nazareth, rise up and walk" ἐν τῷ ὀνόματι Ἰησοῦ Χριστοῦ τοῦ Ναζωραίου περιπάτει! And he took him by the right hand and raised him up, and immediately his feet and ankles were made strong. And leaping up he stood and began to walk, and entered the temple with them, walking and leaping and praising God.

> Many English versions translate two words, "rise and walk" or "rise up and walk" (DBY), "rise up and walk" (ESV), "rise up and walk" (KJV), "rise up and be walking" (YLT). While these versions employ two words and are acceptable translations, the Greek from the WHO employs only a single imperative "walk" περιπάτει. The NIV "In the name of Jesus Christ of Nazareth, walk!" aligns with the WHO. The inclusion or exclusion of "rise" rendering "rise and walk" or only the word, "walk" is disputed among scholars and the *Critical Texts*. Aside from this slight anomaly, The Greek imperative(s), (weather rise and walk or walk) however, is(are) undisputed.

Peter's Imperative to Aeneas
Ac 9: 31-35 So the church throughout all Judea and Galilee and Samaria had peace and was being built up. And walking in the fear of the Lord and in the comfort of the Holy Spirit, it multiplied. Now as Peter went here and there among them all, he came down also to the saints who lived at Lydda. There he found a man named Aeneas, bedridden for eight years, who was paralyzed. And Peter said to him, "Aeneas, Jesus Christ heals you; rise and make your bed" Αἰνέα ἰᾶταί σε Ἰησοῦς Χριστός· ἀνάστηθι. καὶ στρῶσον σεαυτῷ And immediately he rose. And all the residents of Lydda and Sharon saw him, and they turned to the Lord.

> Here Peter publically affirmed that the anointed messiah Jesus was the healer, not Peter. Luke was intentional in quoting Peter as having spoken two imperatives, "rise" and "make." Peter did not stop with one imperative. His second imperative commanded that the bed was to be made or that work was to be completed to make the bed. The reason for having been risen was to accomplish the work that started with straightening bed linens. Work affirmed and indicated healing.

Peter's Imperative to Tabitha
Ac 9: 35-42 And all the residents of Lydda and Sharon saw him, and they turned to the Lord. Now there was in Joppa a disciple named Tabitha, which, translated, means Dorcas. She was full of good works and acts of charity. In those days she became ill and died, and when they had washed her, they laid her in an upper room. Since Lydda was near Joppa, the disciples, hearing that Peter

was there, sent two men to him, urging him, "Please come to us without delay." So Peter rose and went with them. And when he arrived, they took him to the upper room. All the widows stood beside him weeping and showing tunics and other garments that Dorcas made while she was with them. But Peter put them all outside, and knelt down and prayed; and turning to the body he said, "Tabitha, arise." καὶ ἐπιστρέψας πρὸς τὸ σῶμα εἶπεν Ταβιθά ἀνάστηθι. And she opened her eyes, and when she saw Peter she sat up. And he gave her his hand and raised her up. Then calling the saints and widows, he presented her alive. And it became known throughout all Joppa, and many believed in the Lord.

In English phrase from the two men, "Please come to us without delay."[17] conveys an English command sense from the Greek imperative form. Other translations more accurately reduce the imperative idea, "beseeching him, Thou must not delay coming to us" (DBY), "desiring him that he would not delay" (KJV), or "calling on him not to delay to come through unto them" (YLT).

Luke recorded that Peter spoke the imperative "arise" to Tabitha after Peter had called her by name. Luke did not include any narrative between the time Peter spoke and when Tabitha opened her eyes and sat up. Note that Luke did not record that many believed in Peter. Luke also did not record that many believed in the Lord by working through Peter. Luke simply and accurately recorded that "many believed in the Lord." Big difference.

Paul's Imperative to the Man in Lystra Crippled from Birth
Ac 14: 8-12 Now at Lystra there was a man sitting who could not use his feet. He was crippled from birth and had never walked. He listened to Paul speaking. And Paul, looking intently at him and seeing that he had faith to be made well, said in a loud voice, "Stand upright on your feet" Ἀνάστηθι ἐπὶ τοὺς πόδας σου ὀρθός. And he sprang up and began walking. And when the crowds saw what Paul had done, they lifted up their voices, saying in Lycaonian, "The gods have come down to us in the likeness of men!" Barnabas they called Zeus, and Paul, Hermes, because he was the chief speaker.

There is a reference to the likeness of Paul to Hermes a sometimes overlooked insight for English readers. Hermes was significant to the Greeks as a messenger to whom they compared Paul. Brownrigg clarifies:

> "Hermes is the Greek name for the messenger of the gods, translated sometimes as 'Mercury,' in Acts 14: 12, where the voluble and mercurial character of Paul is contrasted with the dignified appearance and bearing of Barnabas, who was mistaken for Zeus, the father of the Gods."[18]

Paul's imperative, "Stand upright on your feet" Ἀνάστηθι ἐπὶ τοὺς πόδας σου ὀρθός with the result that the man immediately sprang up and began walking conveyed to those in Lystra the presence and power of the Spirit within Paul. Those Greeks who had heard Paul's imperative perceived Paul as having comparable power to Hermes, the messenger of their gods. Every New Testament recorded healing by

---

[17] Dotted underline indicates the Greek imperatives spoken by the two men to Peter
[18] Brownnrigg, Ronald, "Hermes" in *Who's Who the New Testament*, 83.

Peter and Paul is preceded by their spoken imperatives. The presence and power of the Holy Spirit combined with their articulated imperatives was effective in the category of "greater works."

## The Father's Will within Jesus

During Jesus' earthly life the Father's will was unmistakable through the presence and power of the Holy Spirit. Jesus taught his disciples that his will was the will of his father and that his mission was the will of his Father. Everything Jesus said or did was the will of his Father. Thus, Jesus' life and words through the power and presence of the Holy Spirit were then and are today the will of the Father. Additional affirmations of the Father's will are Jesus' words concerning where his authority came. Matthew closed his Gospel with Jesus having established that all authority has been given to him:

> And Jesus came and said to them, "All authority in heaven and on earth has been given to me." Mt 28: 18

The Greek morphology, the word construction is significant. Challenging to glean in English, Matthew recorded an indicative aorist passive verb, "all authority in heaven and on earth has been given," which meant that without the Father's will, and the power and presence of the Holy Spirit were inconsequential. Readers and hearers of the aorist passive recorded by John and Matthew in their time likely were not confused. To simplify, early followers of Jesus after his resurrection held no doubt that Jesus had authority because of the Father's will Jesus had been given all authority.[19]

---

[19] For reader ease, below are selected passages regarding Jesus and the Father's will:

For I have come down from heaven, not to do my own will but the will of him who sent me. Jn 6: 38.

So Jesus said to them, "Truly, truly, I say to you, the Son can do nothing of his own accord, but only what he sees the Father doing. For whatever the Father does, that the Son does likewise. For the Father loves the Son and shows him all that he himself is doing. And greater works than these will he show him, so that you may marvel. For as the Father raises the dead and gives them life, so also the Son gives life to whom he will. The Father judges no one, but has given all judgment to the Son, that all may honor the Son, just as they honor the Father. Whoever does not honor the Son does not honor the Father who sent him. Jn 5: 19-23.

My sheep hear my voice, and I know them, and they follow me. I give them eternal life, and they will never perish, and no one will snatch them out of my hand. My Father, who has given them to me, is greater than all, and no one is able to snatch them out of the Father's hand. I and the Father are one. Jn 10: 27-30.

If you abide in me, and my words abide in you, ask whatever you wish, and it will be done for you. By this my Father is glorified, that you bear much fruit and so prove to be my disciples. As the Father has loved me, so have I loved you. Abide in my love. If you keep my commandments, you will abide in my love, just as I have kept my Father's commandments and abide in his love. Jn 15: 7-10.

Matthew did not record an aorist active, an undefined past action about something that Jesus had done. Jesus was passive in receiving the authorization. Jesus did not ask for the authority. Jesus did not demand the authority. Jesus did not go and get the authority. Jesus affirmed that he had been given the authority. Big difference.

First-century readers and hearers understood where and how Jesus received his authority. Their grasp of the will of his Father combined with the power and presence of the Holy Spirit was much different for them in their day than perhaps to us in our day. Jesus fulfilled his Father's will through the power and presence of the Holy Spirit. With his focus on the will of his Father through the presence and power of the Spirit within, Jesus was then and is today the quintessence of the working Trinity.

## The Father's Will and the Disciples

Each Gospel writer recorded insight on the Father's will and Jesus. John went deeper. In chapters 13, 14, 15, and 16 John extensively recorded Jesus words that described Jesus' relationship with the Father. Further, the Disciples' relationships with the Father through Jesus had been established. Luke recorded the will of the father at the betrayal of Jesus just before his crucifixion:

> And he withdrew from them about a stone's throw, and knelt down and prayed, saying, "Father, if you are willing, <u>remove this cup from me παρένεγκε τοῦτο τὸ ποτήριον ἀπ ἐμοῦ. Nevertheless, not my will, but yours, be done πλὴν μὴ τὸ θέλημά μου ἀλλὰ τὸ σὸν γινέσθω</u>." And there appeared to him an angel from heaven, strengthening him. And being in an agony he prayed more earnestly; and his sweat became like great drops of blood falling down to the ground. And when he rose from prayer, he came to the disciples and found them sleeping for sorrow, and he said to them, "Why are you sleeping? Rise and <u>pray προσεύχεσθε</u> that you may not enter into temptation." Lk 22: 41-46

Within his prayer, Jesus' first two imperatives were to his Father. Significant is the phrase immediately preceding Jesus' first imperative, "Father, if you are willing." Jesus first imperative to the Father demanded the removal of what his Father had planned he endure. The second imperative demanded that the Father fulfill the Father's will. Note that immediately after his second imperative, that the Father fulfill the Father's will, there appeared an angel.

After Jesus' imperatives to his father, pray (v46) is the only imperative Luke recorded that Jesus gave to his disciples. Although "rise" reads like an English command, the Greek is an aorist

---

You are my friends if you do what I command you. No longer do I call you servants, for the servant does not know what his master is doing; but I have called you friends, for all that I have heard from my Father I have made known to you. You did not choose me, but I chose you and appointed you that you should go and bear fruit and that your fruit should abide, so that whatever you ask the Father in my name, he may give it to you. Jn 15: 14-16.

Then he said to them, "My soul is very sorrowful, even to death; remain here, and watch with me." And going a little farther he fell on his face and prayed, saying, "My Father, if it be possible, let this cup pass from me; nevertheless, not as I will, but as you will." Mt 26: 38-39.

active participle, "having risen" not a Greek imperative. The YLT translation "having risen pray that ye may not enter into temptation" rather than "rise and pray…" more accurately conveys the aorist active participle. Mk 14: 32-42; Mt 26: 36-41

## John 14: 1

Perhaps the most explicit passage affirming the relationship between the Disciples and the Father is John 14: 1. English construction, however, sometimes make that relationship challenging to understand. (See Chapter 12: John 14: 1 for more detail.)

Let not your hearts be troubled. Believe in God; believe also in me. Μὴ ταρασσέσθω ὑμῶν ἡ καρδία· πιστεύετε εἰς τὸν θεόν καὶ εἰς ἐμὲ πιστεύετε

Most English translations correctly convey the present passive imperative mood of the first sentence, "Let not your hearts be troubled." Some Bibles, however, have made the Greek word καρδία which is single into "hearts" which is plural. However, the Greek word καρδία is singular as is the preceding article ἡ. Also, some translations go beyond translation fundamentals by having created English sounding commands out of present active indicatives verbs.

The Greek word construction, however, leaves possibility for either indicative or imperative. Hence, the ESV is not alone in translating "Believe in God; believe also in me" to both read and sound as English commands even though the Greek indicative case is more accurately translated as "believing in God and believing in me."

Jesus did not likely command his disciples to believe in God and believe in him. A healthier translation not creating an English sounding command from a Greek present active indicative verb is, "Do not let the heart (singular) of you (plural) be troubled believing in God and believing in me." Perhaps the reason Jesus told them that their collective singular heart as a group should not fear to believe in him and the Father is because at that time they were not able to comprehend the Father, Son, and Spirit Trinitarian one God. Remembering that Judaism was and is monotheistic here Jesus prepared his followers for what they would encounter believing and him and the father and the Spirit as one.

Identifying that English translations sometimes make imperatives out of indicatives may seem insignificant. The disciples of Jesus in their day, however, might have wanted you today who have read John's words to know that they believed in God and believed in Jesus. They also likely would have wanted you to know that they were well aware of where their belief in God and the Messiah Jesus would lead them. Given the failure of ruling Jewish leaders to accept the Messiah combined with Roman rule, what the disciples accomplished could not have been done had they not believed in God and Jesus.

In Jn 14: 1 Jesus affirmed himself and also pointed his followers to the Father beyond himself. The translation, "Believe in God and believe in me" conveys Arianism, the idea that Jesus is subordinate to the Father. The will of the Father, the Holy Spirit, and Jesus were and are inseparably Trinitarian linked. More importantly, Jesus' early follows might have given you the same encouragement today. We need not let our own heart as a faith community be troubled believing in God and Jesus as Messiah given what Christians have historically endured, endure today, and will endure.

Big difference.

## Place of the Trinity

There is no more excellent example of the Trinity in full power exhibited for the Kingdom than through Jesus. The early church perhaps understood and employed the Trinitarian working power more deeply than we do today. Early Jewish converts did not limit Jesus to only his Messiahship. Nor did early Gentile converts limit Jesus only to salvation. Instead, both early Jew and Gentile believers embraced and employed the Trinitarian power that Jesus had commanded. There is no question that Matthew was intentional having recorded Jesus' imperative "disciple and the nations" and Jesus present active participle "baptizing in the name of the Father, Son, and Holy Spirit."[20]

Today, however, the Father's will, combined with the presence and power of the Holy Spirit is seldom perceivable to contemporary confessing Christians or church bodies. Today Christendom seems to limit Jesus only to salvation. Kingdom efforts are often limited to church, missions, and evangelism. Seldom does the will of the Father and the role of the Holy Spirit and Jesus in Trinity come to mind for most of Christendom. Because the Trinity and Jesus' imperatives are seldom a focus, we miss that experience. We inhibit ourselves through lack of knowledge and lack of belief in the Kingdom and his righteousness that Jesus had commanded his followers seek.[21]

## Discontinuation of the Presence and Power of the Holy Spirit

Cessationism vs. Continuationism refers the ceasing (not for today) or the continuation (for today) of charismatic gifts found in 1 Co 12: 8-10.[22] In simple terms, some people believe healings and miracles continue for today. Other people believe healings and miracles have ceased. More specifically, however, is the question: Does God work through people today as he worked through people of the Bible? Cessationists in general hold that the Holy Spirit has ceased working in and through people for healing, miracles or spiritual unknowns. The term Cessationism advocates that miracles and healings that occurred in the Bible have ceased. The term Continuationism advocates that miracles and healings, which occurred in the Bible continue and are possible today.

Of course, both Cessationists and Continuationists cite scriptural support inclusive of presuppositions at best or faulty exegesis, hermeneutics, and interpretation at worst. Few theologians, pastors, clerics, or laity delve into this exhausting and emotional debate because the dispute often becomes divisive. Instead, both sides often go their own way. Some churches and people within those bodies hold cessation views, and other churches and their congregants hold continuation views. Many churches are silent on the topic preferring not to discuss to avoid opening a can of worms. Exegesis, hermeneutics, interpretation, and exposition surrounding the

---

[20] And Jesus came and said to them, "All authority in heaven and on earth has been given to me. Go therefore and make disciples of all nations [more accurate Greek to English is "disciple all the nations"], baptizing them in the name of the Father and of the Son and of the Holy Spirit, teaching them to observe all that I have commanded you. And behold, I am with you always, to the end of the age."
Mt 28: 18-20.

[21] But seek first the kingdom of God and his righteousness, and all these things will be added to you. Mt 6: 33.

[22] For to one is given through the Spirit the utterance of wisdom, and to another the utterance of knowledge according to the same Spirit, to another faith by the same Spirit, to another gifts of healing by the one Spirit, to another the working of miracles, to another prophecy, to another the ability to distinguish between spirits, to another various kinds of tongues, to another the interpretation of tongues. All these are empowered by one and the same Spirit, who apportions to each one individually as he wills. For just as the body is one and has many members, and all the members of the body, though many, are one body, so it is with Christ. 1 Co 12: 8-12.

debate are often mixtures of both subjective and objection verbiage. Hence the Cessation vs. Continuation debate is not within the scope of this book.

Nowhere in scripture are there literal, metaphorical, objective or subjective indications within any Greek imperatives spoken by Jesus that the Spirit's presence and power were to abate or continue. Same for the Father's will and the Kingdom of God. Instead, Jesus' affirmation that he sent and sends the comforter, counselor, helper, and advocate via the Paraclete with presence and power is a comfort for those hearing what the Spirit says to the churches. For this study, there are no imperatives from Jesus indicating either cessationism or continuationism. Matthew, Mark, Luke, and John are silent on imperatives regarding tongues, miracles or healings or concerning cessation or continuity of them. What is entirely clear, however, is that wherever miracles, healings, or casting out demons occurred in the New Testament, spoken imperatives preceded them.

## Application

The Father's will, the Holy Spirit within Jesus as well as within Peter, and Paul and others who spread the Gospel after Jesus ascended are without question. Matthew, Mark, Luke, and John each affirmed the presence, power, and working of the Holy Spirit. Original hearers and readers better understood in their context that power perhaps better than what we understand today. Jesus, Peter, and Paul healed by the presence and power of the Holy Spirit working within. The Trinitarian presence and power are absolute. In the Nazareth synagogue after reading the scrolls Jesus affirmed the Spirit upon him:

> And he came to Nazareth, where he had been brought up. And as was his custom, he went to the synagogue on the Sabbath day, and he stood up to read. And the scroll of the prophet Isaiah was given to him. He unrolled the scroll and found the place where it was written, "The Spirit of the Lord is upon me, because he has anointed me to proclaim good news to the poor. He has sent me to proclaim liberty to the captives and recovering of sight to the blind, to set at liberty those who are oppressed, to proclaim the year of the Lord's favor." And he rolled up the scroll and gave it back to the attendant and sat down. And the eyes of all in the synagogue were fixed on him. And he began to say to them, "Today this Scripture has been fulfilled in your hearing." Lk 4: 16-21

Luke quoted Jesus, "The Spirit of the Lord is upon me." Following his baptism and time in the desert, Jesus knew that accomplishing his mission would be impossible without the Holy Spirit. The Holy Spirit had indwelled him at his baptism, led him into the desert, and provided the presence and power to withstand Satan. Without the Spirit, Jesus was unable to fulfill his Father's will, and he knew so. There is no surprise that Jesus focused on blasphemy of the Holy Spirit for anyone who denied the presence and the power of the Spirit working within. Agreeing with Streett:

> Apart from the Spirit, Jesus cannot fulfill his mission.[23]

---

[23] Streett, Alan R., *Heaven on Earth: Experiencing The Kingdom Of God In The Here And Now*, 79.

Similar to Peter, Paul, and all who spread the Gospel during the first-century, apart from the Spirit, the Father's will, and Jesus they could not fulfill their mission. The same applies today. Christians, sensing a call toward any ministry type be that missions, teaching, preaching, evangelism, healing, service, prayer, pastoral, speaking, prophecy, and others are wise to discern not just a calling, but the will of the Father and the power of the Spirit.

The will of the Father and the power of the Spirit are not reserved solely for those feeling a call toward ministry. Pew sitting Christians sometimes mistakenly come to believe that the Father's will and the Spirit's power are reserved for those with a calling, a ministry or a foreign mission. Worse, those in ministry work come to think that the Father's will and the Spirit's power are unique to their ministry calling. Being oblivious to the Father's will and Spirit's power working in others results in a sad loss of fellowship. The will and the power of God apply to anyone who identifies as a Christian regardless of call or employment.

## Jesus Immanuel and His Imperatives

Apart from the Spirit's indwelling (the indwelling with which Jesus was empowered) and apart from knowing the will of the Father (the same will of the Father that Jesus knew) and apart from Jesus Immanuel (God with us) we today cannot fulfill our mission. His name "Immanuel" and his promise of his ever presence are sometimes mistaken for English metaphors, similes, or allegories despite numerous passages affirming His presence and power.[24]

The Father's will, the power of the Holy Spirit, and Jesus Messiah Immanuel is what Jesus taught his followers. His teachings and his imperatives have not changed. The Father's will, the power of the Holy Spirit and Jesus Immanuel extol his Kingdom work for salvation and maturity that discerns good from evil.[25] Jesus affirmed his ever presence to his followers, those who believed. Jesus affirms now his ever presence to his followers, those who believe. Jesus declared then the power he gave to those who believed. Jesus declares now the power he gives to those who believe.

His Kingdom, Lordship, and presence as Jesus Immanuel have not changed.

---

[24] The name "Immanuel" (God with us, ever present) affirmation passages:
    Therefore the Lord himself will give you a sign. Behold, the virgin shall conceive and bear a son, and shall call his name Immanuel. Is 7: 14.
    Behold, the virgin shall conceive and bear a son, and they shall call his name Immanuel" (which means, God with us). Mt 1: 23.
    No man shall be able to stand before you all the days of your life. Just as I was with Moses, so I will be with you. I will not leave you or forsake you. Js 1: 5
    I have been young, and now am old, yet I have not seen the righteous forsaken or his children begging for bread. Ps 37: 25
    We are afflicted in every way, but not crushed; perplexed, but not driven to despair; persecuted, but not forsaken; struck down, but not destroyed; always carrying in the body the death of Jesus, so that the life of Jesus may also be manifested in our bodies. 2 Co 4: 8-10
    I will never leave you nor forsake you. Hb 13: 5
    Go therefore and make disciples of all nations, baptizing them in the name of the Father and of the Son and of the Holy Spirit, teaching them to observe all that I have commanded you. And behold, I am with you always, to the end of the age." Mt 28: 19-20

[25] For though by this time you ought to be teachers, you need someone to teach you again the basic principles of the oracles of God. You need milk, not solid food, for everyone who lives on milk is unskilled in the word of righteousness, since he is a child. But solid food is for the mature, for those who have their powers of discernment trained by constant practice to distinguish good from evil. Hb 5: 12-14.

If you love me, you will keep my commandments.

Jn 14: 15

# 18 Keeping His Commands

If you love me, you will keep my commandments. Jn 14: 15

## Keep or Obey

This chapter focuses on the Greek to English exegesis of Jn 14: 15 and John's word usage. What did they hear and what did they interpret? What did Jesus' words mean to them? How were Jesus' disciples to know his commands? Who had the responsibility to draft and write documents to recall what he had commanded them? At the time Jesus spoke what John recorded in Jn 14: 15, Jesus had had not been crucified, nor resurrected, nor ascended. So, what did Jn 14: 15 mean to his disciples in their context?

Again, we focus on the Greek text and compare the numerous English translations from Greek. As referenced in earlier chapters, English Bibles are not alike. English Bibles having developed from different translation philosophies have produced a variety of words, phrases, different numbers, different tenses, and passages. Jesus' words, particularly his Greek word τηρήσετε recorded by John in Jn 14:15 has historically been translated into various English sentences and has produced numerous rendering inconsistencies:

> If you love me, you <u>will keep</u> my commandments. (ESV, CSB, NRS)
> If ye love me, <u>keep</u> my commandments. (KJV)
> If ye love me, my commands <u>keep</u>, (YLT)
> If you love me, you <u>will obey</u> what I command. (NIV)
> If you love me, you <u>will obey</u> my commandments. (NET)
> If you love me, <u>obey</u> my commandments. (NLT)
> Ἐὰν ἀγαπᾶτέ με τὰς ἐντολὰς τὰς ἐμὰς <u>τηρήσετε</u>· (WHO)

Note the various English phrases that have developed out of a single Greek text:

1. Two different English words, "keep" and "obey" rendered from one New Testament Greek word recorded by John, τηρήσετε.

2. Different numbers singular and plural: command, commands, and commandments. John's Greek is plural, not singular.

3. Different time aspects of some being future "you will keep" and "you will obey" and others are present "obey my" and "keep my." John's Greek is future active, "will be keeping."

These examples affirm that different translation philosophies through history have produced dissimilar translations that have resulted in diverse interpretations.

Jn 14: 15 is a verse often cited by contemporary Christians sometimes in context and sometimes out of context. The verse has sometimes been interpreted to convey the idea that disobedience is an indication of sinners not loving Jesus. The verse has also sometimes been interpreted to convey the idea that obedience is an indication that the sinner loves Jesus. However, a more in-depth study refutes both of these interpretations.

The essential concern, however, is that the Greek word "τηρήσετε" has been rendered to produce two different English words, "keep" and "obey" depending on the English Bible in question. Today, "keep" and "obey" are sometimes contemporarily considered to be English synonyms. However, in Greek from the critical texts, there is but one Greek word.

Mingling words such as "keep" for "obey" or vice versa that carry vague English meanings would not have been what hearers or readers of Greek in Jesus' day would have understood. The language they shared at that time was more precise or less ambiguous than so many English words today. Of course metaphors, allegories and parables are found throughout Scripture. However, here a contextual, etymological, and morphological understanding of the Greek word τηρήσετε is required to discern the difference between "keep" and "obey" in English.

## Concerning Commandments

Most Christians are familiar with the Ten Commandments from Ex 20: 2–17 and Dt 5: 6–21.[1] Similarly, most Christians are also aware of the answer Jesus gave to the question about the most important command Mt 22: 35–40 and Mk 12: 28–34.[2] However, seldom are Christians familiar with the 613 Jewish laws from the 3rd century found in the Mitzvot. Bank provides a summary:

> Tradition holds it that on Mount Sinai Moses received the Torah, which includes the 613 *mitzvot* (or commandments). According to the Book of Exodus, God had

---

[1] For reference ease, following are passages from Ex 20: 2 – 17: [2] "I am the LORD your God, who brought you out of the land of Egypt, out of the house of slavery. [3] "You shall have no other gods before me. [4] "You shall not make for yourself a carved image, or any likeness of anything that is in heaven above, or that is in the earth beneath, or that is in the water under the earth. [5] You shall not bow down to them or serve them, for I the LORD your God am a jealous God, visiting the iniquity of the fathers on the children to the third and the fourth generation of those who hate me, [6] but showing steadfast love to thousands of those who love me and keep my commandments. [7] "You shall not take the name of the LORD your God in vain, for the LORD will not hold him guiltless who takes his name in vain. [8] "Remember the Sabbath day, to keep it holy. [9] Six days you shall labor, and do all your work, [10] but the seventh day is a Sabbath to the LORD your God. On it you shall not do any work, you, or your son, or your daughter, your male servant, or your female servant, or your livestock, or the sojourner who is within your gates. [11] For in six days the LORD made heaven and earth, the sea, and all that is in them, and rested on the seventh day. Therefore the LORD blessed the Sabbath day and made it holy. [12] "Honor your father and your mother, that your days may be long in the land that the LORD your God is giving you. [13] "You shall not murder. [14] "You shall not commit adultery. [15] "You shall not steal. [16] "You shall not bear false witness against your neighbor. [17] "You shall not covet your neighbor's house; you shall not covet your neighbor's wife, or his male servant, or his female servant, or his ox, or his donkey, or anything that is your neighbor's."

[2] For reference ease, following are passages from Mk 12: 28 – 34: [28] And one of the scribes came up and heard them disputing with one another, and seeing that he answered them well, asked him, "Which commandment is the most important of all?" [29] Jesus answered, "The most important is, 'Hear, O Israel: The Lord our God, the Lord is one. [30] And you shall love the Lord your God with all your heart and with all your soul and with all your mind and with all your strength.' [31] The second is this: 'You shall love your neighbor as yourself.' There is no other commandment greater than these." [32] And the scribe said to him, "You are right, Teacher. You have truly said that he is one, and there is no other besides him. [33] And to love him with all the heart and with all the understanding and with all the strength, and to love one's neighbor as oneself, is much more than all whole burnt offerings and sacrifices." [34] And when Jesus saw that he answered wisely, he said to him, "You are not far from the kingdom of God." And after that no one dared to ask him any more questions.

dictated the commandment to Moses in order to provide the framework for a way of life for the people with whom God had established a covenant.[3]

The 613 Mitzvot commands were intentioned to set aside a way of life for those inside the community. The Mitzvot commands were purposed to differentiate those inside the community from those outside the community. Commandments mattered because acceptance or rejection and obedience or disobedience identified a community. Bank clarifies obedience to halakha that identified a community or communities:

> In Judaism, the rules that the Jews must obey are known collectively as the *halakha*, and it is astonishing how comprehensive they are. *Halakha* is an interesting mixture of the secular and the religious. Some rules concern themselves with worshipping God and civic matters, while others cover such topics as dietary habits, hygiene, and sexuality. Some of the commandments apply exclusively to certain individuals or groups of people such as the *kohanim* (temple priests) while others are pertinent only to the land of Israel.[4]

In Jn 13: 31–35 John recorded that Jesus had given them a new commandment.[5] Jesus' words, "A new commandment I give to you," ἐντολὴν καινὴν δίδωμι ὑμῖν, verified that Jesus knew the power of commandments. His use of the word, "new" καινὴν emphasized that Jesus had not negated prior commandments. The commandment he had given was a "new" commandment. Matthew, Mark, Luke and John recorded nine times Jesus' use of the word, ἐντολὴν translated to commandment or charge in English Bibles.[6] Here Jesus did not speak an imperative. Jesus could have said, "I command you to love one another." Here, Jesus did not speak and John did not record a Greek imperative.

Obedience to commands does not make nor keep people faithful. Obedience, however, can be outward expressions of faith. But not necessarily. Jesus' statement, "that you love one another just as I have loved you, you also are to love one another." does not contain a Greek imperative. Jesus did not command them to provide outward expressions of faith intentionally. Instead, he affirmed to them that the love they would show toward one another would be their outward expressions of faith. Their love for one another preceded and had priority over obedience.

Big difference.

---

[3] Bank, Richard D., Julie Gutin., *The Everything Jewish History & Heritage Book*, 31. (Rabbi Simlai from the 3rd Century is credited for originally calculating the 613 laws. Numerous Rabbis beyond Simlai codified and categorized the 613 commandments. Moses ben Maimon also known as Maimonides is recognized for the most traditional enumeration and categorization of the 613 commandments.)

[4] Bank, Richard D., Julie Gutin., *The Everything Jewish History & Heritage Book*, 32.

[5] For reference ease, following are passages from Jn 13: 31–35: [31] When he had gone out, Jesus said, "Now is the Son of Man glorified, and God is glorified in him. [32] If God is glorified in him, God will also glorify him in himself, and glorify him at once. [33] Little children, yet a little while I am with you. You will seek me, and just as I said to the Jews, so now I also say to you, 'Where I am going you cannot come.' [34] <u>A new commandment I give to you</u>, that you love one another: just as I have loved you, you also are to love one another. [35] By this all people will know that you are my disciples, if you have love for one another."

[6] Mt 15: 3; Mk 7: 8, 9; 10: 5; Lk 15: 29; Jn 10: 8; 12: 49; 13: 34; 14: 31.

## Obedience to Commands was not a Means to Become a Person of God

Loose yet functional coalitions of Jewish, Roman, and Herodian leaders sought internal protection and mutual gain. Their associations and agreements through politics and faith that were centered on the Temple were self-serving. Jesus' new commandment was different from political and faith alliances. Jesus' new commandment was not the same as a camaraderie, collusion, and collaboration of the Chief Priest Caiaphas and his Temple Priests. His new commandment was not the same as the military and political alliance of Roman soldiers, Pilate or Caesar back in Rome. His new commandment was not the same as the complicity of the Sanhedrin.

His commands were purposed to exemplify their love for one another. This outwardly and obvious love and concern for one another distinguished his followers from others. This inwardly and experiential love and concern for one another created a community or an ecclesia, a church. Both their love for one another and keeping Jesus commands were intended to be seen by political, civil, Temple authorities, and other communities. Communities in Jerusalem, Judea, Samaria, and the whole world saw how they loved one another. The people of God in communities that kept Jesus commands and loved one another exemplified the people of God. Lalleman clarifies how God intended his commandments to apply to Israel:

> Israel does not *become* the people of God by keeping his commandments, but they will show themselves outwardly to be his people by keeping his commandments. On the one hand, the covenant with Israel is exclusive: God has set these particular people apart from other nations. On the other hand, God's covenant with Israel is not exclusive, because God will not neglect the other nations. God intended the blessing of Israel to extend to others. The blessings, as well as the law that God gave to Israel, was intended to show other nations insight into the wisdom of the God of Israel.[7]

Jesus did not command his disciples to love one another as a means of salvation nor as a means of self-protection nor as a way to become the people of God. To love one another was the exact opposite of what Caiaphas, Temple Priests, Roman leadership, Roman soldiers, and Sanhedrin members exemplified. Christian love for one another went against both political and religious powers of their day. This new command from Jesus was neither Roman politics nor Jewish Temple based. This command separated them from what they once were. Forty years later in AD 70 Roman armies destroyed the Temple and Jewish practices were be gone. But, the command of Jesus to his followers to love one another continued.

Big difference.

## The word "Keep" is Neither a Simile nor a Metaphor for "Obey"

In Lk 17: 6 Luke recorded Jesus' use of the word ὑπήκουσεν commonly translated as "obey" in English.[8] Luke's accuracy is supportive. In this passage, Luke affirmed that Jesus knew the difference between the two words, ὑπήκουσεν and τηρήσετε from Jn 14: 15. Jesus spoke two

---

[7] Lalleman, Hetty, *Celebrating the Law? Rethinking Old Testament Ethics*, 41–42.
[8] And the Lord said, "If you had faith like a grain of mustard seed, you could say to this mulberry tree, 'Be uprooted and planted in the sea,' and it would obey you. Lk 17:6 ("would have obeyed you." YLT)

different words, and Luke and John recorded two different words because each word held significant contextual and morphological meaning.

In the context of Jesus' words in Lk 17: 6, he was clear in specifying obedience related to the uprooting and planting of the tree. Contextually, there was no ambiguity in their understanding. Jesus conveyed true obedience that the tree would be uprooted and planted in the sea.

Greek word formation is helpful to understand the meaning (contextual hermeneutics) in their day. Morphologically, the Greek word, ὑπακούω is formed with the prefix, ὑπα meaning beyond and from the root, κούω meaning to hear. In English the prefix "hyper" is appropriate. The meaning is not merely audibly hearing or intentionally listening. There is significance beyond hearing only an audible sound. Action or a response is expected or implied.

Mounce defines and delineates two Greek words, τηρέω and ὑπακούω:

> Verb: τηρέω conveys the idea of watching over something closely or guarding – "to keep, obey; guard, protect." Verb: ὑπακούω means to obey, do what one is told to do."[9]

Danker more profoundly defines, clarifies, and distinguishes the differences between τηρέω and ὑπακούω:

> τηρέω: 1 to retain in custody, keep watch over, guard, 2 to cause a state, condition, or activity to continue, keep, hold, reserve, preserve, 3 to persist in obedience, keep, observe, fulfill, pay attention to.[10]
>
> ὑπακούω: 1 to follow instructions, obey, follow, be subject to, 2 to grant one's request, hear, 3 to answer a knock at the door.[11]

Brown goes deeper distinguishing between τηρέω and ὑπακούω and provides definitions that discerning the two words from one another:

> τηρέω: Preserve, keep; observance; watch, observe; observation; NT (a) guard, keep watch (b) keep, keep blameless, uninjured (d) protect (e) hold fast (f) hold, follow, e.g. the law, the Sabbath, traditions, the commands of Jesus.[12]
>
> ὑπακούω: Listen, obey; obedience, obedient; NT In Acts 12: 13 means to open in the sense of "answering the door." Elsewhere the word group denotes obedience.[13]

Jesus knew the meanings of these two distinct Greek words. He also knew the differences between their meanings. John and Luke also knew. What distinguishes these two words from one

---

[9] Mounce, William D., *Mounce's Complete Expository Dictionary of Old & New Testament Words*, 477.
[10] Ibid, 1002.
[11] Danker, Frederick William, ed. Walter Bauer, *A Greek-English Lexicon of the New Testament and other Early Christian Literature, 3d ed.,* 1028 – 1029.
[12] C. Brown, "Guard, Keep, Watch" in Brown, Colin, ed., *New International Dictionary of New Testament Theology*, 133.
[13] W. Mundle, "Hear, Obey" in Brown, Colin, ed., *New International Dictionary of New Testament Theology*, 179.

another is that ὑπακούω carries with it an action or act of obedience while τηρέω does not emphasize an act as much as observance or watching over.

More significant, however, is that John in Jn 14:15 did not record that Jesus spoke an imperative. The Greek word τηρήσετε is a Greek indicative mood form, not an imperative mood form. While many English translations read as if Jesus gave a command, the imperative is absent. Jesus could have spoken, and John could have recorded the word ὑπακούω meaning obedience. However, the word ὑπακούω rendered as obedience is not in John's text.

Big difference.

## Some Key Words

A word study can illuminate the importance of obedience and Jesus imperatives. Below are critical Greek words with succinct short meanings from various dictionaries and lexicons.[14] The reason to identify these particular Greek words is to convey to you the reader the challenges translators encounter with words and the variety of meanings that can make their way into the English text.

Greek words from which is derived the English word, "obey."
    ὑπακοή meaning obedience
    παρακοή meaning disobedience

Greek words from which is derived the English word, "keep."
    φυλάσσω meaning watch, guard, defend
    τηρέω meaning keep watch over, guard, preserve

Greek words from which is derived the English word, "listen" (not audibly hear).
    ἀκούω meaning listen,
    εἰσακούω meaning hear, listen to, heed, hearken

Greek word from which is derived the English word, "custodial."
    κουστωδία meaning a guard of soldiers having custody to watch over

Greek words from which is derived the English word, "belief."
    πιστεύω meaning believe, believe in, trust in,
    πίστις meaning faith, trust, commitment
    ἄπιστος meaning unbelievable, incredible, faithless, unbelieving
    πείθω meaning to convince, persuade, appeal,
    ἀπειθέω meaning to disbelieve which is disobedience

---

[14] See various Greek dictionaries and lexicons below:
Brown, Colin, ed., *New International Dictionary of New Testament Theology*.
Danker, Frederick William, ed. Walter Bauer, *A Greek-English Lexicon of the New Testament and other Early Christian Literature*, 3d ed.
Friberg, Timothy, Barbara Friberg, Neva F. Miller, *Analytical Lexicon of the Greek New Testament*.
Mounce, William D., *Mounce's Complete Expository Dictionary of Old & New Testament Words*.

Greek words from which is derived the English word, "watch."
προσέχω meaning turn one's mind to, pay attention to, give heed to
γρηγορέω meaning keep watch over, be on guard, be alert,
θεωρέω meaning see, look at, observe, perceive

Greek words from which is derived the English word, "see."
βλέπω meaning to see, to look at, to watch
θεάομαι meaning to see or look at in a stronger sense than simply sight.
ὁράω meaning see, catch sight of, notice

The nuances of Greek words weigh heavy upon choosing an equivalent English words. English translators because of the development of the English language have numerous English words to choose. Considering the depth and breadth of world languages, Bible translating is an arduous task in any language especially if translators are not able to grasp the Greek of Jesus' day.

## τηρήσετε

The Greek word, τηρήσετε in John 14: 15 is a future indicative mood form active and second person plural verb. To capture the future active second person indicative verb from John's Greek an appropriate expanded translation is:

Ἐὰν ἀγαπᾶτέ με τὰς ἐντολὰς τὰς ἐμὰς τηρήσετε

"If you [plural] love me, you [plural] will be keeping my commandments."

The English phrase "will be keeping" conveys the Greek future active indicative. None of the English translations listed above capture the Greek future, active, indicative that John recorded.

To apply John 14: 15 today means that, others see those who love Jesus outside of the faith community by the way those inside the faith community love one another. Those inside the community of Jesus are aware of his imperatives, his commands, his will and will be keeping them in the sense of being aware of his imperatives, his commands.

There is a big difference between interpreting a command to be obeyed compared to a way of living that indicates faith and love among one another.

## Progression Toward Godly Obedience

Progression from hearing to listening, to understanding, to believing, to having faith ultimately makes way for obedience. There is a process or a progression toward faith. Obedience is not the first step. Obedience is a result of having heard, listened, understood, believed, and after having had faith. Obedience is not where lovers of Jesus start. Faith exhibits trust that progresses toward true obedience as a result, not as a means. Thus translating the Greek word τηρέω to mean "obey" in English context stretches the Greek text. Believers start with faith, not obedience.

Big difference.

Jesus spoke, and John chose τηρήσετε over numerous other words that could have conveyed a more definite meaning to obey. John chose the word that Jesus spoke. Just as obedience to OT laws was not salvific, obedience to Jesus' commands was neither salvific.

Obedience, however, stems from belief, as belief stems from understanding, as understanding stems from listening, and, as listening stems from hearing. There is a progression:

Hearing to    Listening to    Understanding to    Believing to    Obeying.

Obedience that does not come from believing, understanding, listening and hearing is not the obedience Jesus is talking about. Jesus never linked obedience to salvation. He did, however, link keeping his commands (meaning to watch over, to guard, after having heard, listened, understood, and believing his commands) as an indication of saving faith and love for him. Keeping through belief in his commands is indicated by keeping his commands, not obedience.

As previously stated, often overlooked in Jn 14: 15 is that there are no Greek imperatives within the text. In other words, John did not write that Jesus gave a command to obey that implied perfection. Some English translations convey through syntax and sentence structure that Jesus made an imperative command to obey without having an imperative within the sentence. Instead, Jesus spoke a future indicative, not an imperative which is significant to meaning then and meaning now. Conveyed in context, loving Jesus was then (and still is now) indicated not through obeying his commands, an impossibility, but by keeping his commands.

Big difference.

Sometimes Greek indicatives are conveyed as imperatives which sometimes happens within some English translations. In Jn 14: 15 John conveyed that Jesus focused on the faith that precedes obedience. Jesus did not focus on a human attempt at obedience to prove faith. He taught that true obedience follows faith. Faith that keeps commands is obedience to prove faith

Big difference.

## Summary of Keeping His Commands

The indicative mood given the absence of the imperative is powerful. Jesus did not need to give a Greek imperative as most English translations convey through making Jn 14: 15 read and sound like an English command. The indicative mood, meaning what people outside the faith community see or perceive from lives lived and indicated by those inside the faith community when they love one another was intentional by Jesus and correctly recorded by John. Use of the indicative case is significant. The lesson to his disciples was that knowing or keeping Jesus commands would be the visible evidence of their love for one another. Remembering their time with him, and what he said and taught, and love within their community had highest priority.

In Jesus words, those who love Jesus will be seen by others as people in a community who are keeping his commands, not by obedience, but by knowing, keeping, and sharing what he had said to them. Jesus would never have made obedience a requirement because obedience to the law was impossible.

While obedience was and continues to be the mode of many practicing a works based faith, those who kept Jesus' commands, recalling and sharing his teachings distinguished Jesus' followers from law practicing Jews and gentiles. His words, "Do not think that I have come to abolish the Law or the Prophets; I have not come to abolish them but to fulfill them." Mt 5:17 did not negate or refute the law. Keeping his commands and knowing what he said set his followers apart for all others. His words recorded by Matthew, Mark, Luke, and John for them then and us today are what Jesus commands to be kept.

Big difference for those with ears to hear.

If you love me, you will keep my commandments.

John 14: 15

# 19 Conclusion and Summary

This is the disciple who is bearing witness about these things, and who has written these things, and we know that his testimony is true. Now there are also many other things that Jesus did. Were every one of them to be written, I suppose that the world itself could not contain the books that would be written. Jn 22: 24-25

## Language and Culture

This book has focused on Jesus' use of the Greek Imperative mood. Agreeing with John 22: 25, it does not contain all Jesus did. At the very least, this is one of the books that has been written to share his Greek imperatives to English commands as recorded in the New Testament. But language in and of itself is limited. Simply understanding Greek morphology, word form, and meaning, is insufficient without understanding both language and culture. Effective translating is not relegated solely to language. Language and culture cannot be separated. Walton affirms:

> As complicated as translating a foreign language can be, translating a foreign culture is infinitely more difficult. The very act of trying to translate the culture requires taking it out of its context and fitting it into ours. The minute anyone (professional or amateur) attempts to translate the culture we run the risk of making the text communicate something it never intended. Rather than translate the culture, then, we need to try to enter the culture. We must make every attempt to set our English categories aside, to leave our cultural ideas behind, and try out b3st (as limited as the attempt might be) to understand the material in its cultural context without translating it.[1]

Jesus imperatives recorded by Matthew, Mark, Luke, and John were deliberate and effective in their culture. In other words, the Gospel writers wrote for their culture. Their Greek imperatives spoke to their culture. Translating Jesus' Greek imperatives into English commands is not merely a translation issue. Both language and culture then influenced meaning then. Both language and culture now influence meaning now.

The Gospels were critically proofed and edited before dissemination. The original Gospels were perfect for readers and those sharing the message in their culture. Perhaps to our benefit God saw to it that those original manuscripts are lost to time leaving us with the Critical Texts and Critical Analysis. Perhaps if we had the original manuscripts today, they would be treated as icons that come to be worshipped or held in higher esteem than the message. The four Gospels are special because Matthew, Mark, Luke, and John focused on the message through language and culture.

Understanding language and culture is absolute for professional scholarly translation teams or a layperson preparing a group study. Without language and culture of that time, English translations can develop some wide-ranging options. (See Chapter 18, Jn 14: 17 excursus.) That sounds simple, but over or under translation is an issue even Greek 101 students must address. Language, culture and context matters.

---

[1] Walton, John, H., *The Lost World of Genesis One: Ancient Cosmology and the Origins Debate*, 8 – 9.

# Timing and History

Chapter 4 focused on timing and history and emphasized that God chose when Jesus arrived. God chose the time, place, language, and culture. The 400 year period after the last book of the Old Testament Hebrew Scriptures sequence Genesis to Malachi and the first New Testament Scriptures sequence beginning with Matthew to Revelation is called "Time between the Testaments." This era of both Judaism and Greek culture is central to understanding the New Testament. The language and more specifically the Greek imperatives of the language is fundamental to context. In other words, time and history are essential to understanding what Jesus said, what his hearers heard and what they understood.

Beginning chapters provided an overview of the Greek language and culture where and when Jesus walked. The reason for a synopsis is because with God and his creation, time matters. When is important. Christians often overlook time. Believers today tend to be concerned with the present and immediate relevance. What happened in the past and what will happen in future is often moot to Christians today.

History and time effect faith. Relevant to the Greek imperatives of Jesus translated into English commands is the issue of time. Faith then, faith over time, faith now, and faith in the future are God's will. Past, present, and future time matters to God. The Hebrew language and culture and surrounding cultures had influence. Similarly, the Greek language and culture and surrounding cultures influenced the writers.

Jesus' coming and comings, his Theophanies, and Christophanies found throughout Scripture are always linked to time. Paul to the Ephesians, Galatians, and Timothy affirmed the fullness of time, the right time, and the proper time were central to meaning.[2] The timings of Jesus' comings are within God's divine plan. Timing mattered then. Timing matters now. Noe clarifies prophesied Theophanies, non-prophesied Theophanies, comings, Parousia's and Christophanies. Specific to Jesus' death and resurrection Noe affirms that the evidence of Jesus' many comings and presence is overwhelming:

> Hundreds witnessed Jesus' death on the cross. But on the third day He arose and during the next forty days hundreds more witnessed his physical presence. After his resurrection, the writers of the New Testament documented many post-Resurrection pre-Ascension and post-Ascension comings and appearing of Jesus.[3]

People saw Jesus as he lived and after he had been crucified. Whom they saw is one absolute. When they saw Jesus is another absolute. There is perfection in Jesus' timing of his words and his comings. Jesus' spoke his words at a precise time in history. Matthew, Mark, Luke, and John recorded their Gospels at a particular time in history.

---

[2] However, when the fullness of time had come, God sent forth his Son, Gal 4:4;
For while we were still weak, at the right time Christ died for the ungodly. Rm 5:6; For there is one God, and there is one mediator between God and men, the man Christ Jesus, who gave himself as a ransom for all, which is the testimony given at the proper time. 1Ti 2:5-6.
[3] Noe, John. *Unraveling the End: A Balanced Scholarly Synthesis of Four Competing and Conflicting End Time Views*, 270-271.

Cullman affirms the importance of Greek and a continuous time process:

> Revelation and salvation take place along the course of an ascending timeline. Here the strictly straight-line conception of time in the New Testament must be defined as over against the Greek cyclical conception and over against all metaphysics in which salvation is always available in the "beyond," and we must show how according to the Primitive Christian view revelation and salvation actually "occur" in a connected manner during the continuous time process.[4]

Regarding time, Jesus' words mattered then. Jesus' words matter now. Jesus's words will matter in the future. No surprise Matthew, Mark, Luke, and John recorded Jesus' words. His Greek imperatives in the context of their day are to be understood first in their context and then in our day. Same for all future generations. The process is continuous. The culture and Greek language where Jesus walked and talked are forever linked to the Gospel message. Words are not dead.

## Gospel Author Remorse

Author remorse, that sense that as an author you could have done better is common for everyone who has written a personal letter, a high school term paper, an article for publication, or a book. Every author laments, "I should have changed that sentence." or "I should have moved that paragraph." or "I should have eliminated that chapter." You get the idea.

Not so for Matthew, Mark, Luke, or John. Their final recorded Greek in their context that came to be copied and disseminated was flawless. Matthew, Mark, Luke, John, Paul, Peter, James, Jude and the writer or writers of Hebrews had no author remorse. They never said, "Oops."

## Bible Translations

Bible translations and translation philosophies matter because the Logos, the incarnate Word, the written Word, and God's gift is the core. Few Christians in the pews consider why we have so many English translations. Word-for-Word or Thought-for-Thought translations philosophies, however, are not always the challenge. What pastors, teachers, professors, or laity do with their teachings derived from the Bibles they choose is at the core of glorifying God.

Chapter 5 *Bible Translations* provided an overview of English translations, a synopsis on translation philosophies, insight on the power of presuppositions, understanding theology or pastoral translation influences, a summary foundation and location of the Greek texts, the importance of Critical Texts and Critical Apparatus, and a brief comparison of popular English Bibles.

Responsibility to rightly handle the Word is no small issue. Both those who translate and those who interpret Scripture have responsibilities that are consequential. In other words, jots and tittles, dotted i's and crossed t's, words, sentences, phrases, chapters, and books matter. Translating and interpreting the Word is not to be taken lightly. Efforts to contemporize ancient texts at the cost of ambivalence toward historical languages, culture, and context is egregious. Disregarding languages and culture when translating or interpreting can produce conspicuous or flagrant

---

[4] Cullman, Oscar, *Christ and Time: The Primitive Christian Conception of Time and History*, 32.

conclusions. Not only do Bible translations matter, but those who translate and those who interpret from any Bible have grave responsibilities to consider ancient languages, cultures, and contexts. Sometimes even the best English efforts to contemporize ancient texts with sincere energies to convey understanding can in the end abuse the original historical context.

Chapter 6 *Exegesis, Hermeneutics, Exposition, and Interpretation* was written to clarify for laity words sometimes heard from pulpits or classes but often misunderstood. The Grammatical-Historical Method is key to translating and interpreting because ancient languages, grammar, and cultural history are indivisibly linked to the texts. In other words, removing grammar and history from the original language is impossible. Any attempt to get the text right without knowing the Greek language and culture at the time of Jesus can be perhaps not fruitless but certainly less than fruitful.

## From Knowing to Understanding to Keeping

After having read this book perhaps you have a deeper appreciation for historical languages, culture, context, meaning then, and meaning now. Certainly, you now have easy access within the book to Jesus' Greek imperatives or more simply his English commands. Perhaps, more importantly, you have found that knowing Jesus' imperatives builds faith. Perhaps you have learned how to love God with a will to first know his commands, understand them and then keep them. The process is irrefutable.

Numerous biblical examples depict the consequences of disobedience. Scriptures detail the consequences upon Adam, Moses, Pharaoh, David, and others for their disobedience as well as God's mercy. Peter's three denials affirm that obedience was not possible for Peter on his own. The disciples had to learn that Jesus' perfect obedience, not their obedience was their only link to his Kingdom. His imperatives mattered. Jesus clearing the Temple (Mt 21: 13; Mk 11: 17; Lk 19: 46) affirmed that Pharisees, Sadducees, and Jewish leaders engulfed in their fruitless attempt at obedience to law and Temple practices became abusive to those God had given them to serve. We should not be surprised that many of today's faith communities reflect the abusive Temple practices when obedience becomes the means of salvation rather than the fruit of salvation through the justification of Jesus.

Big difference.

## God Loves Your Effort to Know

God's laws, commands, and will are always intended to protect and bless. The 10 Commandments were intended to protect and bless. Jesus' imperative commands were intended to protect and bless. You get the idea. The 613 mitzvoth within their context were intended to protect and bless. But sometimes man's laws do not protect. Man is sinful. God is holy.

Big difference.

Failing to realize that God's laws were always intended to protect and bless, comes with consequences. Jesus' imperatives, his commands were purposed to protect and bless. In every biblical example regarding obedience, there existed a prior faith or trust or confidence in the law. In other words, making an effort to know the law or command precedes and surpasses effort toward obedience.

Every biblical record of disobedience resulted in some form of death, end, end of an age, end of an era, or change. Consider Adam, Eve, Moses, David, and Solomon, Jonah, Jew, Gentile,

Pagan, and even those called by God as leaders, prophets, holy men and women. Ends or more specifically ends of ages are unavoidable. Consequences for obedience or disobedience are unavoidable. Because God's laws are intended to preserve life and relationship with him, faith that produces obedience is a precursor for love, inclusion with God and one another.

God is glorified when the effort to know his will and commands is made. When we try to know and keep his commands (not to be confused with obeying his commands) God is glorified. Jesus glorified the Father because Jesus always wanted the Father's will. Jesus is the quintessential example of being fully man and fully divine seeking the will of his Father. In short, God loves your effort to know his will and his commands.

## Belief and Obedience vs. Disbelief and Disobedience

Without faith, without trust, without belief, any attempt at obedience is vanity. Concerning belief and obedience compared to disbelief and disobedience, Hafemann is worthy of quoting at length:

> Every *command* of God is built upon a *promise* from God. Therefore every divine call to action (obedience) is, at the same time, a divine summons to trust in God's promises (faith). After the Exodus, God *promised* Israel that it would rain bread from heaven every day except the Sabbath. God therefor *commanded* Israel not to gather more than their daily ration, except on Friday. God's promise was inextricably linked with a prohibition. Conversely, trust in God's promise would mean obedience to his commands.
>
> When the people subsequently refused to rest on the Sabbath, it was therefore a lack of *faith*, which, as we have seen is the heart of sin. Disbelief always shows up as an act of disobedience, since every promise carries with it a command. Every time we disobey it is because we are not trusting him. For this reason, when Israel fails to trust God's promise concerning manna on the Sabbath, God plaintively asks, "How long do you refuse to keep my commandments and laws?" (Ex 16: 28)[5]

For Hafemann faith and obedience from an Old Testament perspective is the same faith and obedience from a New Testament perspective. Just as God affirmed that trust in his promises is a faith that precedes obedience, Jesus affirmed that trust in his imperatives is a faith that precedes obedience.

In other words, obedience was never the goal. Faith and trust are God's first desire for a man of which acting justly, loving tenderly, and walking humbly follow (see Mc 6: 8). From Adam and Eve, Abraham, Moses, Saul, David, the Prophets, Peter, and Paul the story is always the same. Godly obedience only comes from faith.

The use of the English word "obey" in Jn 14: 15 seems applicable but is an interpretive problem. A person is not justified by works of the law but by faith. Conveying that obedience to either Old Testament or New Testament commands was a false Gospel then and is a false Gospel today. The use of "obeying" in English in reference to Jesus' imperatives sways to the side of works righteousness. Use of the English word "obey" was a translation attempt to motivate readers toward

---

[5] Hafemann, Scott J., *The God of Promise and the Life of Faith: Understanding the Heart of the Bible*, 87.

obedience which sounds appropriate. With a translation that focuses on obedience without consideration of the Greek future, active second person, indicative verb, readers are motivated toward a works righteousness or obedience righteousness mindset.

## Imperative Proof

From the record of the Gospel writers, Jesus' spoken imperatives verify who he was, always has been, is, and forever will be. Matthew, Mark, Luke, and John are consistent regarding Jesus' use of Greek imperatives. After Jesus said to Matthew in Mt 9:9, "Follow me." Ἀκολούθει μοι, Mathew's next written words recorded that Matthew followed. After Mark penned in Mk 4: 39 that Jesus said to the wind and waves, "Peace. Be still." Σιώπα πεφίμωσο Mark recorded that immediately a great calm followed. After Luke wrote in Lk 6: 10 that Jesus said, "Stretch out your hand Εκτεινον τὴν χεῖρά σου Luke recorded, "And he did so and his hand was restored." After John transcribed in Jn 2: 7 that, "Jesus said to the servants, "Fill the jars with water" Γεμίσατε τὰς ὑδρίας ὕδατος John also recorded, "And they filled them up to the brim."

Having Jesus' imperatives readily available is a good place to start. Jesus' commands to them in their language, culture, and context are good news.

Big difference for those with ears to hear all that Jesus commanded them.

# Bibliography

Bank, Richard D. Julie Gutin, *The Everything Jewish History & Heritage Book*. Avon, MA: Adams Media Corporation, 2003.

Bloesch, Donald G., *The Holy Spirit: Works & Gifts*. Downers Grove, IL: InterVarsity Press, 2000.

Brown, Raymond E., *An Introduction to the Gospel of John*. New York, NY: Doubleday, 2003.

Brown, Colin, ed., *New International Dictionary of New Testament Theology*. Grand Rapids, MI: Zondervan, 1986.

Brownnrigg, Ronald, *Who's Who the New Testament*. New York, NY: Oxford University Press, 1993.

Bruce, F. F., *Paul: Apostle of the Heart Set Free*. Grand Rapids, MI: William B. Eerdmans Publishing Co. 1977.

Bruce, F. F., *The Canon of Scripture*. Downers Grove, IL: InterVarsity Press, 1988.

Bruce, F. F., *The Gospel of John*. Grand Rapids, MI: William B. Eerdmans Publishing Company, 1983.

Carson, D. A., *Exegetical Fallacies, 2d ed*. Grand Rapids, MI: Baker Book House, 1996.

Chapell, Bryan, *Christ Centered Preaching: Redeeming the Expository Sermon*. Grand Rapids, MI: Baker Books, 1994.

Charlesworth, James H. *The Old Testament Pseudepigrapha, Volumes 1 and 2*. New York, NY: Doubleday, 1983.

Comfort, Philip Wesley, *Early Manuscripts & Modern Translations of the New Testament*. Grand Rapids, MI: Baker Books, 1996.

Comfort, Philip Wesley, *Encountering the Manuscripts: An Introduction to New Testament Paleography & Textual Criticism*. Nashville, TN: Broadman and Holman Publishers, 2005.

Comfort, Philip Wesley, Wendell C. Hawley, *Opening the Gospel of John*. Wheaton, IL: Tyndale House Publishers, Inc., 1994.

Comfort, Philip Wesley, *The Complete Guide to Bible Versions*. Wheaton, IL: Tyndale House Publishers, Inc., 1996.

Comfort, Philip Wesley, *The Origin of the Bible: A Comprehensive Guide*. Wheaton, IL: Tyndale House Publishers, Inc., 1992.

Cullman, Oscar, *Christ and Time: The Primitive Christian Conception of Time and History*. Philadelphia, PA, MCML, 1950.

Danker, Frederick William, ed. Walter Bauer, *A Greek-English Lexicon of the New Testament and other Early Christian Literature*. 3d ed. Chicago, IL: The University of Chicago Press, 2000.

Demoss, Matthew S., *Pocket Dictionary for the Study of New Testament Greek*. Downers Grove, IL: InterVarsity Press, 2001.

Dever, Mark, *Nine Marks of a Healthy Church*. Wheaton, IL: Crossway Books, 2000.

Douglas, J. D., ed., *The Illustrated Bible Dictionary*. Downers Grove, IL: InterVarsity Press, 1998.

Douglas, J. D. and Merrill C. Tenney, eds. *The New International Dictionary of the Bible*. Grand Rapids, MI: Zondervan Publishing, 1987.

Eisenberg, Ronald L., *The 613 Mitzvot: A Contemporary Guide to the Commandments of Judaism*. Rockville, MD: Schreiber Publishing, 2005.

Elwell, Walther A., *Baker Commentary on the Bible*. Grand Rapids, MI: Baker Book House, Second printing 2002.

Elwell, Walter A., *Baker Theological Dictionary of the Bible*. Grand Rapids, MI: Baker Book House, 2000.

Elwell, Walter A., *Evangelical Dictionary of Theology, 2d ed*. Grand Rapids, MI: Baker Book House, 2001.

Eusebius, *Ecclesiastical History*. Translated by C. F. Cruse, Peabody, MA: Hendrickson Publishers, Inc., 1998.

Grenz, Stanley, J., David Guretzki, and Cherith Fee Nordling, *Pocket Dictionary of Theological Terms*. Downers Grove, IL: InterVarsity Press, 1999.

Fee, Gordon D., and Douglas Stuart, *How to Read the Bible for All Its Worth: A Guide to Understanding the Bible, 2d ed*. Grand Rapids, MI: Zondervan Publishing House, 1993.

Friberg, Timothy, Barbara Friberg, and Neva F. Miller, *Analytical Lexicon of the Greek New Testament*. Grand Rapids, MI: Baker Books. 2000.

Josephus, Flavius, *The Works of Josephus*. William Whiston, Translator, Peabody, MA: Hendrickson Publishers, 1987.

Hafemann, Scott J., *The God of Promise and the Life of Faith: Understanding the Heart of the Bible*. Wheaton, IL: Crossway Books, 2001.

Kaiser Jr., Walter C., Peter H. Davids, F.F. Bruce, and Manfred T. Brauch, *Hard Sayings of the Bible*. Downers Grove, IL: InterVarsity Press, 1996.

Klein, William, Craig L. Blomberg, and Robert L. Hubbard, Jr., *Introduction to Biblical Interpretation*. Nashville, TN: Thomas Nelson Publishers, 2004.

Ladd, George Eldon, *A Theology of the New Testament*. Grand Rapids, MI: William B. Eerdmans Publishing, Co. 1974.

Lalleman, Hetty, *Celebrating the Law? Rethinking Old Testament Ethics*. Waynesboro, GA: Paternoster Press, 2004.

Lamerson, Samuel, *English Grammar to Ace New Testament Greek*. Grand Rapids, MI: Zondervan, 2004.

Litfin, Bryan, *After Acts: Exploring the Lives and Legends of the Apostles*. Chicago, IL: Moody Publishers, 2015.

Lowi-Nida Lexicon within *Bibleworks 8*. Bible Software, Version 8.0.020u.1, 2013.

Marshall, I. Howard, *Beyond the Bible: Moving from Scripture to Theology*. Grand Rapids, MI: Baker Academic, 2004.

McRay, John, *Paul: His Life and Teaching*. Grand Rapids, MI: Baker Academic 2003.

Mounce, William D., *Basics of Biblical Greek*. Grand Rapids, MI: Zondervan, 1993.

Mounce, William D., *Basics of Biblical Greek, 2$^{nd}$ Ed*. Grand Rapids, MI: Zondervan, 2003.

Mounce, William D., *Greek for the Rest of Us, Mastering Bible Study without Mastering Biblical Languages*. Grand Rapids, MI; Zondervan, 2003.

Mounce, William D., *Mounce's Complete Expository Dictionary of Old & New Testament Words*. Grand Rapids, MI: Zondervan, 2006.

Mounce, William D., *The Morphology of Biblical Greek: A Companion to Basics of Biblical Greek and the Analytical Lexicon to the Greek New Testament*. Grand Rapids, MI: Zondervan, 1994.

Moo, Douglas J., *We Still Don't Get It: Evangelicals and Bible Translation Fifty Years After James Barr*. Grand Rapids, MI: Zondervan, 2014.

Noe, John. *Unraveling the End: A balanced scholarly synthesis of four competing and conflicting end time views*. Indianapolis, IN: East2West Press, 2014.

Pierson, Cheri L., Lonna J. Dickerson, and Florence R. Scott, *Exploring Theological English, Reading, Vocabulary, and Grammar for ESL/EFL*. Carlisle, England, Piquant Editions. 2010.

Douglas, J. D. and Merrill C. Tenney, eds. *The New International Dictionary of the Bible*. Grand Rapids, MI: Zondervan Publishing, 1987.

Ryken, Leland, *The Word of God in English: Criteria for Excellence in Bible Translation*. Wheaton, IL: Crossway Books, 2002.

Soulen, Richard N., and Kendall R Soulen, *Handbook of Biblical Criticism, Third Edition*. Louisville, KY: John Knox Publishing, 2001

Scott, J. Julius, *Customs and Controversies: Intertestamental Jewish Backgrounds of the New Testament*. Grand Rapids, MI: Baker Books, 1995.

Streett, R. Alan., *Heaven on Earth: Experiencing The Kingdom Of God In The Here And Now*. Eugene, OR: Harvest House Publishers, 2013.

Virkler, Henry A., *Hermeneutics: Principles and Processes of Biblical Interpretation*. Grand Rapids, MI: Baker Books, 1981.

Wallace, Daniel, B., *Greek Grammar Beyond the Basics: An Exegetical Syntax of the New Testament*. Grand Rapids, MI, Zondervan Publishing, 1996.

Walton, John, H., *The Lost World of Genesis One: Ancient Cosmology and the Origins Debate*. Downers Grove, IL, InterVarsity Press, 2009.